1337192

Co
8/20/07

D1595801

Southern Farmers and Their Stories

NEW DIRECTIONS IN SOUTHERN HISTORY

SERIES EDITORS

Peter S. Carmichael, *University of North Carolina at Greensboro*
Michele Gillespie, *Wake Forest University*
William A. Link, *University of Florida*

*Becoming Bourgeois: Merchant Culture
in the South, 1820–1865*
by Frank J. Byrne

*The View from the Ground:
Experiences of Civil War Soldiers*
Edited by Aaron Sheehan-Dean

Southern Farmers and Their Stories

Memory and Meaning in Oral History

MELISSA WALKER

THE UNIVERSITY PRESS OF KENTUCKY

Publication of this volume was made possible in part by a grant
from the National Endowment for the Humanities.

Scholarly publisher for the Commonwealth,
serving Bellarmine University, Berea College, Centre
College of Kentucky, Eastern Kentucky University,
The Filson Historical Society, Georgetown College,
Kentucky Historical Society, Kentucky State University,
Morehead State University, Murray State University,
Northern Kentucky University, Transylvania University,
University of Kentucky, University of Louisville,
and Western Kentucky University.
All rights reserved.

Editorial and Sales Offices: The University Press of Kentucky
663 South Limestone Street, Lexington, Kentucky 40508-4008
www.kentuckypress.com

06 07 08 09 10   5 4 3 2 1

Library of Congress Cataloging-in-Publication Data

Walker, Melissa, 1962-
Southern farmers and their stories : memory and meaning in oral history / Melissa Walker.
p. cm. — (New directions in southern history)
Includes bibliographical references and index.
ISBN-13: 978-0-8131-2409-4 (hardcover : alk. paper)
ISBN-10: 0-8131-2409-3 (hardcover : alk. paper)
1. Southern States—Social life and customs—20th century—Historiography.
2. Farm life—Southern States—History—20th century—Historiography.
3. Southern States—Rural conditions—Historiography.
4. Farmers—Southern States—Interviews. 5. Oral history.
6. Memory—Social aspects—Southern States.
7. Interviews—Southern States. 8. Southern States—Biography.
I. Title. II. Series.
F208.2.W35 2006
975'.03072—dc22
2006010201

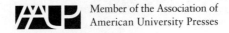

To my aunt, Laura Ann Walker Tate,
who planted the seeds for this project more than thirty years ago,
when she taught me to read the silences as well as the words in
the stories people tell about their lives

Memory's filled with what we think we've lived.
—Rick Mulkey, "Midlothian"

Contents

Acknowledgments

In the course of this project, I accumulated more debts than the average southern farmer, and I am grateful to those who made this project possible and those who made it better. My deepest gratitude goes to the narrators who graciously shared their life stories and all the interviewers who generously archived their work for the benefit of other researchers. A project of this scope would have been beyond my reach if I had tried to conduct all the interviews myself, so I thank the narrators and the interviewers whose years of work made this project feasible.

I am grateful to many institutions and individuals for their support of this project. An appointment as visiting scholar at Baylor University's Institute for Oral History funded my first major foray into archived oral histories and got this project under way. Additional support included two summer research grants from the Converse College Faculty Development Committee, a John Hope Franklin Research Grant from the Perkins Library at Duke University, a Guion Griffis Johnson research grant from the Wilson Library at the University of North Carolina at Chapel Hill, and a Franklin Research Grant from the American Philosophical Society. I deeply appreciate the support of all these institutions.

Thanks to the Converse College Faculty Development Committee and Jeff Barker, vice president for academic affairs, for the gift of a yearlong sabbatical to draft the manuscript. To make that sabbatical a reality, members of my department cheerfully juggled schedules and shouldered extra advising duties. As always, my department chair, Joe P. Dunn, encouraged my scholarship with as flexible a schedule as can be managed at a small college. He daily combines the roles of cheerleader and nagging parent for all the members of the department.

Librarians and staff members at many collections helped me ferret out the most interesting interviews. Thanks to Ellen Brown and the staff at Baylor University's Texas Collection, the staff in the manuscripts division at Duke University's Perkins Library, Laura Clark Brown and the staff in the manuscripts division at the University of North Carolina at Chapel Hill's Wilson Library, Bonnie Ledbetter at the University of Alabama at Birmingham, Dwayne Cox and Martin Ollif at Auburn University, and the staff in the manuscripts division at the Library of Virginia. The staff at the National Museum of American History's Archives Center, especially Susan Strange, Deborra Richardson, and Rueben Jackson, deserve more than the usual measure of thanks for cheerfully wrestling oversized boxes of unprocessed interview files from shelves poised high overhead. Lois Myers and Becky Shulda at Baylor's Institute for Oral History also provided valuable assistance during my stay in Waco. The library staff at Converse College regularly performs miracles with a meager budget. Thanks to Wade Woodward, Becky Poole, Becky Dalton, Mark Collier, and especially to interlibrary loan wizard Shannon Wardlow for tracking down the misplaced, the obscure, and the just plain odd.

Thanks to the editors of journals where earlier versions of portions of this material appeared for permission to include that work in the book. Portions of chapter 1 first appeared in somewhat different form in the *Oral History Review* as "Culling Out the Men from the Boys: Concepts of Success in the Recollections of a Southern Farmer" (Summer 2000, © 2000 by the Oral History Association). Portions of chapter 2 appeared in different form in *Agricultural History* as "Narrative Themes in the Oral Histories of Farming Folk" (Spring 2000, ©2000 by the Agricultural History Society). Thanks to Rick Mulkey for permission to use a portion of his poem "Midlothian" (from *Bluefield Breakdown* [Georgetown, Ky.: Finishing Line Press, 2005]) and to Mike Corbin for permission to use his wonderful photographs for the cover.

Dozens of others have been supportive of this project. Those who provided valuable comments in conference sessions include Ann Short Chirhart, Bob Korstad, Gaines Foster, and audiences at the 2001 Southern Historical Association, 2004 Organization of American Historians, and 2004 Oral History Association. Thanks to Pete Daniel, Sally Deutsch, and Catherine Clinton for all kinds of help and encouragement. Pamela Grundy generously shared her book about Clay County, Alabama, and her understandings of country people. Ted Ownby offered important insights on the study of memory. Lu Ann Jones read chapter 1 and made several important suggestions. Charlie Thompson read the conclusion and gave me new ways to think about the stories told by farm people. Anita Gustafson read chapter 5 and shared insights from her own work on immigrant communities. Members of my writers group at Converse College— Laura Feitzinger Brown, Anita Rose, Suzanne Schuweiler-Daab, and Cathy West—read drafts of several portions of this manuscript and provided sustaining encouragement as well as sound advice that helped me hone my arguments. I am also grateful to my colleagues Corrie Norman and Monica McCoy for their comments on portions of this work. I owe big thanks to my student assistants, Madison Boyd and Kaitlin Brown, for meticulous fact-checking in the final stage of manuscript preparation; they saved me from countless careless errors.

Several friends have gone above and beyond the call of friendship by reading the entire manuscript at various stages of muddlement, and they have saved me from careless errors, irrational interpretations, and oversimplifications. (Any remaining errors are mine alone.) Thanks to Steve Reschly, Mary Rolinson, Kathy Cann, John Theilmann, Brooks Blevins, and Mark Schultz. Fitz Brundage and Michele Gillespie gave the manuscript a careful reading for University Press of Kentucky and made astute suggestions. Joyce Harrison and Michele Gillespie helped me sort through organizational issues. The team at University Press of Kentucky has been superb. I owe them all a huge debt.

During my visits to Baylor, I got to know Rebecca Sharpless, a woman whose skill as a historian and conscientious care in her practice of oral history are a shining example of the best our profession can be. In the years since, Rebecca's kind humor, good sense, and insightful understanding of the lives of southerners have made my work much better, and her friendship has enriched my life. I don't even know where to begin thanking her for her help on this project, including a careful reading of the entire manuscript, yeoman's work checking demographic data, helpful comments on a paper at the 2004 Oral History Association, and endless encouragement along the way. I am grateful for all her support and for the hospitality she and Tom Charlton extended when I visited Waco.

My family provided plenty of moral support during the years I worked on this project. Thanks especially to my parents, Guy and Rachel Walker. Most of all, thanks to my husband and partner in this academic life, Chuck Reback. He has accompanied me to archives, tolerated my distraction, and helped me maintain some perspective on life outside the pages of my manuscript.

Introduction

Texan Leota Kuykendall explained, "Farm life of later years became like a factory in town really. It was a totally different kind of farm life." Interviewed in 1992, Kuykendall offered a detailed description of the changes in southern agriculture since her 1936 birth. As she outlined the impact of specialization, mechanization, and expansion on farm families, Kuykendall was not sure that twentieth-century transformations constituted progress for farm people. She said, "I believe, personally, that the farm life of my childhood had more potential for a lot more personal fulfillment than the farm life of the later years. Even my own father's farm, in the later years, I do not believe was as personally rewarding as the much earlier years. For example, when I was a very young child, . . . my father might be in the barnyard training the horses and mules or he might be fixing fences or out on the cotton farm, or the corn, or the maze [sic], or the oats, or the garden, or the peach orchard. The variety of work was tremendous, which I believe creates a lot of potential for a lot of personal fulfillment in the work." When Kuykendall asked her father whether he would choose farming again, he told her, "All I ever wanted to do is be a farmer and I did what I wanted to do." She went on, "So he had that kinship to the soil. . . . [But in] later years modern mechanization took that in a whole different direction, which I think created . . . from my point of view anyway, less opportunity for that real personal fulfillment. And for the woman on the farm, it would be the same way, because in the early farm days there was all this . . . diversity in the home. . . . And the focus was not on a pretty house and a clean house and all the things that we talk about today." Instead, Kuykendall explained, farm wives of an earlier generation focused on the essential task of providing food for their families. "So methods were . . . perhaps harder and less convenient, but there was a lot of opportunity for a lot more fulfillment. And I hear this particularly when I talk to my aunt because . . . she talks about her mother and her family . . . with

1

a lot of view of the creativity and how to have a little extra income, like in the sorghum molasses production. . . ." Kuykendall summed up her critique of modern farm life by describing later visits to her parents' farm: "When I would go home to visit my parents in the last days before they retired, [they had] these huge, huge chicken houses with thousands of chickens. . . . This work was an entirely different kind of work than the farm of my childhood. So it changed the whole . . . character of farming and life on the farm."[1]

Like Leota Kuykendall, hundreds of rural southerners told oral history interviewers stories about how late-twentieth-century agriculture was "totally different" from farming earlier in the century. The very act of telling stories about the past is a way of making meaning—of interpreting and explaining. By telling stories about life on the land, rural southerners searched for order and meaning in economic and social changes. Storytelling is, in the words of historian David Blight, part of "the human quest to own the past and thereby achieve control over the present."[2] Storytelling is also a method of drawing connections between events and people, past and present. Such stories aim to illuminate the past for a younger generation. Although Leota Kuykendall is more philosophical and articulate than many oral history narrators, the way that she uses memory to give meaning to the changes she witnessed is typical. In their stories of southern transformation, rural southerners weave an intricately designed fabric from the weft of narration and the warp of interpretation. Oral historian Alessandro Portelli reminds us that "there is no narration without interpretation."[3] Oral narratives about the rural South incorporate the "what happened" of the past with the "why," the "how," and the "so what." For example, Kuykendall did not confine herself to the "what happened"—the shift from diversified general farming to "these huge, huge chicken houses" or from farm women's work that focused on providing necessities to work designed to create "a pretty house and a clean house." Throughout her account, she interprets the meaning of agricultural change for farm families: less personal satisfaction, less daily variety, and fewer opportunities to exercise creativity. She approaches this interpretation using conceptual tools drawn from the popular psychology of the 1970s and 1980s. Kuykendall's reservations about late-twentieth-century agriculture were rooted in memories of the farmwork of her childhood and framed in the analytical and interpretive terms of late twentieth-century ideas about work as a form of personal fulfillment.

Kuykendall's account illuminates the tangled relationship between memory and history. The stories that rural southerners tell about changes in the countryside are based in memory, and memory is forged in the crucible of a lifetime. It is the product of a complex alchemy of recall, interpretation, and reinterpretation. Later experiences and cultural forces filter and reframe memories so that stories about the past morph and twist over time. Even nostalgia, that vague longing for an earlier time that often tints memories with a rosy glow, serves a purpose. Seventy-five years ago, Southern Agrarian writer John Crowe Ransom astutely characterized nostalgia as a psychic growing pain, an "instinctive reaction to being transplanted."[4] Historian David Anderson agreed, noting "nostalgia occurs most forcibly after a profound split in remembered events and experiences," and that nostalgic memories become a way for the rememberer to preserve "a thread of continuity" in the face of present-day change and upheaval.[5] Historian Dan T. Carter put it another way: "we constantly recreate memory so that our past can live comfortably with the present without the jarring dissonances that inevitably accompany change through time."[6]

The challenge for the historian who uses oral narratives and other memory-based sources is not simply to sort out the truth from the falsehoods, but rather to consider the shape of the memory stories and to explore what the shape of those stories tells us about the storyteller and his or her world. In considering multiple narratives, we must examine the patterns that emerge in the ways narrators tell their stories. David Blight has argued that though memory is not history, "written history cannot be completely disengaged from social memory."[7] If we cannot disentangle memory from history, we must learn to explore the meaning of the memory and incorporate that exploration into our writing about the past.

Southern Farmers and Their Stories provides a case study in how ordinary people construct and use memories about the personal and national past in their daily lives by examining rural southerners' stories about the social and economic transformations they experienced in the twentieth century. By studying the shape of memory-based stories, I seek to map the intersections of history and memory in order to tell a more nuanced story of the past. In short, I will use memory as a category of cultural and historical analysis in order to gain new insights into ordinary people's experiences of historical change. This study seeks to answer three main questions. First, what experiences molded rural southerners' sense of shared past? Second, how did they remember rural transformation? Third, what does the shape of their stories about change tell us about how people use memories and knowledge of the past to make sense of the world in which they live today?

My own interest in this topic emerged gradually. After repeated readings of my own oral history interviews with rural Tennesseans, I began to focus less on the details of their stories about agricultural transformation and more on the recurring patterns in their narratives. Over and over, in ways both subtle and explicit, the people I interviewed asserted that country people were different than those who had not lived on the land. Such stories resonated with me because I grew up on a farm and had early absorbed from my own family's storytelling a certainty that country people were different. As I read and reread interview transcripts, I began to understand that my narrators were delineating the boundaries of their community of memory. My fascination with the recurrent narrative themes in my interviews led me first to the literature on interpreting oral history and then to scholarship on collective memory and on relationships between history and memory. I also headed back to the archives to read nearly five hundred interviews with rural southerners from other states. I found that rural people all over the South shared a similar mental map of the boundaries of their community of memory. However, I also began to notice dissonances, ways in which narrators' memories of similar events diverged and detoured. Nowhere were these dissonances more pronounced than in their stories about the twentieth-century transformations of southern agriculture. I also began to note textual evidence that the present was molding narrators' stories about the past. My own understandings of rural transformations and of how ordinary people experienced those transformations were becoming layered and more complicated.

Communities of Memory

Southern farm people peppered their oral history narratives about life on the land with observations about how that life made them different from "town folks." By telling stories about life on the land, twentieth-century rural southerners forged a community of memory. Sociologist Robert N. Bellah and his team of researchers developed the concept of "communities of memory" to describe the communities constituted by a shared past.[8] Creating a community of memory for a particular group is, in part, a process of constructing group boundaries. As historian Edward L. Ayers has observed, this process is "inherently political; it is about defining us against them—whether the 'us' is the nation-state, ethnic group, geographic population, family or organization—any group with a recognizable past to which it can lay claim." Groups develop their communities of memory by talking with each other—by creating a shared understanding of the world in which they lived and the characteristics that make them different from others who did not live in that world. Over time and with repeated conversations about shared experiences or a way of life from the group's shared past, a community of memory emerges.[9] The oral history narrators in this study mapped the boundaries of their community of memory by telling stories about their shared rural past—about the nature of farm life and work. Though rural southerners created a recognizable community of memory through their oral history narratives, that community was by no means monolithic. Recurring narrative themes reveal significant gender, class, racial, and generational divides among storytellers and their stories.

Southern farm people used memory to understand their past, their present, and the possibilities looming in their future. Rural southerners did not, however, engage in such memory work simply to express the boundaries of a community of memory or to help interviewers understand the past. They also used their stories to address serious matters in their present worlds. Individuals' recollections of the past were colored and continually redrawn by subsequent experiences; thus narrators see the past through the prism of everything that came afterward. Southern farm people framed their stories about the past by consciously contrasting those days to the present. Stories about the past also served didactic purposes; rural southerners believed that some values were being undermined in contemporary society, and they told stories about the idealized past in an attempt to convince a younger generation that these values were worth preserving. In this instance, memories of the past provided narrators with a tool to convey a sense of what was possible—of what the future might look like if it combined the best features of past and present. Perhaps the didactic nature of their stories grew out of the fact that rural southerners—even those who no longer worked the land—saw themselves as a group in decline. French scholar Pierre Bourdieu argued that when a group (he used the term "class") is in decline, when they feel their collective future is threatened, they may seek to "maintain their value by binding themselves to the past."[10] Rural southerners use their stories about the past, their assertions that we have lost something important by turning away from life on the land, to assert the value of the life they had lived.

A clarification of terms is in order at this point: I will not use the term "class" to refer to the community of memory formed by people who experienced twentieth-century agricultural transformation, though in some ways it seems apt. Many scholars have defined "class" broadly—as a group of people who share the same categories of interests, social experiences, values, traditions, and ambitions. Thus broadly conceived, "class" might seem an appropriate word to describe rural southerners' sense that they shared a set of interests and values shaped by their experiences on the land. As sociologist Scott McNall has argued, groups of people develop class consciousness from shared categories of lived experiences. Such consciousness includes both material and cognitive dimensions. In other words, through shared experiences, people develop a disposition to define themselves as a class in relation to other social groups and to behave in ways that further their own class interests.[11]

Such broad usage of the term "class" might prove misleading, however. Class is one of those terms that scholars bandy about freely, assuming that all readers understand how we are using it. Most often the word is used to describe the relative socioeconomic positions of various groups, particularly vis à vis that group's relationship to the means of production. Rural southerners—landowning and tenant alike—did indeed share many interests, experiences, values, traditions, and ambitions, and they did define themselves in opposition to non-rural people. Nonetheless, sharp material differences separated the landowning and landless who participated in the same community of memory.[12] These material differences could shape significantly different experiences of rural transformation—and different modes of articulating memory—even among members of the rural community of memory. To avoid confusion, I will use the term "community of memory" to refer to the shared experiences that bound rural southerners together, across economic lines, and the term "class" to refer to the economic differences among farm families.

Historians and the Study of Memory

In recent years, American historians have sought to understand the relationship between history and memory. Most scholars use the term "collective memory" to refer to the shared understanding of a particular group's past. The group might be a nation, but racial or ethnic groups, socioeconomic classes, communities, organizations, workers, and families all hold collective memories. Collective memory, according to psychologist Susan Engel, is a term that expresses "the idea . . . that each person in the community, group, or society has an overlapping or similar narrative or collection of details and facts about an event" from the past.[13] Numerous studies have focused on the ways that a national collective memory is constructed and how political leaders manipulate that memory to promote nationalism and to suppress dissent. Other studies have examined the ways that collective memory is expressed in public commemoration, popular culture, or political rhetoric.[14]

Yet not all collective memory is national collective memory and not all of it is publicly articulated. Often collective memory—particularly memories of local life or daily experience—is articulated only when small groups of people get together to discuss the past. In other cases, individuals include elements of collective memories in personal recollections from times gone by. Only rarely have historians paid attention to the ways ordinary people construct and use collective memory in their daily lives.[15] For that reason, most studies of collective memory provide us with, at best, an incomplete picture of the relationship between history and memory. Collective memory must be located in the individual and articulated by the individual in order to play any role in social or political life. Understanding the ways that individuals use memories about the past—especially memories about shared life-transforming experiences—is therefore essential to understanding the role of memory in our society. Indeed, examining memory as it is expressed in oral history narratives can reveal dissonances between individual and collective memory.[16] Oral history provides a powerful tool for examining such memory, especially the role of memory among society's least powerful groups. As historian Michael Frisch put it, oral history provides us with a look at "the processes by which the past is received, digested, and actively related to the present, and an opportunity to see how a broader class consciousness is expressed in the ways people communicate that memory or experience in the social context of an interview."[17] Although oral narratives are shaped in myriad conscious and subconscious ways by the larger culture, they nonetheless are individual forms of expression in which personal memories and the meanings of those memories may be more openly expressed.

While ordinary people often form "communities of memory," it is important, as I have already suggested, not to overstate the extent to which such memories are homogeneous. Indeed, the very concept of collective memory can be problematic when applied to the recollections of individuals. Historian Alessandro Portelli cautions against using the term "collective memory" to refer to the recurring patterns of memory expressed in individuals' oral history narratives. The danger, he believes, is that in doing so we will distort or oversimplify the past. As he put it, "[T]he act and art of remembering is always deeply personal. Like language, memory is social, but it only materializes through the minds and mouths of individuals. . . . Though we are working to construct memories that can be shared and used collectively, yet we should be wary of locating memory outside the individual."[18] He adds:

> If all memory were collective, one witness could serve for an entire culture—but we know that it is not so. Each individual, especially in modern times and societies, derives memories from a variety of groups, and organizes them in idiosyncratic fashion. Like all human activities, memory is *social* and may be *shared*, . . . however, . . . it only materializes in individual recollections and speech acts. It becomes *collective* memory only when it is abstracted and detached from the individual: in myth and folklore (one story for many people . . .), in

delegation (one person for many stories . . .), in institutions (abstract subjects—school, church, State Party) that organize memories and rituals into a whole other than the sum of its separate parts. [his emphases][19]

I agree with Portelli that scholars should not use the term "collective memory" to refer to individually articulated memories. For that reason, rather than "collective memory," I have chosen to use the term "communities of memory" to describe the shared memories of rural southerners. Collective memory exists, and elements of collective memory are often embedded in individual recollections. The extent to which the collective memory—the abstracted memory of commemoration and myth—shapes individual memory and the extent to which individual memories inform and shape expressions of such collective memory are nearly impossible to sort out. Individual and collective memory work as a dialectic process. The focus here is on individual memory and patterns in individual memory.[20]

There are dangers inherent in the study of memory. Just as the dominant powers in any given society can appropriate and manipulate memories of the past to serve their own political purposes, so can historians. Scholars can exaggerate the extent to which "cultural leaders," to borrow historian John Bodnar's term, use collective memory to dominate the masses. They can also read too much resistance into the shared memories of subaltern groups. Similarly, social and cultural theory can be a powerful tool for such appropriations. Theory can illuminate the way people make sense of the past, but it can also obscure meaning and distance the interpreter of history from those who lived it. Either sin does a disservice to the rememberers. For this reason, I have remained sparing and cautious in my application of theory to the study of rural people's memories.[21]

For all its potential pitfalls, the study of memory provides a point of entry into the past that leads to sharply different perspectives on social history than those offered by examining traditional historical documents or even the straightforward content contained in oral history. By exploring how ordinary people remember the past, historians can better understand what social reality felt like to those who lived it. Such a study can also lend new insights into the choices those people made in the past as well as those that they make in today's world. Finally, an examination of communities of memory reminds historians that it is crucial to seek multiple perspectives when examining historical change. The nuanced complexity of rural southerners' stories of transformation suggests that historians have tended to oversimplify the process of agricultural change and its effects on farm people. Careful attention to stories of transformation, particularly to shifts in the ways those stories are told, lends new insights into how larger social forces can reshape ordinary people's understandings of change.

The Place, The Sample, and The Method

The rural South in the first half of the twentieth century provides a unique opportunity to examine how ordinary people make sense of historical forces that shape their lives. Few places and periods in American history have been as well documented by scholars as the Great Depression/New Deal–era South. Scholarly accounts have been complemented and enriched by thousands of letters that ordinary Americans wrote to Franklin and Eleanor Roosevelt, appealing for help with their dire economic problems, and by the efforts of Depression-era social scientists to document the living conditions of the rural South.[22] In recent years, oral historians have gathered thousands of hours of oral interviews in their attempt to preserve the experiences of ordinary southerners. By studying historians' accounts, contemporary documents, and oral history interviews together, it is possible to gain a better understanding of how people understand large national events that shape their lives and the ways they construct and use memories about a shared past.

Though I have focused my study on the rural South in order to create a project of manageable scope, this is as much a rural study as a southern one. Many rural areas in other parts of the United States underwent similar changes in the twentieth century, and my limited reading of oral history interviews from the Midwest suggests that the memories of rural folk there resembled those of southerners in many ways. Nonetheless, race mattered more in the South than in any other part of the nation. Legal segregation and socially sanctioned discrimination dominated the lives of whites and blacks during the first half of the century, and the slow but steady breakdown of those racial barriers in the last half of the century generated unique stories, particularly among black farmers. Poverty was also more pronounced in the rural South, and tenancy rates were higher there than in any other part of the nation.

By using interviews gathered for a variety of purposes, I have been able to amass a fairly representative sample of early-twentieth-century rural experiences. If I simply interviewed southern farm people today, my sample would be limited to people who had managed to persist on the land. However, this study uses collections of interviews gathered to document southern textile and steel mill life, black life in the Jim Crow South, and even southern Appalachian folklore. Such interviews often contain details of the narrators' lives on farms. Of the 475 interviews with 531 people included in this study, more than half were intended to record details about the nature of rural life, whether the goal was to document changes in agriculture, the history of rural churches, home extension work, or southern rural communities. The rest were conducted for other purposes, but the narrators nonetheless describe life on the land at some point in the interview.

As a result, my sample includes interviews with people who were forced to leave the land as well as those who managed to stay. Many who left the land were tenants. Nonetheless, tenants are underrepresented in my sample. In 1920, 50.9 percent of southerners were tenants of some kind, but only about one-fifth of the interviews included in this study were with landless farmers. Of 475 interviews, 260 (54.7 percent) were conducted with landowners while only 97 (20.4 percent) were non-landowning farmers. (The rest lived in the countryside but earned most of their livelihood through off-farm activities.) Roughly 61 percent of the whites in my sample were landowners compared to 60.4 percent in 1920. By contrast, 35.4 percent of landowners in my study were black compared to 22.4 percent in 1920. (See the Appendix for more demographic data on the interviewees included in this study.)[23] Thus, landowners, especially black landowners, are overrepresented in this study, suggesting that my sample was somewhat more prosperous than southern rural farmers as a group.

Most interviewees in this study were born before 1930, and all had lived in the countryside at least part of their lives. All would have identified themselves as rural, and those still farming at the time of the interview saw themselves as family farmers. A few farmed five hundred or more acres, but all lived on farms that were subject to family management and control, and family members worked the land themselves. Over half of the interviewees included in this study (287, or 54 percent) were women, a figure that is not surprising given the fact that most were elderly and that women tend to outlive men. One-fourth of interviewees were African American, a figure that roughly reflected the proportion of total African American residents in the rural South throughout the period. Interviewees represented all eleven of the former Confederate states plus three of the border states, Kentucky, Maryland, and West Virginia. The largest numbers of interviewees hailed from Alabama, Texas, and North Carolina, in part because several large oral history projects were launched in those states. The education level of nearly half the interviewees was impossible to determine from the material available, but for those who gave information on education, nearly half had attained some education beyond high school, suggesting that people in this sample were far more educated than average rural southerners of the period.

While using interviews conducted for a wide variety of purposes by a wide variety of interviewers provided me with a large and somewhat representative sample, diverse interview goals and interviewers also meant that the shape and content of the interviews varied widely. I accommodated those differences by conducting close textual readings of narrators' comments about several categories of shared experience including agricultural transformation, government intervention, the Great Depression, World War II, leaving the land, new opportunities off the farm, the virtues of rural life, and the values that have been lost from the rural past.

I chose to use archived interviews in order to access an exceptionally large sample of oral history interviews. It would have taken me a lifetime to conduct, transcribe, and analyze the 475 interviews used for this project, and a project of a smaller scope would not have offered the same insights into patterns of memory. Scholars must nonetheless approach the use of archived interviews with caution. In cases where I conducted an interview, I not only remember details about my interactions with the narrator, but I also know why I chose that interviewee and why I focused my questions on particular topics while ignoring others. In short, I understand the context of an interview that I conducted myself more deeply than I will ever understand the context of an archived interview. As a result, the danger in using archived interviews is that I may misread an interview in ways that the interviewer would not. For example, in an earlier analysis of one interview used in this study, I interpreted the omission of a topic from the narrator's account as a "silence," and I speculated about the meaning of that silence. When I asked the original interviewer to read my draft, however, she explained the context in which the interview was done and noted that indeed the omission was probably not a "silence," but rather was simply "an artifact of the particular line of questioning" that she had pursued.[24] With this caution in mind, I have tried to be careful not to overstate the "silences" and to read them in the context of actual questions and topics pursued by the interviewer.

The Oral History Process and Memory

The literal and figurative space in which the recalled past is invoked matters. When an interviewer asks an individual to participate in an oral history project, the narrator knows instinctively that he or she will be asked to recall the details of past life, to reflect on the meaning of that life, and to place it in some larger context. Even before the interview, a narrator is considering which stories to tell and what those stories mean in the bigger picture—whether that bigger picture is southern farm life, race relations in the Jim Crow South, or the impact of southern industrialization. In short, memories are shaped to include both narration and interpretation in order to meet the expectations of the oral history process. Reflecting on the ways the oral history process molds the stories told by narrators lays a foundation for an analysis of memory in oral history.

Oral history narrators shape their narratives around their interactions with the interviewer. Oral history is a dialogue, a conversation between an interviewer and the narrator. Thus, the interviewer plays a significant role in shaping memory as it is expressed in the narrative. The questions an interviewer asks help determine the contours of the story. Leading, suggestive, or repeated questions can distort memories. Open-ended questions may elicit more accurate memories because the narrator is not trying to direct an answer to the interviewer's specific agenda, but open-ended questions may also elicit less information than more detailed questions. An interviewer who says, "tell me your life story" will get a far different set of recollections than an interviewer who says, "tell me about life during the Great Depression." An interviewer who fails to listen and ask follow-up questions may not obtain significant details or explanations.

Narrators respond to different interviewers and audiences in various ways. They will often shape their stories based on what they perceive to be the expectations of the interviewer or on whom they think might "listen" to the story. For example, an older narrator who maintains racial beliefs that have become unacceptable in our twenty-first-century world may not share them with a younger interviewer. Black subjects are often not forthcoming with white interviewers and vice versa. Even if speaking decades after the Civil War, a southerner may not provide certain details of southern life to a northern-born interviewer. Women usually will not share some intimate details of childbearing or marital relationships with male interviewers. In short, the narrator will share information he or she believes is appropriate for sharing with that particular researcher or audience. The way a narrator tells a story is based on his or her assumptions about who is listening, so that oral history narratives are always filtered through a web of social relationships.

Most of the narrators whose oral histories were used for this study told their life stories during old age, a fact that also shaped their stories. Late in life, we realize that we are among the last living witnesses to a time period or particular way of life. We may engage in "life reviews" at this point, and older people become acutely aware that their own generation has witnessed events or experienced a way of life that subsequent generations will not. These narrators possess a sense of being "memory bearers." Many understand that they lived through a period of remarkable transformation, and this self-consciousness helps shape the way they tell their life stories.[25] Rural narrators were acutely aware that they were helping to preserve knowledge of a disappearing past, and they shaped their stories in ways calculated to help defend particular interpretations of that past.

Painful memories sometimes disappear from narrators' life stories, particularly near the end of life. Nearly one hundred years ago, Hull House founder Jane Addams noted that elderly members of the urban immigrant population served by Hull House engaged in such life reviews, in the process romanticizing the pleasant elements of the past and erasing many of the more traumatic features of their personal histories. As Addams put it, older people, "in reviewing the long road they have traveled, are able to transmute their own untoward experiences into that which makes even the most wretched life acceptable. This may possibly be due to an instinct of self-preservation, which checks the devastating bitterness that would result did they recall over and over again the sordid details of events long past."[26]

As I have already suggested, the present also shapes oral history narrators' stories about the past. Folklorist Elizabeth Tonkin has noted, "People talk of 'the past' so as to distinguish 'now' from a different 'then.'"[27] It is important for historians to understand this fact and to understand how the current moment in the narrator's life shapes his or her stories about past events. The way narrators frame stories about the past tells us much about the way they view the world they live in today and the things they feel have been lost in the wake of modernization and change. In addition, narrators interviewed in different eras may tell the story in different ways. Roughly 38 percent of the interviews in this study were conducted before 1985—that is, before the farm crisis of the 1980s. Those narrators' perspectives on changes in southern agriculture are often profoundly different from those interviewed after 1985, when the publicity surrounding the farm crisis reshaped understandings among even those narrators personally untouched by the crisis.

Whether or not major historical events become part of the elderly narrators' set of detailed memories depends on several factors. For the most part, rural southerners began their stories about the past not with major national events, but with what historian George Lipsitz has described as "the local, the immediate, and the personal."[28] Narrators turned first to stories about themselves, their families, and their geographic communities. They then tied this individual history to broader contexts, especially economic changes. National events appeared in rural southerners' stories primarily when the event touched the life of the storyteller. Narrators connected the major national events driving rural transformation—events such as the implementation of New Deal programs, World War II, and the development of an increasingly global market for farm commodities—to their own stories of change in vague and highly personalized ways. A major historical event may be remembered in some detail if it was connected in memory with intense emotion or if it proved a turning point in the narrator's life. For example, men who had served in World War II often recounted vivid memories of their own wartime service. Many of them also knew a great deal about the larger political and military context of the war, perhaps because they continued to read about the war in later years. In most cases, they have talked frequently about the war with other veterans, thus rehearsing their stories. By contrast, male narrators who were not veterans interpreted the war as an economic turning point for the South rather than a triumph over fascism. Unlike men, most women remembered little about the war itself, focusing instead on the ways the war altered daily life. Women recalled worrying about loved ones in military service and dealing with shortages and rationing, but few mentioned the details of the military or political history of the war. Such differences in narrative recollections of the war may or may not reflect deep-seated gender differences in what narrators deem important to remember, but the differences in men's and women's stories do reflect the gendered nature of their World War II experiences.

Not only do narrators remember national events in personalized ways, but they also sometimes confuse details of such events. Historian Alessandro Portelli noted that narrators often portray a long series of separate though related events as "one protracted event."[29] Many narrators in this study conflated the Great Depression with World War II. For example, Kentuckian Mary Fouts said, "[The Depression] was called 'hard times,' but to me, I couldn't tell very much difference because our times was hard anyway. . . . I remember the soup lines . . . and I remember the ration stamps. We had to have rations to get sugar and to get shoes."[30] Fouts saw both the Great Depression and World War II as "hard times," and she did not discriminate between the two events in recounting her memories.

The Southern Countryside Transformed

Twentieth-century southern rural transformation was driven by economic crisis, government intervention, technological innovations, and structural changes in the agricultural economy. Although some people remained in the countryside, by the end of the twentieth century, most southerners had ceased cultivating the land in favor of off-farm jobs. The few who remained in agriculture usually adopted large-scale commercial farming methods. Many of those who continued to farm also continued to struggle as increased operating costs, fluctuating prices on the world commodities market, and a bewildering array of federal programs made farming a risky and complicated business. Economic changes brought social changes in their wake, profoundly altering rural southern communities. Many traditional mutual aid networks disintegrated, replaced by impersonal social service programs that provided a complex and often inconsistent safety net for the poor, the unlucky, and the elderly. Chain stores drove local merchants out of business, changing the nature of individuals' relationships to the local business community. Improved transportation and communication enabled rural people to participate more fully in national popular culture. The scholarly story of this southern rural transformation has been told—and told well—elsewhere.[31] The reader who is well acquainted with the contours of twentieth-century agricultural transformation may want to skip the next few pages, an overview of the nature and shape of the changes in southern agriculture, but readers unfamiliar with the story will find the background they need to contextualize rural southerners' memories of this transformation.

The early-twentieth-century South was shaped by the aftermath of the Civil War, a cataclysm that devastated the southern countryside. Much of the South's physical and economic infrastructure lay in ruins. In many regions, such as Virginia and middle Tennessee, the land itself had been ravaged by battles and raiding troops on both sides. Most of all, the South's distinctive labor system, chattel slavery, had been swept away by emancipation, leaving landowners to grapple with the mammoth task of rebuilding without cash and without an ample supply of forced labor. The South was compelled to remake itself economically, and southerners built first on the economic enterprise they knew best—agriculture. Yet the economic winds of the late nineteenth and early twentieth centuries rarely blew as felicitously on agriculture as in the decades before the war.

After the Civil War, many areas of the South cultivated a single crop. In parts of Kentucky, Virginia, Tennessee, North and South Carolina, Georgia, and Alabama, the crop was tobacco. The Gulf

Coast and parts of the Arkansas Delta grew prairie rice, and many Louisiana farmers continued to raise sugar cane. In much of the South, however, cotton remained king, and as one historian has put it, "cotton was a cruel tyrant."[32] Southern farmers' familiarity with cotton cultivation, an existing cotton marketing system, and a favorable climate combined to make the staple crop attractive to farmers. Unfortunately, during the Civil War, European manufacturers had developed other sources of cotton to feed their textile mills. In spite of high prices immediately after the war, as southern cotton production recovered and grew, prices fell. Cotton also quickly drained the soil of fertility in the days before chemical fertilizers, rendering barren thousands of acres of already marginal southern farmland. In most years, cotton was not particularly profitable. In spite of its shortcomings, however, tens of thousands of southerners staked their futures on cotton cultivation.

The production of some crops, notably tobacco and cotton, proved extremely difficult to mechanize, and in any event, most southern farmers lacked the capital to buy expensive laborsaving equipment, so they persisted with timeworn labor-intensive methods well into the twentieth century. The abolition of slavery forced southerners to reorganize the farm labor system. Most newly freed African Americans found it impossible to accumulate the cash they needed to purchase land. At the same time, many cash-strapped plantation owners struggled to find willing laborers among freedpeople seeking independence from white control. Gradually a new system of labor known as sharecropping emerged, a negotiated solution that provided landowners with farm labor and the landless with access to land and hope for some measure of autonomy. Typically, a landowner provided the sharecropper and his family with a plot of land and a small house in exchange for a share of the crop or occasionally a cash rent payment. The specific tenancy arrangements varied, depending on whether a sharecropper owned his own work stock and tools or whether he could afford to buy his own seed or pay cash rent.

The sharecropping system recreated many of the most exploitative features of the antebellum plantation system, offering widely varying levels of autonomy. A sharecropper's entire family labored in the fields throughout the year. In the best situations, the family labored without close supervision from the landowner, but in the worst, the landlord or his hired foreman interfered in every aspect of the sharecropping family's work and lives, even prohibiting them from growing a garden or keeping livestock, both activities that would provide a landless family with some independence from landlord control. Many landlords made additional demands on the sharecropping family's labor, insisting that croppers work an owner's fields as well as their own or that sharecropping women do domestic work for a landlord's wife. Because landless farmers were dependent on the landlord for more than land and housing, elite white landowners exercised considerable control over the lives and fortunes of dependent blacks (and eventually an increasing number of whites). Since cash flowed only with the sale of the crop after harvest, farming families lived without income much of the year. Sharecroppers often devoted so much time and so many resources to one-crop farming that they raised little of their own subsistence, leaving them dependent on store-bought food and clothing. The landowner or another local merchant usually advanced the sharecropper food, clothing, seed, and other supplies throughout the year. This advance of goods was known as a "furnish," and the furnishing merchant held a lien against the future crop to secure the sharecropper's debt. At harvest time, the landowner took his share of the harvest while the furnishing merchant totaled the sharecropper's debt plus interest and subtracted it from the value of the remaining harvest. Anything that was left over constituted the sharecropper's profit for the family's labor that year. Much of the time, there was little left, and some years sharecroppers were not able to pay off what they owed, instead sinking further and further into debt. Avaricious landlords also used the furnishing system to gouge tenants with high interest rates and outrageous prices, and some landowners cheated tenants outright. Tenants who challenged the landlord's control could face arrest, eviction, or violence. At its best, the sharecropping system provided the landless with access to land and an opportunity to accumulate savings and thus climb the agricultural economic ladder. At its worst, and the system was often at its worst, sharecroppers remained utterly dependent on grasping landowners.

As the South's farm economy stagnated in the late nineteenth century, sharecropping spread. Many white yeoman landowners slipped into tenancy. A cycle of overproduction, volatile commodity prices, and indebtedness sucked many southern landowners, black and white, into farm tenancy and the crop lien system. By 1900 about one-third of white farmers and three-quarters of black farmers in the South worked land they did not own.[33] That year, per capita income in the South was half the national average, and much of that differential was due to the terrible conditions in the southern countryside.[34]

Southern agriculture began its long transition to modernity in the 1910s and 1920s. Historian Deborah Fitzgerald has argued that the early decades of the twentieth century saw the emergence of an industrial ideal in agriculture. A new class of experts including university professors, U.S. Department of Agriculture (USDA) employees, bankers, and agribusiness executives urged farmers to apply industrial notions of specialization, mechanization, efficiency, and economies of scale to the farming enterprise. Interconnected systems of production and consumption emerged, tying together economic sectors and geographic regions as never before and leaving farmers more vulnerable to economic fluctuations. Southern farm families confronted this new industrial agricultural milieu at a disadvantage compared to their counterparts elsewhere in the United States. Thanks to high levels of tenancy, the lingering economic effects of the Civil War, undercapitalized and undermechanized farms, and dependence on particularly volatile agricultural commodities, post–Civil War southern farmers did not enjoy the same level of prosperity as farmers in other parts of the country; in the words of economic historian Peter A. Coclanis, "the region's agricultural sector in 1900 seems like a textbook model of agricultural underdevelopment."[35] As agriculture became increasingly "industrialized" throughout the nation, southern farmers were tied to supply, credit, and distribution networks geared to a commercial agriculture that they could not yet practice.

In the South, a constellation of agricultural and rural reformers promoted the adoption of industrial farming methods. Their efforts were rooted in the ideas of the Country Life Movement. Believing that American agriculture was backward and that young people dissatisfied with rural life were abandoning the land in droves, many urban Progressive-era reformers feared that a youthful flight from the land would in turn spark a food shortage. Though these reformers often drew on the report of President Theodore Roosevelt's 1907 Country Life Commission to support their recommendations, recent scholarship suggests a wide gulf between the Country Life Commission's vision of a "self-sustaining agriculture" reformed at the grass roots and the Country Life Movement's patronizing view of farmers as ignorant practitioners in need of "expert advice."[36] Nonetheless, the Country Life Movement's promotion of scientific agriculture, which used the new machinery and techniques being developed in the nation's land-grant colleges and agricultural experiment stations, soon gained currency among the agricultural establishment.

The need for rural reform was especially obvious in the South, where most farmers remained mired in poverty and substandard living conditions. Here the USDA led the efforts to improve agriculture with the assistance of the Rosenwald Fund, a Sears-Roebuck executive's charity, and the Rockefeller family's General Education Board (GEB). Both private agencies were dedicated to improving southern health and education. Reformers not only sought to improve rural schools, but they also taught farm men and women better agricultural and homemaking practices. Most of this adult education took the form of agricultural extension work. Pioneered in Texas in 1902 by a scientist named Seaman Knapp, agricultural extension work took university-trained agriculturists directly to farmers to demonstrate the advantages of adopting new and better practices. Knapp's methods soon gained the attention of Country Life reformers and of the USDA. The Rosenwald Fund and the GEB provided funding to expand agricultural extension work in the South, including a separate program for black farmers. In 1914, Congress passed the Smith-Lever Act, providing federal matching funds to help states expand extension programming.

Agricultural extension agents taught landowning southern farmers improved methods of cultivation designed to increase their productivity and profits. They encouraged farmers to adopt modern soil conservation methods, to purchase hybrid seeds and chemical fertilizers, to use laborsaving equipment, and to specialize in one or two staple crops. Agricultural agents' female counterparts, home demonstration agents, encouraged farm wives to be effective helpmeets for their farmer husbands. Home agents taught farm women improved gardening and food preservation practices, techniques for providing the family with a balanced diet year-round, and ways to inexpensively make fashionable clothing or home accessories. The primary goal of all these extension activities was to make the farm a more comfortable, attractive, and prosperous place to live.

For all their efforts to improve the lives of southern farm families, extension agents enjoyed limited success. Steeped in the USDA philosophy that the poorest and most inefficient farmers should be encouraged to leave the land while ambitious progressive farmers expanded their operations and adopted the methods of scientific agriculture, agents focused their efforts on landowners. Extension services for African Americans were segregated, and they suffered from understaffing and underfunding that limited black agents' ability to help black farmers. In addition, the poorest farm families of both races lacked the capital to adopt the modern methods advocated by extension workers. The structure and philosophy of extension work became a major force in reshaping the face of southern agriculture, providing government support and assistance to prosperous landowners while providing limited service to the neediest farmers.

Southerners' disadvantage in the new industrial agricultural economy became apparent during the first two decades of the twentieth century, a period so prosperous for most American farmers that the period from 1910 to 1914 has been dubbed the "golden age of agriculture." During those years, national farm income more than doubled, and demand for farm products was high. Although some southern farmers did enjoy good years during the so-called golden age, most continued to struggle because of the high rate of tenancy and, for cotton farmers, the arrival of the crop-destroying boll weevil.

The boll weevil ate its way from Texas to Georgia between 1890 and 1920, sparking sustained intervention by government experts who advocated industrial agriculture. USDA officials taught farmers better cotton cultivation practices that helped discourage the dreaded pest, and they also urged farmers to diversify with other crops and with livestock production. Most southerners resisted diversification, often turning to part-time or seasonal off-farm work rather than changing to another crop.[37]

Outside the cotton-growing regions, farm life also remained uncertain during agriculture's golden age. Most of the South's tobacco growers raised bright-leaf tobacco for use in cigarette manufacturing. Tobacco farmers battled low commodity prices, cutthroat industry purchasing practices, and expensive production costs by organizing fertilizer and implement-buying cooperatives and entering into production-cutting agreements. Their efforts met limited success, for several reasons. Independent-minded southern farmers often resisted the adoption of voluntary production and marketing controls, undermining attempts to organize effective cooperatives. Tobacco prices also remained low thanks in part to the entrenched power of several large tobacco companies bent on keeping prices down. Rice farmers faced similar obstacles. In the first decade of the twentieth century, overproduction flooded rice markets, driving down prices. In addition, rice cultivation required expensive inputs such as equipment and irrigation. Like tobacco farmers, rice growers' attempts to organize proved unsatisfactory, and rice prices continued to fall well into the Great Depression.

Even in the southern Appalachian highlands, the early twentieth century's economic uncertainties challenged rural people. In some ways, the minority of southern farmers who lived in the southern Appalachians embodied the independent small family farmer. Large landholdings were rare here, and tenancy had never been as widespread as elsewhere in the South. Most southern mountaineers owned their land and engaged in subsistence farming with a small amount of production for the market. The independent yeoman culture of the mountaineers gradually eroded in the late nineteenth and early twentieth centuries as timber and coal companies discovered the riches available in the southern Appalachians. Company towns sprang up in the timbering and mining regions, luring local farmers to logging or mining jobs. Many eventually became dependent on off-farm wages. Some families succumbed to pressure to sell their land to timber and mining companies. Extractive industries caused environmental degradation that affected neighboring farmers. Those who remained on the land found it increasingly difficult to make a living farming in the face of rising property taxes and higher expectations for an improved standard of living. Many southern Appalachian people faced as much uncertainty and hardship during agriculture's golden age as their staple-crop-producing brethren elsewhere in the South.

For a brief time during the First World War, many rural southerners believed that things were looking up. With the outbreak of fighting in Europe, demand for American farm products skyrocketed.

Once the United States entered the war, a number of government programs encouraged farmers to increase their production in order to feed war-torn Europe as well as supply the American army. For example, the Food Administration, an agency created by Congress to help the federal government control food production and distribution, adopted the motto, "Food Will Win the War," imbuing farming with a sense of patriotic purpose. Congress also appropriated funds to hire additional extension agents for agricultural counties, and these agents fanned out over the South and the nation to promote industrial agriculture to new converts. Farm credit strictures were eased, enabling farmers to borrow large sums of cash for land, livestock, hybrid seed, and chemical fertilizers.

During World War I, many southern landowners took advantage of high profits to improve their lives, and especially to improve their farms, while some landless farmers left the countryside in search of better opportunities. Landowners bought additional acreage in hopes of increasing their long-term profits. Some purchased tractors and implements to help them work additional land and replace fleeing laborers. The wartime draft drained the southern agricultural regions of some farmworkers while northern labor recruiters also flooded the South offering workers free transportation north and the promise of good factory jobs. Between 1916 and 1921, as many as half a million southern blacks left the South, mostly sharecroppers fleeing the poverty and racial violence of the rural South for better opportunities in the industries of the North and West.[38]

Families who remained on the land enjoyed some prosperity into the first half of 1920. Then, as European farmers began to recover from the wartime disruptions, world demand for American farm products plummeted, followed by farm prices. Cotton prices dropped from 40 cents a pound in the spring of 1920 to 13.5 cents in December of the same year. Tobacco fell from 31.2 cents a pound to 17.3 cents in the same period. Prices recovered slightly after 1922 only to fall again after the onset of worldwide depression in 1929.[39]

Rural southerners usually marked the end of World War I as the beginning of the Depression. The economic downturn hit southern farmers, especially tenants, hard. Operating costs remained high even as commodity prices plunged. Credit that had been freely available during the war now dried up. Families were less self-sufficient and had higher standards of living than before the war, and they were often deeply in debt. The downturn in the farm sector proved particularly galling in the face of perceived urban prosperity of the 1920s. Radio and magazine advertising as well as popular movies reminded rural people of a glittering array of consumer products that they could not afford to buy and a lifestyle far beyond their reach.[40]

Farmers who had borrowed money for land or equipment found themselves unable to meet mortgage or tax payments. Thousands of southern families lost their farms to foreclosure in the 1920s, long before the stock market crash signaled the beginning of the Great Depression. As a result, tenancy grew still more, reaching 41 percent in Tennessee and exceeding 64 percent in South Carolina by 1920. Small landowners frequently fared little better than the landless. Although they were independent from landlords, small landowners were often deeply in debt and depended on outside wage work to remain financially afloat.[41]

Farm prices recovered slightly in the mid-1920s, but conditions for southern farmers improved little. The onset of the Great Depression caused another plunge in commodity prices in the early 1930s. In 1931, cotton farmers produced their second-largest crop in history, a production success that only exacerbated their problems by creating an oversupply of the fiber. Cotton prices declined from 17 cents a pound in 1929 to 5 cents a pound by 1932, a far cry from the 1919 high of 41 cents. Using the slogan "Grow Less, Get More," President Hoover urged farmers to voluntarily cut production, but most did not comply, reasoning that unless most farmers reduced production, the few who did cut back would suffer disproportionately from reduced incomes.[42]

To address the poverty and hardships of southern farmers, the federal government aggressively intervened during the Great Depression. President Roosevelt's New Deal reshaped the farmer's relationship to his government. In the end, most New Deal programs did little to help the poorest southern farmers remain on the land, but they did lay the groundwork for the profound transformation of southern agriculture, a transformation that aided large landowners at the expense of small owners and tenants.

The major New Deal agricultural program, the Agricultural Adjustment Act (AAA), provided incentives to reduce production.

Southern landowners, themselves strapped by the economic depression, realized they could reap gains from AAA. They accepted cash payments to reduce their output of certain overproduced commodities, using the money to mechanize their farming operations. Both mechanization and the removal of land from production diminished landowners' need for farm labor, so they often evicted sharecroppers, leaving many landless people without a means of earning a living. Though cotton farmers still needed manual laborers to chop and pick cotton, they began to rely on local day laborers rather than year-round sharecroppers. For example one historian found that in two Black Belt counties of Georgia, the percentage of black farm families who were sharecroppers fell between 1927 and 1934, while the number of farm wage laborers in those counties rose from 20.5 to 34.5 percent of all the county's workers. At the same time, due to the oversupply of available laborers, daily wage rates for agricultural laborers fell throughout the South. Sharecroppers were shortchanged in other ways by New Deal programs. Although the law required that landowners share their AAA crop reduction payments with sharecroppers in the same proportion as the sharecroppers shared the crop, landlords often failed to comply. Government officials classified farm tenants as self-employed farmers, and thus local relief officials declared most ineligible for work relief programs such as those sponsored by the Works Progress Administration (WPA).[43]

Displaced sharecroppers struggled to cope in a variety of ways. Those who had the skills or resources to move to towns and cities in search of jobs did so, though high urban unemployment and the cost of moving a family prohibited many from taking this approach. Some sharecroppers pioneered interracial organizing in an attempt to pressure landowners to comply with federal law and the federal government to intervene on their behalf. With the help of the Communist Party, black and white Alabama farmers established the Share Croppers Union (SCU) in 1931. Sharecroppers in and around Tyronza, Arkansas, formed the Southern Tenant Farmers' Union in 1934 to protest massive evictions of tenant farmers by landowners in the wake of AAA crop reduction programs. In spite of landless farmers' efforts, local, state, and federal authorities caved in to political pressure from powerful landowners and crushed the tenant unions. Still other displaced landless southerners became migrant farmworkers. The eviction of southern sharecroppers provided many East Coast fruit and vegetable growers with a cheap seasonal labor force to harvest truck crops. Migrants followed the harvest north, beginning in the winter with citrus and early vegetables in Florida, moving to New Jersey to harvest summer vegetables, and harvesting fruit in the Carolinas and New England in the fall. Exploited by growers who provided squalid housing and paid inadequate wages, whole families worked in the fields.

By the close of the Great Depression, farming was no longer a viable option for most landless southerners, and many landowners maintained an increasingly precarious hold on the land. At the same time, new federal minimum-wage policies made industrial jobs more attractive and integrated the southern labor force into the national market, a trend that lured people from the land. Most displaced tenants eventually made their way into service and manufacturing jobs in cities inside and outside the South, but often they endured years of suffering before they found permanent homes.[44]

The New Deal may have set in motion the changes that transformed the southern countryside, but rural southerners themselves almost always marked World War II as the "great divide," in the words of historian Pete Daniel.[45] The war tied the South to the rest of the nation—economically, socially, and politically—as never before. Many native-born people left the South, and outsiders moved in. The South's farm population declined by 22 percent during World War II, partly because of young men entering the military and partly as a result of wartime off-farm job opportunities. Farm laborers and sharecroppers made up most of the population leaving the southern countryside.[46] Millions of southerners served in the military, and many lived outside the South for the first time, developing new expectations and new ideas. Federal military installations in the South brought millions of men from other parts of the country, and some stayed after the war ended. Wartime industrial mobilization created thousands of jobs in southern cities—in shipyards on the Gulf and Atlantic coasts, in the steel mills of Alabama, in Piedmont textile mills, and in federal installations such as the top-secret uranium enrichment facility at Oak Ridge, Tennessee. Expectations soared as some southerners saw more comfortable lives off the farm, and many veterans and defense workers who returned to the

South after the war demanded material comforts like electricity that they had once considered luxuries.

The war also transformed southern agriculture in profound ways. Farmers again enjoyed high commodity prices due to wartime shortages, and as in World War I, federal officials urged them to increase their production levels as a matter of patriotic duty. New challenges arose, however. Out-migration sparked a farm labor crisis. For the large plantation owners in the cotton and rice belts, the sharecropping labor system rested in part on coercion of workers and in part on their dependency. World War II transformed labor relations among large landowners, giving workers real bargaining power. As historian Donald Holley put it, "The farm labor shortage of World War II suddenly swept away both dependency and control."[47] Black men left the land for military service or defense jobs, often taking entire families of farm laborers with them. Black women who remained in the countryside, now receiving money from relatives who were in the service or held defense jobs, declined to pick cotton, infuriating white landowners.

In fact, the war struck a deathblow to the old Jim Crow system. African Americans who served in the military refused to show the same level of deference after the war, and they demanded better conditions when they worked as tenants. Racial tensions intensified as African Americans challenged discrimination, and whites worked to shore up the color line, often attempting to manipulate federal agencies into helping them maintain white supremacy. During the war, ordinary southerners found that the federal government was an ever-increasing presence. In addition to old friends at USDA, new agencies such as the Selective Service Administration, the Office of Price Administration, the War Manpower Commission, and the U.S. Employment Service intervened daily in the lives of ordinary people, particularly in the business of landowning farmers seeking to command a labor force. Though they chafed at restrictions imposed by the federal government, landowners did not hesitate to use these agencies to force laborers to work on the planters' terms.

World War II sparked a revolution in agricultural productivity that would transform rural life and bring industrial agriculture to the South at last. This revolution was due to three factors: the introduction of improved varieties of crops and animals, made possible largely by advances in genetics; mechanization; and the use of new chemicals to kill weeds and insect pests and to fertilize the land.[48]

The productivity revolution was particularly powerful in the South. If the New Deal had provided landowners with the where-withal to begin mechanization, World War II created the labor shortage that made mechanization and improved farming methods vital to survival. The introduction of improved mechanical cotton pickers during World War II clinched the southern agricultural transformation. Southern farmers bought tractors and mechanical pickers, used dichloro-diphenyl-trichloroethane (DDT) to eliminate the boll weevil and other pests, and applied new herbicides to eliminate the need to chop cotton by hand. In the 1950s and 1960s, many southern farmers diversified, giving up cotton for new strains of grains and livestock that were more suited to the peculiarities of the southern climate. The impact of improved productivity was dramatic. For example, in 1900, the production of one hundred bushels of corn had required just over one hundred hours of labor. By 1985, the labor requirement to produce the same one hundred bushels of corn would be five hours.[49] The shift to new crops and to the mechanical cotton picker rendered most of the South's remaining sharecroppers obsolete, though many landowners still used day laborers on a seasonal basis. As a result, between 1940 and 1960, about half a million sharecroppers left the land.[50]

Government agricultural programs also contributed to the shift to large-scale commercial farming. A complex allotment system, one legacy of the New Deal, assigned each landowner a specific number of acres for overproduced commodities like cotton, rice, and tobacco. The allotments quickly became assets in their own right. As allotments grew in value, landowners bought and sold them like commodities. To mitigate the price declines sparked by flooded commodities markets, the federal government frequently cut allotments. These cuts were distributed to local farmers by county-based agricultural boards dominated by large landowners. Small landowners often found their allotments too small to be profitable. Many responded by selling their farms and their remaining allotments to large landowners who could afford to offset allotment cuts by using more fertilizer, pesticides, and technology to increase their per acre yields. By the 1960s, a new capital-intensive form of agriculture had replaced the old labor-intensive system.

The transition to commercial agriculture was not monolithic in the South. Some areas resisted the shift to specialized large-scale commercial farming. In much of middle Georgia, for example, a vast area stretching from Macon southward and eastward toward the coast, few landowners ever bothered to turn to tractor cultivation because their land was too worn-out to make such a transition worthwhile. Instead, those who remained on the land persisted with their traditional combinations of subsistence and market-oriented activities until they abandoned farming for other means of making a living.[51]

The social transformations accompanying the economic and structural transformations of southern countryside reshaped daily life for most rural southerners. Thousands took off-farm jobs, learning to organize their lives around time clocks instead of the sun and the seasons. Many eventually moved to towns and cities where they learned to cope with neighbors who lived within arm's reach. For rural southerners who had never had to worry about whether they disturbed the neighbors or whether anyone else approved of the appearance of the front porch, the demands of city life proved stressful, and some returned to the country in response. Farm people who had once depended on family and friends to help them cope with poverty, illness, and death learned to turn to social service agencies for assistance. Rural church congregations gradually diminished and sometimes disappeared as young people left rural communities. In the name of improving education, rural school districts consolidated schools. Yet school and church had been the glue that bound many small rural communities, and without these institutions, community ties were undermined. Neighbors complained that they didn't know their neighbors anymore. Small southern towns dried up and died as the farmers who had once patronized small hardware, grocery, and feed stores left the land. National chain stores such as Wal-Mart drove locally owned retailers out of business, but they also provided rural people with access to the same types of consumer goods enjoyed all over the country. Large regional banks swallowed up local financial institutions, undermining the personal relationships with local bankers that farmers had once enjoyed and leaving them to depend on unseen bureaucrats far away to make decisions about operating loans and mortgages. Increasingly farmers turned to government and quasi-government agencies such as the Production Credit Association and the Farmer's Home Administration for operating loans.

The last third of the twentieth century saw a continuation of the changes in the southern countryside as increasing numbers of small landowners sold out to bigger commercial farmers and took off-farm jobs. Unlike cotton farmers who had always competed in the world marketplace, most other farmers in the region produced for domestic buyers until late in the twentieth century. By the 1980s, however, American agriculture was fully integrated into a world market, making efforts to reduce production largely useless in raising commodity prices. The federal government continued to play a major role in shaping agriculture across the nation, including the South. The USDA did not completely abandon production restrictions, but it turned to other devices in an effort to regulate the supply of farm commodities and boost farm prices, including marketing quotas, price support programs, and expanded lending programs. Farmers remained dependent on the federal government, and many also became dependent on large agribusiness firms. A major structural change in the last half of the twentieth century was the use of production contracts with farmers that gave the contractor control over many aspects of the farm operations, a practice pioneered by poultry processors. Other farmers turned to new crops, especially soybeans and peanuts.

A new speculative boom in agriculture brought hope for prosperity during the early 1970s. This boom was fueled by a combination of factors including government tax policies that encouraged agricultural investment, the ready availability of government-backed loans at below-market interest rates, high inflation that allowed borrowers to pay back debts with inflated dollars, President Nixon's Soviet grain deal, and a strong demand for U.S. agricultural exports (fueled in part by a weak dollar). Farmers met the increased demand by ratcheting up production. As a result, land values soared, increasing landowners' collateral and in turn encouraging farmers to borrow ever-increasing amounts of money. Farmers expanded landholdings, but they did so largely through debt. As a result, even as their equity increased, they experienced cash-flow problems. Agricultural experts who, in the words of economist Barry J. Barnett, simultaneously played "the roles of coach, cheerleader, and fan," encouraged this rapid expansion. Between 1970 and 1973, net farm income doubled. Many southern farmers briefly prospered, but prosperity proved illusory.[52]

By the end of the decade, the boom began to slip away as highly leveraged farmers experienced difficulties. Increased production had resulted in lower commodity prices. Foreign nations recovered from the droughts and other natural disasters that had temporarily increased the demand for American products. President Jimmy Carter's grain embargo, part of the American response to the Soviet invasion of Afghanistan, hit American farmers hard. In the late 1970s and early 1980s, the Federal Reserve tried to curb inflation by raising interest rates, a particular hardship for farmers who depended on annual operating loans. At the same time, the Reagan administration cut taxes. The result was a mounting federal budget deficit that in turn increased the level of government borrowing, further raising interest rates. The dollar appreciated, reducing foreign demand for American agricultural products. Land values plummeted as commodity prices dropped and interest rates rose. Between 1980 and 1987, the value of net farm assets declined 30 percent. Lenders would not refinance farm loans. Because many overextended farmers could not meet their debt payments, agricultural banks failed.[53]

Some southern farmers responded to the farm crisis by joining the American Agriculture Movement's tractorcade to Washington, protesting low commodity prices and demanding increased levels of government price supports, restrictions on agricultural imports, and increased farmer input into federal agricultural policy. Others lobbied Congress through farm organizations. Their efforts garnered a great deal of media attention but little immediate action. The farm crisis slowly faded in the last half of the 1980s as the Federal Reserve eased interest rates and the federal government made massive increases in direct payments to farmers. The 1985 Farm Bill provided some debt relief and bankruptcy protection to small farmers, but it continued to provide incentives for expansion and to favor bigness in agriculture. For many southerners, federal programs provided too little relief too late. Thousands more left agriculture during the 1990s.

At the end of the twentieth century, federal farm policy proved inconsistent and ineffectual. Federal farm policy remains geared to a time when domestic markets determined American commodity prices and is thus inadequate in addressing the major changes that reshaped the agricultural economy in recent decades, including the influence of the world commodities market on domestic prices, consolidation of farm operations (a consolidation encouraged by federal programs), and the use of production contracts. Lawmakers have vacillated between weaning farmers off of federal support and pouring federal dollars into the heartland to ease the suffering of rural communities. Federal programs are structured in ways that encourage farmers to farm more intensively—to use more fertilizer and chemical herbicides and pesticides—practices most available to large landowners and policies that benefit the powerful agribusiness lobby more than family farmers.

Most southern farm families who remained on the land at the end of the century enjoyed a higher standard of living than did their early-twentieth-century ancestors, but they did so because of off-farm income. Economist Bruce Gardner notes that while farm household income grew steadily and consistently in the 1980s and 1990s, the growth was largely due to nonfarm activities. Farm earnings account for only a minority of the income earned by most U.S. farm households. As he observed, "Farms selling less than $100,000 annually in farm products, which amounted to 80 percent of all farms in the late 1990s, earn more than 90 percent of their household income from off-farm sources."[54]

At century's end, most southern farmers struggled to stay in business in the face of continued overproduction, steadily falling commodity prices, rising production costs, and cuts in federal agricultural subsidies. African American farmers waged yet another battle in their long war against discrimination. In 1997, a group of black farmers filed a class-action suit against the USDA. They charged that the department had been engaged in a pattern of racial discrimination throughout the twentieth century. Among other things, plaintiffs accused the agency of systematically denying Farmer's Home Administration loans to black farmers, unnecessarily delaying the processing of black farmers' loan applications, and holding African American loan applicants to higher financial standards than white farmers. They also accused the department of failing to investigate hundreds of complaints lodged by black farmers against it between 1983 and 1997. By the time the case was settled in 2000, at an anticipated cost of $1 billion to the USDA, over twenty-six thousand black

farmers had joined the lawsuit, but many told reporters that the settlement was "too little, too late" to keep them in business.[55]

Scholars have assigned the federal government a large portion
of the blame for the most recent farm crisis and the decline of family farms. For African Americans in particular, farming was mostly
about freedom and independence from white control. Small black
and white landowners often practiced a blend of diversified commercial and subsistence farming calculated to help families remain on the
land. Yet federal programs were oriented to farmers who adopted the
practices of industrial agriculture, and such programs either ignored
or seemed irrelevant to small farmers who tried to remain independent of the demands of large-scale commercial agriculture. As historian Catherine McNicol Stock put it, "While paying lip service to
the family farm, government agencies had encouraged expansion and
indebtedness and had affirmed the ambitions of large landholders
and multinational agribusiness corporations." The evolving institutions of the USDA did not foster the needs of small farmers, but
rather favored large-scale producers. Political scientist William P.
Browne argues that "the destruction of African American agriculture was in large part the work of American governing institutions
and the politics of institution building." To a lesser degree, the same
could be said of farming by small white landowners.[56]

This transformation from one kind of agricultural uncertainty to
another—from small-scale farming in an uncertain market to specialized, large-scale commercial agriculture in an equally uncertain
market—provides the backdrop for rural southerners' memories of
life on the land. The meanings that they give to the choices they made
are shaped first and foremost by their lives on the land and their
experiences with agricultural transformation.

This book is organized around the major themes in rural southerners' narratives of change. The first two chapters explore the ways
that rural narrators use oral history interviews to articulate a sense
of both individual and shared identity. Chapter 1 looks closely at the
stories told by three narrators, stories that illuminate the varieties
of ways that southern farm people saw themselves as different from
people who did not live on the land and the ways they viewed rural
transformation. Chapter 2 examines the threads of common experience that oral history narrators emphasize: rural self-sufficiency, a

strong work ethic, persistence through hard times, neighborhood mutual aid, an attachment to the land, and a sense of relative socioeconomic equality. These themes formed the boundaries of rural narrators' communities of memory.

The last three chapters explore the ways that rural southerners gave meaning to the social and economic changes that swept their lives in the twentieth century—the what happened, the why, the how, and the so what of agricultural transformation. Chapter 3 examines rural southerners' descriptions of ways that southern agriculture changed throughout the century. Chapter 4 explores the reasons for and significance of rural transformation. In other words, the focus in chapter 4 is on how farm people interpreted change. I pay particular attention to the significant generational, class, gender, and racial divides in the ways farm people explain transformation and how these differences are shaped by the larger culture. Finally, chapter 5 analyzes narrators' comments on the nature of modern life, comments they usually frame by describing rural life in the early twentieth century and explaining how "it's not like today." Values and beliefs rooted in their experiences on the land provide narrators with the standards for criticism of modern life, and their stories about the communities of their rural pasts are particularly powerful critiques of today's world. A brief conclusion draws together the major themes of the book and discusses the implications of this study for understanding the impact of rural transformation on ordinary farm people.

Careful attention to memories of transformation—particularly to shifts in the ways those memories are shaped into stories—lends new insight into how larger social forces such as shifts in federal policy and advances in education and communication can reshape ordinary people's understanding of the world in which they live. My study suggests new ways that oral historical methods can be used to explore the process of constructing historical memory—that is, how people connect personal experience with the larger historical context—and how they use historical memory to interpret their lives and the world around them. Most of all, *Southern Farmers and Their Stories* demonstrates that we have not yet exhausted the possibilities for using oral history to better understand people's experiences of lived history.

Chapter One

Three Southern Farmers
Tell Their Stories

Ruth Hatchette McBrayer operated a peach orchard in South Carolina for nearly forty years, but the white landowner gave up peach farming in the mid-1980s. She explained, "I about stayed in peaches too long. . . . It was costing me too much. In the beginning, I counted 25 percent for expenses and 75 percent profit. Then it got to 50 [percent for expenses], then to 60, then it got to 75, then it was break even, and then it was going the other way, so it was time to quit. Past time to quit for me. Because it's too hard work. And there are other things." She leased her land to truck and livestock farmers and enjoyed her retirement.[1]

African American renter Woodrow Harper of Georgia farmed for most of his life, first specializing in cotton and then soybeans. He blamed the rising cost of seed and fertilizer as well as skyrocketing land rents for making farming untenable. He also noted that federal agencies discriminated against African American farmers in granting operating loans and providing other forms of support. He said, "There are numbers of black farmers got out of this thing because they wasn't able to support it financially."[2]

John West's oral history narrative stands in marked contrast to the stories told by Harper and McBrayer. The white landowner raised grain and livestock on a Tennessee farm until he sold his land in the mid-1980s. West lived through a period of profound agricultural change, but he scarcely acknowledged the transformation of southern agriculture. He never mentioned trends in the agricultural economy, and he referred to national events such as the Great Depression and World War II only when they directly affected his own life. His story was the story of a self-made man, "standing on my own feet."[3]

Three southern farmers, and three different approaches to telling the story of transformation. All three were born in the decade of the 1910s. All three farmed until late in life. All three shared a commitment to farming, in spite of having other, more lucrative options. Clearly the privileges and limits imposed by race and class shaped each farmer's experience of rural transformation and the resulting stories about change in the countryside. Nonetheless, other factors also molded their oral history narratives.

Considered as a group, oral histories of people with similar experiences often display persistent and striking patterns, patterns that will be explored in some depth in later chapters. These patterns, however, can only be discerned and interpreted by careful consideration of individual stories. Only by probing the repetitions and the silences, the events that narrators emphasize and those they gloss over or dismiss, can a student of the past begin to understand how people experience and give meaning to the past. This chapter focuses on the autobiographical stories of three southern farmers in an attempt to understand what agricultural transformation meant to them. In the process, I hope to illuminate not only the infinite varieties of individual experiences of similar events but also the ways individuals connect personal experience with the larger historical context.

An individual uses a life story not only to describe and interpret past experiences, but to express a sense of personal identity. Individuals construct personal identity through a process that is both conscious and unconscious, incorporating values, the major activities that shape daily life and fill one's time, and memories of past experiences into some sense of personal uniqueness. Sociologist Joseph E. Davis argued, "Individuals search for self-understanding by imposing narrative structure on their lives, an interpretive process that both looks back in time and projects into the future. The self-narrative configures key experiences into a meaningful whole, introduces a sense of coherence and temporal unity to one's development and future direction, and at the same time serves as the basis by which individuals represent themselves to others."[4] Through autobiographical narratives, a person in essence says, "This is the kind of person I am."

Individual identity is shaped in part by the various communities of memory to which the individual belongs. These groups may include racial or ethnic groups, gender groups, socioeconomic classes, generations, occupational groups, neighborhoods, or even the nation-state. Because most people belong to several communities of memory, an individual may draw elements of his or her personal identity from the collective identity of several groups. For example, the oral history narrative of an African American sharecropping woman from the American South might share elements of her identity with other women, with fellow African Americans, with poor people, with farm people, with southerners, with other people her own age, and with Americans.

Nonetheless, it important not to conflate identity with fixed categories such as race, sex, or class. The fact that individuals belong to many groups whose communities of memory play roles in shaping individual identity is ample warning against this type of essentialism. Race, class, and sex set limits on the range of options available to narrators and thus helped to shape their identities, but other factors were also at work in fashioning identity. Farm people exposed to similar transforming forces responded in a wide variety of ways that the constraints of race, class, and gender alone do not explain. Factors such as personal desires and ambitions and family concerns also motivated individuals to choose various courses of action. As the narratives of the farmers in this chapter suggest, the ways in which southern farm folk negotiated changes in rural life could vary, as could the meanings that they gave to these changes.[5]

These interviews were not chosen because they were representative of some larger portion of the sample used in this study. Instead, they were chosen because their narrators were unusually articulate in expressing their sense of identity as farmers and in describing early-twentieth-century rural life and the changes that swept the rural South. All three narrators came of age during the Great Depression, and all three experienced sweeping changes in the practice of agriculture.

John West

The first narrator, John West, entered adulthood during the Great Depression and farmed with considerable success into his seventies. A white middling landowner from Tennessee, West began farming before ideas about industrial agriculture took hold in the rural South.

Though he always directed his energies toward producing for the market, he never focused on specialization or building a large agribusiness enterprise to pass on to his children. He didn't want wealth, but rather enough to make "a living," to be independent, and to give his children choices in life. He did not embrace the tenets of commercial agriculture wholesale and reject the traditional rural values of his youth. Rather he blended the two sets of values, a feat he was able to accomplish thanks to his success in commercial farming.[6]

West began farming during a time of widespread change in the east Tennessee countryside. The region's farmers, mostly small landowners, increasingly produced for the market, but they also clung to traditional subsistence practices as a means of reducing their need for cash. Many also turned to off-farm work in the region's expanding manufacturing sector, using their incomes to subsidize farm operations. Most farmers who came of age in the years around the Great Depression managed to stay on the land using similar strategies as John West; they were small, diversified farmers. In 1945, over half of east Tennessee's farms were run by landowners who held between thirty and one hundred acres and produced three or more products for the market. (West farmed more land, but he farmed in much the same way.)[7]

Like several of the people I interviewed, I had been acquainted with John West all my life. I interviewed West and his wife, Martha Alice, at their home in Friendsville, Tennessee, on August 12, 1993. (John West's first wife died in 1981. He married Martha Alice McDaniel, a local widow, in the late 1980s.) We talked for two and one-half hours. West was a large, soft-spoken man, his face showing the marks of years spent working outside in sun and raw weather. After explaining the purpose of my interviews, I asked him to tell me his life story, focusing on his life as a farmer. Although I occasionally asked clarifying questions and prompted him to elaborate on things he had mentioned in passing, for the most part, he directed the conversation. Clad in overalls and relaxing in a big, well-worn easy chair, he reflected on eight decades of rural life, on his work as a farmer, and on the successes of his children.

John West was born in 1912 in a rural area of southern Blount County, Tennessee. The son of a landowning father with ten children, West grew up steeped in the tradition of hard work extolled by so many rural narrators. His father accumulated five hundred acres through a combination of careful management and ceaseless effort by the entire family. John recalled:

> Dad was a thrifty fellow. Dad . . . was in debt to a man. And in that depression, people lost their farms. I know one man that had 200 acres, and he owed $800, and he lost his place. My daddy paid, we paid for it; every one of us worked, girls and all. I mean, my gosh, everybody worked. . . . Dad paid off that debt, and he bought a new truck and paid something over $700 for it. He paid for it. . . . He'd buy a farm, you know, and get it paid for, and he'd buy another.

West applauded the fact that his father succeeded in paying off his land and even increased his holdings despite hard times. He saw neighbors losing their farms and their way of life while his father was able to persevere. He learned several lessons from his father's example. First, he learned that paying off debts was important, a symbol of both his honesty and his ability as a farmer and a manager. Second, the fact that his father was willing to take the risk of mortgaging land would help the adult John West take similar risks. And his father's example of gradual accumulation taught him a third lesson—that the process of building a farming operation was a slow and steady one, built on hard work and careful management.

Indeed, in both his example and in the work he demanded of his children, West's father taught that hard work and thrift were the keys to achieving goals. He urged his children to be independent by insisting that they earn their own spending money. As John remembered, "I don't remember my daddy giving me but one quarter. . . . When I was growing up, he had four or five barns, and he said, 'Now boys, you can put you some chickens down here, and the feed's here. If you want some spending money, make it.' I bought my own clothes, bought my books to go to school, and I bought a tire if I needed it, all from the chickens." As an elementary school student, West became a poultry grower. Beginning with a small flock, West reinvested some of his profits in expansion so that by the time he was a teenager, he kept chickens in two barns on land owned by his father. These land-holdings were scattered around the community, so each night after supper, West rode a mule three and a half miles one way to care for the chickens at another barn. Early in his life, he was developing the discipline he would need to be his own boss as a commercial farmer.

This early ambition went beyond the poultry operation, however. John went on to explain that he had always been something of an entrepreneur, even in elementary school. He used his chicken and egg money to buy a stock of whatever toy was faddish with elementary school children at the time. He said, "Kids, they'd take spells, they had tops, spin tops you know. Well, I had tops to sell. And if it was marbles, I had marbles to sell." He laughed at the memory, saying, "And these old . . . Barlow knives, I could buy them for fifty cents a piece. And I'd sharpen them real good, and have them good and sharp and sell them for a dollar. . . . And I'd buy new inner tubes and make flips, you know flips [a toy similar to a slingshot]? . . . I'd sell flips. I'd buy a tube for 98 cents, and I'd sell [the flip] for ten cents. Good gosh, I don't know how many hundred there'd be in one [inner tube]. They sold like hot cakes." As this anecdote suggests, even as a child, West showed remarkable ambition and a willingness to work at a variety of tasks to earn the things he wanted.

Although West respected his father's thrift and determination and would later model his own desire for landholding independence on his father's example, as a teenager West sometimes resented the ceaseless hard work. A hint of buried anger tinged his voice as he recalled, "We worked every day. I mean, we'd go up there, we had a place there at Binfield [a community school]. That's the place he [his father] owed on. And we'd hear them hollering at the ballgames on Saturdays. And I loved to play baseball, you know, and I was working." It was galling to a teenage John West to work seven days a week while friends and neighbors were enjoying his favorite game. He resented laboring in the fields all day for his father and then working at night caring for his own poultry flock. Although he later understood his father's demands, this adolescent outrage played a role in West's decision to marry in 1932 at the age of 20. He explained, "My dad was working my butt off, and I wasn't getting much out of it. So my wife was 16, and I was 20, and we got married." Marriage provided an escape from his father's control and a chance to be his "own man."

Marriage and entry into the wider world made West aware of the Great Depression, an economic situation he had not much noticed before. He recounted, "We really didn't have the depression as much as a lot of people who lived on the farm. We raised what we ate. But course more after I got through high school in '32, I realized more then than I did before that because we didn't want for anything. . . . I've seen men walking the roads wanting to work for a piece of meat or just anything they could get to eat. I had fellas come to me and told me they didn't have a crust in the house." West went on to talk about the abundant and varied diet he was able to raise for his family on the farm. Like most rural people he took pride in the autonomy that self-sufficiency gave him. John realized that farming gave him some advantages over wage earners in the economic downturn. Yet, being on his own raised his awareness of his own and others' vulnerability in a world increasingly driven by cash.

Depression or no depression, West proceeded to set up an independent farming operation. Still, he did not cut all ties to his father. As generations of young American farmers had done, he depended on aid from his father in beginning his own farm, aid that he repaid with periodic labor. For a few years, he rented a farm not far from his family, where he began an operation with the poultry flock he had built himself. He borrowed tools from his father until he was able to afford his own. "I had $375 when I married," he recalled. "And I threw $200 of it for a pair of mules. And we bought us a cookstove, fifteen dollars." From the beginning, the farm operation consumed most of the couple's resources. Mules were essential to independent farming; thus, a set was his first purchase. A few other secondhand furnishings and hand-me-downs from family members were all the young couple needed to set up housekeeping in the small house on their rented property. As he remembered it, their expectations as a young couple were modest. He said, "We didn't require a lot. You know, you didn't, if you never had it, you don't miss it." His comments echo those of many rural narrators who insisted that the lack of material goods rankled less when one had never enjoyed such goods.

On this rented land, John gradually accumulated cattle and equipment while painstakingly saving for his own land. He combined a variety of strategies to earn and conserve cash, as he recounted:

I had a cow, two steers, and a sow and five shoats [yearling hogs]. . . . I had 350 hens when I married, and eggs six cents a dozen. You could buy six loaves of bread for a quarter. I'd go to the stock sale at Knoxville about every Wednesday. There was an old man by the name of Blum that ran a whole-sale house; he was a Jew. And you'd just go in there and buy stuff from him. . . . He'd sell it to you wholesale. He used to pack oranges in a 20-pound box with a paper around them; that's the way they came, you know. And you could buy a 20-pound box for 80 cents. And California dried peaches the same way. And I bought soap by the case. You know it's a lot cheaper.

We lived off those chickens, and I paid my fertilizer bills and stuff like that, you know.

But it was just one thing like that, and I finally got up till I had 17 cows that I raised, and I started milking them. I started there, and I went up to about 25, milking by hand. And sold cream, separated it and sold the cream for . . . about 20 cents. . . . We'd get about $25 a week out of our eggs and the cream. We thought we's really pulling in money. Well, they was making $12 a week at the Aluminum Company. And we just kept a-growing.

West's comment about the Aluminum Company of America (ALCOA) was telling. In 1915, ALCOA had opened a smelting oper-ation near Maryville, a few miles from West's home. For many rural Blount Countians, jobs at ALCOA, or "the plant" as it was known locally, seemed to be a ticket out of the poverty and uncertainty of farm life. Hundreds left the farm for factory jobs and company housing during World War I and the 1920s. Even during the Great Depression, the company attempted to keep everyone employed while cutting hours and wages, and for many, ALCOA remained a symbol of the promise of a better life. Yet John West was clearly proud of the fact that he had usually earned far more than workers at ALCOA through his diversified combination of subsistence and commercial farming.

Thanks to his thrift and hard work, five years after his marriage, in July 1937, West was able to purchase 126 acres of land for $3,500.

He paid $2,300 in cash and assumed a $1,200 mortgage on the farm. The property included a good barn, a large old farmhouse, and 60 acres of corn nearing maturity. He recalled that he had moved to his rental farm in 1932 with a single wagonload but because he had accumulated so much in the way of cattle, equipment, feed, and household goods, it took more than one hundred loads to move to the new place. "I started moving in August and got through on Thanksgiving Day," he explained. "We moved 100 loads of hay down there, and I had about 40 head of cattle, and about that many hogs and about that many sheep."

The new land was not exactly ready to farm. Concerned about the quality of the land, he had asked his father's advice before closing the deal: "Dad told me when we was down there looking at it, 'Son, land that can grow weeds as big as these can grow anything if you can get the chance.'" West chuckled at the recollection, adding that the land certainly "looked blue. There was fence rows thirty feet wide. . . . I'd turn weeds under with Dad's old D John Deere tractor and plow. Actually they [the weeds] was as high as that thing yonder [about 8 feet]."

His father turned out to be right. John went on to explain that his first year on the new farm, he planted a wheat crop that "made 33 bushel to the acre," a very respectable yield at the time. Chemical fertilizers and herbicides would more than double his productivity over the years. He said, "[In] the same field . . . , there was 18 acres there, and it made 75 bushels to the acre . . . [in 1981]."

West's strategy for success, like that of many farmers of his generation, violated all of the then-current U.S. Department of Agriculture's advice to southern farmers with ambitions of commercial farming. The agency advocated specialized farming and suggested that farmers focus their efforts on a single crop or livestock product and on mechanization. But West showed little interest in this brand of commercial farming. Although his operation was deeply entrenched in the market, he saw diversity as a hedge against a downturn in a single market or a bad year for a particular crop. He engaged in many agricultural pursuits, raising corn for a cash crop and for livestock feed, as well as wheat, poultry, sheep, and hogs. In his earliest years farming, he milked cows and produced both raw milk and butter for the market. He also trapped rabbits and muskrats in the late fall and winter, selling their furs for a nice premium. He did mechanize, but he did so slowly, borrowing equipment from his father or hiring other farmers to do the work using their equipment until his operation was large enough to justify going into debt to buy a particular piece of machinery. John West's strategy of engaging in multiple types of farming even as he became dependent on cash for everything except food demonstrates one way he blended traditional practices and modern ones.

Although he may have rejected overly specialized farming, West was not afraid to take other risks inherent in modern commercial farming operations, so long as those risks did not undermine his commitment to self-sufficiency. For example, as his operation grew, West leased more land for expansion. Ultimately he leased two farms, one belonging to a distant neighbor and the other belonging to his aging grandfather. Though he may have eschewed excessive debt, West also borrowed modest amounts to buy additional cattle and equipment. He had begun doing this a year after he began his own operation on rented land. He described it this way:

> After the first year, I started expanding. I bought cattle at Knoxville in the sale, 2 cents a pound. Borrowed the money at the Bank of Maryville to pay for them. I'd go up there and talk to them [bank presidents] just like I's talking to you; tell them what my ideas was and that we needed some money, and I never was turned down.
>
> People's always been good to me. Dad said, "They wouldn't give it to you if they didn't think you'd pay." But it's still accommodation. [One bank president] said, "All I know to do is let you have it. Everything you ever tried works."

West understood the risks inherent in borrowing money. He had watched other men lose their farms to creditors when farm prices fell, and he had watched his own father struggle to pay a mortgage. Yet, like his father, he saw the loans as a calculated risk, and he trusted his own judgment in farming. West took great pride in the bank presidents' respect for his abilities as a profitable farmer. To him, the way the bank presidents treated him demonstrated that they thought of him as a careful businessman, not unlike themselves. West once advised his oldest son to ask for a raise by talking to his boss as an equal. "You just go talk to Mr. Brown just like you're talking to me, not in a demanding way. In a business way," he coached. "He knows what [kind of work] you're doing." This was advice drawn from West's own experience in dealing with men of authority like those bank presidents. He believed that his performance as a farmer—the kind of work he was doing—was evidence that he was something of a peer of the bankers, another competent businessman who dealt with them as equals—man to man—"in a business way," as he put it.

Indeed, West believed that his careful, businesslike management had as much to do with his success as his hard work. He said, "You know if I was a millionaire, I'd still be conservative. It's been a part of my life. And I don't think it's bad. . . . It's more in managing than it is in working." West took pride in his management skills, products of his intelligence. He believed that endless hard work, while admirable, was useless without wise management.

West's anecdotes about bank presidents and his conclusions about the importance of management revealed much about his own conceptions of masculinity and of farming success. Indeed, West's views on masculinity, like his farming strategies, were a mix of the traditional and the modern. In the nineteenth-century South, although there were local variations, manhood for yeomen farmers had generally involved acquiring land, commanding the labor of household dependents (usually family members), and participating with planters in the political process. A "self-working" yeoman farmer also worked his family hard. Even his women might work in the fields, under his supervision. The yeoman valued hard work and often quietly disdained planters whom he viewed as living off the labor of others, even as his own level of prosperity was determined in part by how many others' labor he controlled. By the early twentieth century, these definitions were shifting in the countryside. Several factors contributed to this shift, including the short-lived prosperity of the World War I–era, USDA calls for farmers to see themselves as businessmen, concerns that farm women were leading an exodus from the land because of their dissatisfaction with the quality of rural life, and the growing influence of a popular culture that emphasized a new consumer economy. Middling landowning farmers did not see themselves as yeomen; rather they began to acquire material goods and to aspire to middle-class urban and suburban standards of living that had first emerged in industrializing nineteenth-century cities. Along with aspirations for a middle-class standard of living, many adopted the ideology of separate spheres for men and women. White farmers who aimed for middle-class status saw the ability of men to support their homemaker wives and women's consumption and leisure as markers of that status. John West would not have described himself as a yeoman farmer; he aspired to be middle-class. He hoped to be respected by men of means. Although he referred to himself at one point as a "little farmer," he believed that the fact that professional men such as bank presidents treated him with respect was symbolic of his equality with them, much as nineteenth-century yeomen had believed that planters' political deference was a marker of their shared manhood.[8]

To West, another sign of his rising status was his ability to help lesser men. As his operation grew, he needed additional help, so he hired farm laborers. Aside from seasonal hands, in the early years of farming, he usually had at least one employee year-round who helped him with feeding, milking, and fieldwork. These men also assisted West's wife with heavy household chores such as laundry. West's farmhands were usually African American. (By the 1960s, however, black men could find better opportunities off the land. West had been able to accumulate considerable equipment by this time, so he was able to get along with seasonal workers.) In West's relationships with his workers, we again see a blending of traditional rural values and modern market-driven ones—a mix of paternalism and pragmatism. John West believed he had been fair with his employees. In general, West claimed he paid twice as much as the prevailing wage at ALCOA throughout the 1930s, 1940s, and 1950s. This statement is perhaps less generous than it might at first seem. ALCOA cut hours during the Great Depression, resulting in reduced income for its workers, so it wasn't hard for West to pay more than the prevailing wage at the factory. Given the dismal job market at the time, farm laborers were happy to find a steady job. Moreover, by 1940, when ALCOA's demand for workers to help fill defense contracts far outstripped the local labor supply, West likely had to pay high wages in order to get any help at all. He nonetheless took pride in his belief that he was a fair and generous employer. He emphasized:

Now I ain't no saint, and they say I'm tight [with money]. But if a man done me a good day's work, I wanted him paid for it. . . . If we was working hard, he'd [John, the hired man] eat three meals a day with me. He lived over there by himself [in a house belonging to West]. But John had to go in and cook. I know if he was like anybody else, he got tired, too. And if he could sit down to a good warm meal, I wanted him to. And of course, we milked those cows, and he'd take him a half gallon of milk every day. And my wife would give him a pound of butter, and you know different things that way all the time. . . . And I'd go, I'd buy me a pair of overalls and a jumper, we called it a jumper [a jacket]. And I'd buy John one, too. . . . I don't think you lose anything by being good to people.

To some degree, West's ability to provide jobs for young men and to pay them well with supplemental benefits such as work clothes, food, and housing was a measure of his success. He rarely mentioned mutual aid exchanges in his narrative, but he was gratified to be able to be "good to people." As he explained when he recalled assisting a young father who came to his door during the Depression, begging food for three small children, "I didn't really need it; I had a little backlog coming all the time, you know, out of them chickens and cream and stuff." West was pleased with his ability to help others, an ability he achieved through his hard work and shrewd and careful management. The fact that he could assist less successful men not only made his success more visible to others, but it helped cement his view of himself as a man of means. Indeed, in other interviews I did, neighbors' statements indicated that they respected West as a "good man," and one woman referred to him as a "fine farmer."[9]

Another mark of West's middle-class notions of masculinity was his determination to provide his children with an education and to spare them from some of the work his father had forced upon him. Although he noted several times that his children helped on the farm, he also made it a point to explain that he encouraged his sons to participate in sports in spite of the fact that these activities took them out of the fields. To John West, one measure of his success was his ability to give his children good educations and choices in directing their own futures. All of the couple's six children graduated from high school, and five attended college or business school. West had a touch of wonder in his voice when he noted that:

> I made sacrifices all my life, you know. A little farmer sent six kids to school. I know it didn't cost like it does now to go to college, but it cost. It was hard to get. . . . Me and my wife talked about it. We'd go to bed at night and talk about it. I said, "Well, honey, if we can give them an education, nobody can take it away from them unless they lose their mind or something." And I told [our oldest son], "Now, son, if you work and help, we'll get it." And we did. They made good grades and made the honor roll in college.

West's memories of the decision to send the children to college suggest that he and his wife shared family if not farm decision making. In the course of our conversation, it became clear that West was close to his first wife. He felt protective of her, and they worked out a division of labor that fit his (and perhaps her) notions of what was appropriate work for her. He noted that she was not strong or in good health and that he often had his hired hands help her with heavy tasks around the house. When asked whether she helped him with fieldwork, he didn't answer the question directly but instead recalled an incident early in their marriage when they had negotiated this division of labor: "My wife helped me chop out corn one evening, and we got hot, and we's under the apple tree in the shade, and her face was red like Alice's [his current wife] gets when she gets real hot. And I told her, I said, of course, we [already] had two kids. Oh, she'd pick stuff out of the garden and stuff. She was always doing something. She was a workaholic. She worked all the time. But I said, 'You just take care of the house and the children and I'll make the living.'" Perhaps West was exercising selective recall here. Possibly his wife did do fieldwork early in their marriage when they couldn't hire labor and her childcare burdens were light, but she apparently moved increasingly out of the fields as they grew older and more established. Certainly West's version of the story fit his view of himself as an excellent middle-class provider. He had definite notions about the type of work he wanted *his* wife to do, notions that probably had more to do with his definitions of his own masculinity than his definitions of femininity. As his account of how he had purchased mules (a farm purchase) while "we" purchased a cookstove (a household purchase) exemplifies, West always remembered farming decisions as his own, not "ours." At no point did he say that his wife should not be doing some kind of work. In fact, he was quick to point out that she worked steadily and hard, and his story about providing hired men with hot meals carried the implicit assumption that cooking for farmhands was part of his wife's contribution to the family economy. He nonetheless viewed his work as the income producing work, something he indicated when he said, "I'll make the living." A farmer whose wife did not need to work in the fields was a successful farmer. Like his ability to "take care" of his hired hands and help the poor, his competence at "making the living" was very much a part of proving John West's success, his middle-class status, and his manhood.

Indeed he saw his success in farming as the ultimate proof of his masculinity. He recounted the story of a local farmer who had lost all his assets in the post–World War I crash in farm commodity prices. As West told the story, "He had a big herd of registered Angus cattle and was rolling in luxury, and he bit off more than he could chew and lost everything he had. And to show you what kind of fellow he was, he come back and made another fortune. He was a *farmer* [emphasis his]. That culls the men out from the boys." As this account suggests, John West saw persistence and the ability to turn failure into success, adversity into prosperity, as markers of manhood—of maturity. "Boys" failed to recover from farming setbacks, while "men" persisted and overcame. "He was a *farmer*," he said, with a fervor that implied that real farmers engendered masculine ideals.

West's values and motivations were embedded throughout his oral autobiography. He spoke of his choice of diversified farming as a conscious one. He knew what was important to him. His laughing recollection of the time in the 1940s when he himself took a job at ALCOA speaks eloquently of his motives. The plant was expanding, due to a number of profitable defense contracts. Moreover, a new union contract and a shortage of labor had driven wages way up. West recounted, "I took a notion I was going to get rich quick, and I took a job at the Aluminum Company. [Chuckle] It didn't take me long to know I was in the wrong place. I worked six months and quit." His wife reminded him that if he had stayed with the company for his entire working life, he would now be drawing a generous pension from ALCOA's union-negotiated retirement plan. He scowled and raised his voice impatiently, "I'd have been dead. I wouldn't be drawing anything. If you're not doing something you like to do, you've missed the boat. I was the only boy in my senior class that knew what he was going to do. . . . Farming was all I thought about." Farming was more than a job to West—more than a means of making a living. It was a vocation—a calling. He was happy to have been able to do exactly what he wanted to do with his life. Yet West maintained he was not aiming for large profits. Nor did he ever, in the whole of a two-and-one-half-hour interview, lament the fact that his sons had not chosen to follow him into farming. If an ongoing family operation had been a central goal for him, he did not mention it now. Looking back on his life, he insisted, "Let me tell you something: if you've got a living, that's all you need anyway. Just like I told my boys."

To some degree, West romanticized his life as a farmer. He recalled some hard work and hard times, but he had little to say about how he and his family may have struggled. He never mentioned a farming setback though his briefly taking a job at ALCOA suggests that he was dissatisfied with his farming income at that moment. When pressed, he insisted only that he was motivated to enter the industrial work force by his "notion that I was going to get rich quick."

West's choice of memories to recount may have been shaped, in part, by his efforts to justify and give meaning to his life choices. Although his farming had been successful by his own definition, his wife's battle with cancer had left him with substantial medical bills, over and above their Medicare coverage. Shortly after her death, he stopped farming and sold his machinery, perhaps because his heart was no longer in farming but possibly also because of the financial blow of the medical bills. He continued to raise large patches of truck crops in retirement and explained that this was due to his love of farming, but he may also have been motivated by efforts to supplement a meager Social Security check. West and his second wife lived modestly in a small house, furnished with mismatched accumulations from a lifetime, but such a lifestyle was not unusual for even some of the wealthiest retirees of his generation. Still, Martha Alice's comment about the large retirement check he'd be drawing if he had stayed at ALCOA, and John's angry and defensive reaction hint that he may have felt that he did not have a great deal to show for his years of farming.

Neither did West ever see himself as buffeted by larger impersonal forces in the agricultural economy. He referred to the Great Depression, but only in terms of his relative prosperity compared to some neighbors. Like many farmers who came of age before World War II, he never mentioned the farm crisis of the 1980s or various federal agricultural policies. He discontinued his small-scale dairy production in the 1950s, probably because stricter USDA sanitation regulations made it prohibitively expensive to upgrade his milking equipment to minimal standards. Nonetheless, he never described federal interference in farming, although at two points during the interview, Republican West and his Democrat wife sparred over what he saw as government's excessive interference in daily life. Like many people of his generation, John West believed that each person controlled his or her own fate. One historian has noted that many of the people Studs Terkel interviewed about the Great Depression attributed their hardships to personal failures rather than the collapse of the economic system. West seemed to have a similar reaction. Although his narrative occasionally hints at outside influences shaping his farming career, to have explicitly attributed any hardships to larger structural forces would have undermined his belief in his ability to control the circumstances in his life.[10]

By the same token, West never acknowledged any advantages that his race, class status, or gender might have given him. He certainly benefited from his father's status as a successful farmer, with tools to loan and advice to give. As a white man, he enjoyed opportunities that a black man would not have enjoyed in Jim Crow–era east Tennessee. For example, he was able to obtain a mortgage for his first farm and subsequent loans for equipment and cattle, loans that no Maryville bank would have granted to an African American farmer at the time. Like most of the prosperous white farmers I interviewed, these advantages remained invisible to West, and to have acknowledged them would have undermined his steadfast belief that he was a self-made man.

John West's narrative repeats many of the themes emphasized by other narrators in this study. He clearly belonged to the rural community of memory that they shared. Nonetheless, many elements of his story are unique. His narrative was shaped most of all by his need to present himself as a self-made man. What John West valued most was his own independence. Farming made him his own boss. Working the land provided him with the opportunity to prove to himself and the world that he could stand alone. It brought him a secure belief in his own abilities. He chose to recount memories that buttressed this self-image. Near the end of the interview, he mused, "I got a kick out of it, standing on my own feet. I was the only boy in school that had money. I had money to do anything I wanted to do."

Ruth Hatchette McBrayer

Like John West, Ruth Hatchette McBrayer came of age during the Great Depression and farmed into the 1980s.[11] She came to farming reluctantly and in the wake of great personal tragedy, fifteen years later than West. McBrayer also came to value her independence and skill as a farmer above all else, but unlike John West, she placed her own success within the context of a supportive network of family, employees, and friends. Notions of femininity had no place in her oral autobiography, although she remembered that many of the men in her community did not expect her to succeed at farming because she was a woman. Her description of how she came to farming was matter-of-fact with no apologies or justifications for taking an unorthodox path. McBrayer's background was somewhat more affluent than John West's. Although she married into a prominent family that owned land and various businesses, her middle years were marked by financial struggle because her husband died in considerable debt.

I interviewed Mrs. McBrayer at her handsome brick home outside the small town of Chesnee, South Carolina, on August 20, 1998. Writer/photographer Mike Corbin, another scholar of upstate South Carolina peach farming, suggested that I interview Mrs. McBrayer because of her articulate descriptions of this way of life. We talked for about two hours in her book-lined den. Mrs. McBrayer was carefully but casually dressed, and she settled into an easy chair next to doors opening onto her screened porch to relate her life story.

Born around 1910, Ruth Hatchette McBrayer was the youngest

in a family of seven children. Her family lived in a community called State Line on the border between North and South Carolina. She described her landowning father as a general farmer who was a good provider but one who "didn't make a lot of money." He grew cotton, corn, and small grains as well as raising livestock. Ruth's mother died when she was only seven. Feeling overwhelmed at the prospect of farming full time while trying to look after a seven-year-old (her siblings were apparently much older) and perhaps desolated by grief as well, her father sent her to live with an older married sister in the town of Spartanburg, twenty miles to the south. According to Ruth, he believed that in Spartanburg Ruth could attend better schools and benefit from the motherly attentions of her elder sister. She explained, "I was very unhappy [living in town]. But it was good for me because I learned to fend for myself and went to a better school than I would have if I had stayed home in the country." Losing her mother and being torn from her childhood home all at once must have devastated young Ruth. Living in town from a young age also distanced her from farm life. She enjoyed visiting with the family on the farm during school breaks, but she said that she was never asked to do any work on the farm. She noted that when she visited her father and the rest of the family, "I was treated like a guest."

McBrayer attended Winthrop College (now Winthrop University), a state-supported college for women in Rock Hill, South Carolina. After two years of college, she taught school for a time before marrying Vernon Eugene Hatchette in 1933. Hatchette and his family were among the leading citizens of Chesnee, a small market and mill town in northern Spartanburg County, not far from Ruth's birthplace. Gene Hatchette's father owned a car dealership and a large farm, and he was also president of a bank in Chesnee that failed during the Great Depression. In addition, the senior Hatchette owned a peach-packing shed, where seasonal workers sorted and packed growers' fruit for shipment to distant markets. After her marriage, Ruth worked part-time in the car dealership alongside her husband. During World War II, she also worked in the peach shed upon occasion. Ruth and Gene Hatchette never had children, a subject she did not address and about which I did not ask.

Peach farming was just taking hold in the northwestern counties of South Carolina when the Hatchettes built their first packing shed.

In the early years of the twentieth century, upstate South Carolina farmers had focused on producing cotton for the market, in spite of the poor fertility of upstate soil. Many also pursued subsistence activities. In the 1920s at the urging of agricultural extension agents based at Clemson University, a number of upstate farmers turned to peach production as a way to recover from the ravages of the boll weevil, rock-bottom cotton prices, and horrific soil erosion. By the 1950s, the upstate counties were among the largest peach producers in the state.[12]

Details of the Hatchettes' married years emerged piecemeal during the interview, mostly in the context of explaining how Ruth had learned about peach farming. She explained that her husband did not serve in the military during World War II. Instead, she recalled, he stopped working at the car dealership to become a full-time farmer, planting a peach orchard and unsuccessfully experimenting with commercial chicken production. McBrayer implied that by undertaking farming on a full-time basis, Gene Hatchette sought to obtain exemption from the draft, since the federal government considered farming an essential wartime occupation. Even as she described adult life on the farm and various commercial farming ventures, McBrayer never mentioned subsistence activities. She did not describe a garden or raising livestock for home consumption. Most likely, given their prosperity and focus on producing for the market, the Hatchettes purchased most of their food and clothing.

Gene Hatchette's father was diagnosed with cancer during the war and died in 1944. Gene carried on with farming, building another packing shed on the farm in 1945. Tragedy struck Ruth again in 1947 when her husband shot himself in the barn on their farm. Ruth did not explicitly tell me that he committed suicide. Instead, she said, "after Daddy Hatchette's death, the responsibility of all this was just too much for Gene. He had been protected for all his life. And he missed his father tremendously. And he had had a serious breakdown while I was at Winthrop, and he began to have troubles again after his father's death." During the interview, I did not press Mrs. McBrayer to be more explicit about her husband's death, but later I located a newspaper article confirming the cause of Gene Hatchette's death.[13]

After Gene's death, Ruth took over the peach operation. The pampered youngest child of a doting and relatively prosperous family had grown up to marry into a prominent local family. A woman of her status would never have expected to perform farmwork, particularly not the hands-on farming that McBrayer eventually did. Instead, she had taught school, done occasional office work in her father-in-law's car dealership, and helped out in the peach shed office during the wartime labor shortage. Indeed, she explained that on the rare occasions she had accompanied Gene to the farm before his death, she had remained in the car. During her husband's lifetime, much of her energy had been expended on her home and her husband. Neither her class status nor her life experiences had prepared her to run a farm. With Gene's death, Ruth McBrayer not only had to cope with her grief, shock, and anger, but she also had to learn how to run an orchard. At first, she resented the heavy responsibility. As she put it, "then the farm and everything was just dumped on me." She soon discovered that Gene had left behind a considerable number of debts, including the mortgage for the brick home she inhabited for the rest of her life. She said, "I was lost. I didn't know what to do really. But fortunately, I learned. And with a lot of good help, I paid his debts which at that time seemed very, very large." At no point did she discuss the tragedy in gendered terms, though the underlying message was that as a woman, she had not been expected to know much about the farm operation or to share responsibility for the couple's financial well-being. Although it seems logical that the crushing burden of debt may have played a role in Gene's suicide, Ruth apparently knew little of their financial condition until his death.

It is not clear why she did not sell the farm, and I failed to ask her. She may have shared title to the land with her mother-in-law; in other contexts, she mentioned that the two co-owned a number of real estate parcels in and around Chesnee. If this indeed was the case, perhaps the elder Mrs. Hatchette was unwilling to sell the farm. Whatever her reasons, Ruth Hatchette McBrayer threw herself into learning how to farm.

Unlike John West, Ruth McBrayer did not portray her success as an independent accomplishment. By her own account, her success was due to her own hard work, her willingness to learn, the help of others, and her faith in God. In a pattern common to the autobiographical narratives of women, she saw herself as embedded in a caring network of people who helped her succeed, as the beneficiary of "a lot of good help."[14] She remained close to her mother-in-law, "Mother Hatchette," until the end of the older woman's life. Though at first McBrayer knew little about peach farming, she said, "of course, I did have the desire to learn." She recalled that she learned a great deal about peach farming from a skilled foreman who worked for her and from the ordinary hired hands. "I worked with the men. I learned to prune. I learned to thin. I actually didn't know much. I had sat in the car when my husband would give directions to the men as we were maybe leaving to go someplace, but I didn't know I absorbed any of it. But actually I did. I had absorbed some." She also took advantage of educational opportunities provided by the Agricultural Extension Service. In addition, she benefited from the help of family members. Two brothers assisted her at harvest time. An orphaned niece whom McBrayer raised eventually ran the packing shed. All these people were part of the network that helped McBrayer persist as a peach farmer. At several points during the interview, she also referred to help from "the good Lord."

The help proved essential because she described herself as being at first "ignorant" of farming and the peach operation in general. To illustrate her own lack of knowledge, she told a story:

> One thing that's nothing more than to prove how ignorant I was: [one year] we had a freeze. The peaches were killed, I thought. And I had a peach grower friend that came over [to look at the orchard]. We walked down through the Red Haven [variety of peach] field and they kept looking at the field and kept looking at the field and kept looking at the field. And my mind was made up. They [the peaches] were all gone. They kept telling me that "no, you have a peach crop. This is a crop of peaches." Finally I said—this proves how ignorant I was—I said, "Well, I know peaches when I see them." And I had a beautiful crop of peaches that year.

McBrayer realized that she faced many challenges, and she soon learned that one was posed by the male farmers in the community who did not expect her to succeed. She said, "All the men in the community believed that I would fail and they would own this property.

And I had one friend who came to me and warned me that people were—his words were, 'They are staying awake at night trying to figure out how they're going to get everything you have.' That made me more determined, of course." Hatchette succeeded in proving herself to the skeptical men around her. Later in the interview, she told me that, "After the men in the community and around saw that . . . I had the determination and the courage and the ability, I guess, to do it, they began to try to help me."

She remembered the adjustment to running the farm as hard, "real hard. I would get up at five in the morning, sometimes even four in the morning. At one time, it was three straight days and two nights." After a few years, McBrayer managed to pay off all of her husband's debts. She remembered that at the point of her husband's death, "I was so discouraged and so grieved that I thought if I ever got his debts paid that I was just going to go somewhere else." Success fueled her interest in farming, however. As she put it, "After I did that [paid off his debts], I thought, well, if I can make that much money, I'll make some for myself. . . . So I became interested in my work. And I worked day and night for several years. I worked in the peach orchard and ran the packing house." Hers is the story of a woman who found a vocation. McBrayer's description of becoming absorbed in "my work" suggests the extent to which she came to identify farming as that vocation.

McBrayer was modest about her success, asserting, "My late husband had a beautiful young orchard at the time of his death, which was just coming into a good bearing stage of peaches. So I was attributed with being extremely smart. I didn't deserve all that because the orchard was already planted, and the trees were good." Nonetheless, she took credit where credit was due. She became active in the local growers association, and she adopted new farming methods when she believed they would prove profitable. She expressed pride in the fact that she was the first peach grower in the area to install an air cooler in her packing shed and an irrigation system in her orchard. Soon she became known as an innovative farmer, and other farmers watched her work. She said, "people came from all around to see us out there in those fields barefoot in our jeans and with our tractors waiting for the water to come on. . . . But irrigation paid off." Other peach farmers in her community expressed admiration for her skill as an orchardist and her use of progressive farming strategies.[15]

By the mid-1950s, Ruth Hatchette McBrayer was known as one of the best peach growers in the area, and she took pride in her reputation for growing and packing high-quality fruit. For example, she told me, "It was said one time a long time ago that next to Louis Caggiano, I put up the best pack in the area. I thought that was a compliment." Louis Caggiano, the child of Italian immigrants, established an orchard in neighboring Cherokee County early in the twentieth century and became one of the region's top peach farmers. To "put up the best pack" was to pack peaches so carefully and well that few spoiled or were damaged in transport. McBrayer was pleased to have her work compared favorably to Caggiano's. She had her own label designed for her peach crates. Emblazoned with a red hatchet, the label identified Hatchette peaches to consumers far and near. As a result of the label, she heard from a satisfied customer one thousand miles away, another story she told with great pride. As she explained, "One year I had packed peaches in bushel baskets. They were shipped north in the area of Martha's Vineyard, and I got a letter from this person. . . . I had my own personal label and stamp on my packages. . . . And this lady wrote me a beautiful letter, which I appreciated very much, and . . . it [the letter] was read one time at one of the peach conventions. She only found one bad peach in our bushel. I really valued that letter, and I, in return, wrote her and thanked her."

McBrayer ran a large operation, and she depended on sizable numbers of seasonal workers in addition to a small staff of year-round hands. She remembered the task of managing her workers as one of her greatest challenges, and she described the management lessons she learned over the years in great detail.

> I had said to my husband one time, when he was having a little bit of trouble [with workers]—I thought he was doing too much for the help. I said, I will be darned if I would haul them and beg them to work and haul them and pay them and loan them money and do all the things that you do. I just wouldn't do that. You know, I didn't have any experience. I didn't know.

I soon learned. I really soon learned, that if they didn't like you, even if they were hungry, they would not work for you. So I went to the field when they went in the morning. I worked. Just any kind of clothes that I needed to wear. And if it were raining [*sic*], the only way I could get them to pick peaches was to go and pick peaches with them or be in the field with them—I didn't do much picking—until time for the shed to start. It was all right when you had to leave when it was time to operate the shed, and they'd pick on, but I must go in the morning and pick with them until I had to leave. So I worked with the people. And really I had respect. I had a lot of respect. They were kind; they were good. Some of them would come back to see me. I was really most fortunate. But I did change. *I* changed. Because I knew that if I didn't change—see, I didn't know the people. They lived down here all their lives, and I had, too. But I really didn't know the people that were going to work in the fields, so I had to learn them and they had to learn me and they had to like me or they wouldn't bother working.

Over the years, her labor force changed. As "the black people began to get better jobs in the different areas and places of work," she explained that she turned to Mexican migrant labor crews. McBrayer seemed to respect the work ethic of all her workers, concluding that, "But they were good workers. They were real good workers."

The previous passage is revealing because it alludes to serious class divisions between landowner and farmworker that could have handicapped McBrayer's orchard without careful management. She never explicitly referred to racial or class differences, though she hinted at their existence several times during the interview. Nor did she acknowledge that her own class status had given her distinct advantages in terms of inheriting land and access to capital. Nonetheless, she acknowledged the importance of landless workers to her own success, and she lends insight into the complex power dynamics embedded in relationships between landowner and farmworker. She points out that she did not "know the people"—at first, African Americans—in spite of the fact that she had lived among them all her life. Moreover, in spite of their poverty, McBrayer's laborers worked on their own terms. They would not work for an employer who had not proven herself to be hardworking as well as respectful of their work ethic and abilities—an employer who would not work beside them. By working in the orchard, she sent a message that she did not see herself as "too good" to work in her own fields. Only by earning workers' respect could McBrayer count on a stable, reliable workforce. Perhaps gender played a role in this dynamic as well; because she was a woman, she may have had to prove to workers that she was a competent farmer.

Ruth McBrayer also proved to be a shrewd businesswoman who was not afraid to take risks on unorthodox ventures or to stand up to men who tried to take advantage of her. Like John West, McBrayer took pride in this entrepreneurial spirit, pointing out the risks she took more than once during the interview. This trait emerged even before the death of her husband. She explained that during her father-in-law's last illness, "I was put in the packing house to look after it, which I didn't know much about." Although a man was hired to supervise the day-to-day packing of peaches, Ruth was expected to manage the office and the sale of culls, bruised peaches that cannot be sold as fresh produce. Culls are usually sold to food processors at a much lower price. That year, the Hatchettes were packing their own peaches as well as those grown by Ruth's brother and by one other local grower. Ruth said, "And for some reason—we must have not done a good job growing peaches that year—and we had oodles and oodles of culls. And not very many customers [for culls]. They were packed from the floor to the ceiling." Culls must be processed quickly before they spoil. Unable to locate a cannery or baby food processor to buy the culls, Ruth tried a new approach.

> I don't know how I came to do this, but I got on the telephone calling people, and I called a winery in Charlotte. I do not know to this day how I did that. . . . I called the Tennent Brothers Winery in Charlotte. And they were interested. And they came. One of the owners came and talked with me. And I felt so inadequate. But I must have done a pretty good job. . . . I sold those culls to Tennent Brothers Winery. . . . Why I did all these things I don't know, how I did them. I guess it was 'cause I was so young and venturesome.

We made more money off of the culls than what we packed. And I did buy some of the wine that Tennent Brothers sold. [laughs] It was good.

On another occasion McBrayer recalled "an interesting experience" with a Charlotte fruit broker. He visited her office in search of a railroad carload of fruit, and "he offered me so much more money than I had been quoted that summer that I sold a little to him which I should not have done, though I called my broker in Spartanburg and more or less asked and told at the same time that I had done it." Mrs. McBrayer meant that she had already contracted to sell all her peaches through another broker at a particular price. By selling peaches to the Charlotte broker who offered a higher price, she violated her agreement with her own peach broker. She soon learned the proverbial lesson: deals that seem too good to be true often are. She explained, "So when the returns came, I was paid considerably less [than I was promised] by this man from Charlotte and of course, I would not cash the check. I called him, and he called me an impulsive woman. He said, 'Lay the telephone down; I can hear you all the way from Chesnee.' I was talking so loud." She laughed at the memory and continued, "I mailed the check back to him and threatened him. So he paid me the full amount. But he was testing me." Apparently the Charlotte broker was impressed with her peaches and with her business acumen. McBrayer went on, "Later he came to visit me at my home during the winter and wanted me to associate myself with him. And he would operate the shed, he would operate the orchard, he would furnish all the money that I needed." The broker was offering to serve as Mrs. McBrayer's operating lender, providing money for equipment and operations each year in return for the right to buy all her crop. She quickly rejected his offer. She explained, "I looked at him. I was young, very young. I looked at him straight on and I said, 'I own this now. But if I did that, you would own me.' I said, 'I appreciate your offer, but no thanks.' I guess the good Lord helped me [make the right decisions]." She went on to be friends with the broker until his death.

As the previous story suggests, Ruth McBrayer was determined to maintain her independence. Resolved not to allow anyone else to control her operation—to "own me"—she kept a firm hand on all

aspects of her operation. Her determination to maintain her independence played into her lack of interest in remarriage. For many years,
she focused on her work and did not pursue finding another life partner. McBrayer finally remarried in 1969, once she found a spouse
who would not interfere with her orchard and packing shed. Her second husband, Charles McBrayer, was a cattle dealer whom she met
when he tried to buy some property from her. The land deal never
materialized, but she was struck by his good looks and nice manners.
The two became close friends. As she put it, "He had never been
married, and I was not wanting to be married; I had business on my
mind." After several years of friendship, however, the two decided to
marry. She described him as "having his business" while she had her
own. By her account, it was a close and good marriage, and he was
"a very good man, very good man. I've been most fortunate to have
two good husbands." Charles McBrayer died in 1995.

McBrayer witnessed the growth and the decline of peach farming
in South Carolina. By the 1980s, the forces of increasingly unpredictable spring weather, rising operating costs, and fierce competition
from California and foreign growers combined to drive peach prices
down and to make peach farming increasingly risky for upstate farmers. At the same time, explosive economic growth in the area caused
land values to skyrocket. Many peach growers retired or sold their
orchards for housing developments. Like John West, Ruth McBrayer
had always been a cautious farmer, investing selectively and carefully
in new equipment and expansion. In spite of her caution, however,
"The years got leaner and leaner. I operated very frugally. I didn't buy
a lot of new tractors like a lot of people did. I operated with as few
spraying machines and equipment as I could get by [on]. I did not
buy a lot. I bought what was necessary and only what [was] necessary. Through the years, I got smaller and smaller. I replanted several
orchards. The first orchards were the best orchards we had. . . . After
the older orchards began to get less productive, I became a smaller
operator." In the mid-1980s, she closed down her packing house and
ceased to farm.

Unlike West, McBrayer was reflective about the changes she saw
in agriculture. At no time did she mention federal intervention as
having a negative impact on agriculture, not particularly surprising considering the fact that peaches were never subject to federal

production controls or to most types of federal payments. In short, her contact with the federal agricultural apparatus had been limited to the assistance of agricultural extension agents and an occasional drought relief payment. Nonetheless, she had a thumb on the pulse of the changing farm economy. When I asked her what she thought had driven so many peach farmers out of business, she explained,

> The heyday in peaches is over for this area. I haven't kept up with the actual prices, but the fertilizer and labor and necessary packaging that you would have to buy is all so expensive and the freight and the marketability, the brokerage fee. If you want to do hard work, there'd be years that you'd make money. But the young people today, like if I had a son, he would not want to be in the peach business if he grew up in it, because he would know how hard it is. I think it's a wonderful business. And it's a beautiful operation to see the trees in full bloom and the beauty of the trees and the land when it's really growing and underneath the trees, it's real pretty, and when it's loaded with fruit.

Implicit in her praise for the beauty of the orchard is the same sense of attachment to the land and the natural world that appeared in the narratives of so many other landowners. McBrayer had obviously enjoyed farming, but she did not see it as a wise choice for young people. In her view, the rising cost of farm supplies, falling and unpredictable peach prices, and the difficulty of obtaining the necessary labor force combined to make peach farming largely untenable.

McBrayer's previous statement is interesting, too, for its gendered assumptions about who might consider farming. She said, "like if I had a son, he would not want to be in the peach business." In spite of the fact that McBrayer farmed on her own for most of her life, it did not seem to occur to her that a daughter might choose to farm. She ignored conventional gender roles in her own life, and indeed, she made no comments about appropriate roles for women and men, on the farm or in society. But when she considered the possibility of passing farming on to a new generation, she assumed that only a son might want to farm.

The silences in Ruth Hatchette McBrayer's autobiographical

narrative are telling. She recognized that farming has changed irrevocably, and she understood many of the structural forces driving that transformation. Her life story offered clear evidence that race and class had provided her with numerous advantages in farming, but like John West, she is silent about those advantages. She readily shares the credit for her success with other individuals, but at the same time her narrative is marked by a strong streak of individualism—by stories about her own accomplishments. Like West, she shaped her memory stories to bolster her own view of herself as an independent and successful farmer.

Woodrow Harper Sr.

Woodrow Harper Sr.'s story contrasts sharply with Ruth Hatchette McBrayer's and John West's. Though he also came of age during the Great Depression and farmed all his life, his family did not own land. Cash renters, the Harpers faced the additional disadvantage of being African Americans in the Jim Crow South. Like West, Harper described farming as the best work a man could hope to do for a living, and like both West and McBrayer, he took great pride in his farming skill. Yet he was never able to earn a living by farming alone; from the 1950s until the time he was interviewed, Harper worked off the farm in a variety of jobs in order to support his family and cover the high costs associated with farming.

Historian Lu Ann Jones interviewed Harper in his Hartwell, Georgia, home on April 17, 1987. Part of the Oral History of Southern Agriculture project sponsored by the National Museum of American History, the interview focused on the nature of twentieth-century farm life and on the changes in southern agriculture over the course of the century.

Woodrow Harper Sr. was born in 1917 in Hart County, Georgia.[16] Hart County, located on the South Carolina border in northeastern Georgia, was then a predominantly agricultural area where farmers produced cotton for the market. Many also produced subsistence crops for home use as well. In 1930, roughly one-fourth of the county's farmers were black, and three-quarters of all farms were operated by tenants.[17] Like farmers in upstate South Carolina, Hart County farmers suffered from the effects of declining cotton prices, soil depletion, and the boll weevil. Some turned to new grain crops and others to poultry farming by mid-century.

Self-sufficiency was an important theme in Harper's memories of his childhood on the farm. His parents rented land in Hart County, where they grew cotton for the market and raised a garden, cattle, and hogs for the family's use. More prosperous than many landless farm families, the Harpers owned their own mules and tools. Woodrow Harper's mother died when he was young, but his father soon remarried and had more children with his new wife. In all there were twelve children in the Harper family.

During the agricultural depression that commenced in the 1920s, Harper's father sought work elsewhere, a strategy adopted by many landless African American farmers. He traveled to Florida for three or four months at a time, working on road building projects in order "to make money to support us that next year." The elder Harper's cash wages would have freed the family of the necessity of borrowing from a furnishing merchant, thus enabling them to maintain some measure of autonomy from white control. While Mr. Harper was away, Woodrow's mother kept the farm going with the help of her children and neighbors. According to Harper, a large number of young black farmers in Hart County journeyed to Florida for long periods for similar work.

Harper placed more emphasis on the importance of community mutual aid networks than either John West or Ruth McBrayer, apparently because mutual aid networks had been so crucial in helping his family weather a difficult economic time. Harper explained that the men too old to leave the county in search of work would assist the children of absent farmers in cutting firewood to sell or in planting the spring crop. He recalled:

> The working men had gone on to Florida, and the elderly men who was too old to shovel asphalt, they stayed here. There was quite a few of them. They supervised the people in the families whose father had gone on to Florida to work. All that was charity work. They didn't charge you anything, because there wasn't anything to pay. I mean they were just Christian-hearted enough to do that type of thing. In other words, we had good old men left here to take care of the

ladies who remained here with their children. They'd come around every once in a while to see that everything [was] going well.

Jones asked Harper whether that kind of "Christian-hearted" behavior was common in the neighborhood in later years. Harper lamented, "Well, folks ain't hardly got time to fool with you now much. It's quite a difference. We talk about that in church sometime, how people used to—if a neighbor in the community got sick, a man especially, . . . [then] my daddy would send us over there to help work that man's crop out. We'd just completely work it, have enough folks to work his crop plumb out, with no charges because he was sick. I mean, that was church people. So we don't have that type of thing existing right now because most everybody is working, man and wife." Harper's comments about strong early-twentieth-century mutual aid networks and about the decline of those networks and of community ties late in the century reflect the memories of many narrators included in this study. As Harper noted, employment off the farm helped alter the mutual aid networks in rural communities. People who worked full-time no longer had the flexibility to pitch in any time the neighbors needed help.

Like his father, Harper wanted to farm. When Woodrow was nearly twenty, his father died. His stepmother moved away, leaving Woodrow to finish raising two of his younger brothers, the children of his mother. Newly married, Woodrow continued to farm in his father's tradition, growing cotton for the market and subsistence products for his family's use on rented land. He and his wife had six children in all. His wife worked in the family garden, but she never worked off the farm. Harper does not say whether she worked in the fields, but his children did provide important farm labor.

Another way that Harper's life resembled that of his father was the fact that he also found it impossible to make a living through farming alone. Harper explained that when his children were small, he took a "public job" to supplement the income from the farm because "cotton liked to went down to nothing, almost." "Public work" and "public jobs" were terms used by rural southerners to describe off-farm jobs. He worked first as a dockworker for a trucking company and later as a machine operator in a manufacturing plant that made bobbins for textile mills. He explained that he "wasn't getting enough out of the farming business. I had to supplement it with a public job."

Harper was not content to be a struggling "dirt farmer," as farmers in his area who barely scraped by were called. He was ambitious and sought to build a substantial enough operation to provide a good living, a goal he was never able to reach. He expanded slowly but steadily during his young adulthood, at one point farming a total of 280 acres of rented land. Like McBrayer, he took every opportunity to learn about farming and was willing to try new crops and new equipment. During the 1950s, the owner of the grain elevator where he occasionally did business advanced him the money to experiment with a switch from cotton to soybeans. He started with roughly 30 acres and eventually had about 200 acres of soybeans. As he described it, "We got away from cotton because of help. See, my help [his children] was small then. It took a pretty good crowd to gather a sizeable cotton farm. So we stopped raising cotton and went to soybeans, something that one man could take a machine out there and gather it by himself." Like most struggling farmers, Harper hired labor only occasionally. For the most part, he depended on family labor, a strategy that conserved precious cash resources. At first, soybeans proved profitable, but by the 1980s, competition from foreign producers had driven prices down.

To a greater extent than West or McBrayer, Harper dwelled on the changes in southern agriculture. One change that he emphasized was the improvement in the rural standard of living over the course of the twentieth century. He told Jones, "I came along when times was pretty tight. You folks seen good time." In spite of better living standards, though, farming became increasingly difficult. One problem faced by landless farmers was the rising cost of leasing land. In the early 1960s, the Army Corps of Engineers built Hartwell Dam at the confluence of the Seneca, Tugaloo, and Savannah rivers. Intended to provide flood control and hydroelectric power, the dam flooded fifty-six thousand acres in the Savannah River Basin, much of it in Hart County.[18] The lake removed much prime farmland from production and made other land attractive for lakefront real estate developments. As a result, competition increased for the remaining land available for rent, and leasing costs rose. Small farmers found themselves pushed off of rental land by large commercial farmers who could afford to pay premium rates. Harper explained this dynamic: "Say for instance, I was paying $10 per acre [annually] for the land that I worked. Maybe just to get the number of acres and get the amount of money that some farmers needed, they would offer maybe $12 or $15 per acre. That freezes us out. Naturally, a landowner is going to go for the top price unless you have been mighty nice or he liked you pretty good or something like that. But landowners rented to bigger farmers just because they were friends and they were paying more money than the smaller farmer could pay." The requirements of lending agencies added to small farmers' dilemma. In order to qualify for federally backed operating loans, farmers had to cultivate a minimum number of acres. Harper said, "I've paid some $20 a [*sic*] acre to have enough land to qualify for the amount of finance it took to operate. I've done that, but it didn't pay."

Harper talked at length about the dramatic decline in the number of black farmers in Hart County. "I think we only have about four [black] farmers in Hart County, which doesn't speak well for as big a county as Hart County. Four black farmers, tried to hang in there," a marked contrast to 1950, when 469 Hart County farms were operated by black families.[19] Jones asked Harper what caused the dramatic decline in the number of black farmers in the South. He cited the difficulty in achieving financial success through farming. "Like I said before, there are numbers of black farmers got out of this thing because they wasn't able to support it financially. And it was a few landowners, the majority of the landowners was white and they saw fit to do other things with their land [than rent it for farming], which they had all the priority to do that if they want to." Given the financial hardships of farming and the difficulty the landless faced in finding available land, Harper said that many turned to higher-paying off-farm jobs. He explained, "So, after jobs opened in Hart County pretty good, our younger people saw that they could make more cash money working publicly than they could out here on the farm, which the income mostly comes once a year."

Another factor pushing farmers out of farming, according to Harper, was the high costs of inputs:

The concern is fertilizer and chemicals is eating us up. We can't do it. Let's say, for instance, a bushel of soybeans bringing you around $4.30, $4.40 a bushel, but the fertilizer and the chemicals are the same, they haven't fluctuated any. So it's too unbalanced, you see. We maybe could do all right now with farming, even though the prices of our production is low. But if fertilizer and chemicals come down according to that thing [the decline in commodity prices], then we probably could do all right still. But the fertilizer's way up here and the soybean—I'm just using soybean—mostly everything else is down here low, you see. And if you use much fertilizer then you've got to go somewhere else to get the money to pay for it, you see.

In other words, high operating costs and low commodities prices eroded profits. In some cases, such as "if you use much fertilizer," a farmer would actually have to take money earned from a source outside farming to cover the costs of farming. Many people who preferred farming could no longer see the point if an off-farm job was required to subsidize the costs of working the land. As Harper put it, "That's the reason we find a whole lot of people that would be farming, maybe, rather than public [work]. But if they've got to work public and take money to support this farm over here, they say I might as well to leave the farming off and go and work and public [sic] where I can get my check every Friday."

Lack of federal support for black farmers was another factor Harper cited for the decline of black farmers. Harper was explicit and outspoken in his comments about the federal government's treatment of black farmers. He said, "This is one thing that I think can help any county—if we had a supervisor among our people or ag people among our folks that we could get more blacks to remain on the farm." Jones asked if there had ever been agricultural extension agents in Hart County assigned to serve the needs of black farmers. Harper explained that two agents had briefly been assigned to work with black farmers, but "They only stayed here a few years, and they shifted them on out into another position, you see, because of the fact that they was digging in too much truth." He implies that an extension agent who attempted to help black farmers was perhaps reassigned for exposing discriminatory practices. Jones asked him for an example of a case in which the agents were "digging in too much truth," and he told her a story about his own experience with the Farmer's Home Administration (FmHA). He recounted an occasion when he sat down with his FmHA lender to work up his financial plan for the year. Though he does not specify the race of this lender, a Mr. White, it is clear from the narrative that Mr. White took Harper's needs as a farmer seriously and was prepared to ask FmHA for a loan large enough to meet those needs. Harper said,

> Then the assistant supervisor [of the local FmHA office] redone the whole thing. Financial-wise, cut it about half in two, which is going to get me in dutch. Of course, all of it's an estimation, but you get out here and make an estimation about your farming and home plan and most of the time it works if you do according to the recommendations. They majored in those fields and they know what it takes to grow a bushel of soybeans or a pound of cotton or a bale of cotton, so far as that's concerned. . . . They can come within a few dollars of telling you what you're going to make on that farm, you see. Then they multiply it by the number of acres and there you are. Got your production and your expenditure. You know how much it's going to cost you to do an acre of land and that type of thing. In this particular case, that was done two years ago. Mr. White sat out there on the porch with me—it was in the summertime—and we made our farm and home plan for the coming year. That was early. It was probably in August or September. I submitted this farm and home plan, and they went over it with me and redone the whole thing, which amounted to about half as much you see. But that got me behind the eight ball. So that's been the general trend of farmers in Hart County. Some getting too much money and some not getting enough, getting about half enough.

The relationship between the reassigned extension agents and the preceding story is unclear, but Harper is clear that he believes that the federal government has not provided black farmers with the support they ought to have.

Harper also complained that FmHA "just took a long time to process it [his loan application] and everything. That's been one of the major issues, especially black farmers. We've been getting too little financing and not getting it on time." He cited an example of a farmer in a neighboring county who submitted his application for an operating loan to the FmHA in December but did not receive approval on the loan until May or June, far too late to finance his spring planting:

> It was too late. So he's behind the eight ball on that. That's one of the things that got him behind. Mr. Long, he's a nice fellow. He used to be an ag teacher. He's been pretty progressive. . . . As an ag teacher, he tried to get FHA [Farmer's Home Administration] to loan to certain black farmers. I believe only one black man qualified for a loan in Elbert County. Whole big Elbert County. And it was almost the same thing in Hart County. . . . It appears to me that, like I said before, the big fish is eating up the little ones, and they're going to freeze us out.

Later in the interview, he reiterated that, "the federal government was against us [black farmers]."

Harper's 1987 criticisms of the way federal agricultural agencies discriminated against black farmers were echoed by thousands of plaintiffs in a class-action lawsuit against the USDA, a lawsuit in which Harper was a plaintiff. According to the lawsuit, which the USDA settled in 2000, FmHA had engaged in a systematic practice of delaying the processing of black farmers' loan applications, holding them to higher financial standards than white farmers, and other types of discrimination.[20] Long accustomed to discrimination, Harper seems resigned to the way federal agencies treated black farmers, but he is forthright about his belief that such treatment helped push them off the land.

Although he was acutely conscious of racial discrimination, Harper nonetheless gave a complex and nuanced account of rural race relations. Juxtaposed with stories about racist whites were stories about supportive ones like the grain elevator operator who financed his shift to soybean production. At another point in the interview, he explained that a white storekeeper named Fleming had bought some equipment that Harper was about to lose to foreclosure by the Production Credit Association, an agricultural lender. Fleming allowed Harper to continue using the equipment. As Harper put it, "a friend . . . bailed me out. Went to the bat and bought some of the equipment that I needed to farm with, to keep going." Later, Harper explained, he was able to borrow money from the Farmer's Home Administration to buy the equipment back from Fleming, but in the meantime, Fleming's favor enabled him to continue farming. Calling the white man who "bailed him out" a "friend" is significant. Friends are equals who support each other in tough times and do favors without expectation of repayment in kind. Later he emphasized that Fleming was a "good friend" whom Harper had known "ever since he's been in the grocery business." Such stories illuminate the contingent nature of race relations in the countryside. Harper knew that racism was rampant and that it undermined his efforts to remain on the land, but he also knew that some whites saw him as a friend and were willing to treat him as an equal.

Near the end of the interview, Harper summed up the changes in southern agriculture during his lifetime:

> So for the last five or six years, it's been tough with the Georgia farmer. It's been dry. . . . Right at present I'm down to about 64 acres. In '59 I was working a total of 280 acres, and each year I had to take money from somewhere else to support that. I mean, the expenditure. So I had to kind of get away from that. In other words, the only reason why I'm trying to hold on now, I owe a little money for the equipment that I have and I'm trying to hang on to farming so I can repay that.

In spite of the hardships, however, he told Jones, "I like farming and that's all I ever done in my life." She asked whether he ever thought about leaving the land, and he replied, "No, I never did. I don't care too much for the city. I never did think about leaving. My thought was trying to do what my daddy did." Jones probed further, asking him what he liked about farming, and he answered,

> Well, out here on the farm you can—of course, it's important that you work when you're needed, but your freedom. And

it's just a good thing to look at stuff grow. Grow cattle, grow swine and that type of thing, that's the kind of farming that— in other words, it takes diversified farming to survive now. That's all I ever known is farming. So I just like farm life. It's growed up in me. My daddy was a farmer, my granddaddy was a farmer. And we used to do pretty good on the farm. We used to didn't have to go to the grocery store for anything, scarcely, except maybe sugar and salt because we had our own milk, we had our own meat and that type of thing. So, farming was a good life and is a good life now. If a person look at it right and if he can get into the situation, farming is one of the greatest things that a man can do to my thinking. Nothing beats seeing a big herd of cows out there in the pasture or out there in the field where you used to grow cotton and that type of thing. In other words, diversified farming, the type of farming that we used to do, raising cotton and corn[,] needs to be revived and take in other type farming to make the livelihood better for the farmer.

For Harper, farming offered a kind of freedom and independence available in no other occupation. That independence was particularly characteristic of the diversified farming that combined subsistence and market-oriented production that Harper had practiced at mid-century, and he believes that more diversified farming is the only way to survive on the land today. Like McBrayer, his admiration for "seeing a big herd of cows" in the pasture implied an attachment to the land, one not usually articulated by the landless, but an attachment that helps to explain his determination to continue farming in spite of the hardships involved. Moreover, Harper believed that farming provided a link to past generations, a type of continuity: "my daddy was a farmer, my granddaddy was a farmer." Yet he does not seem disturbed by the break in continuity with his children's generation. He simply notes that all six of his children had taken off-farm jobs and that most had moved away from Hart County.

Woodrow Harper's narrative is marked by his commitment to farming and his sense that farming is an act that connects him with the past. He shaped his memory stories to emphasize his identity as a farmer, but unlike John West, he does not hesitate to complain about the external forces that are obstacles to his farming success. Unfortunately, farming paid dubious rewards. In semi-retirement, he supplemented his Social Security and farming income by driving rural folks to various social services. The local welfare department paid him for providing transportation, wages that helped him pay his annual farm-operating loan. The forces of landlessness, poverty, racial discrimination, rising operating costs, and declining commodity prices had all combined to thwart Harper's effort to attain financial security through farming. He is silent about his family's role in farming and about the impact of persistent financial insecurity upon them, but he is not silent about the causes of that insecurity.

In the end, these three narrators shared a commitment to farming as a satisfying form of work. Farming was all John West thought about, and he believed that "if you're not doing something you like to do, you've missed the boat." In farming, he found an autonomy that was life affirming. Ruth McBrayer believed that farming was a "wonderful business," and she loved to "see the trees in full bloom and the beauty of the [orchard] when it's loaded with fruit." She also enjoyed the independence that farming offered her, the way it enabled her to "make some [money] for myself." Woodrow Harper echoed West's and McBrayer's belief that farming offered him a level of autonomy not available in other lines of work, noting that "out here on the farm, . . . [you have] your freedom." Like McBrayer, he enjoyed watching "stuff grow," but he also experienced farming as a kind of continuity with previous generations of men in his family. As he put it, "Farming is one of the greatest things that a man can do." The oral history narratives of John West, Ruth Hatchette McBrayer, and Woodrow Harper Sr. provide powerful testimony as to why thousands of rural southerners went to great lengths to persist on the land during the twentieth century.

Chapter Two

Rural Southerners and the Community of Memory

Black North Carolina sharecropper Susie Weathersbee told an interviewer, "And when I come up, I was a farmer. . . . And that's all I ever done, any work on a farm." Arthur Little, the son of a prosperous white landowner in Catawba County, North Carolina, concurred. Little was born on a 250-acre cotton farm. College-educated, he farmed for five years as an adult and then became an accountant and a glove-factory owner. He told an interviewer that all of his brothers and sisters "farmed as a main occupation" even though most worked full-time as textile industry owners and managers. When asked to which class he belonged, he replied, "We belong to the farming class. We're basically farmers." The interviewer asked if this was so even though Little ran a glove mill. "Yes," he answered. "I travelled [*sic*] across Europe for six weeks, and I told everyone I was a farmer."[1] Weathersbee farmed all her life, struggling along as an economically marginal sharecropper. Raised on a prosperous farm, Little rose to prominence and relative wealth as a textile mill owner. Yet at the end of their lives, both possessed a clear and succinct vision of who they were—farmers. Although they probably never met, Little and Weathersbee would have seen themselves as belonging to a community of memory formed by shared experiences on the land.

Though most oral history narrators did not articulate their sense of belonging to a community of memory in such clear and explicit terms as Weathersbee and Little, the recurring stories in their oral narratives reveal the experiences that shaped and bounded that community. Many scholars have noted that people preserve their community of memory by telling stories about the past. As Sherry Lee Linkon and John Russo have pointed out, "Communities of memory continually retell their stories, and this process creates a sense of shared history and identity, out of which they develop vision and hope for the future." Robert Bellah has pointed out that such stories also contain "conceptions of character, of what a good person is like, and of the virtues that define such a character."[2] Through the stories that rural people tell about their lives, we can begin to discern elements of their common experiences that created the context for their sense of belonging to a distinctive community of farming folk as well as their notions of what traits constituted a *good* country person. When asked to talk about farm life during the twentieth century, individuals focused on several categories of shared experiences including rural self-sufficiency, a strong work ethic, persistence through hard times, neighborhood mutual aid, an attachment to the land, and the relative equality of rural folk. Often, perhaps most of the time, narrators made statements that revealed the characteristics shared by members of their community of memory spontaneously rather than in response to particular questions. Sometimes a narrator returned to an element of identity over and over during the course of the interview. The spontaneity of these recollections and the recurrence of similar themes in interview after interview indicate the importance of certain elements to narrators' sense of shared identity.

Many elements of this rural community of memory have been extolled in the work of generations of agrarian thinkers from Thomas Jefferson to Wendell Berry. From the time of the early American republic, the yeoman farmer has represented independence, sobriety, a commitment to hard work, and special ties to nature and to nature's God. To Jefferson, the yeoman farmer was the superior citizen because he had a vested interest in the health of the republic and because his seeming economic independence freed him from political or economic subservience to less virtuous men. In the South, Jeffersonian ideals had been forcefully reiterated in 1930 when a group of intellectuals known as the Southern Agrarians issued a controversial manifesto entitled *I'll Take My Stand: The South and the Agrarian Tradition*. The writers and philosophers who contributed to the volume warned that industrial capitalism, including scientific agriculture, would destroy the soul and conquer the spirit of the agrarian South. Historian David B. Danbom noted that agrarianism has both rational and romantic elements. In contrast to rational agrarians like Jefferson who emphasize the contributions that rural people make to the nation's economic and political well-being, Danbom argues that romantics like the Southern Agrarians emphasized the "moral, emotional, and spiritual benefits agriculture and rural life convey to the individual." Agrarian ideals have permeated American literature, political rhetoric, and popular culture for generations, and rural people's oral narratives clearly indicate that they have absorbed elements of both rational and romantic agrarianism.[3] Their stories focus on both the contribution that farmers make to the community and the larger society as well as the benefits that life on the land brings to the individual.

Rural narrators use elements of agrarian ideology to tell stories about the experiences that bind rural people together across time and space. Historian Alessandro Portelli has noted that memory can serve both symbolic and psychological functions for narrators. Symbolic memories represent a category of experiences or the experience of a whole group, while memories that serve a psychological function may heal a psychic wound or salve injured self-esteem. The storytelling that creates a community of memory involves recounting memories that serve both functions. For example, stories about the relative equality of rural people often served the psychological function of soothing the pain inflicted by the past experience of poverty. By contrast, stories about self-sufficiency, mutual aid, and the work ethic functioned as symbolic representations of the common experiences that bound rural people together in a community of memory. As Portelli put it, such stories "amplified the meaning of an individual event . . . into a symbolic and narrative formalization of a culture's shared self-representations."[4]

Personal and collective referents in symbolic stories overlapped and reinforced each other. Some of the common experiences—such as self-sufficiency—were personal ones. In other words, the narrator told some types of stories that were focused on individual experience and located in a personal place—the household, the family, or the home farm. Other experiences—such as mutual aid—were collective, focused on the neighborhood or proximate community. Narrators described the development of a strong work ethic as a personal experience, forged in the family through the discipline of working the land. Yet the rural work ethic was closely related to a collective experience—that of mutual aid. For narrators the shared labor that constituted mutual aid came to represent rural life as a whole. The central activity in mutual aid was work, and the goal of such shared work was the good of one's neighbors and kin.

Using memories of life on the land, twentieth-century rural southerners constructed stories about the experiences that made them different from city people in fundamental ways. Over and over, narrators recounted the experiences that separated them from those who had not lived on the land. Some elements of farm people's autobiographical narratives recur so often that a listener might believe they were rehearsed. Certain themes appear again and again in the stories of sharecroppers and wealthy landowners, blacks and whites, males and females, North Carolinians and Texans alike—in spite of differences in the personal identities and life experiences of individuals. Thus, it becomes clear that these themes formed central elements of an agrarian consciousness and marked the boundaries of a particular community of memory.

Self-Sufficiency

The theme of self-sufficient farm families recurred perhaps most commonly in rural people's oral narratives. At the time of the oral history interview, most narrators had not achieved anything resembling self-sufficiency for decades. Yet almost without exception, regardless of economic status or whether they had persisted on the land, at some point in the interview, narrators spoke with pride about the past self-sufficiency of rural families. For example, John West, son of a landowning Tennessee farmer, recalled life on his father's farm: "[We] raised everything we ate. . . . [W]e'd buy a little sugar and coffee. . . . We usually made our own soap." Similarly, his wife, Martha Alice West, daughter of a sharecropper, noted that, "The Depression didn't hurt us because we made everything. Even our chickens and eggs, we had on the farm."[5] Self-sufficiency is a persistent theme in agrarian writings. For example, the Southern Agrarians touted (indeed exaggerated) the historical self-sufficiency of southern yeomen farmers as an antidote to the perils created by industrial "progress."[6] Oral history narrators agreed. Nearly every person interviewed about rural life in this period mentioned the self-sufficiency of farming folk, suggesting that stories about self-sufficiency had been retold over and over again, and that in some sense being rural meant being self-sufficient.

Many narrators returned to the topic of self-sufficiency again and again, a further measure of its importance. For example, Pinkey Hall made self-sufficiency the center of her interview. Hall was the youngest of twelve children of prosperous African American landowners in Mississippi. The fact that her family "raised most everything" was one of the first things she told an interviewer about her childhood. She explained that the family had raised a wide range of crops and livestock for home consumption. Her father grew sorghum and had his own mill for grinding molasses, a service he performed for neighbors as well as his own family. Each winter, the family slaughtered at least twenty hogs for the family's table, and they shared much of their meat with poor sharecropping neighbors. She said, "We had plenty, plenty. . . . [W]hen the Depression was on and other people were hungry, we were never hungry." Hall added that her mother made most of the family's clothing. In fact, the first two pages of the transcript of Hall's interview are filled with her descriptions of the family's subsistence activities. Then Hall moved on to a discussion of community mutual aid. When asked how World War II affected her family, she explained that one of her brothers served in the military, a fact that worried the family. Nonetheless, she emphasized, "during the war, we still was on the farm and . . . doing good." Hall again described the family's subsistence activities. In all, Pinkey Hall returned to the theme of her family's self-sufficiency four times over the course of the interview.[7]

Some rural southerners pointed out that self-sufficiency was not simply a choice but rather a necessity because of economic conditions. Pierre Bourdieu has pointed out that working-class people tend to focus on food "as a material reality, a nourishing substance which sustains the body and gives strength."[8] Certainly, rural southerners focused on the material benefits of the ability to produce their own food, and most spoke with pride of their ability to feed themselves and their families in the face of dire poverty. For example, Frances Read Phelps was born in 1909, in Fitzgerald, Georgia. Her father was a railroad worker. He and the family also sharecropped. She described their subsistence efforts—raising and butchering hogs, raising cane with which to make syrup, and growing a garden. Phelps recalled: "I have seen the time more than once when I couldn't mail a letter [because she had no money for a stamp]. But I had plenty to eat. We had chickens, cows, hogs, corn, potatoes. Oh we didn't have to buy anything except flour and sugar and coffee. Things like that." Similarly, South Carolina farmer Irene Jackson explained that her family survived the Depression largely by raising their own food. "We was lucky, you know, 'cause we owned a little house and had a farm. It wasn't big, but it was plenty big enough to feed us all. . . . We never went hungry," she said. Then she repeated it for emphasis, "We never went hungry. We grew food and had a cow and some pigs so we could always eat. We was lucky. . . . We always had food to eat."[9]

Never "going hungry" mattered in more than a physical sense; it provided narrators with a sense of autonomy. Self-sufficiency was the opposite of dependence, and dependence was anathema to farm people, perhaps especially to African Americans like Pinkey Hall. Historian Ted Ownby has noted that for many black and white rural southerners in the early twentieth century, home production assumed a moral significance far beyond its material importance. By producing many of the things they needed instead of buying them, farm people could avoid debt. Most rural people of the time believed that debt posed a serious threat to independence.[10] Over and over, narrators emphasized their self-sufficiency in producing foodstuffs as a means to underscore their lack of dependence on others. In reality, many southern farm families were not so self-sufficient. Numerous studies of the South's staple crop economy have noted that the focus on producing cotton for the market led some sharecroppers to abandon efforts at self-sufficiency and some landowners to forbid their sharecroppers to waste time and land on garden crops. Ironically, a family's ability to provide its own food increased in direct proportion to its economic resources. A 1926 USDA study found that landowning southern farm families produced 66 percent of their own food and enjoyed a higher standard of living than sharecropping families who produced only 47 percent of their own food.[11] Nonetheless, self-sufficiency figured largely in narratives of sharecroppers in this study, as in Martha Alice West's account above, suggesting that memories of self-sufficiency functioned to minimize memories of dependence among the poor and the landless. A black Alabama sharecropper,

Rosa Tensley, explained that one of her landlords tried to insist on claiming half her garden produce. She refused, instead growing a garden on land her father owned.[12] To Tensley, a garden made her family less dependent on the landlord. Thanks to the vegetables she produced, her family did not have to buy large quantities of groceries on credit, which would have made them dependent on the landlord or a furnishing merchant for a balanced diet. Having her own garden not only preserved some measure of independence from the landlord but also put Tensley one step closer to realizing the agrarian ideal of self-sufficiency.

Narrators often described self-sufficiency as "living at home," a phrase popularized by agricultural extension agents who promoted rural self-sufficiency. Narrators used the phrase to describe the process of producing as many of their needs "at home" as possible, thus reducing their dependence on cash. Narrators' pride in their ability to "live at home" was related to the autonomy provided by such self-sufficiency. For example, white South Carolinian Lurline Stokes Murray told historian Lu Ann Jones:

> I want to tell you something. In all these years this woman has never been hungry. We've lived at home, and I practically live for the most part at home now. I raise the chickens for food. I've never bought milk nor butter. We used to have home-cured meat to spare. [The smokehouse] would be hanging with middlings and shoulders. I know we used to dry apples and dry peaches. So, as far as food was concerned, never been hungry. But there's many, many years I didn't know what a piece of money was.
>
> Listen to me, if you live at home and you have money, you can put it on your indebtedness. And there's no excuse for people out here in the country not to be able to live at home.[13]

For Murray, "living at home" was part of a total strategy of self-sufficiency. By living at home, she saved money. That money could be used to pay off her debts. Being debt-free in turn made her more independent and self-sufficient. And country people, in Murray's view, had no excuse for being dependent.

As most rural southerners told it, "everybody" in the country "lived at home," at least until the last quarter of the twentieth century. Narrators from a range of socioeconomic levels described this self-sufficiency as a "good living." By a "good living," they meant that it provided a comfortable and enjoyable living, rather than a livelihood marked by scrimping and barely getting by. Elizabeth Lasseter, the wife of a white Alabama cash-renting farmer, described her family's Depression-era experiences. The couple raised most of the family's food. She raised and sold chickens. She also milked two cows and sold her milk and butter. She sewed dresses for neighbors, charging 50 cents each for her labor. She made sheets from guano sacks. She said, "We had a good living because we raised all our lard and our meat and chickens. We could do that at home. We had a good living but we didn't have any money. There was just no money to be had." Lasseter implies that farm people could survive hard times by producing most of the things they needed: "we could do that at home." Similarly, Georgian and African American Jurl Watkins, daughter of a landowning farmer with twelve children, told an interviewer, "You know, most people said back in those days they had hard times. But we never had a hard time, never suffered, because my daddy would always prepare—he would even plant his rice. . . . And my mother would can. We had jars all around the walls in the house. . . . And everything you can imagine we had it."[14] As these accounts suggest, families achieved their self-sufficiency through hard work and the practice of a wide range of productive skills—sewing, canning, hunting, gardening, butchering, and more.

"Good living" was not universal, however. On rare occasions, memories of self-sufficiency were not so rosy, and narrators admitted that the self-sufficient diet could be monotonous. Irene Jackson, the white South Carolinian quoted above who took pride in never going hungry, nonetheless confessed, "We always had food to eat. Now it wasn't good food, mind you. I know I never ate so many grits in my life as during the Depression. That's all we could afford. We didn't go to the store just to buy food like we do today, you know. I ate grits almost everyday. I got so tired of them; I don't even eat them no more."[15] Similarly, Monroe Wood, son of an African American sharecropper, described his family's self-sufficiency in producing their own food. He told an interviewer, "My daddy raised us all during the Depression, you know, and it was rough. . . . You couldn't hardly make it. . . . Never did starve, but you got tired of what you had, but you couldn't do no better."[16]

Narrators who bragged about their self-sufficiency asserted their sense that though cash may have been scarce, they were not victims of abject poverty. Watkins says that most people had hard times, "but we never had a hard time." Careful planning and production of their own food staved off poverty and hard times. Male and female, black and white, landowning and landless, these narrators asserted that because they were self-sufficient, they were not poor even though their incomes might suggest otherwise. Narrators also believed their self-sufficiency distinguished early-twentieth-century farm families from people today. South Carolinian Virginia Harris recalled her farm childhood:

> But you know, living on the farm, you learn to live with what you have. If you don't have it, you substitute with something else, you know. 'Cause I've seen my mother substitute things in food. . . . [W]e had a lot of food, and we canned. . . . I hated it when pear time came. Those hard pears, you know, were hard to peel and made your hands so sore. But we'd do our part, and everybody did their part. And we had a big pantry filled with shelves filled with food, and we had everything that we could can in it, you know. So we lived at home except for those, sugar, and salt and the things that you could not grow.

Living within one's means, living "at home," living "with what you have," constituted the major virtue of self-sufficiency in the eyes of these narrators.[17]

Not only did rural self-sufficiency help rural people survive the hard times, but several expressed the belief that this self-sufficiency distinguished their experience of the Depression from that of town dwellers. Worth Jewell believed that because of the family's self-sufficiency, he and his siblings lived better on the Florida farm belonging to his grandparents than later when their father moved the family to a cotton mill town in Georgia. He said, "We had a good life for as long as we stayed on the farm and I ain't got nothing to say about it, as far as eating and wearing stuff was." Although many families who lived in mill villages worked large gardens and kept livestock, Jewell's family apparently did not. To him, farm life provided a plentiful diet; mill village life was marked by a meager table. Ann Smith agreed. She took a mill job at age thirty-five, after she and her husband tried farming and storekeeping in Lee County, Alabama. She told an interviewer, "But when we lived out in the country, which everybody knows is a hard life, we didn't think we were better, but we knew we was having it better than people that lived in mill villages. . . . And as everybody knows, there wadn't [sic] ever a time that we didn't have a balanced diet, because we raised our vegetables, had our milk and butter and meat. And so I'm glad that I wasn't raised in a mill village." Tennessean John West explained it this way: "Now they was a lot of people, now in these cities and everything, that's where they hurt if they's out of work. We [farm people] didn't know what it was to want for something to eat, and good food, too."[18]

The shared experience of subsistence production and the skills honed in this experience formed a key boundary of rural southerners' community of memory. They maintained that their material lives had been markedly different than those of urban dwellers, and they understood that the fact that they were not yet fully integrated into urban material culture had lessened their sense of relative deprivation. They could produce many of their necessities at home, making them less vulnerable to "hard times." As a result, they believed they had been better off than urban people. By the time they were interviewed, most narrators no longer "lived at home," though some still had large gardens. Nonetheless, subsistence practices remained central to their sense of what it meant to be a rural person.

Work Ethic

Self-sufficiency required hard work, and to hear many rural southerners tell it, farm people might have invented the Protestant work ethic.[19] The idea that work had value for its own sake was expressed implicitly or explicitly in the narratives of most rural southerners in this study. Hard work figured prominently in oral autobiographies, and like stories about self-sufficiency, memories about hard work came to symbolize an aspect of the larger experience on the land.

The work ethic valued by rural southerners was composed of several elements including a willingness to engage in hard physical labor, a sense of duty to complete tasks competently, and a readiness to carry one's own share of a larger burden and contribute to a larger good. The work ethic also included the self-disciplined commitment to delaying gratification in order to achieve greater gain later. Parents or other authority figures may have initially imposed a work ethic on country children, but gradually most rural people internalized the idea of a work ethic until it became a voluntary practice and a substantive component of both personal identity and shared memory. Work was sanctified. Many landowning and landless narrators, like urban working-class people, saw work as a form of moral purity, and they used their commitment to hard work as a way of drawing distinctions between themselves and those who did not work so hard. Historian Carl R. Osthaus has noted that antebellum southern yeomen "discovered self esteem and reputation in their work-related accomplishments and independence."[20] The work ethic remained just as important to southern farmers in the early twentieth century. Narrators believed themselves to be different and even superior to other people who did not live on the land because of their strong work ethic. Texan Ora Nell Moseley, granddaughter of landowning German immigrant farmers, told an interviewer that her mother never had hired help "because our family were [sic] not wealthy. And they were hard-working people, and everybody . . . pulled their own weight. They worked."[21] To Moseley, being willing to work hard and pull one's "own weight" was an important virtue, one closely related to self-sufficiency. Mealie Diggs, an African American woman from Waynesboro, Virginia, agreed, contrasting the work ethic of her childhood to the less-demanding world of today. She recalled her farm upbringing, telling an interviewer, "We had to work for our living, them times things wasn't like it was now. . . . All of us had to work together . . . on the farm."[22]

Many narrators remembered that farming parents took care to instill a strong work ethic in their children. Hard work disciplined children, taught proper values, and kept them out of mischief. White North Carolinian Dema Lyall described the childrearing of her youth to an interviewer: "[Parents] used a lot of common sense. They used a lot of firm discipline. And they used a lot of work. My dad always said it kept our brains out of the devil's workshop."[23] Georgia African American Jurl Watkins, daughter of a landowner, also remembered that her father taught her to work hard. She said, "My father just knew how to raise his children, you know, and we all worked."[24] White Texan R. H. Linam grew up on leased land near Elmo, Texas. He credited his father with teaching him a strong work ethic. He said, "A part of it was his great pride in what he was doing: believing that anything that was worth doing was worth doing right. And he wanted to have the best farm in the community. . . . Because he was a firm believer that we should all work and we should work hard, we should produce, we should be punctual. And we should live the kind of lives that would be exemplary and he lived that kind of a life before us." As both Watkins and Linam suggest, work was a way to teach children responsibility and the key to leading an exemplary life.[25] Linam's fellow white Texan, Elmin Howell, linked the work ethic to the well-being of the family. He spent much of his childhood under the tutelage of his landowning grandfather, a general farmer. As he put it, "my father and my grandfathers were always hard workers. . . . I remember being taught to work before I ever went to school. I remember there were certain jobs that were mine and it was very important to the family that I take care of my responsibility."[26]

Narrators—white and black, rich and poor, landowning and landless—invariably presented their own family as hard-working, but they occasionally acknowledged that not all rural people possessed a strong work ethic. For example, Sara Brooks, the daughter of an African American landowner from Alabama, noted that "a lot of people didn't work, just like they don't work now."[27] Members of landowning families like Brooks's were the narrators most likely to acknowledge that not all rural southerners demonstrated a strong work ethic, and these narrators rarely referred to lazy landowners. Perhaps by assigning the sin of laziness on the landless class, landowners could explain their own status—they were landowners *because* of their hard work. Nevertheless, landowners rarely dismissed *all* landless people as lazy. White Texas landowners Dovie and Etta Carroll explained to historian Rebecca Sharpless that they sought "good" sharecropping families to work on their farm. Dovie said that a "good" sharecropping family was "a family that liked to work and [was] easy to get along with." His wife added, "some of them, they didn't care whether they worked. . . . You'd want nothing like that. You'd want somebody that you can depend on doing the work whether you was in the field or whether they's out by themselves."[28]

Though most narrators embraced the ideal of hard work uncritically, a few rural southerners expressed a more ambivalent view of the work ethic. Such narrators were not lazy. To the contrary, details in their narratives make it clear that they spent their lives engaged in back-breaking physical labor in order to support themselves and their families. Nonetheless, in these interviews conducted late in life, they articulated a suspicion that hard work for its own sake might lead them to miss out on other rewards in life. For example, one or two landless farmers expressed a belief that extraordinary effort on their own part would benefit only the landowners. This sentiment is implicit in an interview with John and Estelle Heard, African Americans from rural Alabama. The Heards described his work as a pulpwood cutter and hers as a day laborer in other farmers' cotton fields. John Heard cut timber year-round until his health failed in his early fifties. In later years, Estelle helped him by running the machine that loaded logs onto the truck. Of cutting timber, a grueling and dangerous task, John said, "I loved it. I just liked to cut it down and load it." Timber cutting was a challenging task, one that gave him an opportunity to demonstrate his strength and stamina. As Heard put it, "I'd show them how strong I was, you know. In a way it was fun, to us young boys. We would see which one could carry the largest one [log]." Estelle explained, "He liked to work like he wanted to. He could go early if he wanted to. Quit when he wanted to. If he had two loads early, he'd quit early. If he didn't, he'd stay there until he did." John went on, "That's about all a black man could do. Pulpwood or sawmill, one or the other." Estelle interrupted, "Or pick cotton. The women picked cotton and the men pulpwood." Later Estelle explained: "We didn't really work that hard. Just to make a living and pay the bills. I mean, I can understand a person working to get ahead. But good Lord, you work and kill yourself and die and not enjoy it."[29]

Several elements of this exchange prove revealing. John Heard obviously did not fear the hard physical labor involved in cutting timber. In fact, he enjoyed the challenge of his work, but he also enjoyed the independence it offered him. He believed that as a black man, he had few other options for earning a living, and he implied that cutting and hauling pulpwood was far superior to picking cotton or working in a sawmill, both occupations that placed workers under the close supervision of (usually white) foremen or crew bosses. Although Heard does not explicitly say so, he suggests that cutting timber offered him the opportunity to direct his own labor and work at his own pace. In spite of their willingness to work hard, however, the Heards were committed to balancing work with other aspects of life. As Estelle put it, one could "work and kill yourself and die and not enjoy it." John concluded with a story about his brother, a man who logged from dawn until dark each day in spite of the fact that "everything he's got is paid for." Heard wondered aloud about this, "I don't know why he does that. . . . He still goes out there like he ain't got a dime." Perhaps their landless status and their lack of opportunities for upward mobility as black people in the rural Jim Crow South fostered the Heards' ambivalence about the commitment to work for its own sake espoused by so many farm folk, but so did their observations of others who worked relentlessly, long after the need for such dogged labor had passed.

Landowning white Tennessean John West also expressed ambivalence about the balance between work and other pleasures of life. West himself was a hard worker, and he approvingly described his wife as a "workaholic. She worked all the time." Later in the same interview, he expressed great admiration for a hard-working neighbor, a farm wife who had lost an arm in a childhood accident. He laughed and said, "That gal had a lot of nerve. Just one arm, make a farmer's wife. She was a go-getter. You say John West told you that. I don't care. I admire her." Yet particular life experiences also led West to share Estelle Heard's desire to balance hard work with enjoying life. Later in his interview, he sat forward in his chair and said emphatically,

Let me tell you something: if you've got a living, that's all you need anyway. Just like I told my boys, I told John Burton [his son]. He called up here and wanted to know about selling part of his place down there. He was in 30 miles of Atlanta. And he said, "I can sell 50 acres . . . for more than I paid for the farm." Wanted to know what I thought about it. I said,

"Sell it!" Then I said, "Live a little. You've not done anything all your life, just work like a slave." He said, "I don't wanna sell it." I said, "Well, you're the doctor about that. That's what I'd do." And he sold the timber off of it for $50,000. And they hadn't cut the timber when he died. Found him dead on top of the house. Wind had blown the antenna over, and he was putting up the antenna. He had a heart attack.[30]

With this story, West expressed his late-life concern that a man or woman could work hard over a lifetime without having time to enjoy the fruits of one's labors. His son had worked hard but died young, long before he could spend his accumulated material wealth. These expressions of ambivalence about the value of work for its own sake are striking precisely because they are so rare among rural southerners' oral histories. Most narrators—even the Heards and West—bragged about how hard they and their families had worked in the past, disdained those who did not work hard and, like John West, expressed admiration for those who did.

Narrators believed that a strong work ethic remained a valuable skill later in life. Texan Ray Summers, the son of a cash-renting white farmer, said, "We worked hard [on the farm]. We were there in the fields in cotton-chopping time as early as you could see to tell the grass from the cotton. . . . We stayed as the old farmers called it, 'from can till can't' [from "can see till can't see"]." Later in the interview, Summers added, "So I would say that it was good wholesome work; it gave you an appreciation for work so that you weren't afraid of it at all. . . . I think all of us got a good wholesome respect for work and never were afraid of it; never felt that we were abused at all." Alabama farm wife Rita Harwell declared, "Growing up on the farm has helped [my children] learn the value of work."[31]

To hear most country folk tell it, the work ethic they learned on the farm led to future success. Woodrow Fetner was born to a white farming family in Cragford, Alabama. A retired school bus driver, he still lived on his family's tiny farm at the time he was interviewed. He explained, "The poorest fellow in the country back whenever I started growing up could have had as much as I've got. I didn't have anything. Started out farming on halves. I'm not rich, but I've got a living. . . . I just come in at the bottom rung in my set and just worked hard and saved a little and worked all the time, and by doing that, accumulated what I have got. I never had nothing gived [*sic*] to me. . . . I'm proud that I could work, make what I have got." Texan Howard Matthies believed that the work ethic learned on the farm made men more desirable to off-farm employers. As he put it, "the people were leaving the farm on account of price [low commodity prices], and they sought employment here and there. It was a whole lot easier for . . . a boy from the country to go to town and get a job than the city boy to get a job in the city . . . because they [country boys] were better workers. They all learned to work."[32] Black Mississippian William A. Butts recalled childhood on his landowning parents' farm. Butts described his family as better off than many neighbors, but he nonetheless recounted hardship and struggle on the farm. He said, "Something about the lonely and meager situation like that though; it disciplined us to become men and women . . . because everyone had a responsibility. . . . You had to do that job to make sure that everything functioned."[33]

Delaying gratification through hard work was also a way of learning to appreciate one's blessings. An interviewer asked Louisiana farm wife Irene Clause if she had any unfulfilled dreams at the end of her life. She replied,

[My husband] had prepared [financially] for the future so that neither one of us may have to worry. I guess it is because we have had to work so hard for the things we have. It was not handed to us on a so-called silver platter. For this, we feel so grateful for what we have. Oh, I am sure that I have felt disappointment at one time or another. One [disappointment] was that I had plans for a new home that we would one day build, but then when we bought this land and remodeled this house, I knew that I would never have a new one. But I kept my plans and I would look at them once in a while and dream. And I would quickly think of my family and how blessed we were, and I was so glad to have this home and a beautiful family.[34]

A white Kentucky farm woman agreed, saying of her Depression-era childhood, "Of course, we didn't have all the things that people have today, but I'm not sure that we really needed all of them. I think that we appreciated what we had more growing up in the time that we did and having to work to do things on the farm and help preserve the food for the winter and also to have a better appreciation of it."[35] Through hard work, rural people achieved an adequate living, and because they had earned it instead of having it "handed to them," they valued their material success. They saw this commitment to hard work as something they shared with other farming folks—another trait that set rural people apart from those who did not live and work in the country.

Mutual Aid

Noting that Americans have always valued self-reliance and that this self-reliance often focused on the "work ethic," sociologist Robert Bellah and his team of researchers have argued that "an emphasis on hard work and self-reliance can go hand in hand with an isolating preoccupation with the self."[36] Narratives of rural southerners refute Bellah's findings. In fact, rural southerners often explicitly linked a devotion to self-reliance and a strong work ethic with a sense of obligation to one's community. Landless black Arkansan Helen Howard explained that helping neighbors "was just a tradition and everybody fell in line with it and just kept up that tradition on down through. And a lot of people do that right today. They share with one another."[37] Landowning white Texan Howard Matthies said, "We helped a . . . lot of people out, great number of times. And we used to borrow. Let's say, when a fellow broke something and the neighbor had it, you go over there and borrowed it from them till you got yours fixed . . . and all the neighbors . . . were neighborly. Neighbor knew neighbor. Everyone was concerned [with] what each one was doing."[38] Rural southerners' oral history narratives repeated stories like these over and over, indicating the importance of strong mutual aid networks to their community of memory.

Since the time of settlement, American farm families relied on the types of mutual aid described by Howard and Matthies to survive an uncertain environment and an unpredictable economy. Historian Robert S. Weise has noted that in the South, the focus of civic society was traditionally the household. Plain folk southern farmers preferred informal approaches to meeting community needs at least in part because those informal approaches were organized out of households, the primary locus of power for farm men.[39] Indeed, the narrators in this study noted a preference for locally based efforts to address people's needs. Rural people depended on kin and neighbors for many of the necessities of daily life. Farm families shared labor and tools in order to get through the busy seasons of planting and harvest. They cared for their extended family members and neighbors in times of sickness or death. A person with an abundance of green beans, for example, shared the bounty with neighbors who might later reciprocate with gifts of turnips or apples. Pitching in to help a nearby farmer harvest wheat or build a barn was more than an act of friendship; farm families who participated in mutual aid networks accumulated a benefit that sociologists have called social capital. By participating in the community's mutual exchange network, a farm family was earning the right to benefit from reciprocal exchanges in times of need. Social networks like those described by farm people provided individuals with influence, with companionship, and with access to material resources. Such networks built norms of trustworthiness and reciprocity in communities. As political scientist Robert D. Putnam puts it, "If we don't have to balance every exchange instantly, we can get a lot more accomplished. Trustworthiness lubricates social life."[40]

The oral narratives of southern farm people bear out this analysis of the efficacy of social capital. To most rural narrators, labor exchanges were as much a matter of self-interest as of charity. When asked about mutual aid efforts in his community, white North Carolina landowner Dean McGee said,

> I did work with neighbors every year that I farmed, either in harvest and a lot of times in the planting season, too. That's not very common anymore. Every man's looking after his own. . . . [We would go] from farm to farm, more or less borrowing time from them and returning it, you know. I wouldn't say it was an act of charity, unless, like I said, in some cases I know people who were sick or something, we'd go and help them harvest their crop. But most of it was just the convenience of getting yours out maybe faster, you know. In other

words, if you have a field that's good to cut, you're anxious to get it [the crop] out before a storm comes or something, so you get help, you get it out [of the field and into the barn] quicker, and your neighbor may have some the following day. It was a convenience thing. It wasn't being that charitable, as a rule. It was just more convenient for us to do it in that manner.[41]

In some ways, the centrality of mutual aid activities to rural narrators' community of memory is not surprising. Anthropologist Douglas Harper has argued, "From a cultural perspective, you might expect that participants' social identities led them to actions which were consistent with the needs of the group. Farmers were farmers and little else. This occupation was actually a lifestyle—a master identity. For a long time, this master identity included exchanging labor with one's neighbor's, and in these moments the farmer played out his role, which included how others who were his peers defined him."[42] Doing one's share for others was a way to earn respect from one's peers and even influence in one's community. On the other hand, failing to do one's share not only resulted in a failure to accumulate social capital but also in a loss of regard from friends and neighbors.

A commitment to doing one's share for others could cross racial boundaries and minimize class differences. In the process of exchanging labor for material goods or helping each other through crisis, the barriers that separated the prosperous from the struggling might seem less visible, especially in retrospect. Narrators often noted that farm families "helped each other" in spite of class differences. In addition, numerous narrators of both races told stories about interracial mutual aid. For example, white South Carolina farm woman Lurline Stokes Murray told historian Lu Ann Jones about an incident during her childhood. Murray and her parents were struggling to move a crop of oats from the field and into the barn before a rainstorm hit. Two African American farmers plowing cotton in the field next door observed their plight and came to help. She explained,

That cloud, oh, it looked awful in the west. We looked back and they [the black farmers] had taken out and went back to their house and hitched up their wagon and they was back there throwing oats on to help us.

Now, listen, you can have some of the best times in the world if you be a neighbor. I'm telling you. There ain't no need of people living fussing and fuming. And I just want to inject that because if people would just have feeling for one another, you can work together. Now, it doesn't work every time, but for the most part.[43]

As Murray saw things, one had to "*be* a neighbor" to earn neighborly aid from others, and neighborliness mitigated conflict, "fussing and fuming." She saw a lesson in stories like this one: even racial boundaries could be overcome by "being a neighbor."

Dovie and Etta Carroll, white landowners from Texas, echoed Murray's observations about the reciprocity inherent in neighborly exchanges, reciprocity that could cross the color line. Etta explained that "If you got a good [sharecropping] colored family . . . and could depend on them, they'd go help you do things and they wouldn't charge you for them. A lot of times, we'd give them milk or we'd give them butter because they were good to us." Carroll added that in return, she and her husband tried to provide their sharecroppers with a garden spot or space to pen a hog or raise chickens. She said that mutual aid across racial or class lines depended on "how you treat your hands. If you got some hands and treated them good, they were good to you. They would be there to help you when you needed them."[44]

The social capital generated by strong mutual aid networks performs several important functions in communities. First, it allows citizens to resolve collective problems more easily. Social capital widens our awareness of the ways in which our fates are linked. In that sense, social capital can overcome barriers such as class or racial differences, as it did in the case of Lurline Murray's family. Social capital also improves individuals' lives—making them better able to cope with traumas, hard times, and illnesses. The social capital accrued in strong mutual aid networks can minimize the effects of poverty. As Putnam has noted, where social capital is lacking, the effects of poverty are magnified. As he put it, "Precisely because poor people (by definition) have little economic capital and face formidable obstacles in acquiring human capital (that is, education), social capital is disproportionately important to their welfare."[45]

Not all mutual aid efforts were rooted in labor exchanges. Rural narrators often related stories of mutual aid that helped minimize the effects of poverty or provided assistance in times of personal crisis such as sickness or death. Ben and Earlien Engelbrecht described the mutual aid networks of their central Texas German community. Ben said, "I don't think it's quite as prevalent like it was in the old days, but in the old days, . . . when somebody got sick, that party line went to work, and we'd go there. My dad sat up with a lot of sick people." LaVerne Farmer, a white Tennessean who lived with her parents and grandparents on a prosperous dairy farm, noted that "If there was serious sickness or deaths or needs of the community, the neighbors would just . . . go, no matter how much work they had to do. And if they needed food during garden season, they'd take surplus food to the neighbors. You know it was just kindly an extended family." Texan Della Folley recalled that during her childhood, rural women helped each other. She explained, "Whenever anyone got sick, well, instead of hiring a nurse . . . the women go over and help them to nurse. . . . [T]hat's the way they did it on the farms; they just helped one another." She recounted that her mother served as a midwife in the community. "[S]he helped—even do the Negroes, she helped bring their babies in the world. She'd go from place to place where they could—if it was close enough to where she could walk or where they could come and get her and take her. But she worked as a midwife. She didn't get any money for it; it was all free gratis." Folley's fellow white Texan Dovie Carroll recalled an incident when he was about ten. His father asked a neighbor about another neighbor. They visited and found the neighbor had been sick for days. According to Carroll, "Papa said, 'Well, I'll take my two planters over there in the morning, go to planting!'" The neighbors had their ailing friend's fields planted in two days. Carroll concluded, "You take back in those days, people helped one another. They don't do it now."[46] Most farm families could not afford to hire nurses to care for sick relatives or laborers to replace a farmer sidelined by illness. Mutual aid networks thus minimized the combined impact of poverty and illness on farm families.

The mutual aid networks developed and maintained in rural southern communities during the early twentieth century provided economically struggling farmers with important social and material resources and tied more prosperous farmers to others in the community. Yet idealized memories about mutual aid networks functioned to minimize economic, status, and racial differences that structured the interactions among neighbors and friends. Gaps between rich and poor were real realities in the early-twentieth-century southern countryside. Stories about mutual aid efforts bridged such material gaps and presented all country people as virtuous folks committed to the good of the larger community. Farm narrators identified a strong commitment to rural mutual aid networks as an essential component of country life and yet another marker that distinguished them from town folks. In fact, many rural people seemed to believe, erroneously, that people in towns lacked a commitment to mutual aid.

Love for the Land

Like mutual aid, another value that many rural narrators believed distinguished them from urbanites was their attachment to the land. The theme of attachment to the land appeared less often than most other themes. Unlike most other characteristics of the rural community of memory that farm people recounted more or less spontaneously in their interviews, narrators rarely discussed a devotion to the land unless specifically asked about the differences between country people and city people. For example, when a narrator asked white North Carolinian Nancy Holt what made rural people different from people in town, Holt explained that people in town did not have "a real tie with the land and a real tie with what we considered the . . . way to live." The "way to live" seemed inextricably bound to the country's person's devotion to the land, in Holt's view. Other narrators emphasized the fact that farming strengthened one's ties to the natural world. Holt's fellow North Carolinian, white farmer Edna Harris, expressed a similar view. Farming, she said, "just puts you next to nature, I guess. And as some of 'em said, I'm just cut out to be a farmer. [Chuckle]"[47]

While some narrators focused on the land as symbolic of nature and others formed attachments to the land because they loved the act of farming, still others associated a love of the land with a sense of a particular place and a particular history. Arthur George, the son of African American landowners from South Carolina, described his family's attachment to the land in more specific terms. George's parents farmed near Bishopville, South Carolina. When her husband died in 1945, George's mother, Leler George, was pregnant with her ninth child, but she insisted on continuing to farm. She struggled to pay off a mortgage, and then she mechanized so that her children could attend school instead of staying home to work the land. She sent all nine of the children to college even as she managed to accumulate 174 acres. None of the children farmed, but they often visited their mother in Bishopville and did chores on the family land. Arthur George tried to explain the family's feelings about the farm to an interviewer: "One of the things that's really sort of background on the whole thing is where we got our beginning and what forethought was put into not only just farming, but *this* farm [emphasis his]." In other words, the family was attached to this particular farm—this particular piece of land—because of all the work their parents, particularly their mother, had put into holding on to it. Arthur's attachment to the land was complex, however, and he had clearly internalized much of the rhetoric of agrarian ideology. He said, "The other strong thing is the love and the independence, love for the land and for the farm and for the independence that it gives Mother, even though we have our own vocations." Arthur George had become a Virginia insurance executive as an adult, working on the farm only intermittently. Yet the land remained important to him, and it tied him to his family. He also saw life on the land as the source of his values. The interviewer asked George what the land symbolized to him. He replied, "The land symbolizes two things. Not just land, not just dirt. But the land symbolizes my father's work and toil before his death, and it also represents my mother's since that time. . . . And then it represents our success where we are, because it did come from here. Our work ethics, our beliefs, our teaching, our whole social and psychic being came from the land and from what it represented, because it did give them the independence."[48]

Unlike other elements of rural identity, whether a narrator discussed a love for the land seemed directly linked to socioeconomic class status. The few narrators who articulated an attachment to the land as an element of rural identity generally proved to be landowners. Although men and women, blacks and whites, mentioned closeness to nature and attachment to land, few landless farmers in this study mentioned those factors, and they did so in less detail. A sense of ownership, of permanent connection to the land, shaped landowning narrators' sense of attachment to that land and their sense that such an attachment set them apart from other people.

Relative Economic Equality

One of the most surprising elements in the stories told by many of the farm folk in this study was the theme of relative equality. As many of the narrators told it, "everybody was in the same boat" financially. Yet distinctive class and racial differences emerge when one looks at how rural southerners remember this economic equality. The landless and marginal landowners might proclaim that their rural communities boasted relative economic equality, but at another point in the interview, they often told more complex tales, outlining clear economic differences among families in the neighborhood. African Americans often mentioned economic disparities among blacks, but they were most likely to couch economic differences in racial terms. The people most likely to proclaim that "we were all in the same boat" without contradicting themselves with stories of economic differences elsewhere in the interview were among the most comfortable farmers in their communities. These prosperous narrators usually remained silent about significant gaps between rich and poor.

I have written at some length elsewhere about the complex and dynamic ways that early-twentieth-century rural southerners defined and assigned class status.[49] A brief summary is useful in assessing farm people's memories of relative economic equality. In general, the South's white farm folk believed that they and their neighbors belonged to one of three tiers of a class hierarchy: elite, middling, or poor white. Economics alone did not determine one's position in the hierarchy. Elite families were always landowners, and they were usually, but not always, wealthy. Elites dominated local politics, thus wielding considerable power over their neighbors. Families of moderate means might be considered local elites because of longevity in the community or kinship ties to the community's founding families. Middling farm families might be small landowners or prosperous tenants. They gained respect in the community because they were seen as hardworking folks of good character. Poverty distinguished white families at the bottom of the class ladder. Middling and elite whites often blamed the poverty of the poorest whites—people they dismissed as "poor white trash"—on a lack of industriousness, while poor whites recognized that the privileges enjoyed by powerful elites could also serve to keep them in an inferior economic position.

Black farm folk, too, fit into a class hierarchy, one recognized by people of both races, though defined somewhat differently by whites and blacks. Many blacks on the top tier of the African American economic ladder called themselves "better class blacks."[50] These black families, some landowning and some prosperous tenants, valued hard work and upward mobility. Although they recognized the reality of racism, they deftly negotiated the shifting power relations of the local white community for their own advantage, often cultivating assistance from white elites. Whites saw these "better class blacks" as people who worked hard, stayed out of trouble, and "knew their place." African Americans in this group were among the "good sharecroppers" that landowners like the Carrolls sought to employ. By contrast, African Americans on the lowest rungs of the rural economic ladder, often dismissed by whites as being lazy and untrustworthy, recognized the forces of racism and economic discrimination that denied them opportunities to advance, and they often rejected the notions of respectability and industriousness promulgated by white rural society as well as "better class blacks."[51]

There were marked racial differences in the ways blacks and whites remembered socioeconomic disparities. In spite of these very real class differences in rural communities, over and over white southern farm people minimized or ignored these differences in their oral history narratives, while African American narrators frankly acknowledged them and often recognized that they had much in common with poor whites. In interview after interview, whites—landowning and landless, male and female—asserted that southern farm families "were all in the same boat" in the years before World War II. Tennessean Wilma Williamson, the daughter of a white lumber worker who spent much of her childhood on her grandparents' hardscrabble mountain farm, explained, "You know," she said, "we all grew up together like that [in the mountains]. One person didn't have much more than the other. You didn't feel better than somebody else." Similarly, LaVerne Farmer noted that during her childhood years in the mountains of

Blount County, "I don't recall anybody being much better off than anyone else. They just shared what they had." Yet Farmer came from one of the wealthiest families in the community. Her parents and grandparents ran a successful dairy farm and bottling operation, selling milk to the nearby lumber and Civilian Conservation Corps camps as well as to residents of the nearby town of Maryville.[52] Landless white Louisiana farm wife Billy Lee Jones reported that the 1920s and 1930s, her early married years, were hard times. "Times were hard but everyone was in the same boat. . . . We did not feel poor or underprivileged. Every time a new Shirley Temple pattern would come out I would buy it and make my daughters a dress just like Shirley's." Jones's comments are striking because she links the ability to participate in the same consumer culture enjoyed by more affluent urban dwellers with her feeling that she was not poor. Nonetheless, it was her rural skill of self-sufficiency that enabled her to make a consumer item available for her daughter. Texan Etta Carroll said, "We didn't never think that we were that poor because we had plenty to eat and plenty to wear and your health was pretty good, why, that was the main thing back in those days."[53]

Perhaps white narrators present their communities as places of economic equality because relative wealth and poverty were not the most salient aspects of identity and daily existence. If most farm families were self-sufficient in terms of food, if they ate diets similar to their neighbors, if they worked together in times of crisis, then poverty *may* have been less visible. As white South Carolinian Mary Webb Quinn, the daughter of sharecropping parents, put it, "We were poor people, and we knew that we were. We didn't really know it because everybody was poor. And we had friends and they were in the same boat we were in. If somebody was a little better off, well everybody helped each other."[54] As Quinn suggests, strong mutual aid networks mitigated some of the most debilitating effects of poverty. Certainly in an era in which there were fewer consumer goods, class differences in consumption patterns might have been less visible. Whatever the reason, narrator after narrator said, "we were all in the same boat."

Even in the face of their own contradictory accounts of some families being better off than others, again and again, storytellers characterized all rural families as suffering more or less the same hardships. Ethel Davis and her husband owned a small dairy farm in Loudon

County, Tennessee, a farm they nearly lost when they were unable to pay the mortgage in the 1930s. Davis recounted that they held on to the farm because a neighbor with available cash loaned them enough money to meet their payments. Yet in spite of this explicit admission that at least one neighbor was better off than the Davis family, later in the interview, Ethel said, "We was poor and all of our neighbors were." Farm wife Betty Newman, daughter and wife of small land-owners, noted that "I never realized that we were as poor as we were when I was growing up . . . I always had everything I thought we needed. . . . There wasn't a distinction at the time that I was growing up between poverty level and wealth level and all that like there is now. But I think I have a different value about things than I would have if I was born today."[55]

Occasionally poor and middling white narrators acknowledged that some class differences existed in early-twentieth-century rural communities. For example, Mary Quinn, the South Carolina woman quoted above, may have seen her family as being "in the same boat" as most of their neighbors, but she went on to explain that, "Yet, we knew that there were other ways of making a living, that there was money out there, and that some people had nicer clothes."[56] Bill Lewellyn gave a slightly more accurate and more nuanced account of class differences in his neighborhood than many narrators, but he came back to the theme of relative equality. He lived with his grandparents on a tiny rented farm in Blount County, Tennessee. The large extended family survived on subsistence crops and money his grandmother earned taking in boarders from a nearby textile plant. Lewellyn recalled, "Most everybody was in the same boat. In some cases, some people were better off, such as those who had steady jobs. . . . Some were a little better off than others. . . . But some had had money and lost their money when the banks failed." Lewellyn's account recognized that the Great Depression years brought down even the most prosperous of families, but that some were "better off than others." Nonetheless, the theme of relative equality persisted in his story.[57] White South Carolina farm daughter Pat Gates also admitted that in retrospect, she realized that some people had fared better than others during the 1930s. When asked about the daily wage during the Depression years, Gates recalled an old man who offered to plow for her landowning father all day for ten cents. "We were as poor as church mouse [*sic*] ourselves, but we evidently had more than some in that Depression era."[58]

Poor or not, white narrators often presented class differences in ambiguous and misleading terms, but occasionally an interviewer teased out the contradictions in stories about class. Recalling life on a Texas cotton farm in the 1920s and 1930s, Myrtle Dodd noted, "It's a hard life. I can tell you now. But we didn't know it was hard then. Wasn't any harder than anybody else's." During her childhood, Dodd's father rented a series of dry farms in west Texas, unable to afford to buy land until around the time Myrtle married. Later in the interview, however, historian Rebecca Sharpless probed more deeply at Dodd's picture of relative economic equality, asking, "There are always people who have more and people who have less in any given community. Where would you say your family fit into that?" Dodd replied: "I would call it middle class." At that point, Sharpless asked, "How did the people who had more than you all had live?" Dodd replied, "Well, I'm not really too sure, but they owned the land. But you know, those owners of land then had to, of course, pay taxes and keep up with their things. They may have been the first ones to get a car. I don't know. But it seems to me like we were just about first in the neighborhood to get a car, and that was in 1912 when we had our first car." The interviewer persisted in exploring the theme of class differences by asking, "How did the people who were poorer than your family live?" Dodd answered, "Oh, any way they could. Most of them worked, labor, you know, for farmers about. . . . After they began to have a little store and a bank . . . and a doctor's office in Hewitt. . . . Some of them worked there." Then she referred again to a more prosperous landowner: "And now, Mr. Chapman, of course, had several farms, but he worked because he went from one farm to the other to see about it." She went on to discuss Mr. Chapman's children attending college. "And lots of the—what we called renters and middle-class kids didn't get to go to college, but we was lucky enough, and my father was energetic enough and prosperous enough that we all got to go some. Boys, too." Significantly, she linked her family's relative prosperity to her father's work ethic: they were prosperous because he was "energetic enough." Dodd implies that less prosperous families might have been less prosperous because they were less energetic. Again, Sharpless probed more deeply, "How did the sharecroppers, let's call them, and the laborers live compared to the way your family lived?" Dodd responded:

> Well, I really just can't tell you except—I don't know too much about any of them except the blacks, and I know it was from hand to mouth with them. . . . They begged. Just horrible. In the wintertime, the blacks there in the parts of Hewitt would go out and pick up sticks and decayed trees and things for wood . . . Ada was a good old black woman. . . . And she had dozens—had a whole lot of children, and I can remember us laughing yet about [this incident]—we were getting ready to go to school and she had brought one of her sons to draw the water out of the well to wash and he was leaning way over the well looking in and she says, 'You gets away from that well! You might fall in and you knows I ain't got no money to bury you with!' . . . They were just really poor. Good people, too, some of them. . . . [T]here were some poor whites, I'm sure, that I didn't know too much about. I thought we were just about as poor as there was around there, but I don't know if that's true or not.

Sharpless asked, "Did you think you were poor when you were little?" Dodd replied, "Well, I guess I did because I didn't have things that I'd hear about. You know, I read the paper, and read books. . . . Of course, we all had the idea of going to town and having better things, and that's what most of us did [when we were grown]."[59]

Several components of this exchange reveal that the relative economic equality Dodd claimed to have existed early in the interview was actually more complex. Until the interviewer's probing questions forced Dodd to elaborate on the economic conditions of her childhood community, she presented a one-dimensional picture of the rural class structure: her childhood had been no poorer or richer than anyone else's. Although Dodd first maintained that her family's life was no "harder than anyone else's," she later admitted that socioeconomic differences existed in her rural community and that she had been aware of those differences during her childhood. Some families were better off. Nonetheless, she pointed out that well-off families also had additional financial responsibilities, such as property taxes.

She asserted that the landowning Mr. Chapman "worked because he went from one farm to the other." Reading between the lines, one senses that Dodd was ambivalent about Mr. Chapman. Perhaps her general impression was that prosperous people did not usually work since she hastened to clarify that Mr. Chapman *did* work. Or perhaps she wanted to emphasize that Mr. Chapman was like her father, a hard worker, thus raising her father's status by comparing him to someone better off. She said she had little contact with poor whites, but she knew that many poor blacks struggled to survive even though they were also "good people" like Dodd's own family. Dodd's belief in her family's relative prosperity was central to her image of her family as hard-working, virtuous country folk who earned their way in the world, so until pressed, she clung to that notion and extended it to the other families in the neighborhood.

Like Dodd, some white narrators acknowledged socioeconomic disparities when pressed. Texan Carl Neal was the middle son of a blacksmith and sharecropper. He remembered his family's farm as "just an old hardscrabble farm over on the middle branch of the Bosque [River]." While the family continued to run the farm, in 1929, Neal's father took a job at a nearby cement plant "so we actually had it a lot better than a lot of people did because he was a hardworking man, and he managed to make . . . money continuously. Not a big amount, but to provide for the family." Neal's father's wage work supplemented the farm's income, enabling the family to have "it a lot better than a lot of people." Like Myrtle Dodd, Neal links this prosperity to his father's work ethic: "he was a hardworking man," and his prosperity was the well-earned fruit of his hard work. When an interviewer asked Neal about poor families in his community, he explained that he did not know any black sharecroppers in his community but knew of a couple of landowning black families. He said, "Even with the hardships we might have had, the [landless] blacks did have it much worse because about the only income they had was day labor—not all of them, but I'm talking about the majority of them was picking up a day's labor when they could. At harvest time on the farms, yes, there was work, but when harvest was over then it was cutting cord wood or whatever they could find to do to exist." He added that most of the racial tension in the community grew out of economic competition. For example, blacks and whites both gathered dewberries from roadsides and woods to supplement the family diet. As he put it, "That's mostly the antagonism I remember was in competition. There wasn't any hate. The race—the color of your skin didn't make any difference, they were getting all the dewberries."[60] Neal's assertion that racial animosity was nonexistent was probably wishful thinking, but his insight that much racial conflict grew out of competition for limited economic resources was important.

Blacks, too, saw economic competition as a source of racial conflict. African American narrators often acknowledged class differences between whites and blacks, and they were more likely than white narrators to articulate some sense of kinship with poor whites. According to this narrative line, large white landowners controlled the labor of sharecroppers and thus oppressed poor blacks and whites alike. When an interviewer asked black Alabaman Rosa Tensley if her landowning family was well off compared to the neighbors, she replied, "Well they [the neighbors] was living like we was. They was doing the same thing we was doing. And plenty of them, just like they is now, ain't have nothing; just work on halves. . . . They just worked the land and the white folks got half of everything." After she married a sharecropper in the 1920s, Tensley remembered knowing white sharecroppers who also struggled financially. She recalled that poor whites "all of them that didn't have nothing, they worked on halves." She explained that poor whites had little more than black sharecroppers because white landowners "just wanted everything they could get—and you, nothing."[61] Black Arkansan Cleaster Mitchell described several white families in her community that:

> were in the same shape we was—extremely poor. At that time, if you was extremely poor, regardless to what color you was, if you was really, really poor, then you was treated like you was poor. So they [the poor white families] had to live in a little shotgun house like we did, and my mother fed them. See, they could come to our house and eat. And his little wife [the poor white man's wife], she really wasn't nothing but a kid, you know, but she had two children, and my mother worried because she said she didn't know how to take care of the children. So my mother would take her and show her how to care for her kids and sew for them and take [them]

things. . . . Maybe the little children wouldn't have survived if my mother didn't help her. . . . But the catch was, if they pull up a little bit [the whites got in a better financial position]—they have to get out from down there. They can't stay, because then they won't be recognized, you see. . . . See, to get recognition—I worked for one that was poorer than I was, but to get some recognition, some status among the white people, then he got somebody to work for her. But she didn't have any more than what I had.

In other words, the white man marked his improved economic condition by hiring Mitchell as a domestic servant for his wife. When asked if working for the poor white family was different than working for richer whites, she said, "I had more fun working for the one that was as poor as I was than the one that was rich . . . because the one that was poor was more down to earth. We had something we could talk about, . . . and she knew what hard work was. You worked, but she didn't worry about you killing yourself." Mitchell went on to say that this was not the case with many richer whites who worked their domestics relentlessly.[62]

Not only did black narrators remember that they had a great deal in common with poor whites, but unlike white narrators, they also were quick to acknowledge class differences among their own race. For example, black Texan Vera Malone recalled a neighboring black family named Tolbert who had two daughters. The family was better off than Malone's parents who owned land but nonetheless struggled because Malone's father was an alcoholic. Vera enjoyed playing with the daughters of the prosperous family, apparently because they had more interesting playthings. She said, "They had a surrey. Oh, and we just admired it, all of us. It was so lovely. . . . They were very good farmers. . . . Very prosperous farmers, and so, that was a highlight in our lives, to be with those girls sometimes."[63] Similarly her fellow Texan Lonnie Graves, son of a landowner, recounted that:

there were a group of black people in this community, and as I'm sure in other communities as well, who had a lot of pride, who worked hard, who earned their living, who made their land pay off. And they could spend their money for what they wanted. . . . They bought new cars, just like the white people did. . . . Sent the kids off to finish school in Marlin and Waco or Austin or wherever they could send them to stay with relatives and finish high school and go on to college. And they did this in spite of, you know, the hard things, the disadvantages that they had to live with. . . . Some of these people made great people out of themselves and out of the community.

Graves's language—"a group of black people," "some of these people"—suggests that not all black people worked so hard to make "great people out of themselves." At another point in the interview, Graves was more explicit about class differences among African Americans in his community:

There were many sharecroppers. . . . But they were not all sharecroppers. . . . These people [black landowners] had a kind of social level of their own—not that they looked down upon the sharecroppers, but they were just—they were better off. They were able to afford—you know, to buy better clothes. . . . Now, some of the sharecroppers did real well. . . . And a lot of these people worked hard, and they worked well, and they lived well. They bought wagons, too. And some of them bought . . . surreys at the times, which was sort of a—in today's language, it would be a Cadillac.[64]

A certain level of prosperity and respectability not only eased the material conditions of life for rural blacks, but it also made for smoother interactions with white people. Alabaman Kenneth Young explained that both sets of his grandparents were landowners, "which was unusual for blacks in those days." He went on, "Back in those days and even now, not much respect was given to black folks who didn't own their homes and very few did. Most of them were tenants on white folks' places. . . . If you were what you considered a prosperous black person, owned your home and owned your land, the whites respected you, liked you better than they did that black man who had nothing."[65]

White narrators' reticence about class differences and their insistence that neighbors were "all in the same boat," even as they described clear economic disparities, undoubtedly has several sources. In part, such notions can be traced to Jeffersonian agrarian ideology that suggests that all independent yeomen farmers are free and equal participants in the nation's political life. In a few cases, such erasures can also grow out of childhood nostalgia or the child's lack of awareness of class differences. Some narrators' accounts were childhood memories, and they may have tended, like most of us, to wax sentimental about childhood years. Certainly LaVerne Farmer's privileged position may have made the poverty of others less visible to her. On the other hand, Myrtle Dodd and Bill Lewellyn were acutely aware of their relative poverty. Earlier in his interview, Lewellyn described his embarrassment at being sent to pick up the family's allotment of federal food commodities. His was not the account of a man nostalgic for an idyllic childhood. Neither would childhood nostalgia explain Ethel Davis's, Rosa Tensley's, or Wilma Williamson's references to the relative equality of rural people; all three were adults struggling to establish independent households during the period they recall. In many cases, white narrators may have insisted on their own families' relative prosperity as a way of marking racial difference. Myrtle Dodd seems to use her story this way: black people suffered poverty while Dodd and her fellow white families did not suffer.

Such stories are also shaped by the context in which they are told. Any kind of fieldwork, including oral history interviewing, is historically conditioned. A narrator may tell the story in a dramatically different way at another time. If these white narrators had been interviewed in the 1940s and 1950s, when the divergent realities shaped by material differences had been acute, often painful, and more salient in shaping the conditions of daily life, they might have been more likely to recount stories about class differences instead of insisting that "we were all in the same boat." Instead, these farm people were interviewed in the 1970s, 1980s, and 1990s. By this point, nearly all enjoyed a much higher standard of living than they had early in the century. In addition, by the end of the century, rural narrators were conscious that they were members of a rapidly vanishing group. Their sense of having shared experiences on the land served to bridge—at least in memory—many of the gaps created by race and class.[66]

Moreover, the myth of relative economic equality served an

important psychological purpose among many rural white narrators. Mississippi-born Will D. Campbell grew up to head the Farm Security Administration and later became a prominent white civil rights activist. Campbell grew up on an eighty-acre farm in Amite County, Mississippi. He told an interviewer that "My father always taught us 'we were of the middle class.' Well, now if a family [today] were living on the financial scale that we were living under then, they wouldn't be middle class at all, they would be lower low class. But we were taught that 'you are of the middle class'; that instilled a sort of pride in you and yet it told you there are people above you and there are people below you, but you are all right, you know. You don't have anything to be embarrassed about."[67] As Will Campbell suggests, seeing oneself as part of the "middle class" and as sharing the economic struggles of one's neighbors rendered the memories of poverty less painful. Since "everybody was in the same boat," poverty was not a result of laziness or personal failings. This narrative strategy reinforced narrators' sense of personal identity and of belonging to a rural community of memory.

Narrators themselves understood that they had not fully recognized their own poverty until many years later. Will Campbell expressed it this way: "When you didn't know what affluence was, there was nothing to be sorry that you didn't have. Of course, a lot of the gadgets and machines, and so on, that exist today simply didn't exist then, so there was no way you could think you were culturally deprived because you didn't have a television, because there was no such thing." He added, "Life was generally hard work, which nobody complained about because that was what life was, you know. I never recall words like 'happy' or 'boredom,' ever being a part of our vocabulary. That wasn't part of the commitment."[68] Hard times were simply a fact of life to be endured by one and all. And hard as times were, rural folk believed they were better off than city folk who were dependent on wages.

The Differences between Town and Country

Implicit in many of the things narrators say about rural life is the idea that country life was far superior to life in town. Occasionally narrators made explicit statements about this belief, sometimes spontaneously and sometimes in response to an interviewer's specific questions. Narrators cited privacy and freedom to live without neighbors looking over their shoulders as important elements of their preference for country life. When asked why he returned to the family farm in Burton after thirty-five years in Houston, black Texan Grover Williams Sr. replied: "Well, see, I still have this little piece of property here, and things were getting so hectic in town, you know, you get out where you can spread your wings and just have a little solitude every once in a while. And I like the country, and I like farming if I have the proper equipment and stuff." Landless white Alabaman J. C. Chapman told an interviewer, "I'm a country person. . . . I wouldn't have been living in town if it hadn't been for my work. [I like] anything that's country. Of course, these country towns here aren't like these other towns outside the South. You don't even know who's next door to you. . . . Well, [here] you have good neighbors, you can holler as loud as you want to, and do sort of like you want to. You don't have to think about the man next door a-raising Cain because you done it."[69] White Texan Etta Carroll said, "Back then you had more freedom in the country. You could get up and do what you wanted to do. And when you're in town, you do what the other person wants you to do. . . . I'd just as soon live in the country."[70]

North Carolinian Mary Harrington spent her childhood on a farm in Virginia and her adulthood working in mills and living in Burlington. When asked where she preferred to live, she said, "I'd rather live in the country. I've spent most of my life here [in the town of Burlington], but I like country life. I am so glad that I experienced both, because I think it's real good. But I really prefer the country life." Nonetheless, Harrington noted that country life was changing at the end of the twentieth century. She said, "People used to visit more in the country than in the city, but there's no difference there now. Their lifestyle is getting to be like people in the city. I just like the wide open spaces a little bit more. There's not too many wide open spaces even in the country now, but I think it's the greatest life there is. I can remember people would say 'that old farmer.' It's been quite a few years now that people have recognized that the farmer is the backbone of the nation." Later in the interview, she added, "I prefer the country. A place like this is not big enough. When you go out, you're almost in somebody else's yard. I like privacy. I like to get out without coming face to face with somebody every time you step out one way or the other."[71]

At least one African American narrator expressed the belief that race relations were better in the countryside. Black Alabaman Flossie Ward told an interviewer: "Here out in the country, people has always been nice to us. But back in town, you know, . . . they didn't want to live beside the blacks. . . . And our children, you know, growing up. . . . *All* [emphasis hers] the children played together . . . out here in the country." Her husband explained that this difference was because blacks lived and worked on whites' farms and had close personal relationships with white people, a marked contrast to race relations in the cities.[72]

Rural Identity and Personal Character

The life stories of rural southerners suggest that farm folk built their community of memory with stories about shared experiences on the land that they believed made them both different from and in some senses better off than city people. Their oral narratives convey a belief that rural life molded people of superior character. Their rural experiences provided them with strength to survive a rapidly changing world, strength that not everyone acquired. As white South Carolinian Virginia Harris put it, "We thank God for our life on the farm. We learned to cope with situations when we were young—circumstances help to make you stronger. We thank God for living on the farm."[73]

As Harris suggests, some narrators saw their rural experiences as gifts from God. Others talked about their faith as an important element of character and a source of hope that sustained them on the land. For example, North Carolinian Edna Harris explained that to be a good farmer, "You've got to have faith, you've got to have hope, and you've got to have perseverance. You've got to have faith things is gonna work out and you've got to have hope for tomorrow and looking forward to the future." Yet rural southerners were largely silent about religion. Though narrators often mentioned church activities, they rarely discussed the nature of their religious beliefs. Even those who mentioned the importance of faith, always spontaneously, were silent about the shape of the religious beliefs that undergirded that faith. Nonetheless, a handful of narrators like Harris described faith as important to their ability to persevere through hard times. White North Carolina farmer Norbert King Andrews told an interviewer that he was raised on a farm in Orange County, North Carolina. He had nine siblings, and his father had "a rocky farm to raise them on, but he did it. He had a lot of faith. . . . A lot of hard work and a lot of faith."[74]

Frequently, narrators linked their religious faith to the experience of living on the land. According to this view, a farmer's utter dependence on forces beyond his or her own control, forces, such as weather, that lay in the hands of a higher power, taught the farmer to believe in God. Virginia Harris, the South Carolinian mentioned above, explained, "I think a farmer has to have faith in God. You can't put your money in something if you don't have faith that it's going to grow. And I think when people go into farming, . . . they have to have faith that God's going to give 'em rain and he's going to multiply, give 'em a good crop." Fellow South Carolinian Kate Graham agreed. An interviewer asked Graham if she thought anything had been lost with so many farmers being forced from the land. She replied, "We've lost probably the last honest man in the country. We've lost our faith. I think a lot of that comes with the times, but I really do think that a farmer in particular, . . . has to depend totally on faith. We have lost worship of God because farming is totally dependent on God. Really everything is, but you're aware of it every day, every day, every morning when you get up [if you farm]."[75]

According to narrators, strong religious faith was only one element of the superior personal character forged by rural life. Texan Thomas Patterson said of his childhood on the farm, "I've always felt that I developed a set of values because of what I experienced on the farm. I learned to build things, to entertain myself because I didn't have any money with which to buy toys. I learned the value of money, and I learned the value of hard work because we worked from daylight in the morning to sundown at night. I think I also built up some physical resources that have helped immensely in these years when there have been so many responsibilities that I've had to assume." Patterson grew up to be a Baptist minister and one of the most powerful figures in Texas Baptist life.[76]

Bill Lewellyn seemed to best articulate this interpretation that

early-twentieth-century farm life molded people of superior character. He recounted the physical hardships of rural life without electricity and indoor plumbing, without money and without a safety net,
and he concluded that this life created stronger people who were better able to weather hardships than people today. He said:

> I guess we were a whole lot better prepared to endure the
> hardships that came about during the Depression because we
> didn't know any better. . . . It was just a way of life for us, so
> we didn't have to have a lot of things. But . . . young people
> nowadays, they'd have an awful hard time coping with situa-
> tions that we found ourselves in . . . back then. . . . You take
> this generation now, if suddenly they lose all that you know
> and find themselves back like we were during the Depression,
> and, oh, there'd be a lot of nervous breakdowns. And people
> would just give up, I guess, 'cause they wouldn't know what
> to do, you know. But in our case, why we were used to mak-
> ing do with what we had. Therefore . . . it wasn't all that
> much of a hardship for us.[77]

To Lewellyn, hard work and hard times molded strong people who
were capable of enduring and outlasting economic dislocation. Even
as the narrators described people who had not been able to cope with
hard times, who in Lewellyn's words had "nervous breakdowns,"
they insisted that people of their day were better equipped to handle
adversity.

Rural southerners believed that particular elements of their lives
made them different from those who did not live on the land, and
their sense of shared identity remained remarkably consistent across
generational and geographic lines. They believed that the type of
work they did and the way they approached that work made them
unique. They linked productivity with virtue and cooperation. A
commitment to self-sufficiency, mutual aid, and a strong work ethic
were central characteristics of their community of memory. They
linked the virtue of work with the virtue of strong family and community ties. Though class differences existed, something black narrators freely acknowledged, white narrators often minimized those
differences in their narratives, building a collective identity on the

insistence that "we were all in the same boat." Rural people clung to the notion that they were somehow different from urbanites and that they shared a great deal with fellow farm folks even as their world underwent profound change throughout the twentieth century. The community of memory forged on the land helped them negotiate drastic transformations.

Chapter Three

Memory and the Nature
of Transformation

During the twentieth century, waves of change buffeted agriculture. Rural southerners fill their narratives of rural transformation with details about dramatic alterations in the way daily farmwork was done, descriptions of an evolving agricultural economy, and information about a changing countryside. Rural southerners may have shared a community of memory, but their accounts of transformation varied widely by gender, race, class, and especially generation. The accounts of farmers who came of age before World War II (those born before 1920, about one-third of the sample used in this study) and those who entered adulthood during or after the war are profoundly different. The prewar generation told simple stories of change. They described bad economic conditions and technology as the major forces transforming southern agriculture and driving farmers from the land. Even those prewar narrators who farmed until the last quarter of the century remain largely silent about other forces transforming agriculture: integration of the United States into an increasingly competitive global farm commodities market, structural changes in domestic production, and shifting federal agricultural policies. By contrast, narrators who came of age in the wartime and postwar years comment extensively about a wide variety of forces that reshaped agriculture. Their accounts of change are layered, complex, and nuanced.

The Prewar Generation's Accounts of Transformation

The prewar generation's memories of rural transformation are largely one-dimensional and contain many silences. Even those who farmed into the 1970s and 1980s had little to say about the changes in agriculture over the course of the twentieth century. For example, white Tennessee landowner John West began farming in 1932 and continued working the land until he retired and sold his equipment in the 1980s (see chapter 1). He witnessed and participated in major changes, but he did not comment on structural or economic changes in agriculture.[1] His silences were striking because I told him at the outset of our interview that I was studying the changes in farming during the Great Depression and World War II. West, however, had his own ideas about the story he wanted to tell. Details of the transformation of his own farming practice emerged in the course of his description of life on the land, but he did not offer any analytical framework to explain what changed or why.

John West's silences may be striking, but they are not unique. Those few prewar narrators who did describe changes in southern agriculture emphasized technology as the major force transforming the nature of farmwork. Sometimes interviewers asked specifically about changes in the southern countryside, but usually stories about the way technology transformed rural life emerged without prompting. Technology altered day-to-day living more than any other force because it changed the way people worked. Since work formed a central component of rural identity and life, the shift from horsepower to engine power proved significant. Tractors and tractor-drawn equipment enabled a single farmer to complete far more work during a given growing season. Not only did mechanization increase productivity, but it also lightened the physical workload, a benefit embraced by the prewar generation. Black Texan Deola Adams pointed this out in describing the farm where she grew up. Adams's father raised livestock, corn, hay, a garden, and three or four bales of cotton a year on land owned by her grandmother. Adams recalled the hard manual labor their farm required. She said, "We had to work when we was on the farm. Well, now, it's a different day. It's easy. People don't use plows and hoes and things like that. Daddy just used a plow and used horses."[2] Adams's remarks point to the way mechanization altered rural people's understandings of farmwork. Before mechanization, she says, "We had to *work* [author's emphasis]." The implication is that after mechanization, farm people did not work so hard—that "it's easy." Some of her admiration for the hard work of farm people may have been undermined by the advent of tractors and mechanical cotton pickers, but she was clear that mechanization changed farming forever. Over and over, prewar narrators echoed her story.

Farmers who became adults before World War II rarely mentioned other forces that transformed agriculture. Most striking is their virtual silence about the federal government's increasingly active role in reshaping agriculture. Only rarely did the prewar generation mention federal intervention in agriculture as a force in rural transformation, even though many had participated in production reduction programs and other federal efforts both before and after the war. Occasionally narrators mentioned agricultural extension work, but they usually did so in passing, barely pausing to note the Agricultural Extension Service's efforts to promote new types of agriculture. One rare exception was Alabaman A. L. Head, a sharecropper born in 1884. He told an interviewer that by the late years of the Depression, "The type of farming changed. Auburn [University Extension Service] was sending out new methods of farming. Farmers, as a rule, were slow to take it on." Though initially dubious about the "book farming" methods promoted by extension agents, many farmers observed the success of new methods promoted by government officials and adopted them. Head said, "[I]f some man got an Auburn man out and planted his crop . . . , and he cleared a better profit the neighbors would go to patterning after him. He'd watch what the farmer did and then they began to increase the fertilizer per acre. For a period . . . the Auburn plans of farming were ridiculed by people who said they were farming out of a book. But as a farmer would begin to experiment with that and increase his production per acre, his neighbors would follow."[3] In Head's memory, the extension agent brought information about new and improved farming methods to rural communities, and thus was an agent of change.

Another rare prewar farmer who mentioned the federal government as a transforming force was less positive about the results. Ruth Irwin of Mississippi was born in 1905 to a prosperous white plantation owner and married a successful farmer. In 1982, she lamented, "We don't have little farmers anymore. That is, you've got to have commercial farmers now 'cause no more in Warren County can people farm unless they do it commercially. You can't sell your sausage if you make it at home. You can't sell your hogs except through cooperation with others. You can't sell your beef. Everything's different; the program's different, and you've got to have cooperative [government] inspection for everything you do. And that has done away with the little farmer."[4] Irwin's account is notable precisely because it was so unusual among members of her generation. In her view, expansion, commercialization, and excessive federal regulation were factors that made farming prohibitively expensive for most people.

Perhaps it is tempting to attribute narrators' silence about the variety of forces transforming agriculture to ignorance on the part of the narrators—to assume that they did not understand how global commodities markets and federal programs operated or the ways such programs reshaped southern agriculture at the expense of the landless and small landowners. This would be a false perception. There is ample evidence that rural southerners farming in the 1930s understood the impact of federal programs in this earlier period. For example, southerners' reactions to the Agricultural Adjustment Act show that farm people usually grasped both the intended and the unintended consequences of New Deal programs almost as soon as federal guidelines were issued. Acreage reduction programs of the Agricultural Adjustment Administration (AAA) generated consternation among southern farmers who struggled to negotiate the complexities of the program's rules and to keep their heads above the rising waters of financial insolvency; they did not hesitate to protest the programs. Letters poured into local and national AAA offices and to editors of the farm press praising the intent of the programs even as the authors complained about what they saw as the unfair structure of the programs. Landowners and tenants alike expressed dissatisfaction.

For example, on August 28, 1933, farm renter J. D. Hamrick of Mooresboro, North Carolina, penned a letter to Secretary of Agriculture Henry A. Wallace:

Dear Sir:

The recent statement, in the papers, that you would require a further <u>cut</u> in the <u>cotton acreage</u>, promotes me to write, to you.

I am a renter, and pay, for the farm I cultivate, eighteen hundred and fifty (1850) pounds lint cotton per year.

Last year, when I borrowed from the government, I was

required to cut my acreage 35%. This cut my acreage to 19 acres. This year, I was again required to cut 25%, which reduces my acreage, to 14 acres. Then came the plough up campaign, and I plowed up 5 acres, which leaves me 9 acres.

I will have to get over 200 pounds of cotton, to the acre, to pay the rent. This will not benefit me any, even though cotton were 40 cts. per pound, as I will not have any to sell.

Now unless, there is some change, in the renting system, I cannot stand, any more acreage cut.

I appreciate the effort you are making, to help the Farmer, and I will cooperate with you, as long as I can.

I hope you will investigate conditions such as I have described, and will consider them, in making your plans for further reductions, in the acreage next year.

Yours truly,
J. D. Hamrick[5]

Hamrick's was a sophisticated understanding of a complicated issue. He saw federal programs as posing a threat to the survival of small farmers. His letter stands in sharp contrast to the silences about the impact of federal programs found in oral history narratives of his peers who were interviewed years later.[6]

Landowners as well as renters like Hamrick protested the unintended consequences of AAA policies. In 1940, Mrs. H. M C. of Johnston County, North Carolina, wrote the editor of *Progressive Farmer* about the problems created by acreage reduction. "The landowning farmer now has his crop cut so much he can hardly support his own family, much less one or more tenant families. . . . We have one son born and raised on the farm. He is never happier than when plowing a clean, straight furrow and his highest ambition is to be a farmer. Shall I encourage him to stick it out or shall I get him out of it while there is time and send him on to a rotten, crowded city to make a living?"[7]

Southern farmers' New Deal–era commentary indicated that they clearly understood the ways that federal programs were reshaping agriculture. In the early 1940s, Farm Security Administration researcher Arthur F. Raper undertook an intensive study of tenant farmers in Georgia's Black Belt counties. In his landmark book, *Tenants of the*

Almighty, Raper noted that farm people had begun to see the New Deal as a major turning point in rural life. He said, "The people speak of being 'on the government' and 'off the government.' They speak of 'government farms,' 'government chickens,' 'government men.' They say: 'We belong to the government'; 'The government never turns us down.' The phrase 'before the government came' is as definite a way of speaking about times as 'back in slavery times,' and 'before the boll weevil.' People feel they are in a new era. And some do not like it." Raper observed that yeomen farmers, the struggling landowners who worked small amounts of land with family labor, benefited least from New Deal agricultural programs. As a result they were among the harshest critics of such federal intervention. Raper quoted one yeoman farmer as saying, "The gov'ment has helped farmers who were getting along fine in the first place. Just helped them go a little higher. And it's helping farmers who never have had anything anyhow; but it's helped folks like us precious little."[8]

Postwar Transformation: "Farming is Big Business"

In the years during and after World War II, the entire agricultural establishment—the USDA, agribusiness leaders, bankers, and the farm press—sent American farmers a message that one narrator summed up as "get big or get out."[9] In other words, American agricultural leaders told farmers that if they adopted the methods of scientific industrial agriculture, including mechanization, specialization, economies of scale, and efficiency, they would be assured of farming success. The postwar revolution in agricultural productivity, fueled by advances in plant and animal crossbreeding and agrochemicals as well as improved farm equipment, seemed to promise healthy profits for landowning farmers and prosperous renters who thought and behaved like businessmen, strategically specializing and expanding their operations to take advantage of new markets. Farm people's responses to the messages of the agricultural establishment—as recounted in their oral history narratives—lay along a continuum. Many marginal landowners and the landless left the land during and after the war for better-paying jobs off the farm. Some who remained on the land rejected advice to "get big or get out," persisting with traditional farming practices. Others adopted advice from agricultural experts selectively and carefully. Thousands, however, followed the advice wholeheartedly, believing that they were at the forefront of a new era when American agriculture could benefit from adopting the business practices that had made American industry great—an era in which farmers would join the burgeoning American middle class.

Farmers who selectively adopted the advice of agricultural experts even as they continued traditional farming practices, or those who left the land entirely after the war were often the narrators who most clearly articulated the advice of the agricultural establishment. Perhaps they were the most forthcoming with their criticisms of scientific-industrial agriculture because they felt vindicated that such farming practices had not paid off as promised for other farmers. South Carolina farmer Lurline Stokes Murray ran a modern farming operation, using federal agricultural programs and adapting her farm's crop mix to shifting market demands. Yet she also avoided debt and maintained traditional subsistence practices. She told interviewer Lu Ann Jones that in the 1960s, agricultural advisors had promoted bigness in farming, a practice they were not advocating as strongly by the time she was interviewed in the 1980s. She said,

> [My son] Julian's ag teacher came and we talked. He said, "Mrs. Murray, I'll tell you. There's only one thing to do. You're going to have to get bigger." I said, "We are?" He said, "Yeah, you'll never make it." I said, "Well, I'll guarantee you, we will never put a mortgage on this piece of property as long as I live, unless it's a case of life or death. . . . This home tract will not be mortgaged unless it's life or death." And that's why so many people have lost the old homeplaces and everything they got. Somebody brainwashed them into thinking, "You've got to get big; you've got to get big." When you get too big that you can't tend to your own business, you better get out today. The quicker you get out, the better you will be.[10]

For Murray, holding on to her land was a higher priority than large profits. Unmortgaged land offered her independence and security, and she believed she made an adequate living by adopting some modern practices while still maintaining traditional values of thrift and self-sufficiency.

Like Murray, North Carolina apple farmer John Little valued his independence, and thus resisted the temptation to expand his orchard too quickly. He selectively adopted the advice of agricultural experts. He told an interviewer that in the 1950s, he had often attended Extension Service workshops for apple growers where "They used to tell us . . . to get big or get out. I never will forget that. . . . I've set [*sic*] there and listened to them doctors from state college talk and they'd say, 'Get big or get out.' I thought to myself, 'Now, I don't have too many trees and as long as I can do that work by myself I don't have to pay nobody, just the chemicals and a little work. I could do it myself, no expense much, I could make a little.' So I've done that for years. Kept planting more trees and more trees and the first thing I knowed I had too many trees for one man." As long as he could do all the work himself, Little believed he could reduce his overhead enough to earn a profit. Unfortunately, however, when fruit prices stagnated, Little began to expand his operation. Contrary to extension service wisdom, expansion did not equal prosperity. Unable to make an adequate living on the farm, Little took an off-farm job in the mid-1960s, continuing to grow apples part time.[11]

Other narrators who came of age after World War II agreed that this "get big or get out" mentality was a source of difficulty for small farmers. Black Mississippian David C. Matthews grew up in Woodburn, Mississippi, where his family sharecropped. After serving in World War II, he left the land, attending college on the GI Bill. In explaining the changes in the rural community of his childhood, he told an interviewer, "Farming is like these major businesses and corporations; the larger ones are really driving the smaller ones out of business. . . . Huge machinery, chemicals and handling that farm with these machines and combines and things that cost a hundred thousand dollars and equipment to go with it, . . . a small amount of land can't support that kind of operation. You have to have a large quantity of land to support that kind of operation."[12] As he suggests, the enormous capital investment required for increasingly sophisticated farm equipment forced farmers to adopt economies of scale. To maximize an investment in a tractor or combine, a farmer needed to cultivate large amounts of land. As a result, he might increase his indebtedness to purchase additional land so that he could make the fullest use of the equipment he had already gone into debt to purchase. Such farmers usually purchased this land from neighbors whose landhold-ings were too small to allow for profitable farming. Eldred Quinn, the son of a white South Carolina sharecropper who himself farmed briefly before attending college on the GI Bill and joining an agri-cultural equipment manufacturer, explained, "The number of farms decreased and the size of them increased. . . . [T]his one man with that little Ford tractor could plow and cultivate 100 acres, where it would take five men and five mules, 20 acres per mule, per man. So the number of farms decreased and the average size increased." Quinn continued, "But the tenant, sharecropping method of farmers doing those kind of chores and raising their families like they had in the past, . . . that left the countryside. And it's still on that same trend: farms are getting larger and larger, and less people are getting involved in it. The farming business today is becoming, it's big busi-ness. . . . The beginning of World War II and the period following that, farming as we knew it disappeared."[13]

As Quinn suggests, narrators of the postwar generation dated the beginning of southern agricultural transformation to the 1940s and 1950s, and they offered a complex analysis of the multifaceted nature of change. Quinn's fellow white South Carolinian Tom B. Cunningham, a landowner said, "[T]he biggest change . . . took place during the war and years immediately following the war. When I left to go to war, we had those two old Farmall tractors. . . . But imme-diately after the war, there was tremendous change and fast change. When I came home from the service an older brother and I started a partnership. . . . [W]e needed updated tractors, tractors that were capable of doing more work and capable of more variations of equip-ment than could come with those [small Farmall] tractors." After that, he said, "[T]he changes came so fast and so furious and there were so many improvements and changes. . . . We kind of got used to change, I guess, during the '50s. Changes and improvements are still going on at a tremendous rate."[14]

Like their older counterparts, Cunningham and others in the postwar generation of farmers believed mechanization was a major force driving the rural transformation. The similarity to prewar nar-rators' stories ends there, however. The postwar generation's sto-ries about the role of technology are more subtle and complex than those of older farmers. Tractors and tractor-drawn implements were not the only technological improvements that transformed farming. After World War II, chemical fertilizers and pesticides were among the primary weapons in the arsenal of modern farming advocated by USDA officials, the farm press, and agribusiness. Landowner Marvin Engelbrecht of Crawford, Texas, explained that commercial fertilizers had dramatically increased the productivity of farmers. He noted that without commercial fertilizer, "We wouldn't be sending any food across to Russia or anywhere. We'd be doing pretty well to supply our own needs here. That was a blessing—the start of this fertilizer."[15] Tom B. Cunningham agreed. He told an interviewer that chemicals "were our salvation." He went on to explain, "[W]hen all the hand labor and all the people who were there, ready, willing and able to help you out anytime you needed 'em doing any kind of work, when that just disappeared from the scene had we not had chemicals we couldn't have grown cotton, for example."[16] Engelbrecht and Cunningham both use religious language to describe the changes wrought by chemicals: chemical fertilizer was a blessing and herbicides were salvation. To Engelbrecht, the blessing grew out of the fact that a single farmer could feed hundreds. He lauded an American achievement: American farmers, with the help of chemical fertilizers, could feed the world. Cunningham believed that chemical fertilizers saved farmers in the face of a labor shortage. The language used by both narrators reveals their enthusiasm for the positive benefits of agrochemicals. Their attitudes reflect mid-century Americans' faith that science could solve the world's thorniest problems, even those that had plagued farmers for thousands of years.

While many narrators praised agrochemicals as having wrought positive changes in farming, many rural people saw them as a mixed blessing. Rural North Carolinian Dema Lyall observed that "[today] we have so many more [insect] pests . . . that actually, things are much harder to grow now than they were in those days. We could just plant beans in the corn field and have bushels and bushels of beans." When asked why she thought this was the case, Lyall replied, "That I don't know. . . . I can remember when the Mexican bean beetle first came and we'd have to go out and pick the beetle off. And they [plants] didn't have diseases. But now beans have diseases; they have blights; they have so many more things. It's just harder for them to produce like they once did."[17] In some ways, Lyall's memories of

pest-free earlier times were probably the nostalgic and vague memories of a child. (Lyall was born around 1920.) Insect pests and plant
blights have plagued farmers since the development of agriculture.
She nevertheless makes an important point. Monocropping and an
overuse of chemicals created as many problems as they solved. The
testimony of her fellow North Carolinian, landowning dairy farmer
Mike Teer, lends further insight into the new challenges chemical use
brought to southern agriculture. He explained that army worms or
cut worms in corn were a new problem. "A lot of it is brought on by
the fact that there is a limited amount of land and you have to plant
corn year after year. And another way to kill these things is to plow
it and just leave the land open and leave the residue up where it can
freeze and it'll kill it over the winter. But people have gone away
from that practice, a lot of them have, because of expense and things
like this and the fact that you have to keep rolling your land over
and just planting one crop after another and you don't have time to
leave the land open like this. You have to come up with something
else to get rid of that problem."[18] Monocropping created magnets
for the natural predators—insects and diseases—of crops. Insects in
particular sometimes became resistant to pesticides after generations
of exposure. The demands of commercial farming, such as the need
to produce on a large scale in order to justify a major investment in
expensive equipment, meant that farmers no longer had the luxury
of using time-honored natural methods like allowing a field to lie
fallow in order to combat disease and insects. Like Lyall and Teer,
many postwar narrators' memories of chemical technology were profoundly ambivalent; chemicals were both salvation and scourge.

As the prewar generation noted, the shift to mechanized farming
changed the nature of farmwork for small landowners and plantation owners alike, and the changed character of farmwork was a
major theme in the postwar generation's stories. Mechanized farming required knowledge of sophisticated equipment and an ability to
work on it. Farmers could rarely afford to pay professional mechanics
to make minor repairs on farm equipment, nor could they afford the
lost time required to wait for professional mechanics to fix broken
machinery. As a result, many farmers became skilled mechanics. They
also had to supervise hired hands more closely because laborers were
using expensive equipment. After the advent of mechanization, plan-

tation owners performed more of the day-to-day work themselves. Virginia McIntyre, the wife of a white plantation owner in Franklin Parish, Louisiana, told an interviewer that her husband had once employed twenty-two tenant families on their land and that mules pulled all the equipment. "As time went on and things changed," she explained, "after we got tractors instead of mules . . . we ended up the last few years with one colored man helping him, and consequently, he [her husband] did harder work before he retired than he did when he was first farming. . . . Now they can just do it so fast, where it used to take fifteen or twenty to cut hay. . . . Now it's [farming] so much easier."[19] McIntyre meant that as mechanization reduced the need for farm laborers, her husband spent less time supervising the work of others and more time engaged in the hands-on work of farming such as cultivating the land, bringing in the harvest, and repairing equipment. The physical work was less arduous, but as a large landowner, after mechanization McIntyre was more likely to do the physical work himself.

Familiarity with mechanical equipment was not the only new knowledge base required by technological advances in agriculture. The use of chemicals also required specialized knowledge. South Carolinian Tom B. Cunningham said, "We were so uneducated in the dangers of chemicals. I remember the first chemical that I used on a cotton crop destroyed my tobacco crop the following year. Somebody along the way either forgot to tell me or I forgot to remember that you can't put Cotoran on a tobacco field. . . . It would linger in the soil and carry it across to the next year and damage your crop. You could put cotton back there, it would be fine. But you definitely couldn't put tobacco, because I learned that the hard way. . . . But we had a lot to learn about chemicals." He learned about chemicals from reading farm magazines and the pamphlets distributed by pesticide and herbicide dealers. He added, "And it was a matter of burning a lot of midnight oil, reading and studying and knowing you knew sure what you were doing. It required a lot of that."[20] As the memories of McIntyre and Cunningham suggest, the shift to specialized, mechanized commercial farming required more knowledge and a different set of skills. By implication, applying technology to farming may have required greater intelligence and education. The meaning of farmwork was changing. No longer was hard physical labor the only key to success. Brain power became more critical than manpower.

The capital investment required to implement the scientific farming methods advocated by postwar agricultural experts was expensive, and not every farmer could afford to specialize and expand. Those farmers could not compete with their more affluent neighbors, and farmers who did mechanize often found themselves drowning in debt. White North Carolina tobacco farmer Lamas Denning explained that tobacco had once been profitable but that it became less profitable over the years. This was not because tobacco prices dropped but because expenses increased. As he put it, "Equipment is much more expensive, fertilize [sic] is more expensive."[21] A. C. Griffin, a white North Carolina landowner, noted that people had once saved their own seed for the next year's crop, but "nobody now saves the seed peas. They buy 'em. Soybeans, they buy 'em. Cotton seed, they buy 'em. And everything else. . . . The primary reason the farmer's in such bad shape today is keeping up to date to even farm."[22] Hybridizing produced larger plants and plants that were insect- and disease-resistant, but the process also produced seed that varied in quality at the second generation, eliminating the need to save seed for next year's crop. Thus, buying expensive hybrid seed left farmers "in such bad [financial] shape." Rural North Carolinian Norbert King Andrews described the evolution of dairy farms from tiny one- or two-cow operations that produced for home use to larger herds that delivered milk to local markets to USDA-approved operations that generated Grade-A milk sold to commercial processors. These USDA-authorized dairies "required inspection and sanitation. You had to have that, and you had to have running water—hot and cold—and you had to have cement places to milk the cows, and you had to keep it grade A sanitation. And all this evolved from this barnyard milk." New barns and better sanitation required large investments. Unable to afford the upgrades, many farmers abandoned the dairy business, switching to another type of crop or livestock production or even ceasing to farm.[23]

For farmers who gambled by making large capital investments in their operations, unpredictable commodity prices could easily spell financial ruin. The prewar generation of farmers occasionally mentioned low prices as a source of hardship in farming, but they did not discuss foreign markets as a cause of low prices. Indeed, until the 1950s, most American farmers produced commodities destined for domestic markets. As a result, export markets had limited impact on U.S. prices for most (but not all) farm products. Postwar farmers understood that things had changed drastically—that fluctuating prices on world commodities markets in the face of rising production costs had made agriculture more risky than earlier in the century. Over and over, the younger farmers of both races in this study lamented low commodity prices as a force that helped transform southern agriculture, and not usually in positive ways. In their discussion of fluctuating commodity prices, a shift in farmers' self-perception becomes evident: farmers increasingly saw themselves as knowledgeable businessmen, and they described their growing awareness of the impact of world markets. Loudoun County, Virginia, dairy farmer Lehon Hamilton told an interviewer that "I'd say farming was mostly successful in the 1940s, early 1950s. I think because the prices were good. Milk was a pretty good price."[24] His neighbor Curtis Laycock noted that the prosperity Hamilton described did not last. Speaking in 2001, he said, "Over time, prices declined and livestock prices were much lower. Cattle prices are very good now, but hog prices are very low, and wheat, the grain prices, two dollars, and corn two dollars. It was worth that back in the 40s and 50s. And you can imagine what the production costs are now compared to then."[25] White Arkansas landowner Kenneth Gosney said, "See, we're competing with world rice markets, and the world rice market up until recently was about $1.70 a bushel. Well, the United States and Arkansas exports [sic] over half of what they produce. Well, if it costs us $3.40 to produce a bushel of rice, how can we sell it for $1.70?"[26] Like Gosney, many narrators explained that high overhead left American farmers at a distinct disadvantage when competing with producers in less developed nations.

Farmers also understood that they could not control commodity prices. They attempted to cope with fluctuating and unpredictable prices by careful management and calculated investment. Many southern farmers gave up on cotton and other overproduced commodities in favor of more profitable types of farming. Some began to produce soybeans or to contract with poultry processing companies to raise chickens on a large scale. In upstate South Carolina, hundreds planted peach orchards in former cotton fields. As South Carolinian Mary Quinn put it, "King Cotton left. . . . And peaches came in."[27] In yet another shift driven by the global economy, by the 1990s, competition from California and foreign growers was driving South Carolina peach farmers out of business. At mid-century in many parts of Texas, farmers abandoned cotton and grain cultivation for ranching. As a result, according to African American landowner Grover Williams Sr., "The only plowing we do is to make seedbed for Coastal [Bermuda grass] pastures and gardening. That's the only plowing."[28] White Alabama landowner J. Robert Stevenson explained that his family switched from cotton to dairy farming during World War II because "during the war, it was impossible to get labor to gather the cotton" while the market for fluid milk expanded. His father built a Grade-A dairy barn and assembled a dairy herd.[29]

Indeed, southern agriculture became more diverse by the last quarter of the twentieth century. By the turn of millennium, some southern farmers struggled to compete by eliminating the middleman and selling directly to consumers. They also engaged in diverse entrepreneurial ventures: producing organic and specialty crops for restaurants and gourmet foods stores; entering into arrangements with local consumers who buy a share of the farm's harvest each year; or contracting with large agribusiness corporations to produce poultry or crops. Many converted their farms into educational and entertainment complexes. For example, Christmas tree farmers provided customers with hayrides and hot chocolate. Crop farmers sometimes mowed mazes into cornfields to provide fall entertainment to suburbanites and town dwellers. All of these new ventures appealed to an increasingly affluent urban population, eliminated middlemen, and allowed farmers to reap higher profits by selling directly to consumers. Such innovations have enabled many southerners to continue farming. As Loudoun County, Virginia, farmer Jim Brownell explained, "Large scale, traditional farming is history as far as Loudoun County. Now they're talking about vineyards, Christmas tree farms, vegetable farms, exotic animals, and outbackers, llamas. Many of the old farmers, they laugh and snicker at that kind of stuff. 'That's stupid.' . . . [But] that's the future of farming in Loudoun County. The big traditional grain, dairy, beef, that's history. That will never come back."[30]

Shifting patterns of agricultural production were only one change sweeping the rural South. Industrialization and urbanization also transformed the southern countryside. New economic opportunities figured prominently in oral history narrators' tales of transformation. Factories sprang up not only in towns but also in rural industrial parks, providing high-paying jobs within commuting distance of rural communities and a means for some rural people to hold on to their farms. Many narrators explained that they had been able to continue farming because at least one member of the family took an off-farm job. Loudoun County, Virginia, landowning farmers Curtis and Betty Laycock explained that in order to continue farming and still support the family at a standard of living the Laycocks found acceptable, Betty supplemented farm profits with an off-farm salary. Betty said, "I went to work in 1966." Curtis added, "Just wasn't enough income [on the farm]. We were strapped and it was a big help."[31] Many narrators told similar stories. White Texas landowner Van Massirer said, "A lot of families have at least one member of the family, maybe the wife, who has maybe just a part-time job, or in some cases, full-time job off the farm or ranch. There's been a drastic change in the last—say in the fifties to now."[32] Pauline Price and her husband reversed the roles. As the landowning North Carolina woman explained, she and her husband, Gwyn, moved to his grandmother's farm when he inherited it in the late 1920s. The couple began a dairy farm and commercial milk bottling operation, including a milk delivery service. A few years after they moved to the farm, Gwyn, a supporter of rural electrification and a former school principal, was appointed chair of the Rural Electrification Administration board of North Carolina, a post he held for thirty-two years. He lived in Raleigh during the week. "During most of that time, I lived on the farm with the two children," Pauline explained. "They didn't want to go to Raleigh to school 'cause they knew no one in Raleigh. They wanted to stay home. So Mama stayed at home and kept the children, kept the cows, kept the whole farm." She ran the family's dairy operation with the help of two hired men.[33]

The Federal Government and Transformation

The shifts in federal agricultural policy outlined in the introduction made the postwar generation of farmers increasingly dependent on the federal government for financial survival and ever more aware of the federal government's role in reshaping agriculture. Perhaps this was a cumulative effect of the continuation of early federal programs combined with an increasing array of new programs. Whatever the reasons, a major theme in postwar narrators' stories about rural change was the role of the federal government in transforming farming. Narrators praised some aspects of government intervention, described others without value judgments, and frequently criticized the impact of federal programs. Some narrators explicitly blamed the federal government for the decline of family farming.

Besides agricultural extension work, the earliest federal programs that sought to reshape the countryside were those initiated during the New Deal. Similar programs that sought to limit productivity and boost commodity prices have persisted to the present. Prewar farmers may have been silent about these programs, but not so the postwar generation. Younger farmers routinely explained how price supports and production control programs changed the nature of farming. South Carolinian Otto Davis described tobacco price supports as "our salvation,"[34] and his Lee County neighbor William Graham explained the federal allotment program for tobacco and peanuts, "[Y]ou have an allotment. Several farmers have bought up the small farmers' [allotments] and they have a right good sized allotment and they plant that and made more so than [from growing] cotton."[35] As Graham suggests, the commodification of federal allotments encouraged some farmers to expand, driving smaller farmers out of business. African American North Carolina landowner Nathan Murray worked off the farm for many years because his tobacco allotment was too small to allow him to earn a living by farming. He explained, "Tobacco was the one thing at that time where you made your money. If you didn't make it off tobacco, you didn't make it on the farm in this area. And we didn't have no tobacco [allotment]. Just a little bit, but not enough to make no living off. . . ." Clearing some more timberland on their property entitled the Murrays to a larger allotment, and later they purchased land that included a tobacco allotment, eventually enabling them to farm full-time. Murray also hinted that he did not fare as well in the federal allotment program because of racial discrimination. He said, "It was allotments is what it was.

We just couldn't get it. I'm not saying discrimination or nothing like that because there was a whole lot of us didn't get no tobacco, we won't the only ones didn't get no tobacco, so I'm not claiming nothing. But I just said we didn't get any."[36] Murray recounted his story for a white narrator and may have been reluctant to proclaim himself a victim of racial discrimination at the hands of a federal agency, but that is the implication of his story nonetheless.

Extended commentary by white Georgia landowner Dick Benson illustrates the way that technological change, the availability of federally subsidized credit, and shifting federal agricultural policy combined to reshape farming in the late twentieth century. He said, "But somehow or other I think maybe if we hadn't never got into these big tractors and got so big in farming, we might have had more money and might have had more time with our family. 'Cause we got being getting bigger and bigger in this farming. Some of 'em got seeing who could owe the most money and got to bragging about it. Back when I was farming, I'd slip in the bank and borrow money hoping nobody wouldn't see me. But today people wants to see who can buy the biggest tractor." In Benson's memory, the very mind-set of farmers had changed. In the early twentieth century, respected farmers were prudent ones; they planned carefully, saved wisely, and avoided debt whenever possible. They did not engage in conspicuous consumption, even consumption that was also a farm investment. Borrowing money had once been something embarrassing, almost shameful, for an independent-minded farmer, but Benson saw this attitude change. In recent years, he recalled, buying ever-bigger equipment and farming on a large-scale became markers of farming success, and going into debt to farm on that scale was not shameful at all. In fact, he implies that some farmers believed the size of their debt was the mark of a "big farmer." When asked when the practice of taking on significant debt began to dominate farming, he replied,

> End of the late '70s. People started making real good money in the Nixon days. . . . But I never did get too big that I couldn't do any [work] around a tractor. I always planted and looked after my own business. . . . I know a man told me one time, he said, "Dick, when you lay down at night and you can't put your finger on your business, you're going

away from home." And that's the truth. You lay down and just think about it, that you assume you done this or assume that, but you don't know it, and the first thing you know, you're gonna be out of business. Then the government come in there, and they decided they'd loan this 3-percent money. Well, you had these people that never have farmed, they decided they'd get in farming and get some of this 3-percent money, or we called it easy money, and they started farming. Well, it was good and it was bad. It turned out most of it was bad. The government meant well, but the 3-percent money wasn't used where it was supposed to be used. People built fine homes with it. They [the government] didn't mean to be that way. Some people borrowed it and didn't need it, and they put it in the bank, and interest rates was high and they made money with it. Some people bought luxury automobiles and tractors thinking they would never have to pay it back. That's where it all started. If they had never loaned that 3-percent money, these farmers who was farming just to be farming—now, my way of farming was the way of a living. I didn't know anything else to do in particular. But that way, they got in there, and the first ones that started foreclosing were the kind that was trying to farm and didn't really care whether he made any money or not. So they went out. Then there's another type that went out, and they started raising the rent on peanuts, on all farms, and us people that had been on the farm all our lives, we had to compete with this high-priced rent, you see.[37]

Benson's statement exposes what historian Brian Donahue has called "the complex tension between farming for permanence and farming for profit."[38] Benson believed that by doing most of the labor himself and keeping his thumb on the pulse of his operation, he was a better manager and he saved on labor costs. Both practices made him a more efficient and financially viable farmer. Indebtedness in and of itself did not offend Benson; debt was an inevitable fact of farming life. Nonetheless, like the farmers of an earlier generation, Benson believed that debt posed a threat to independence and that a taste for consumer goods signified weakness.[39] In his view, some farmers incurred debt for the sake of conspicuous consumption—to build "fine homes" or purchase luxury automobiles and "the biggest tractor"—an irresponsible practice that Benson scorned.[40] Worse, farmers who used indebtedness to finance rapid farm expansion drove up the cost of renting land for more responsible neighbors. In Benson's view, the federal government exacerbated the risks involved in farming by providing "easy money" in the form of low-interest loans that enticed many inexperienced folks to enter agriculture. Indeed small numbers of people entered farming for the first time in the 1970s, though their numbers proved to be few. Nonetheless, Benson believed that these people farmed "just to be farming" instead of "farming as a way of living," and that they shouldered large debts for fine houses and big equipment. Benson did not see the federal government as the only force transforming agriculture, but he certainly believed that federal policies had accelerated and shaped change.

Rural southerners' oral narratives depict a countryside that is awash in a flood of changes. Most rural people of the prewar generation grew up believing that farming was a means of making a living. Though many enjoyed the autonomy that farming offered them, the prolonged agricultural depression and the financial unpredictability for farming made for a hard life—a life so hard that it shaped the stories they told about transformation in surprising ways. However aware they may have been of the impact of government intervention or global commodities markets early in the century, in later life farmers who came of age before World War II were most conscious of mechanization as the principal agent of change. Perhaps their one-dimensional memories of changes grow out of the fact that they grew up in the era when man and mule power performed most of the work on family farms. Tractors, combines, multi-row cultivators, hay balers, and other equipment profoundly altered the rhythms of daily life and increased the productivity of southern farms. In prewar narrators' minds, the contrast between farming before and after mechanization was striking, and thus mechanization was the major transforming force that they remembered.

Postwar narrators, on the other hand, usually grew up with tractors and some tractor-drawn equipment. Mechanization continued and evolved in their lifetimes, as newer and more productive equipment was introduced, but mechanization was not the only transforming force on their radar screens. As their narratives suggest, the post-war generation experienced an escalating pace of change. Though many postwar narrators had begun their farming careers with high hopes for achieving middle-class living standards—and indeed many did—they also farmed in a more complex environment. Farmers in the last half of the twentieth century struggled to succeed in the face of more and more factors that were beyond their control. No longer were weather and domestic markets the major uncertainties. Competition from global markets, rapid technological change that reshaped the work of agriculture, shifting federal agricultural policy, and an ever-increasing need for both capital and education shaped southern farmers' memories of transformation, and their stories became more layered and complex.

Chapter Four

Memory and the Meaning of Change

Rural southerners' narratives of change are peopled with villains and victims as well as heroes. Some stories are rich and complex; others are flat and one-dimensional. While their descriptions of change reveal the forces that they believed were driving transformation, their analytical and interpretive comments reveal the meanings that they gave that transformation. For the transformation of the rural South did not mean the same things to all members of the rural community of memory. The prewar generation of white landless and land-owning farmers frequently saw rural transformation as the source of new choices and new opportunities for better lives often found off the farm. Although a few who abandoned farming admitted that they would have preferred to stay on the land, most depicted leaving the land as a positive choice that materially improved their lives. African American farmers saw agricultural transformation as yet another example of a process that disadvantaged black farmers—as yet another chapter in the long book that chronicles the disempowerment of America's black citizens. Many African American narrators had abandoned farming by the 1950s, but a stubborn few persisted on the land. Their stories emphasized the persistent impact of racial oppression on black farmers. Some African Americans hated farming, some loved it, but nearly all expressed the belief that racial discrimination, including discrimination by the federal government, worked to make farming untenable. Nonetheless, large numbers of black farmers worked the land long past the time that other doors opened to them. The postwar generation of white farmers, mostly landowners, described agricultural transformation as a convoluted, multifaceted, and protracted process that left farmers at the mercy of impersonal market forces and uncaring businessmen and bureaucrats. Members of the postwar generation of farmers who left the land were quick to blame federal policies as a principal factor in driving them out of farming. Gender differences also appear in the narratives. While the generational, racial, and class divides appeared in the narratives of women and men, women's narratives proved significantly different than men's in several areas. Most strikingly, women were acutely aware of the differences between rural and urban life earlier in the century, and they expressed relief that the gap between country and town had diminished in recent years. Among families who left the land temporarily or permanently, women were more likely than men to express a preference for living in town.

This chapter examines the varied meanings that narrators gave to agricultural transformation by examining several categories of stories: farm women's stories about the transformation of daily life and rural-urban distinctions; landowners' and tenants' accounts of the displacement of sharecroppers; and a range of narrators' explanations about reasons for abandoning farming.

Gender and Memories of Transformation

The main discrepancies between men's and women's narratives fell into three categories: the ways they discussed technology's impact on their work, their impressions of the distinguishing characteristics of country and town life, and the ways that farm and town people were different. When men discussed the impact of technology on farming, they were more likely to emphasize that new equipment had improved productivity. Howard Taft Bailey, a black landowner from Holmes County, Mississippi, was typical. He told an interviewer that a man could work as much land with two or three tractors as he had with forty mules and as many sharecropping families. He emphasized increased production and the lowered production costs that had been brought about by technology.[1] Over and over, men focused on how much more work one man could do, thanks to technology, but they rarely talked about the work being "easier." By contrast, women were more likely to focus on the way technology lightened their workloads. Many, like Virginian Ethel Carter, believed that "Being a farmer . . . is a grinding thing," so any equipment that eased the grind was welcomed.[2] Tennessee dairy farmer Mabel Love said that milking machines eased her workload because she no longer had to milk a sizable herd by hand and that the electric stove freed her from the arduous task of tending and cleaning "that messy wood stove."[3] Louisiana farm wife Zelphia Edwards noted, "All your modern conveniences have really taken the drudgery out of homemaking today."[4] Mary Fouts of Kentucky explained that the advent of electric freezers had eased the task of preserving food from her garden. A hot and miserable task in the days before air-conditioning, canning involved spending hours over a hot stove sterilizing jars and later sealing them in boiling water baths. In her early married years, Fouts recalled that she had canned three hundred to five hundred jars of food each year, but once electric freezers came along, she simply froze the garden produce.[5] An occasional narrator qualified her praise of the way technology lightened her barnyard and household burdens. For example, Texan Leota Kuykendall pointed out that the work may have been easier, but that in later years women felt more pressure to keep a "pretty house and a clean house."[6] When asked if electricity made her housework easier, North Carolina farm wife Lena Boyce replied, "Well, yes, much easier in some ways, especially the washing. But yet it seems that other work comes to take the place; you stay just as busy. [laughter] But maybe it's not quite as hard." She recalled that on the day in 1941 when electricity was installed in her home, she turned on the kitchen lights as her family was eating supper only to realize how dirty her kitchen walls were.[7] In spite of the fact that improved technology had raised the standards of cleanliness and beauty in the farm household, generally, women saw the arrival of technology as an overall blessing in their lives.

Not only did women and men remember the benefits of technology in different ways, but women also proved especially likely to articulate a hatred for farm life. Women frequently found farm life harder than men. Many farm wives were expected to play the quadruple roles of mother, housekeeper, petty commodity producer, and field hand. The rickety homes of many sharecroppers and poor landowners, open to weather, dirt, insects, and rodents, proved nearly impossible to keep clean. A lack of running water or electricity, conveniences few southern farm families enjoyed before World War II, made grueling work of cleaning, cooking, and preserving food. A woman might rise before the rest of the family in order to cook breakfast, then spend her day toiling in the fields while keeping one eye on her children, returning to the house at dark to cook dinner, clean, preserve food for the winter, and sew or mend while the men in the household rested or retired early. The social and economic costs exacted by racial discrimination made farm life particularly bleak for black women. Little wonder then that many women, especially African American women, expressed little nostalgia for farm life. Black Mississippian Amy Jones grew up watching her mother endure country life, and she herself worked in the fields from a young age. She said she came to Memphis because "I had always said, 'If I ever get grown, I won't chop no cotton. And I won't pick no cotton.' So, when I got grown, I left the country and I came to Memphis and got me a job."[8]

Distaste for the farm motivated some women to marry at a young age in order to leave the farm behind. Theresa Lyons, a black North Carolinian born around 1920, described her childhood on her grandfather's tenant farm outside Durham. She told an interviewer, "I remember as a little girl, wanting to get married, because I said I was going to get married and move out of the country and move to the city. And sure enough, when I was 17, I got married. That was my way of getting away from the country." Later in the interview, the interviewer asked again about why she married young. Lyons replied, "I just wanted to move out away from the farm. Wherever my husband was going to move, into whatever city, I would be willing." She met a much older man with a nice car who took her to the movies, the fair, and other places she had never been. She married him because "I felt it was an opportunity for me." The couple moved in with his parents in town. She explained, "It was a nice house with a bathroom. Ah, I thought that was something. We had an outdoor toilet, and we were still getting water from a spring. I thought, oh, they must be rich." Her husband worked at a bakery in Durham and later for Liggett-Myers and IBM. For Lyons, leaving the farm meant leaving behind substandard living conditions without modern conveniences. It meant leaving behind poverty. It meant entering a world where a steady job and commercial amusements made life more comfortable and less tedious.[9]

Black Georgian Viola Carter and her husband moved to Miami from a Lee County, Georgia, farm in 1937. When asked how she liked living in the city after growing up in the country, she said, "I just liked it because I didn't have to go to the field no more; that was the thing I liked about it." She admitted that town life had been difficult at first because she had no family or friends nearby, but she explained that she soon adjusted and made friends. For Carter, life in town was a major improvement over the endless toil of life as a sharecropper's daughter and a sharecropper's wife.[10] Rural white Alabamans L. D. and Lula Walker moved to Birmingham for nine years after their country store in rural Clay County burned to the ground. Lula recalled that in Birmingham, they had enjoyed running water for the first time. She explained that her husband had wanted to return to Clay County, but "I didn't want to move back down here. We moved back during the Depression. I didn't want to move back." In 1934, they returned to Clay County and rebuilt the store. The couple prospered with their country store, but Lula was clear that she had found town life easier.[11]

An exchange between J. C. Colley and his wife, Lizzie, a white couple, proves even more revealing of gender differences in feelings about leaving the farm. Interviewed by historian Pamela Grundy in 1987, J. C. Colley explained that the family moved to Alexander City, Alabama, from Clay County in 1960. There he worked in a factory because "we needed a little more money [than he made farming]. Times began to change, and you had to sort of change with the time. Just to live and to have things like other people had." Lizzie Colley said, "We didn't stay [in Alexander City] but eight months. I loved it. There were lots of people. Where I lived, I had neighbors close by. And there were people, and I could hear the children playing. I just loved it. He wouldn't stay. We ought be [sic] down there now. We'd be close to somebody." J. C. replied, "I just liked home." He went on to explain how he preferred having his garden and his cows, but Lizzie said, "We had everything we needed [in town]. I didn't have any neighbors close to me when we was off in here. I couldn't walk, couldn't drive—couldn't go anywhere unless he carried me. In Alexander City, I had neighbors all around me, and a pretty house. I just liked it. Well, if I can better myself, I want to do it. But he wouldn't stay." Lizzie found country life isolating, especially since she did not drive, and she preferred the nice house equipped with modern conveniences that she enjoyed in town. To Lizzie, town life was a step up. J. C. protested, "I don't know that I was bettering myself [in town]." Lizzie replied, "Well you was, if you could have just took it like that."[12]

Although women were more likely than men to express a preference for town life, a few female narrators insisted that country life was more desirable. For example, African American Georgia field hand Lottie Jackson found herself pushed off the land in the late 1970s when the landowner for whom she had worked for years sold his land to a large corporation. She told an interviewer, "I tole him [the landowner] he ought've looked out for us, though, he ought've leaved a space for us. I ain't goin to no town, not Dawson an not Americus, neither! . . . Lord, I don' like no town, for sure I don'! I like to stay out where I can get somptin for nothin! I kin go to somebody's house they give me some greens, peas, anything. If I go to town, I got to go the market. Town ain't no place to live . . . I fish a lot, I sure do. How come I goin to miss this place, we got a lot of fishin on this place. An I hate to leave here, on account of that fishin."[13] Jackson clearly loved rural life. She preferred the autonomy afforded by her subsistence activities to a cash-dependent existence in town. She was unusual among narrators, however.

With new technology, better transportation and communication, and a higher farm standard of living, the lines between rural and urban people became less pronounced by the last third of the twentieth century. Women who remained on the land praised this development. Rural North Carolinian Dema Lyall told an interviewer that "I used to feel that the people who lived in town were so much better socially than we country people that I was never quite comfortable with them. And now I don't really feel that anymore. . . . [T]here's no difference really. Not anymore, and probably never was. It might have just been my imagination. But I do know that we feel much closer now . . . I think, really, that electricity and the communication it's brought to us has helped in that. That we understand them better, and they understand us better."[14] An interviewer asked another white North Carolina farmer, Fredda Davis, whether the attitudes of town people about country people and vice versa had changed in recent decades. Davis replied,

In my memory it definitely has. People out in the country probably didn't have the income that the business people in town

did have. In other words, we were sort of poor, you know. . . .
We were proud in that respect. We couldn't have the dress to
go to town and wear and get well-dressed as the city woman
did. See, we didn't have as good a clothes. Now we *do*! [her
emphasis] You can't tell the difference between we old hay-
seeders . . . when you walk down the streets of downtown.
You can't tell the difference between the hayseeder girls and
the city girls. . . . They [country people] probably felt like they
wasn't quite [as good as town people] for some reason. Oh,
they was good if not better. But [laughter] you see, back in
those days if I had to go to town I didn't have the fashionable
clothes, the kind of clothes of that city girl, and I'd see her
over there all dressed up so pretty. I'd think she might look
better than me; that's the way you think. [laughter]

Davis added that country people generally thought that town people
"felt, a little superior or something."[15] As Lyall and Davis suggest,
rural women had been acutely aware of the material differences
between country life and town life, differences that male narrators
rarely mentioned. Because many country women perceived town
people as "better socially," as people who looked down on "hay-
seeders," their memories of the rural/urban divide proved persistent
and significant.

The fashionable clothing of town women may have made farm
women uncomfortably aware of their relative poverty and lack of
sophistication, but so did the comfortable homes of town dwellers.
Town households enjoyed many conveniences unavailable on early-
twentieth-century farms. By late century, however, most farm homes
were finally equipped with such conveniences, and farm women's
comments about how they now enjoyed many of the same ameni-
ties as town women speak volumes about their feelings of a bygone
rural world. For example, Dema Lyall said, "We live a more modern
and more convenient and a much easier and better life today. Most
of us have as many conveniences or about as many as you'd find
anywhere. We have good lighting in our homes; we have water both
hot and cold; we have TVs, stereos, movie projectors; we have tape
recorders; we have microwave ovens. You just name it, we have it,
that's available in America today." She noted that late in the cen-

tury, farm women enjoyed more leisure time because technological advances freed them from the burdens of doing the laundry. Then she went on, "but seems like our society we've become more demanding because we get involved more and more and we're much more able to do things just for pleasure than our forefathers. Like lots of things that they never had the opportunity to do because they had manual labor they had to do. And now electricity has given us all these convenient things that we can now have leisure time to go on a vacation, to go on a trip, to go do whatever we enjoy for the afternoon instead of having to do hard manual labor."[16] Lyall's comments were echoed by many women who expressed gratitude and relief that late-twentieth-century farm life had become less arduous for women. Female narrators found both relief and satisfaction at the reduction of material and social differences between themselves and town people.

Displacement: Class-based Stories about Change

The class-based nuances of memories about transformation become particularly visible in the stories that narrators tell about the displacement of sharecroppers. Both generations of farmers included in this study saw mechanization as a driving force behind the displacement of the landless, but landowners and tenants told varying stories. Many white landless farmers and African Americans blamed mechanization for eliminating the need for sharecroppers. For example, black Mississippian Essie Mae Alexander, a sharecropper for most of her life, noted that mechanization left many landless people unemployed. As she put it, "Then a lot of people started using tractors and cotton pickers and things like that. So the peoples on the farm didn't have anything to do." By the 1960s, her husband became a tractor driver on a plantation while she took an off-farm job as an aide in a federally funded Head Start program.[17] Undoubtedly her life was more comfortable and her work less arduous after she ceased to work in the cotton fields, but she did not see leaving the land as a choice. Rather, mechanization forced her to change occupations. Her fellow Mississippian, black landowner Howard Taft Bailey, concurred: "Mechanisms [sic] and herbicides just knocked out the sharecropping."[18] Black Mississippian Maurice Lucas, born in 1950, agreed that technology reduced the need for laborers on large cotton plantations in the Deep South. Lucas grew up in a landowning family that depended on family labor to raise cotton, corn, and livestock on their eighty acres. Nonetheless, he observed the changes that appeared first on the large plantations near his home in Renova. He explained, "Every farm had 15 to 20 boys on it. Everything was done by hand back then. They plowed the land with mules. They chopped all the cotton with hoes and they picked all the cotton by hand. So it took a lot of folks. In Bolivar County in 1930, it was over 300,000 [farm laborers] in our county, and now you're talking about 45,000 people in the whole county. So that can tell you how many people went north when mechanization took over. Man, 40 acres and a mule. It took a lot of mule to work 40 acres back then and now they take one of these tractors and work 40 acres in 15 minutes. So that was the difference."[19] Lucas saw mechanization as setting in motion a chain of events. Tractors replaced mules, displacing thousands of workers who drove the mules and did the manual labor. Displaced workers left the South looking for other ways to make a living. The reduction in the need for laborers first displaced sharecroppers, then renters and tenant farmers, and eventually even day laborers.

A rare white landowner might agree with these narrators that mechanization drove displacement. Clayton Lowder, a landowner in Sumter, South Carolina, farmed a total of 5,500 acres of land, including rented acreage. When asked whether mechanization came first or laborers left the land thus forcing farmers to mechanize, he replied, "If I had to put one first, I'd put mechanization came first. It may have been simultaneously more or less, but I would say we were mechanized before labor got pretty scarce, because there was still a good bit of labor that you could get when we started to mechanize. As I said, you couldn't get enough production out of a mule. We had to speed it up."[20]

Most historians have agreed with the assessment of Alexander, Bailey, Lucas, and Lowder: mechanization displaced landless laborers. Other historians, however, have argued that the flight of people from the countryside and alternative employment for the landless forced plantation owners to mechanize. White South Carolina landowner Tom B. Cunningham shared this perspective. As long as he enjoyed access to plentiful cheap labor, he had no reason to buy machinery. Cunningham was born in 1923 and began farming on his father's land after World War II. He explained, "We did not have a cotton picker until after we discontinued the sharecroppping because . . . the sharecroppers picked the cotton. . . . After all the sharecropping stopped, then it was a year or two there we didn't grow much cotton. But after a few years I bought a cotton picker."[21] Cunningham's memory of the sequence of events is that the departure of sharecroppers from the land first caused him to stop raising as "much cotton," and *then* inspired him to buy a mechanical cotton harvester. In short, he did not lay off his sharecroppers, leaving them homeless and unemployed. Instead, sharecroppers left, forcing him to make a capital investment in equipment to replace the missing laborers.

Some landowners saw both factors operating, although they did not often explain the complexity of the process until interviewers pressed them. Born in 1908, white North Carolina landowner A. C. Griffin began farming during the later years of the Great Depression. When historian Lu Ann Jones first asked him about the advent of mechanization, Griffin explained that the difficulty in finding laborers forced him to shift to mechanized farming and the use of chemical herbicides. "You couldn't get anybody to do anything," he explained. In Griffin's early years of farming, he said he had relied on "[l]ocal people around and about. [Then] all these mills and stuff come in here. Right here . . . in Edenton, we got more factories than any small town I know of. And they pay a whole lot more money. I couldn't . . . get enough help to pick a bale of cotton the whole week. No, sir." As Griffin tells it, better paying job opportunities lured workers from the land. His wife, Grace, agreed, but she also linked better educational opportunities for African Americans to the shortage of farm laborers. As she put it, "I think the main thing is colored folks getting an education. And they moved out of the fields into the stores and offices. That had a lot to do with it." The Griffins also noted that the decline of neighborhood mutual aid forced landowners to use more mechanical equipment. Mrs. Griffin said that her husband had once stripped peanuts from vines using a stationary picker. In this process, neighbors pitched in to pull ripe peanut vines from the ground, and carry them to the stationary picker that stripped the nuts from the vines. Mrs. Griffin explained, "See, neighbors did it [helped with the peanut harvest]. They helped each other." Once the neighbors were not available to help with the peanut harvest, Mr. Griffin switched to a tractor-drawn peanut-picking machine.

As the story progressed, interviewer Lu Ann Jones probed the sequence of the change. She asked, "[D]id machines replace labor that had gone, or did machines come in and then labor left? So far as you're concerned?" A. C. Griffin replied, "Really and truly now, there was a little bit of both there. There was a little bit of both. I reckon the machinery, when it come in, like it is today really, run 'em off the farm. What few there was left. Won't too many left. But they had to go, too. But in preparing the ground, ground wasn't prepared as good with teams as the tractors and stuff done it. . . . You could cultivate a whole lot more land [with machines]."[22] As the Griffins' story unfolds, a protracted process becomes apparent: some workers left the land in search of better prospects. Farmers replaced the lost manpower with equipment that did a better job on many farm tasks, in turn reducing the need for the rest of the landless workers.

Many landowners came to see sharecroppers and tenants as financially draining. John B. Laney, a Mississippi farmer ten years younger than A. C. Griffin, told an interviewer, "[T]hat's when I bought two cotton pickers of my own. I had all those tenants but I had to cut 'em down 'cause I couldn't keep 'em. [In 1954] I had fifty-one tenants on twelve hundred acres. . . . And shoot, that fall I wrote off twenty-some thousand in bad accounts. They couldn't pay me." Laney meant that his sharecroppers had not cleared enough money on their cotton crops to pay off their accumulated furnishing debts. He went on, "I helped 'em find homes. . . . I cut 'em to thirty-three [tenants]. The next year I cut 'em to twenty. And the next year I just cut 'em out. . . . [I]t just got prohibitive. . . . It was just a drag to have tenants. We let 'em work by the day, but they gradually drifted off the farms. Well, some of 'em went to town and some of 'em went north, as they called it."[23] In short, Laney got rid of his sharecroppers because it was not profitable to use them anymore. He presents himself as a benevolent employer: he helped his former sharecroppers find homes. But he also believes himself to be a clear-eyed businessman who mechanized because it made more financial sense to use mechanical cotton pickers than to provide the annual furnish for sharecroppers.

The way landowners constructed the story of the displacement of tenants is striking. Not one mentioned federal agricultural programs, such as acreage reduction plans, as playing a role in their decisions to reduce the number of sharecroppers. This omission is particularly conspicuous given the extensive documentation of landlords' New Deal–era practice of using Agricultural Adjustment Administration (AAA) crop reduction payments to buy farm equipment and their expulsion of unneeded tenants as they reduced acreage during the New Deal.[24] Historians' analysis is supported by letters from sharecroppers who found themselves displaced by federally mandated acreage reductions. For example, in December 1938, Mrs. Minnie Adcock of Joelton, Tennessee, wrote a desperate appeal to President Roosevelt for intervention with local Works Progress Administration officials. She explained, "I don't know what to do I have been all over Davidson [County] and others too and I can't find a vacant house no where they all say no I dont [sic] need no body the acreage is cut. . . . [Y]ou had all this done to help the farmers well it shure has got us in a mess us poor tenants I have no home no place to live the coming year tell me what to do I cant [sic] get a WPA job I have got to move from the place I live."[25] As letters like Mrs. Adcock's demonstrate, federal policy provided powerful incentives for landowners to evict tenants, and they often did so. Even after the end of AAA programs, complex federally mandated allotment programs continued to regulate how many acres a landowner could cultivate. Nevertheless, landowners do not remember federal policy as a major factor in their decisions to discontinue the use of sharecroppers. Instead they often maintain that sharecroppers left for better opportunities, and when they do admit deciding to eliminate sharecroppers, they construct it as a logical business decision. They most frequently describe mechanization as a response to sharecropper flight.

Some of the postwar generation of farmers blamed the flight of farm laborers on social welfare programs provided by local, state, and federal agencies beginning with the New Deal. White Arkansas farmer L. D. Brantley, born in 1926, began farming in the late 1940s on rented land, eventually saving enough to purchase his own farm. He told an interviewer, "We have trouble keeping help on the farm today. But back then, you just could get more [help] than you could pay for, if you wanted it. And it was good help. But today—and I'm not saying it's not good—but all the welfare programs and this type of thing, they haven't got any incentive to work. Like I say, I'm not saying it's not good, 'cause it does a lot of good, but it does a lot of other things, too. My gosh, we didn't know what welfare was back then, I don't guess."[26] Brantley's contemporary, North Carolina landowner John William Andrews, told an interviewer: "I'll tell you who's wrecked the farmer. Them people up in Washington has really wrecked the farmer because they have made it so easy for people to be on welfare. But you know, what's happened people just go out here and get money now without working. And we've got so much of that. People that are able to work, but yet they'll go down here in these offices and they'll start putting on this pitiful tale and that pitiful tale. And the social worker ought to get out here and examine this thing, come out here and see what's going on."[27] In the view of Brantley and Andrews, landowners could not find farmworkers in part because the government paid jobless people not to work. The fact that most jobs for farmworkers would have been temporary and low-wage did not enter into landowners' understanding of landless people's preference for government assistance instead of farmwork.

South Carolina landowner Tom B. Cunningham implicitly acknowledged the shortcomings of farm laborer jobs when he told an interviewer a story about his attempts to hire hands in the 1950s and 1960s. He said, "There again, the welfare people got involved and was furnishing these people, and it was wonderful that they did, during the seasons of the year when there was no work for them." Cunningham's language indicates that he believed that social service agencies had replaced the landlord in the old landlord/cropper arrangement: the "welfare people . . . was furnishing" the poor, providing them with money for subsistence. Landlords had once shouldered the burden of "furnishing" tenants by providing credit for food and clothing throughout the year as a means of assuring themselves a stable workforce throughout the growing season. When landlords no longer needed a stable workforce for most of the year, they depended on government agencies to provide for the landless, and they lobbied local welfare officials to force public assistance clients to do farmwork at peak seasons. For example, during the New Deal, public assistance officials in southern counties routinely fired WPA workers at harvest time in order to force them to work for local farmers at prevailing (usually lower) wages. Cunningham alluded to this practice as he continued his story:

But then they decided that if those people didn't hoe cotton in the spring or pick cotton in the fall, that check would go year 'round. It would continue to come. . . . I had two women that I depended on to get pickers for me, cotton pickers or hoe hands. . . . So I went to visit one of those women one day and she said, "Mr. Tom, I hate to tell you this." I said, "What's that?" [She] said, "The welfare department tell me that if I go in your field and work, they'll cut off my check. And they pay me more in that check than I can make working for you. And I know you can't pay me that much, 'cause if you do you can't pay your debts. I understand that. But I just can't afford not to keep on getting that check." I told her, . . . "I understand." Well, that changed the complexion again as far as farm labor was concerned, and farmers had to turn to chemicals.[28]

Cunningham's story illustrates one way in which landowners believed themselves to be victims of federal interference: various federal social welfare programs had reduced the availability of farm laborers. Federal relief programs offered disadvantaged people an alternative to poorly paying seasonal jobs as farm laborers. Cunningham was willing to concede that government intervention to help the rural poor was acceptable, and in fact desirable, if it did not undermine landowners' efforts to obtain cheap labor at peak seasons. He nonetheless resented social welfare programs that inhibited his ability to hire low-wage workers when he needed them.

Both landowners and laborers understood themselves as reacting to circumstances rather than forcing change. The gap between landowners' and tenants' memories of the process of farmworker displacement reveals something of the way that class-based experiences shaped their understandings of rural transformation. The landless frequently felt that they had been pushed off the land by mechanization. Landowners, by insisting that their farmworkers either left the countryside in search of other types of work or that they declined to do farmwork in favor of social welfare payments, could depict mechanization as a sensible adaptation to the changing labor market and themselves as reasonable and compassionate men who dealt fairly with their workers.

Leaving the Land:
Landless and Landowning Prewar Whites

If stories about sharecropper displacement reveal the way that class shaped narrators' memories of transformation, stories about leaving the land illuminate the complex interactions of class, race, and generation in shaping memory stories about change. The twentieth-century depopulation of the southern countryside and the decline of farming as the primary occupation there wrought a profound reorganization in the lives of millions. Oral history narratives about this diaspora are fraught with contradictions and tensions. Narrators' memories about the process that led to this diaspora gave understanding and meaning to the changes in their own lives.

White farmers in the generation that came of age before World War II tended to shape their stories about leaving the land so as to depict themselves as engaging in a certain amount of choice. This was true whether they owned land or not. Historian John Bodnar, in his study of Ohio autoworkers who lost their jobs when Studebaker closed, notes that their oral histories usually located pain and suffering in the lives of others while they portrayed themselves as survivors who landed on their feet.[29] The landless and the prewar generation of landowning farmers adopted the same strategy to describe leaving the land. Some of them admitted pain and suffering while farming, but they rarely talked about undue hardship and struggle after leaving the land. Rural southerners who left the land by mid-century fashioned their accounts of leaving to reflect personal efforts at improving their lives rather than representing themselves as victims buffeted by uncontrollable forces.

Many whites in the prewar generation explained leaving the land as a product of their dislike for farm life. For example, Avery R. Downing, the son of an east Texas landowner, explained,

> I disliked it [farm life] very much. My father was quite disappointed in me, I think, on that score because I always had my head in a book or paper. . . . So I have a biased opinion about life on the farm. I disliked it intensely. Yes, . . . it was full of work. There was always something that had to be done in the field or on the fences or in the woods or in the barns,

horse lots, or somewhere; there was work all the time and I was very envious of my acquaintances who lived in town and didn't have to work.[30]

Downing did leave the farm as an adult, and his memories are striking. Although the privileged son of white landowners, he nonetheless perceived farming as a life of hard physical labor that brought dubious financial rewards. As a result, he sought better opportunities off the land.

Many landless whites concurred with Downing's analysis of the limited rewards available through farming. Alice Grogan Hardin was born in 1911 to white sharecropping parents in Greenville County, South Carolina. At some point in the 1910s, the family had lost their home and possessions to a tornado, but continued sharecropping on thirds for two or three years. By this time, the mid-1920s, the South was in the grips of a prolonged agricultural depression, and the Grogan family's financial position went from bad to worse. When Alice was fifteen, her family moved to the Woodside mill village. There her mother, father, and the older children, including Alice, took jobs in the textile mill. She explained her father's reason for deciding to leave the farm, "Things got tough in the country the way they started doing, so he just went and asked for a job, and they give us a job and a house." Alice reported that the children enjoyed mill work because they worked their shift and were done, but she added, "I don't think my father liked it at all, because he had rather be on the farm." Later in the interview, she elaborated on their reasons for leaving the farm, "Farming, where you rented, was getting difficult to make a living. That's the reason we moved to the mill."[31] Hardin used the terms "renter" and "sharecropper" interchangeably, a common practice among rural southerners, but her description of the terms of her family's "rent"—one-third of the crop to the landlord, clarifies that the Grogans' legal status was that of sharecroppers. Hardin remembered two factors that drove her family off the land—hard economic times combined with the exploitative system of sharecropping.

Many narrators noted that jobs in town seemed to promise a level of financial security not found on the farm. Some cited visits from relatives who had taken jobs in distant towns as the catalyst for decisions to leave the land. For example, Mary Harrington grew up on a farm near Danville, Virginia. Her sister had left the farm for public work, and other sisters soon followed. Harrington explained, "It all come from her leaving [the farm]. We just ventured out because we didn't have a lot to do down in the country. We had a good chance to come and stay [with the sister in town], and we'd find some work to do."[32] C. P. Horn, a white man born in 1917 on a farm in rural Clay County, Alabama, told an interviewer that an uncle who was a physician in Athens, Alabama, made a real impression on him. The uncle was always clean and wearing a Sunday suit. More important, his uncle was rich in the eyes of young C. P.; he owned two or three farms, apparently worked by tenants. So when C. P.'s sister, a teacher, offered to put him through medical school, he jumped at the chance. Eventually he returned to Clay County to practice.[33] Other narrators reported that parents encouraged them to seek off-farm jobs. When white Texan D. Y. McDaniel finished college at Baylor University around 1920, he told his landowning father that he wanted to join him on the farm.

> [Dad] said: "Well, I'd like for you to get a profession." And he named a man there who was a doctor who had never practiced medicine. But said, "He can go to practicing medicine any time he wants to." He said, "You know I haven't got much education, and I'm just a farmer, and if anything happened to me financially, why I'd have to be a tenant farmer. I don't know anything else. And I don't want that to happen to you. I want you to get a profession, so then, if you want to farm you come home; I'll be glad for you to do it. But get a profession, whatever you want to do, that you can fall back on. . . . That's what I'd want you to do. That's really what, you asked me what about it, that's what I want." Well, that's what he got.[34]

McDaniel became a lawyer and later a judge.

Several narrators remembered that high-paying jobs created by World War II mobilization were a major factor in their own or another family member's decision to leave the land. When asked why people started leaving her community, white Texan Opal Bateman explained that it was mostly because of the war. "The defense work and the army taken [*sic*] a lot of people out of the community, I would say."[35] Loudoun County, Virginia, farmer Curtis Poland concurred, "[The] turning point was in World War II when they took all the young men off the farm. When they come back out of the service the ones that had survived never went back to the farm."[36] Poland implies that once young men had seen the opportunities available off the farm, they never wanted to return to working the land.

Just as they did not mention the federal government's role in transforming agriculture, in their oral history narratives, the prewar generation of whites did not see the federal government as playing any role in their decisions to stop farming. This omission is striking when compared to correspondence that the same prewar generation of farm people sent to New Deal agencies during the 1930s, letters like the previously mentioned one from Minnie Adcock. Instead, whites who came of age before World War II constructed decisions to leave the land as clear choices between prosperity and poverty, between relative ease or significant hardship. To some extent these narrators had been scarred by twenty years of agricultural depression. They depicted themselves as eagerly seizing opportunities for a better life. For most, it paid off. Sociologist Arthur G. Neal has noted that "Through confronting hard times and moving beyond them, an older generation of Americans came to hold a special appreciation for the material abundance of the postwar years. . . . For the generation seriously scarred by the Great Depression, economic prosperity was not taken as self-evident. Knowing what both hard times and prosperity were like contributed to a keen awareness of the limitations and prospects of the human condition."[37] Prewar southern farm people rarely expressed regret at having left the land. Instead, they believed that leaving the farm had offered them financial security and even success.

Racial Oppression, the Federal Government, and Leaving the Land

African Americans also left the land in search of better lives, but their stories about leaving the land are more ambivalent, complex, and varied. To an even greater extent than whites of the prewar generation, African Americans were likely to express outright antipathy for life on the land. Black Mississippian O. C. Gibson's father sharecropped cotton in LeFlore County, Mississippi, "the only way you could farm back then." He told an interviewer, "They stopped farming with mules . . . and I was glad of it. . . . I ain't never wanted to farm. I ain't never liked the cotton. I was born, raised up in it, but I never liked it. I said, if I ever get to the place where I don't have to pick and chop no cotton, [I won't]." Gibson finished high school and worked in a cottonseed oil mill, ran a store, and worked for Baldwin Piano. He never picked cotton again.[38] Mary Shipp, an African American woman from Georgia, told an interviewer, "I hated that farm religiously." Shipp, born in 1927, was the third of five children born to struggling landowners who supplemented their income with day labor for neighboring farmers. The family had inherited the land from her paternal grandparents, and Shipp noted that her father's brothers all left the family farm in their twenties because "they hated the South and they hated their lives." They went to Detroit where they found manufacturing jobs, but her father "was a farmer at heart." Mary Shipp shared the views of her uncles. She told an interviewer that on the farm, the family lived in poor-quality housing. Shipp also complained that she felt isolated in the country, five miles from stores and from schools. She recalled that white children would throw things from their school bus at black children who were walking to school. Mary Shipp remembered her childhood on a marginal farm in the Jim Crow South with a sharp clarity and much pain. She said, "It was so hard I don't even like to recall it, but it was a part of our life." Shipp's father died when she was ten, and unable to pay their father's debts, the surviving family members lost the one-hundred-acre farm. They moved to town to live with Shipp's grandmother. Mary loved living in town. She eventually earned a college degree and then became a teacher and a licensed beautician.[39] Shipp's memories of the material hardships of farm life mixed with memories of overt racism. The only logical choice for a better life, in her mind, had been leaving the land, and she was thrilled to do so.

Like the prewar generation of whites, African Americans remembered that the difficulty in making an adequate living drove them off the land and that relatives who had left years earlier demonstrated hope for a better life elsewhere. African American farmer William Rucker explained, "Most of the people left when the boll weevil came here. I was quite small. 1921. In '21 they started leaving here going everywhere. In 1928 when the bottom dropped out during the Depression, cotton came from 30 cent down to five cent. They just couldn't make it. They started to leaving. . . . A lot of 'em went to Chicago, Philadelphia, Detroit. My brothers—one of 'em went to Cleveland, Ohio, and the other one went to Detroit. My sister went to Charlotte, North Carolina. They just left."[40]

As with landless whites, World War II also created new opportunities for African Americans. Black Texan Ophelia Hall recalled that her older brother R. G. Mayberry married and moved to Waco to work as a porter for Greyhound during World War II. She said that the main reason he left Gatesville was "There wasn't anything to do. . . . He got enough [of farming]. It seemed like that was for the poor starving people there was farming in those days. And the droughts come one right after another and we weren't able to raise too much of anything. So—so he had no desire to stay . . . out on the farm."[41]

The prevalence of stories about hating life on the land among African Americans suggests that racial oppression played a major role in their decisions to leave farming. In the first decade of the twentieth century, journalist Ray Stannard Baker asked southern blacks why their peers were leaving the farms for the cities. He was told it was due to the lack of educational opportunities in the country, ill treatment from landlords, and the "lack of protection."[42] Although 11.4 percent of the interviews included in my study were with African American sharecroppers, stories about the mistreatment of sharecroppers emerged infrequently, and the storytellers were often vague about the nature of the mistreatment. Nonetheless, African Americans' stories about sharecropping were marked by persistent references to race, references that indicate the extent to which black farmers saw racism and economic exploitation as intertwined. For example, black former Texas sharecropper Eugene Webster noted, "Sharecrop—that was the white man furnish everything and . . . you do the work and get half the crop. That's the way they said it was done, but they were taking half of it. . . . They were taking it all away. Black man didn't have a chance."[43] Significantly, Webster couches his indictments of the exploitive sharecropping system in racial terms— "white man furnish" and "black man didn't have a chance." Jessie

Easter, a sharecropper from the Mississippi Delta, also saw race as a key element in the exploitation of sharecroppers. She told historian Valerie Grim that she moved to the Midwest because "Surrounded by cotton and cotton fields, you felt, at times, that you could not get out and no one could get to you because you was livin' in a closed off community where you did not see many things or folks from the outside. . . . So the only way to escape the madness caused by greed and the power white folks got from raisin' King Cotton was to run, run, and run away as fast and far as you could."[44] Other African Americans recalled that economic exploitation could be accompanied by physical abuse, and that women on isolated farms had little protection from abuse from landlords and husbands alike. Annie West, a black woman born in the Mississippi Delta, told Grim that she left the Delta for a Midwestern city because "there was no way to be protected from physical, sexual, and spousal abuse [in the South]. The law was not interested in keepin' black field women safe from any kind of attack, so the fields because they were so far from town and the lack of enforcement of the law, worked together and actually became a form of imprisonment for many women."[45]

One black landowning farmer told particularly detailed stories about the abuses of the sharecropping system, some of which he had witnessed among his neighbors. Georgian William Rucker told an interviewer that "[T]he sharecroppers usually paid for everything— all the fertilizer, all the everything out of the half that they made and a lot of 'em would move off every year. When they moved off they went to somebody that was just about as bad, or maybe worse, than the one that they were working with." The interviewer asked if Rucker knew of cases of sharecroppers being abused, and he replied, "Yeah, they were abused. When I say abused, not necessarily whipping but taking everything that they made. Some of those sharecroppers moved off, [the landlord] even took the cows, the hogs, whatever they had from them." When asked if he knew of specific cases in which that happened, he said, "Well, I wouldn't want to personate. But I do know cases." Another man present for the interview, Welchel Long, a leader in black farmers' fight against the FmHA, interjected, "They run 'em off when they got the crop made." Rucker agreed, "Yeah, yeah, they run 'em off." Long meant that landowners sometimes evicted tenants without compensating them after tenants had worked on the crop most of the year. Rucker concluded, "That's what had been happening all the time. And then a lot of farmers just got tired of it and they left, went on everywhere else. And I don't blame 'em."[46] For black sharecroppers in the Jim Crow South, challenging a white landowner for breaking a contract or otherwise acting illegally was usually fruitless at best and potentially dangerous. According to Rucker, many chose to leave the land after years of exploitation and abuse.

Even relatively prosperous African American farmers who avoided the trap of sharecropping blamed various forms of racial discrimination for black farmers' decisions to leave farming. Born in 1917, black Georgian James Hall grew up on a sharecropping farm in Lee County. As an adult, Hall farmed as a cash renter. He recalled that in 1939, he cleared $1,800 on his crops. With his profits, he had enough money to pay off his bills and to farm without borrowing operating cash the next year. He enjoyed another good year in 1940. Hall explained that in the spring of 1941, his landlord insisted that he agree to turn over the sale of his crop to the landlord. In other words, the landlord planned to transport the crop to market and negotiate the sale, paying Hall from the proceeds. Landlords frequently used this strategy to cheat sharecroppers. Such a landlord would claim that a crop had sold for less than the actual market price, pay the cropper the smaller proceeds, and pocket the difference. Apparently, Hall's landlord hoped to use the same tactic with Hall, a cash renter. The landlord made renewal of the lease on the land contingent on Hall's agreement to allow the landlord to take over marketing of the crop. Hall refused and moved to another rented farm. By the late 1940s, Hall had saved $3,900, enough money to buy sixty acres. He continued farming his own land until 1989, and he and his wife still owned that land at the time of the interview in 1994. In spite of his success, Hall noted the difficulties that black farmers faced. He told an interviewer, "All the Negroes now has done moved to town. . . . They couldn't get nothing to do." His wife added, "The land belongs to the white people. They have the tractors and all this chemicals; they don't have to hoe their crops. Cotton pickers, peanut pickers and all that stuff. . . . So that's what causes black folks to have to migrate to town."[47] Implicit in Mrs. Hall's account is an indictment of institutionalized racism that made it extremely difficult for black farmers to buy land, obtain annual operating credit, or qualify for loans to make capital investments in their operations. As Black Georgian Mary Shipp concluded, black farmers "is almost extinct, especially in the South. . . . It was hard to make it as a black farmer because many of the things that was available to white farmers were not available to black farmers."[48]

Black North Carolinian James Lewis explained that not many people in his childhood community were farming anymore, even if they had held on to their land:

> Much of the land that's owned by blacks is being rented by whites. And that's about the only way I guess that a farmer can make it is use a lot of land. Got to have acreage. . . . [Black people] don't have the facilities. You got to have a tractor. See if you're not farming, I'd say 300 acres, if you're not farm-ing 300 acres, why you'll go in the hole real fast. Fertilizer is high. Seeds are high. Labor is high. And I remember the time when I was growing up, if a farmer went to the fertilizer plant to buy fertilizer they would deliver it and say "you pay me in September." They don't do that no more.[49]

Lewis's story reveals the complex obstacles faced even today by blacks who aspire to farm. First, as he implies, most black landowners held relatively small amounts of land, hardly enough to farm profitably in today's agricultural economy, a world where farming on a large scale is often key to financial survival. He also illuminates the changes in the farm credit system and the unintended consequences for black farmers. In earlier times, most agribusinesses such as farm supply stores and fertilizer manufacturers were small and locally owned. Local businesses usually extended credit to local farmers, men whose credit-worthiness was well established in the community. Respected black farmers as well as white might receive credit from local busi-nesses. Most of this locally based operating credit disappeared by the last quarter of the twentieth century. Farm supply stores often became part of national chains or members of a statewide network of farmers' cooperatives. These larger operations forced farmers to apply for a line of credit in the manner of small businesses, and they rarely deemed the smallest farmers credit-worthy. Federal and quasi-federal agencies became the major source of farm operating loans. In a recent settlement of a class-action racial discrimination lawsuit filed by black farmers, U.S. District Court judge Paul Friedman found that "for decades . . . the Department of Agriculture . . . discriminated against African American farmers when they denied, delayed, or otherwise frustrated the applications of those farmers for loans and other credit and benefit programs."[50] In short, some black farmers could get credit earlier in the century when it was supplied by local businesses, but not after it was supplied by national chains or federal agencies. Lewis's tale indicates that even landowning blacks found it nearly impossible to farm successfully in a modern capitalist economy and that racial oppression persisted. Lewis himself did not attempt to farm. He earned a college degree in electrical engineering with the help of the GI Bill and worked for Douglas Aircraft as an adult.

William Rucker, the Georgia landowner quoted above, had a dim view of federal agricultural agencies' treatment of African American farmers. He told Lu Ann Jones that the federal acreage reduction system had often left black farmers at the mercy of white landowners because it gave the landowners control over acreage reduction payments and allowed them to determine the sharecroppers' share of other returns. He said that the landowners "kept the records and what do you know if you've got a record out there and now you just stand by your memory and somebody putting down a record out there what you getting. How you gonna prove that you did get it or you didn't get it. The system to me, isn't much." Jones asked Rucker to whom he referred when he said "the system" and he said, "I'm talking about the practices that the federal government put out. The intention of the system was good, but the people who carried it out, some of 'em were poor."[51] Rucker had received his own farm loans from the Farmer's Home Administration (FmHA), but he nonetheless criticized FmHA, blaming the agency for the death of another farmer in his community. According to Rucker, "Julian Clark is dead and in his grave. They killed him. Julian Clark died because you're always pushing something on people, you've got to do this." Rucker's friend Welchel Long picked up the story. He explained Clark had purchased a farm. In order to obtain production loans from the FmHA, Clark routinely implemented federal officials' recommended farming practices, borrowing ever-larger sums in order to do so. As Rucker explained, "They had him growing hogs, buying feed. He was losing money. Hogs were selling at 12 cent a pound, on the foot. There's no way in the world you can grow a hog and buy feed and sell it for 12 cent a pound. The black ag teacher trying to tell him it couldn't be done, and that's [raising hogs] the only way they would loan him some money. . . . Every time they would sell hogs, he'd be some 500 more dollars in debt. . . . Finally, they wouldn't let him have no hog money or nothing else. He lost all his credit." Eventually, according to Long, continual pressure from FmHA and threats of a lawsuit from a local bank who held an outstanding loan left Clark "scared to death," and the man died of a stroke. "Worried that old man to death," Long concluded.

Like Rucker and Long, Black Mississippian Howard Taft Bailey was critical of federal agricultural agencies. He dated the federal government's discrimination against black farmers all the way back to the New Deal. When asked about federal efforts at production control, the landowner said, "That put a lot of black farmers out of business. That was in 1932 [actually 1933] when that federal program came in, and they'd give the white man that had a family—sometimes they'd just have two in the family were working twelve and fourteen acres and sometimes a black man couldn't hardly get eight acres." He explained that he had been successful in switching to other crops when his cotton allotment was cut. Bailey noted that until the civil rights movement "shook the [allotment] board up and made 'em kinda equalize the acreage," black farmers had had little recourse for such injustices. Bailey was also critical of FmHA. He said, "You go there and put in for FHA [FmHA] loans, a lot of 'em went to FHA. But the black folks with the FHA loan, they'd give just enough to barely make a crop and the white, shoot, they'd let him have money to hire labor and just do everything."[52]

African Americans told their stories about deciding to leave the land differently than their white neighbors, and their stories indicted the racist systems that disadvantaged black farmers. Some were thrilled to quit farming, and they were happy with the financial security they found through off-farm jobs and the improved social and material life in town. Others expressed bitterness at the forces that made it impossible for many blacks to remain on the land even as white neighbors farmed successfully. Regardless of whether they found satisfaction or disappointment in leaving the land, African Americans nonetheless talked about racism—including institutionalized racism practiced by federal agencies—as a contributing factor to their decisions to stop farming.

Postwar White Landowners and Decisions to Stop Farming

The postwar generation experienced an escalating pace of change. Most landless people left farming by the 1960s, leaving fewer farmers who farmed on a significantly larger scale. Farmers in the last half of the twentieth century struggled to succeed in the face of more and more factors that were beyond their control. High overhead costs, low commodity prices, and increasing foreign competition squeezed American farmers. Moreover, shifts in federal agricultural policy made the postwar generation of farmers increasingly dependent on the federal government for financial survival and ever more aware of the federal government's role in reshaping agriculture. As a result, many blamed the federal government for allowing the development of conditions that forced them and their neighbors off the land. The postwar generation's stories of leaving the land are poignant descriptions by people struggling to understand the changes engulfing them.

People who began farming after 1950 were especially likely to cite the difficulty in covering the expenses of hybrid seed, chemical fertilizers and pesticides, machinery, interest on operating loans, and the high cost of land as reasons they left farming. North Carolina landowning farmer Grace Griffin told an interviewer:

> But the thing now with farming is you don't break even anymore. Farmers have got head over heels in debt with this high-priced machinery. The export business has dropped off. In fact, people are raising so much more on a certain amount of acreage than they ever did before. We raise enough right here in this country to feed the world. What they get for what they sell is not equal to what they pay for what it takes to produce the crop. And they're in trouble. Seriously in

trouble. . . . Money lenders is responsible for part of it. Here a few years ago it was doing a brisk export business. Bankers and home loan folks were encouraging farmers to expand, to acquire more land. Easy credit. . . . You could get credit with no security at all, near 'bout. Everything was on the up and up, at that time. So many farmers, especially out in the Midwest, went ahead and acquired a lot of acreage with a high interest rate. Now the export business has failed. The crop production has exceeded the demand. And they cannot meet their obligations at the bank and the foreclosures is just everywhere.[53]

In Griffin's mind, a complex set of changes in the agricultural economy drove people off the land.

Former Virginia dairy farmer Joan Moore explained why she and her husband sold their dairy operation: "[B]asically what occurred—of course farm prices were down, all produce was down, beef was down. What was more important were the land values in Loudoun County were out of sight. Could we have convinced the cows to have triplets, a time or two a year, we might have stayed in it. We had eight children to educate, and we couldn't do it. . . . It was one of the worst days of my life. We had an auction up at the barns. I could not go up there."[54] In other words, the Moores could not afford to expand their herd at a fast-enough rate to maintain profitability. To make matters worse, real estate development pressures intensified. Loudoun County, Virginia, is home to Dulles International Airport. Land values in this rapidly developing Washington, D.C., suburb had been climbing steadily since the airport opened in the 1960s, and prices skyrocketed during the 1990s. Farmers could no longer afford to buy land for expansion and were lured into selling by inflated real estate prices. Former pastures and fields that the county's many dairy farmers once rented had become the sites of new subdivisions. Skyrocketing valuation of real estate also brought rising property taxes, which farmers found increasingly difficult to pay. Joan Moore constructed her stories about leaving the land as a choice, but a choice between a bad set of options: the family could continue the financial struggle of farming or they could leave the farm they loved in order to support and educate their eight children as they wanted. Although not all southern farmers were pushed off the land by the forces of suburbanization, many who lived near major metropolitan areas like Atlanta, Dallas/Fort Worth, and Charlotte faced similar challenges as the Moores.

Farmers also understood that they could not control commodity prices. They attempted to cope with fluctuating and unpredictable prices by careful management and calculated investment. Charles Bailey of Mississippi was born in 1919 on a sharecropping operation. As an adult, he sharecropped on his own for a time before taking a job with the state highway department. Bailey served in the U.S. Army in North Africa and Italy during World War II, and after the war he worked at a service station and then as a plantation manager. Eventually he was able to purchase land with a Farmer's Home Administration loan. He raised soybeans, cotton, and pecans, but at the time of the interview in 1987, he owed $90,000 to FmHA and was nearly bankrupt. He could no longer borrow operating funds, so he did not farm, instead subsisting on $3,300 a year in disabled veteran and social security checks. He told an interviewer, "Our prices is what we can't deal with." He went on to say that low commodity prices had caused him to go broke. He said, "We planted some beans expecting to get seven dollars [per bushel] for 'em and we turn around and get five for 'em, see. That two dollars a bushel makes a lot of difference."[55]

The postwar generation, though they sometimes praised federal agricultural programs and called for more of them, were also quick to blame the federal government for making farming untenable. Increased federal regulation created new challenges for farmers, and many claimed they left the land because they could not afford to comply with regulations. Loudoun County, Virginia, dairy farmer Lehon Hamilton explained, "Of course you had a dairy inspector that come out of Washington. He was a health inspector, too. Every time he would come around and inspect you, . . . he would say, 'You need to do this, and you need to do that.' More or less, the profit that you made you had to put back into it, modernize. In other words, they wanted pipeline milkers. They wanted tanks, which is what they've got today. . . . That's where all of our profit was going in, to try to modernize. We decided to maybe get into another business."[56] The narrators who tended to blame the federal government for their problems, like Lehon Hamilton, quit farming in the 1980s and 1990s.

Even farmers who managed to continue farming were bitter about what they saw as federal policies that harmed farmers. In 1986, Arkansas rice farmer Jessie Gosney explained that 1983 had been the Gosneys' last good year farming. She said, "But if you remember the government was bringing people from other countries over here, educating 'em in our land-grant colleges. We sent fertilizer; we sent equipment to foreign countries while they embargoed our crops. We were helping Brazil learn to raise soybeans, developing strands in our colleges for their climate and their conditions. They've plowed up the rain forests. They're going to ruin their country." Her husband added, "See, that's what killed us. We raised these expensive crops and then couldn't sell [them]. The cost of production just went up so fast. Of course, we wouldn't be here today if I hadn't loaded up with good equipment in the '70s. Of course, the reason for that is I needed tax write-offs, needed it bad. I was in a very high tax bracket. But after '83, that reversed. . . . This has reversed and we're [rice farmers] operating at a loss now."[57] The Gosneys do not oversimplify. They understand the role of rising costs and global competition in making farming unprofitable. Nonetheless, they blame the government, in the guise of land grant colleges, for providing foreigners with the knowledge that they needed to compete with American farmers. Thus, in the eyes of the Gosneys, even foreign competition was the federal government's fault.

William and Kate Graham told a more complex and bitter story. They farmed inherited land in Lee County, South Carolina, abandoning cotton for peanuts and soybeans by the end of the century. The couple explained that in 1977 they had been forced to turn to Farmer's Home Administration for their annual operating loan—the money they borrowed each spring to buy seed, fertilizer, and other supplies they needed for making a crop. William Graham said, "We had figured out we needed a hundred and fifty thousand or something like that. And . . . that guy [at Farmer's Home Administration] said, 'Well, I figured out you can get more than that.' And we took it. About twenty or twenty-five more thousand dollars." At this point in his story, Graham laughed ruefully before continuing: "And he said, 'Now to pay this back, you'll have to pay thirty-two thousand dollars a year.' And I didn't realize, well, that's above everything. Your living, paying all the bills, they wanted $32,000, and I was a fool to think that I could pay them that above everything else." Kate Graham continued the story:

> And then the next year when we went, we hadn't paid them all back. I went with William [to the Farmer's Home Administration office]. They said, 'Well, now this year, you can borrow this much.' And I said, 'Wait a minute. We hadn't paid last year's yet. We're not borrowing until we can pay that back.' Well the land had appreciated, and we could get this much more. And like William said, you know, they talked us into taking more than there was any way we could ever pay back. I mean, if everything had been perfect, if prices had been good, we still could not have paid it back. So I began, at that point, and I guess William began at that point also, to feel like we were being used and abused. . . . Because if you cannot make a profit, you cannot stay in business. And there was no way that we could make a profit. I think that one year, we made, we got as much for our cotton as William's great-grandfather had during the War Between the States.

The Grahams' statements illuminate the very real pressures that low commodity prices and rising operating costs placed on farmers, pressures that drove them to take on large levels of debt. Significantly, though the Grahams lament their own mistaken choice to borrow more money than they needed—William Graham mentions that he failed to realize that the annual payment on their FmHA loan would be "above everything," in addition to all other expenses—they reserve most of their venom for FmHA. They believe that FmHA had enticed them to borrow too much. Indeed in the boom times of the 1980s, local FmHA officials were often evaluated in part on the volume of loans they made, so perhaps the Grahams' feelings were not entirely misplaced.

The Grahams did not give up on farming without a fight. Both Grahams were part of the American Agriculture Movement's tractorcade, when farmers drove their tractors to Washington to protest federal farm policy in 1979. Kate became active with the farm lobbying organization Women in Farm Economics (WIFE). Organized in 1976, WIFE was a grassroots organization of farm women "dedicated to improving profitability in production agriculture through educational, legislative, communicative and cooperative efforts."[58] WIFE members educated themselves and their neighbors about farm policy issues, lobbied their legislators to support government programs that aided family farmers, and worked with other farm organizations as an effort to survive the farm crisis of the 1980s. Kate Graham's involvement with WIFE made her feel as if she were fighting on behalf of her family farm, but her lobbying trips only increased her disillusionment with the federal government. She recounted the senators' rudeness and lack of attention as she testified before the Senate agriculture subcommittee on behalf of WIFE and farm families:

> The first time I went in there, there were . . . four senators in there. But two of them were sitting and talking and the other two were standing up talking at each other. You know how that is. . . . "My learned colleague this, my learned colleague that." You know I thought that I was going to hear them say, "You know this country really does need agriculture" or something. But do you know what they were talking about? . . . Which school had the number one football team in the nation. I nearly came unglued. I was so angry. I could not believe that. But then . . . I was so angry that when they asked me if I would testify I said, "yes." And so you know, you have to write out your testimony. You have to make 50 copies which they just trash anyway. I don't know why you even bother to do all that. But I started talking, and you know the green light's on while you talk and then the orange one means you have one minute left and then the red one comes on and you have to stop. Well, I let some of my time go by and they said something to me. And I said, "Well, you know, my mother taught me that it was rude to talk when somebody else was talking." [laughs] Talking among themselves, you know, they weren't listening to what I was saying. And we were losing our way of life, our opportunity to make a living. We were losing land that William's grandfather, his great-grandfather had farmed. It was fourth-generation land that we were los-

ing and they cared no more about that than I cared about talking about that football. You know, they DID NOT care. And they care even less now because there are fewer farmers. . . . But I told them in my testimony . . . that it was my prayer that I lived long enough to stand on this side of the Potomac and watch them try and get out of Washington to find food. And that was my very hope, and that's what I said. . . . It was exactly how I felt.

William Graham despaired over their increasing indebtedness, and he considered suicide. He said, "I hated to even admit, it was very hard to tell anybody that I'm quitting. But since that time, farmers that I know are good farmers, I mean they farmed right, they had to quit." Eventually all the Grahams' efforts to remain on the land failed. They staved off foreclosure until 1999, when they sold their land and their home to liquidate their debt.[59]

Antigovernment sentiment on the part of farmers was not new, of course. Farmers have been simultaneously resisting government interference and asking for government help since the nineteenth century. Historian Catherine McNicol Stock notes, "Hatred of and dependence on the federal government has long been a part of rural politics." She locates much of farmers' antigovernment feeling in their opposition to "bigness"—big landowners, big speculators, big business, big government. By the twentieth century, family farmers saw USDA policies as promoting bigness.[60] As a result, farmer criticism of federal policies intensified in the 1980s and 1990s. For farmers like the Grahams, the federal government provided a convenient target for their anger over losing their land. Even as they criticized the government for too much interference in farming, they demanded more government aid. By blaming elected and appointed policymakers, FmHA officials, and others, narrators could hold real people, rather than faceless market forces, responsible for their failures. Indeed, they could even avoid confronting their own miscalculations and poor decisions.

Nor was farmers' anger at the federal government particularly misplaced. In the 1970s, 1980s, and 1990s, farm policy became a constantly shifting political football as Congress and a succession of presidential administrations sought to balance farmers' demands for higher commodity prices in the face of escalating foreign competition with consumers' demands for lower food prices. Even attempts to reduce farmers' dependence on the government failed. For example, the so-called Freedom to Farm Act of 1996 was intended to wean farmers from federal payments over the course of seven years. Instead, the collapse of both the export market and domestic prices drove Congress to pass several emergency appropriations bills in subsequent years, bills that in essence unraveled the goals of Freedom to Farm. Ironically farmers became more dependent on the federal government instead of less so. In 1996, 21 percent of farm income came from federal payments of various kinds; by 2000, the figure had risen to 40 percent. By the end of the century, southern farmers were more dependent on the federal government for financial survival than ever.[61]

Generations and Communities of Memory

Rural southerners may have shared an inclusive community of memory shaped by their lives on the land, but within that community, smaller groups remembered aspects of rural transformation quite differently. Race and class shaped farm people's narratives of change in significant but not surprising ways. The material differences in the lives of the landless and marginal landowners on the one hand and prosperous landowners on the other generated different experiences of transformation and thus divergent stories about change. Sociologist Robert Bellah and his research colleagues have noted that Americans tend to think "of the ultimate goals of the good life as matters of personal choice."[62] Those people who left the land by midcentury saw their choices as efforts to improve their lives, and they were loath to present the move as anything less than positive or to admit that they were victims of forces beyond individual control. These narrators—mostly poor people—did not perceive themselves as powerless victims of poverty or of government mismanagement. In their minds, while economic conditions may have generated hard times on the land, they chose to leave the farm as a path leading to a better life.

Likewise, the experience of racism in the Jim Crow South shaped African Americans' memories of life on the land and twentieth-century transformations. African Americans had long been the victims of discrimination in myriad forms, and their descriptions of change, like their experiences of that change, were distinctly racialized. Though some narrators were reticent about discussing discrimination, many others confronted racism and economic oppression openly, indicting the society and the government that had perpetrated such oppression.

Race and class shaped competing accounts of the collective rural past, yet generational change molded more dramatic differences. Historian Iwona Irwin-Zarecka notes that, like people who have shared similar life experiences, generations can form communities of memory that are shaped by their experiences of key events—despite having very diverse individual experiences of these events. She notes that such communities of memory are comprised of people who shared the same historical events and were thus "strongly affected in their outlook by a particular time in history."[63] Traumatic experiences cement the most vivid shared memories. Unlike some wars or other traumatic events shared by particular generations, the Great Depression rarely inspires public monuments, but the experience of the Great Depression nonetheless lived on in the shared memories of those who witnessed it. Those hard years affected people's views of life, work, and money in ways that a younger generation could not comprehend. Rural southerners' memories of the hardships of depression years on the land shaped their narratives in important ways. They found easier, more comfortable lives off the land, so they were less likely to lament the leaving or to blame other forces for driving them from the countryside.

In some ways, age and the passage of time may also help to explain the prewar generation's silence about federal intervention in agriculture. Most had either left the land or retired from farming long before they were interviewed. All but the most prosperous had experienced grinding poverty during the agricultural depression of the 1920s and 1930s. They had gone on to build satisfying and more economically successful lives off the land, so they felt little need to blame a distant federal agency for helping to drive them out of farming. French sociologist Maurice Halbwachs, the earliest theorist of collective memory, suggested that in later life, people often failed to express bitterness against people or groups that might have wronged them in the past, because the constraints imposed by those people or groups were no longer active forces in the lives of the people recounting memories.[64] Painful aspects of leaving the land were in the distant past and were no longer central to narrators' understanding of the meaning of leaving the land; thus these painful accounts found no place in memory stories.

The prewar generation may have also shaped their memory stories in ways that allowed them to avoid a wholesale critique of the failures in the economic system that gave rise to their problems. Historian Michael Frisch has noted, "Contemporary contexts . . . operate as a sort of rearguard attack on the structure of memory." Frisch points out the structure and content of the narratives found in Studs Terkel's collection of oral history accounts of the Great Depression, *Hard Times*, demonstrate that people turned "history into biographical memory, general into particular" in ways that allowed deeper validation of their lives and society and allowed them to defer cultural and political judgments about the depression crisis. By making it personal, they did not have to examine the larger historical forces at work. Frisch argues that during the Great Depression, "failure forced people to reduce general experiences to personal terms, the intense pain thereby sheltering them from deeper, more profoundly threatening historical truths." Instead of formulating a critique of capitalism that might have led them to doubt the efficacy of the entire American political economy, narrators used memory to tell a personal story about "hard times," rather than a national story about economic collapse.[65]

The community of memory shared by postwar white farmers also grew out of their experiences on the land, experiences that were significantly different than those of the prewar generation. Before World War II, many rural southerners of both races farmed because they had few other options. If they inherited land, their families expected them to farm, and their rural residences made it difficult to pursue professional or business careers. Marginal landowners and the landless also had few choices. They rarely had the resources to obtain the types of education that would have prepared them for better jobs. Beyond domestic work and lumbering, there were few off-farm jobs in most areas of the countryside. While thousands left family behind to take their chances in distant towns and cities, most rural southerners born early in the century saw farming as their only sensible option. The situation changed drastically during and after World War II. New job opportunities appeared in the southern countryside and in nearby towns and cities. Better roads enabled farm people to commute to jobs off the farm. The consolidation of rural schools and the GI Bill improved educational opportunities for many, and opened new career opportunities. By late century, the widespread availability of financial aid made higher education accessible for most who desired to attend college, and college-educated farm youth could enjoy a wide array of opportunities off the farm. After the war, people who remained on the farm were usually there because they wanted to be.

Just as farming became a more conscious career choice after World War II, farmers developed a new self-definition. Many of the postwar generation aspired to middle-class status, an aspiration reinforced by farm magazine editors and political leaders. Historian Lizabeth Cohen has shown how, in the postwar period, politicians and business leaders peppered their rhetoric with promises that mass consumption and the resulting mass prosperity would raise all workers to the middle class. Agricultural leaders pledged that farmers who adopted industrial farming practices would enjoy the kind of prosperity that would bring them into a middle-class mainstream. Even politicians included farmers in their vision of a broad and prosperous American middle class. For example, in a 1955 speech to the first joint American Federation of Labor and Congress of Industrial Organizations (AFL-CIO) convention, President Eisenhower asserted that Marx's doctrine of class struggle did not foresee that "in America, labor, respected and prosperous, would constitute—with the farmer and businessman—[the] . . . middle class."[66]

In an age when middle-class status came to be seen as the norm in the United States, farmers, too, identified with middle-class values and aspirations. They wanted modern comfortable homes, dependable family cars, vacations, and good educational opportunities for their children. Achieving middle-class status required a steady flow of cash, and the farm press, agribusiness, and USDA officials promised the postwar generation that they could earn a comfortable income if only they adopted specialized, mechanized, commercial farming practices. Many farmers bought into this promise, and in the process, they came to see farming in a different light. They now viewed farming as a profession. Instead of perceiving themselves as people of the land, depending on horse sense and conservative money management practices to get by, many in the postwar generation believed that farmers should be educated and shrewd businessmen. Most earned high school educations including courses in agriculture, and many attended college, often obtaining degrees.[67] They read farm magazines, attended extension service institutes, and generally treated farming as a profession requiring constant professional development. To finance a new style of farming and to maintain middle-class lifestyles even in years when commodity prices plunged, they borrowed increasingly large sums from federally backed farm loan programs. The younger generation of farmers studied the constantly shifting rules and regulations of evolving federal farm programs. They also actively lobbied Congress, usually through mainstream farm organizations, such as the Farm Bureau, for legislation that would benefit farmers.

Finally, members of the postwar generation forced from the land needed an explanation for the calamities that they suffered that mirrored the scope of what had happened to them. Historian Alessandro Portelli has pointed out that narrators need to be able to attribute major life-changing events to "adequate circumstances, causes, and consequences." Their stories are shaped around the idea of adequate causation. In this way memory is used to heal wounds.[68] People like the Grahams need an adequate explanation for the destruction of their way of life, and it is more satisfying to find that cause carries a human face. You cannot place a human face on the global commodities market, but you can on an FmHA loan officer who convinced you to borrow too much money or a senator who trivializes your pain and your predicament.

In short, the postwar generation of landowners believed that adopting the advice of agricultural experts would bring financial success. Initially, they accepted that the direction of change in American agriculture was a positive one. They felt betrayed when the realities of the "new" farming drove them out of business. Being forced to leave the land was to be forced to give up one's professional identity. In addition, anxieties about a loss of middle-class status fed their anger and bitterness. They shaped their memories in ways that attributed their losses to real people—real villains—rather than faceless and impersonal forces.

Rural southerners' narratives of agricultural transformation demonstrate the contingent and contested ways that individuals use memory to give meaning to the past. Although many elements of rural southerners' accounts of transformation were consistent, their memories varied according to gender, race, class, and especially generation. Men's and women's different experiences of rural life shaped different understandings of the implications of change. Similarly, material differences in the lives of the landless and the landowning colored narrators' accounts of rural transformation. Racial discrimination in many forms had persistently disadvantaged black farmers, and as a result, the effects of racism dominated their stories of rural transformation. The generational shift in patterns of memory demonstrates how changing circumstances—changing federal policies, improved educational opportunities, broader exposure to mass media—can reshape the stories people tell about the past. Different generations of farm people told different stories of rural transformation not just because the forces pushing them off the land changed but also because the cultural tools they used to understand the world around them changed.

Chapter Five

The Present Shapes Stories about the Past

Stories that southerners tell about life on the land in the twentieth century tell us much about the common experiences of farm people and about the meanings they ascribed to rural transformation, but they tell us more than that. In the late twentieth century, in the words of historian Ted Ownby, "[T]raditional identities rooted in rural *families* gave way to new identities of urbanizing *individuals* [emphasis in original]."[1] As rural southerners confronted sweeping changes in the ways they viewed themselves and their world, they experienced tensions and anxieties that found voice in their autobiographical narratives. As dozens of examples throughout this book suggest, rural people's stories tell us much about the ways narrators view the world they live in today and the things they feel have been lost in the wake of modernization. As historian David Thelen puts it, "people shape their recollections of the past to fit their present needs."[2] In their attempts to come to grips with their vanished rural world, rural narrators describe that world by contrasting it with the present.

People cannot tell stories about the past without reference to the present. As scholarship on memory has shown, human beings constantly re-interpret past experiences through the prism of subsequent ones. In part, storytellers believe that contrasting the world of the past to the world of today—the present with their lost rural world—can help their listeners understand the past. The practice of presenting the past in opposition to the present nonetheless serves another purpose: the past becomes the yardstick for measuring the quality of life in the present. For example, elderly people who shared experiences and thus already understand the past nonetheless persist in peppering their conversations about that shared past with explicit contrasts to today's world. By listening to stories about how the past is "not like today," we hear echoes of dozens of conversations narrators have shared with their peers on just this topic. Scholars of oral history note that narrators often construct their stories around counternarratives—that is, that they describe what their lives were not. In oral narratives, farm folk emphasize that their lives *then* were not like life *today* and that today's world is often lacking when measured by the standards of the past.[3] By examining the present in light of the past and finding that the present does not measure up, rural southerners' stories serve as powerful critiques of modern life. Values and beliefs rooted in their experiences on the land provide the standards of criticism for today's world.

This chapter examines three of the ways that rural narrators believe the past was different from the present: the material conditions of daily life, the way values were instilled in children, and the nature of community life. Although narrators are quick to acknowledge the many ways that their lives have improved since the early twentieth century, more often than not, they do not believe the present meets the high standards set by the past. Many rural southerners long for a return to an earlier world, a world in which hard work seemed to ensure a certain level of stability if not prosperity, where interactions were structured by a set of mutual obligations, and where people knew their place. They express a working-class ethic that laments the loss of a sense of long-term stability in their once-settled communities, a loss that undermines trust and mutual commitment.[4] They agree that life is often easier today, but they are not sure that easier equates with better. Society's focus on short-term profit, individual gain, and easy entertainment, they fear, is creating a weak, amoral America incapable of surviving adversity.

In the early twenty-first century, several social movements seek a return to lost values of rural life and small communities. These movements call on farmers to practice sustainable agriculture, consumers to buy locally produced foods, and homeowners to move to houses in so-called traditional neighborhood developments. These movements are all manifestations of nostalgia for a more nurturing past, and all are rooted in a sense that something has gone deeply wrong in modern American culture. This chapter and other studies that compare the memory of these much harkened past values to their reality can help us better understand whether they can be translated into today's world. Through their stories about communities of an earlier time, rural southerners express their own vision of what community should be—of what common life ought to provide for the people who share it.

I do not argue that the picture of declining community presented by oral history narrators is new. For example, Scottish Enlightenment thinkers expressed anxiety about how the progress generated by Enlightenment rationalism might come at the cost of a stable social order.[5] Similarly, historian Orville Vernon Burton found concern about a "decline of sociality" in the community of Edgefield, South Carolina, as far back as 1851, and the reasons Edgefield people gave for community decline were similar to those used by the narrators included in this study.[6] One of the major concerns of the Southern Agrarians was the erosion of community bonds.[7] Nor is this sense of loss unique to the South or indeed to rural America. Many of the elements in rural people's stories about community deterioration might also be found in the accounts of early-twentieth-century urban dwellers. Nonetheless, rural Americans may be more acutely conscious of the extent to which their worlds changed in the twentieth century than most people. The early-twentieth-century rural South, with its divides of race and class, extreme economic and political disempowerment of the poor, and its overall poverty provides a powerful lens through which to view the impact of social change.

I also do not intend to debunk the "myth" of the idyllic bygone rural world. Strong mutual aid networks, for example, were real and performed essential functions in rural communities.[8] Instead, my aim is to include ordinary people's stories and critiques in our consideration of the past. Instead of dismissing memories as mere nostalgia or simply pointing out the contradictions that reveal the distortions or erasures of memories that threaten to undermine the pristine versions of the past found in most oral history narratives, we must take memories more seriously. Storytellers may well be engaged in deliberate acts of "forgetting" the shortcomings of rural communities. Historian Jacquelyn Dowd Hall has argued, "Turning memories into stories—whether humble life stories or pretentious master narratives—is also a potent form of forgetting. For every narrative depends on the suppression and repression of contrary, disruptive memories—other people's memories of the same events, as well as the unacceptable ghosts of our own pasts."[9] Hall says that, indeed, such forgetting is part of forging a community of memory. Since communities of memory are based in narratives about what people shared, about their common life, then forgetting contradictory memories that would undermine the shared connections becomes essential to forming or maintaining such communities. A community of memory shared by rural people generally is different, nonetheless, from the real, geographically based networks of neighbors that had once formed the center of rural life. Narrators lamented the decline of these geographic communities, thus asserting their interpretations about what was most valuable in the world in which they lived.

Material Improvement: Blessings and Curses

Rural southerners were quick to mark the improvements in country life, and they often cite a higher standard of living and increased material comfort as the chief improvements over the world of their childhoods. Rural Alabaman L. D. Walker told an interviewer in 1987: "Everything's changed a lot. . . . Everybody says, 'The good old days.' Well they were good all right, in their way. But I wouldn't want to go back to not having that water in the house. . . . If you had a job, it'd take a day's work to buy a little old twenty-five pound sack of flour. And now in one hour you could buy fifty if you want to. So they can all go back to the old days if they want to. They [the old days] was good in their way, but I'd rather have them like they is."[10] All in all, Walker is pleased with the world he inhabits today. His labor purchases more products than when he was a young man, enabling him to live better. Technological improvements like running water make daily life easier and more comfortable. Many rural southerners expressed similar sentiments. A series of interviews with rural North Carolinians about the impact of the New Deal–era Rural Electrification Administration reveal country people's affection for the improvements brought by technology. An interviewer asked North Carolinian Yates Abernathy and his wife whether the days before electricity were "the good old days." Yates replied, "We enjoyed 'em; we enjoyed 'em. To some extent it was good, and then another way you look at it, it wasn't so good." Mrs. Abernathy added, "I wouldn't want to change back." Yates agreed, "No, we're not going to swap back as long as we live." The Abernathys went on to describe the way technology had changed their lives. Yates Abernathy explained that his wife was particularly grateful for the way technology lightened her housekeeping burdens. He said, "We got her a gasoline washer before the power came, and she was kind of hungry for something to take some of the work out of it. [laughter]" Easing Mrs. Abernathy's household burdens proved a high priority. The first appliances that the Abernathys purchased after the introduction of electricity to their home included a refrigerator, a radio, an electric iron, and a freezer. Technology also transformed Mr. Abernathy's farming, making it possible for him to raise broiler chickens on a large scale because he could now install electric lights and heaters required to keep broilers warm.[11] In short, technology eased Mrs. Abernathy's workload and created new opportunities for Mr. Abernathy to earn cash on the farm, thus transforming the family's standard of living. To the Abernathys, the changes that technology brought to the countryside were generally good. Technology also reduced the isolation of rural life. Like the Abernathys, many rural families purchased radios as soon as they became available or affordable. North Carolina farmer Fredda Davis praised the coming of the radio because "It gave you contact with the outside world; you knew what was going on in the cities and around. . . . That made you a citizen of the whole world instead of this little valley over here."[12]

Narrators were explicit: modern life was materially improved over the world in which they lived as children and young adults. An interviewer asked North Carolina farm wife Lena Boyce to reflect on whether life is better today with all our modern conveniences. She replied, "For me back there 50 years ago, that's when I was in the prime of my life just about. But so far as conditions and things being better, I don't think there's any question that they're much better for people today. They have so many more opportunities and so many more privileges than there were back then. Of course, we were happy. We didn't know about the convenience of electricity and we were happy with what we had. But we're much better off, living easier, than we did back then."[13]

Like Lena Boyce, many narrators agreed that deprivations of an earlier time seemed less severe because they "didn't know any better." Mississippi-born Will D. Campbell recalled his childhood on an Amite County farm: "[Y]ou would assume that there would be a great deal of boredom with no radio, no television, no movies, no automobiles, you're sitting there on a little cotton farm and you may get to town once a year. This would be the most drab [existence today] but we didn't think in those terms, you know. So I don't recall being aware that I was having either a difficult or unpleasant childhood."[14]

The material improvements mentioned by Will Campbell and other narrators brought rural people a more comfortable life. Narrators explained that even poor people enjoyed a much higher standard of living than earlier generations of the rural poor, but they also expressed uneasiness about modern life on many levels, some implicit and some explicit. When an interviewer asked rural North Carolinian Bill Moore whether he thought life was better fifty years ago, he said, "Lord, no, life is getting better on everybody I feel like today. Today is no where near the hard times the people has had. I imagine that peoples' lives were more at ease and not as much turmoil as they are today as far as that goes but as far as easy living the times are a hundred times better than they were."[15] Moore makes distinctions in the ways life has and has not improved. People today have "nowhere near the hard times" as farm people earlier in the century. To rural people, hard times were synonymous with poverty, so Moore is asserting that people are not so poor today. The conditions of daily life have also improved: people experience "easy living." Still, Moore notes that people did not experience as much turmoil in the past as they do today. Moore does not explain what he meant by "turmoil," and the interviewer does not ask, but he clearly sees some element of modern life as being destabilizing and tumultuous in ways that he believes rural life early in the century was not.

Rural southerners did not universally praise material improvement. Even narrators who insisted, as Moore did, that "we're much better off," saw the improvements wrought by technology as a decidedly mixed blessing. Technology may have lightened the load of manual labor and therefore given people more leisure time, but it also made it possible to accomplish more work more quickly and to travel long distances in short amounts of time. In other words, the pace of daily life seemed to accelerate, and many narrators saw this increased speed as a negative consequence of technology. Yates

Abernathy explained, "The children looks back now . . . when you tell them about these things, they can't even imagine. Even teenagers can't imagine what we went through back then. . . . A lot of walking going on. A lot of riding in the wagons and buggies. And we enjoyed that. There's a lot of things we did enjoy that we don't enjoy now. We're in such a hurry we don't enjoy a lot of things that we could enjoy."[16] North Carolina farmer Jim Foster put it more bluntly. He said, "We're living in a faster lane. Back then when there wasn't any automobiles or anything, you didn't go anywhere. The only people that you knew were people within walking distance, you know. And so you just lived quieter than you do now."[17]

Better transportation encouraged farm people to partake of commercial amusements and "go places." According to many narrators, "going places" and seeking out commercial or private leisure activities undermined community social life. When an interviewer asked North Carolina farmer David Bateman whether times were better before the arrival of electricity or today, he said:

> Well, I think we've had several trade-offs. When some people refer to the good old days, I think they're talking about when people had time to visit or felt like they had time to visit. People were more dependent on one another in the neighborhood at that time than they are now. With the coming of electricity everybody is sort of self-sufficient so far as around the house, especially with the coming of television. I think the good old days was when people had the opportunity to just sit around and chew the fat and socialize and enjoy one another. I think much has been lost through modern technology.

He went on to explain what he meant. Before the arrival of electricity, Bateman recalled, his father would go to the country store at night where other farmers congregated. He said, "Many farmers in the area would go to the store at night. They'd talk about what they had done that day, how their crops were progressing, what they were doing to 'em, what they were selling so far as crops were concerned. Just general exchange of agricultural information that was relevant to them and their particular farming operation." Thus, the social gatherings after supper not only cemented community ties but also provided farmers with an important source of information with which to improve their farming practices. The visits to the store also provided young people with an important (and supervised) social opportunity. Bateman explained that he saw other young people when he accompanied his dad to the store at night. About 10 P.M., David and his father would return home and go to bed. After the coming of electricity, he concluded, people stayed up later watching television. The practice of gathering at the country store gradually faded away.[18]

Nellie Stancil Langley, a farmer from North Carolina, summed up the ambivalence many narrators seemed to feel about the material improvements that rural southerners enjoyed by the end of the twentieth century. She told an interviewer, "We lived good back then. People were closer; they were more friendlier. If somebody got sick, everybody was there. It's just better than it is now. I mean, it's more convenient and we got lights, we got all that stuff. But seems like the closeness is not there like it used to be."[19]

"Young People Today"

David Bateman's story points to another hazard of modern technology lamented by many narrators: it had negative effects on the younger generation. In fact, concerns about today's young people dominated farm people's accounts of how past farm life differs from life today. Many narrators worried that improved material conditions, a higher standard of living, and more leisure time have raised the expectations of younger generations of rural southerners to unrealistic levels. In these stories you can hear grandparents' concerns about the struggles of their own grandchildren to grow up whole in the modern world. One problem was television. Narrators identified television and other commercial amusements as undermining young people's creativity and their work ethic. An interviewer asked Anna Evans, a Kentucky farm wife, "We hear talk about young people today saying they're bored. . . . What do you think about that?" Evans replied, "Well I think they look at too much television. First, a little child has so many toys. They have no initiative to make or build things. When we grew up, we had to make our own toys. . . . Now the growing boy and girl have everything handed to them. . . . I think that's one thing that's happening in our society—giving children too much and not letting them work and not teaching them to work."[20] Similarly Eva Finchum recounted that, on a typical day in the 1920s and 1930s,

> we'd work from sunup to sundown. Everybody got up early. Now there wasn't no children laying in the bed 'til they woke up. Everybody went to the breakfast table at the same time, and it wasn't just our family, it was everybody around that I knowed.
>
> But you know, people was happy then. I don't think people's happy anymore. I really don't. As I said, kids now, they don't know how to work. Parents don't teach 'em how to work. All they know is just to go somewhere and watch TV. My great-grandkids, that's the way they are.[21]

As Finchum suggests, technology was not the only force narrators saw as undermining the work ethic of young people today. In the view of many narrators, permissive parenting was the problem; parents simply did not require their children to work. This theme appeared over and over in oral histories. For example, Letha Anderson McCall of North Carolina said that learning by doing is "the only way [to teach children]. That is partly what's wrong with some of our young people today, that they don't love to do things. They've been brought up to push a button when they wanted something. They've been left to read a book, play the piano, or go visit with a friend, lie and sleep, things like that, when my mother had me doing little things to help. Then when I grew up I did the same thing with my children."[22] In McCall's view, children learned to find satisfaction from work when parents required them to work. Texan Carl Neal agreed, noting that rural parents did not center their lives on their children in the way that contemporary parents do. He explained, "My parents loved me dearly. But they sure didn't spoil you. [laughs] Believe that. And that would be one of the things today's children would find hard to accept is they came last, not first. And really I'm not sure it was not a pretty good idea, because you didn't get to feeling overly important, you know, and it certainly didn't hurt us any."[23] Narrators believed parents had a responsibility to teach their children to take pride in work, and that they were failing their children by spoiling them and allowing them to avoid work.

Television, commercial amusements, and permissive parenting were not hazards for young people alone. Many narrators expressed discomfort with the material abundance of their own lives. White Texan Dovie Carroll noted that today "Things is a lot different. Don't even seem right now to have things like we have now. . . . Now then, when we went to town, we got the necessities. And now we go to town and we buy just whatever we want."[24] Perhaps Carroll feels he is becoming too used to material bounty and has himself become spoiled. Perhaps he finds the rampant materialism of modern America wasteful and repugnant. He does not elaborate, but he is clearly concerned that today's level of prosperity "don't even seem right." North Carolinian Yates Abernathy and his wife agreed that they enjoyed an improved standard of living compared to their early years in the country, when, as Mrs. Abernathy told an interviewer, "we didn't know no better. We had to do with what we had." Her husband concurred, saying, "You had to do with what you had. That's right."[25] The Abernathys believed there was virtue in doing "with what you had," in not constantly striving to fulfill unrealistic expectations or consuming for consumption's sake.

If adults themselves expressed qualms about material abundance, they expressed even more reservations about the impact of this prosperity on children. When asked if she had any advice for young people today, Texan Frances Podsednik said, "I would tell them to better mind their parents, and they shouldn't want too many things from their parents. Today they make a list of the things they want for Christmas. We would get 10c [sic] and a doll for Christmas, that was all. When we picked cotton, we would get 05c [sic] when we picked 150 pounds, if we didn't pick that much, we would have to give the nickle [sic] back."[26] Scandalized by the idea of children making a list of possessions they wanted, Podsednik points out that she and her siblings contributed to the family economy rather than making demands upon it. She implies that today's children do not appreciate their blessings.

Another problem with today's young people, according to narrators, was the decline in their manners and moral standards, faults they blamed in part on parental leniency. Black Texan Eunice Johnson described going to church as a child. On days when the church building was full, Johnson explained, children would sit in the floor to give the grown-ups the seats. "But now children don't give you no seat."[27] In Johnson's view, children were not being taught good manners and respect for their elders. Other narrators believed that parents failed to inculcate strong moral values. African American Georgia field hand Lottie Jackson told an interviewer that she had married around age fifteen or sixteen. "I think I were that old cause they wouldn't let you marry along then fore you got old enough, you know. Chillun nowadays, they don' marry, they jus shack up together, they don' marry no more! . . . But you had to *marry* [her emphasis] along in then. I think it better to get married."[28] When asked about the changes she saw in her grandchildren's lives as com- pared to her own, white Mississippi farm woman Orry Little noted all the opportunities children have for obtaining a good education. She described the variety of courses and the fine facilities available in public schools as well as the wider opportunities for college educa- tion today. When asked if these changes were beneficial, she said, "I don't know whether it is. I can't say that it is. They go too much [go too many places], they have too much. I believe that's the reason we have so many divorces this day and time. The majority of the children never have any homework, anything to do at home; they don't have any responsibilities." She talked about how her children had chores around the house and farm. Little also lamented the behavior of her grandchildren's generation. She said, "Back when I was young, if I did a lot of things the young people do now, whoa, I'd be the worst girl in the country!" Little describes a constellation of problems that she believes are connected: immoral behavior, too many material goods, lack of responsibility in the household. It is impossible to read her mind, and the interviewer did not probe Little's view of the cause and effect relationships among these factors. Nonetheless, she is clear: compared to her own rural childhood, young people today do not grow up to take responsibility for themselves or to uphold basic moral standards.[29] White Texan Mary Simcik also connected a decline in morality among young people to excessive abundance. She said, "Morality is just in a low ebb; it's awful the way people live. . . . I wouldn't raise a family now for love or money. . . . Because everybody's so lenient with the kids. And anything a child wants, you get whether you can afford it or not; that's not right. We were poor. . . . I didn't give them anything we couldn't afford."[30]

Too much material comfort, Simcik believed, undermined children's values.

Perhaps because they saw childrearing as primarily a female responsibility, women were far more likely to express concerns about today's young people in their oral history narratives; nearly two-thirds of the narrators in this study who remarked upon the condition of the younger generation were female. Nonetheless, men, too, worried that today's young people were ill equipped to deal with the world because of their soft upbringing. Men were also more likely to express a belief that corporal punishment was the key to disciplining children in the right way of living. African American Robert Jefferson Spencer lamented that:

> [W]e don't have no job for our young people. That's why I believe most of it like it is. They need to [have responsibility]. What they see on tv, then our children is not raised like when I came up. I think we was raised a little better than some of them coming on now. See now these girls having [babies] and they ain't nothing but kids having kids. They don't have no experience or anything else and they still get that wild edge on 'em. So they forget about the kid. They put them off on somebody else, and then the kids don't get the right love from their parents. They look for the teacher to do it. They look for the preacher to do it. They look for somebody else to do it. See we had, when I was coming up, you had a certain time to be at home and you's going to be there. You didn't miss that but once. See wasn't no child abuse. See now it's parent abuse . . . , 'cause the kid say, "you hit me, I have you arrested."[31]

Spencer is appalled that parents who use physical punishment to discipline their children might be accused of abuse, and he insists that excessive force was not used in his day: "wasn't no child abuse." He goes on to note that when he misbehaved as a child, he could count on a switching from his grandfather, and he believes that such physical punishment kept him in line and taught him appropriate behavior. He seems to believe that restoring the primacy of physical discipline in childrearing practice will result in more responsible young people. By ignoring or forgetting the reality of child abuse in the past—by denying that physical abuse of children took place—he can rationalize his prescription for today's youth. White Texan Dovie Carroll agreed. He explained:

> Well, my daddy, most of all fathers back in those days, they didn't tell you but one time to do something. And if you didn't do it, well, the next time he tells you to do something, you done it. Cause when they got through with you—my dad . . . , he'd say, "Well, son, why didn't you do what I told you to?" Of course, I'd tell him I's playing or something, well, all he'd say to go get in the house. When he went in the house, it may be an hour or something like that, regardless; he had a double razor strop hanging up by the mantel of the fireplace and he'd get that, why the next time he told you, you'd do it.

Carroll went on to tell the interviewer another story about an occasion when his father punished him for disobedience. He concluded, "The only thing he said when he got through, 'Don't let this happen no more.' That's all he ever said. He wouldn't get mad at you or nothing like that. And if you got a whipping at school, you got another when you got home." Carroll's wife, also present for the interview, summed up their concerns by saying, "Children aren't raised nothing like they are now."[32]

Black Mississippian and retired teacher Chris Young also advocated more corporal punishment as a means of bringing young people into line. He explained that the decline in discipline among the younger generation was the result of the elimination of paddling in public schools, a change he linked to desegregation. Young told an interviewer:

> There wasn't no drugs. People drank a little homemade wine . . . and that type of thing. But you didn't have all this drug stuff that you have now. The biggest problem with what's happening now is that when they integrated these schools, they cut out the paddle. They cut the paddle out when they integrated the schools, because I guess they didn't want black teachers to be whooping white children. . . . So then . . . children started child abuse. You couldn't whoop your own children. . . . You didn't have all this stuff they got going on

now. . . . If you can't put a paddle on a kid, he does what he
want to do, you can't raise him. That's the problem.[33]

First, Young says, schools eliminated the use of corporal punishment to prevent black teachers from paddling white children. Then,
he implies, children caught on to the idea that if they claimed child
abuse when they were physically punished, they could avoid such
punishment in the future. As a result, "You couldn't whoop your
own children." In Young's view, parents and teachers could not control children's behavior without physical punishment.

Like Chris Young and the Carrolls, Georgia African American
Anna Bertha Pitts lamented the way children are raised today, and
she offered an extended analysis of the nature and causes of such
changes:

Back then long years ago—I'm talking about before the War
[World War II], when I come on as a child, folks was raising
children better. They had certain times you stay out, boys and
girls, and certain times you had to be home. But now some
of them around here, they don't know where their children's
at. . . . I like the old ways. That's the reason I tell them I don't
follow this new star. It was hard then. I was coming up a little
country girl and hard. On a field, on a farm, picking cotton,
shaking peanuts, doing all that. . . . But I thank God for it
now and I see how terrible it's done got. I thank God for it
I come up the hard way. Because I know how to cope with
this here generation now. What activity do they having going
on—I don't take no part of it because I didn't come up with
it. They say, "Ah, you're old fashioned." I say, "I'm going to
stay old fashioned." That's right. So in one area, it was better back then than it is now. Because every time you can pick
up a paper or turn on the radio, somebody done got killed.
So-and-so done killed. Well, you didn't hear tell all that back
then. All you hear then somebody beat up. . . . The white
Klans come and beat somebody. That's what they'd do.[34]

Pitts's statement is remarkable for several reasons. She holds parents responsible for failing to raise today's young people properly:

parents do not set curfews or keep track of the whereabouts of their children. She implies that, as a child, she resented both material hardships and the endless physical labor that farming required of children, but that as an adult, she is grateful for the lessons she learned from enduring such hardships. Pitts seems particularly alarmed by the level of violence faced by today's youth. She asserts that, in her day, "you didn't hear tell" of so much killing, only an occasional Klan beating. Pitts displays a peculiar and striking historical amnesia as she constructs this account. Even if she never witnessed a Klan murder, it is unlikely that a rural Georgian could have remained insulated from the knowledge of such violence. Moreover, as she notes, Klan violence was racial violence; the "white Klans" attacked black people. The implication here is that she finds black on black violence new and alarming. This, too, is a demonstration of historical amnesia, since black on black violence is nothing new, though arguably it may occur at a higher rate today. Pitts seems to find racially motivated violence in some way more explicable than what she saw as the random violence perpetrated by and inflicted upon the younger generation.

Others blamed the deteriorating character of young people on the influence of the city. Black Arkansan William Malone noted, "Sometimes I think the youngsters of today don't . . . care nothing about his next door neighbor. I don't know whether it's that way in Memphis or not. It may not be. That may just be my thoughts. And again I could be wrong in this." Malone connected city life to economic success in explaining a decline in young people's attachments to families and communities. He went on to describe an encounter with several poor young women from his rural community who had moved to St. Louis, where they enjoyed economic prosperity. He later called on them in the city because "people you were raised around if you see them, you know them and you want to speak to them." However, the former neighbors snubbed him. He said:

These girls acted like they didn't even know who I was. You know what I said to myself? I said you all need to go back to the country because the city's done ruined you. I called them city stricken. Got to the city and they got a good pair of shoes to put on and they don't know you. . . . That's the reason I said prosperity ruined the people. I believe that why people of today is so far apart, prosperity. . . . Because you take some of us, black and white, get a dollar in the pocket and we don't know each other. I guess that's the way it is. . . . It might be some that get more an hour than you, turn their back when they see you coming. . . . And some you've been knowing all your life don't know you.[35]

In short, Malone believed that though city life often brought prosperity, urban living and prosperity also taught people to put on airs and "ruined" people. Material success undermined one's ties to people in the community.

As narrators saw it, the real danger in raising a generation of spoiled, soft young people lay in the threat they posed to the future health of the nation. When asked whether her children and grandchildren are better off living today, Ruth Irwin of Mississippi replied, "In some ways, they are. In some ways, they're not. I don't think that people really appreciate in this day in time the things they have. They are so common they just take them for granted. Our whole nation's that way. . . . They have every opportunity; everybody has money that wants to work. Of course, this relief program—there's people that need to be on relief, but we have some that expect everything for nothing, that don't really need to be on relief, that are physically able to work. And we accept that, too."[36] If our "whole nation" is comprised of spoiled children who don't appreciate what they have and "expect everything for nothing," narrators like Ruth Irwin fear that we will have a nation full of bitter citizens who refuse to work for what they have. Spoiled children became spoiled adults, unable to cope with adversity of any type.

Although she insisted that her children were "good children" who had gotten along well at school and had little conflict at home, Irene Clause of rural Labadieville, Louisiana, said,

I'm so very happy that I grew up in the era I did. The values which we had then, we still have today. I feel that so many of the young people of today have had it too easy. Too many opportunities, too much fun and good times, and too much permissiveness. Many cannot accept responsibilities and all

of their lives are too free sometimes. I'm glad that our children and grandchildren do have the opportunity for better
educations, better schools, good-paying jobs, good entertainment, better living conditions, opportunity to advance in any
field if they strive to do so. I wish that I would have had some
of these opportunities that are available today. As a young
wife I did not have any modern conveniences. . . . I think
if my grandmother would come back today, she would say
"Mein no," which means "oh no," and return to her haven
of rest.[37]

Mae Hartsoe of North Carolina concurred with Clause's analysis. She told an interviewer,

There have been many changes since I was young and growing up. One thing that I really notice is that when couples
get married nowadays, they usually have them an apartment
or a little place to live, and they've got to have everything
furnished, and it's all got to match up just exactly. When we
went to housekeeping, we used what we could get our hands
on. We just mostly had a table and a stove and a bed and
some chairs and, of course, a few other things, a few cookers
and a few dishes. We got along just fine, better, I think, than
people get along now, because they have it all handed down
to them. We worked for what we got. When you do that, I
think you appreciate it more.[38]

Rural southerners' criticisms of young people are not new; for
centuries, mature human beings have lamented that young folks were
headed straight to hell in a handcart.[39] In fact, some narrators realized that all older generations criticize the values of the younger generation. After spending some time complaining about the shortcomings of her grandchildren, Cora Jones, a white woman from Texas,
admitted, "I know that every generation criticizes the younger generation. I can remember that my grandmother was aghast at things."
As an example, she told the story of her own grandmother's shock at
hearing a granddaughter speak of ovaries openly. Apparently Jones's
grandmother saw the open discussion of female reproductive organs

as a sign of impending social decline, in much the way that Jones herself viewed her own grandchildren's insistence on choosing their colleges without parental interference.[40] Both the novelty of narrators' claims about the decline of the younger generation and the accuracy of their perceptions are beside the point. Rather, the point is that their mournful accounts of the faults of the younger generation reveal some of the things that they believe have been lost with modernization: self-discipline, the ability to delay gratification, high moral standards, a respect for one's elders, and an attachment to one's community.

Historians Roy Rosenzweig and David Thelen have argued that the dominant theme in the historical narratives of white Americans is not progress in society, but rather deterioration: the spread of selfishness and hedonism and the decline of traditional values. They found that white narratives about social decline contrasted sharply with African American and Native American narratives, which focused on steady, albeit incomplete progress.[41] An examination of the oral narratives of rural people suggests, however, that Rosenzweig and Thelen are guilty of oversimplification. Narrators of both races saw much progress in the wake of modernity, but both blacks and whites lamented the decline of traditional values and the rise of rampant individualism. When asked about changes she had witnessed in her lifetime, Georgia African American Anna Bertha Pitts applauded both material improvements and diminished racial discrimination in the lives of African Americans. She said,

There's been lots of change since [the early twentieth century]. . . . Because things are better. . . . It's been a mighty big change. There were a lot of things that went on in those days back there. . . . And they [African Americans] had to go along with it. They knew it wasn't right. But they had to go along with it because there wasn't nothing else they knowed to do. So now, it come a time when they don't have to go along with it. If they don't want to, they don't have to. . . . If now, you see them [black people] standing on the street on the side of the corner, they couldn't do it back then. They had to go to work somewhere. The men in white sheets was coming. No! They couldn't do it!

In spite of the improvements for African Americans, however, Pitts saw new problems, many of them related to the decline in morality among young people. She went on, "It was not near as much killing going on among the black as there is now." She explained that she had moved from one neighborhood where crime was rampant, and men loitered on the road near her mailbox drinking and intimidating passersby. "I couldn't get to the mailbox! Standing around there every day! . . . Back then, they wouldn't have had that standing around there! . . . And it wasn't near as much killing! Much robbing! going on as there is now. I sees lots of differences. It's a big change from where I come from on up to now that done been made. A lot of change. Some things were going on back then were better than it is now. And some are worse. Black men killing black."[42] Like many other narrators, Pitts believed that traditional values had eroded in recent years, leading to new social problems.

Changes in Community Life

A recurring theme in narrators' comments about the downside of material improvements and the problems with today's young people is a concern about the decline of community life. Over and over, rural narrators waxed nostalgic about the close country communities in which they lived at mid-century. For example, African American Jurl Wakins, daughter of a landowning Georgia farmer, described life in her community:

> Well, you know, back in those days life was so beautiful because everybody looked after each other. If we killed hogs, you know, we shared with everybody in the community. . . . If we had vegetables, we would share with everybody in the community. You know, it's not like now. We used to share our own peanuts that we planted. And we would have what you call peanut shellings and everybody in the community would come. . . . We would do a lot of exciting things you know.[43]

Jurl Watkins's account contains the elements that recur again and again when rural southerners talk about their bygone country communities. She focused on traditions of subsistence activity and mutual aid that enabled a close-knit community to be largely self-sufficient. She emphasized the harmony of interactions among neighbors. Most important, she described life in her community in terms of what it was *not:* "You know, it's not like now."

As the passage from Watkins's oral history interview suggests, oral history narrators also repeatedly compared today's communities unfavorably to those lost circles of country neighbors from the past. Laments about the decline of community are striking. Narrators come from a diverse range of geographic settings, ethnic and racial backgrounds, farming types, and socioeconomic backgrounds, but their stories repeatedly hearken back to idyllic close-knit communities where neighbors shared their material resources and cared deeply about one another's welfare. Scholars examining oral histories of rural people cannot help but be struck by the way narrators romanticize rural community life. Relatively few narrators mention class differences in rural communities, and only occasionally do rural people hint at episodes of community discord that disrupted community ties. Nor do accounts usually include complaints about neighbors who took aid without returning it, stories of borrowers who damaged farm equipment and failed to repair it, nor even tales of the private conflicts that often mark interpersonal relationships. Of course, we know from examining court records, newspaper accounts, and other contemporary sources that rural communities were marked by as much hostility and strife as any other group of people who interacted regularly. Nonetheless rural southerners have developed something of a collective mythology about the communities of the past. As black Mississippian Minnie Wade Weston put it, "They was real lovely, friendly people together."[44]

Community refers to the place where people interact, to the social system itself, and to the shared sense of identity held by a group of people who lived in geographic proximity. Historian Orville Vernon Burton has argued that in the South, "The meaning of community developed from everyday behavior, social rituals, and experiences as members of families and society."[45] Rural sociologists have found that rural and urban people alike share a set of assumptions about rural communities: that they are characterized by honesty, fair play, neighborliness, and wholesome family life. Yet rural communities, like all communities, vary in the extent to which they provide solidarity—

a sense that members belong. As a team of sociologists headed by Cornelia Butler Flora has written: "A sense of solidarity emerges when the community offers a clear, well-focused set of values, beliefs, or goals with which members identify."[46] As we have seen, rural narrators believed that they shared a set of common values that were forged by their experiences working the land. They felt a sense of community with farmers everywhere, but they focused most closely on the community in which they interacted daily—their neighbors. Historian Steven Hahn has said that for rural people, "the notion of 'community' had immediacy and tangibility. It meant particular people to be encountered in face-to-face relations, as well as a particular place to be lived in and worked on." Hahn notes that rural communities were not necessarily egalitarian or homogeneous. People who believed they belonged to a particular community might also feel sharp divisions among the members of that community. As Hahn put it, "Community did not ordinarily involve or evoke harmonious or egalitarian relations; more often than not it was marked by multiple hierarchies, harsh regimens, and nasty legitimating sanctions. But it was grounded and bounded, with institutional articulations that could promote, at once, deep senses of social identification among members—including those of different rank or class—and deep suspicions of outsiders."[47]

Stories from the narratives illustrate that rural southerners saw community as bounded by face-to-face relationships based in shared values and mutual aid. Rural community members lived in the immediate vicinity and interacted regularly. They believed they shared a common identity and a common set of values with their neighbors. Narrators could and sometimes did point to geographic boundaries to indicate the limits of community, but more often they named families who were part of the community. These families usually went to the same churches or had children who attended the same schools. For example, when asked who was considered part of her childhood community in Spring Creek, Texas, Opal Bateman named a whole list of white families. When asked how a person came to think of himself or herself as part of the Spring Creek community, she said,

I think it was the church and the school. Because there were some that didn't have any children in school off and on, you know. I remember one family that didn't have any children, but they was very much a part of the community because they came to church. But I don't know . . . just how you defined it other than . . . both [church and school] was important as a community. . . . [W]e didn't have too many families that didn't take part in the community.

To Bateman, "taking part" or being actively involved in community life made one a community member. Most community members participated in the church or the school or both, but her ambiguous definition suggests that some neighbors may not have participated in these two institutions and thus did not "take part" in the community. Few narrators mentioned other organizations as being central to community life. Some women reported belonging to neighborhood home demonstration clubs, but school and church provided the institutional backbones of rural community.[48]

Church was a particularly important center to black communities where poor and oppressed people could forge a source of empowerment and independence. As a result, church provided a vehicle for resistance to white domination.[49] North Carolina minister James Samuel spent much of his childhood in a community of migrant farmworkers in Claremont, Florida. He described the importance of the church in that community:

The role of the church in . . . my early life, was the moral and spiritual nerve center for the black family. My family worked six days a week and on Sunday we went to church. . . . For me church was [a] very powerful and very emotionally charged place, a place where I saw . . . people of quiet strength and people to whom I looked to [sic] for stability. . . . There was a sense of empowerment. There was a sense of community that was intense and profound. . . . [T]he church [was] a place where we went, where we talked about freedom and we talked about peace and talked about joy. . . . In one setting, in the migrant fields, I saw my parents being subjected to the supervision of white overseers and farmers and others who were always in charge of the black laborers. And then in the church, I began to see people who were common laborers, people like my father and mother who could neither read nor write. I saw them assume positions of leadership. . . . And so I saw that the church was the arena for the empowerment of a people who otherwise had been rendered powerless.[50]

Churches and schools could be empowering, but they could also be tools of exclusion. For example, blacks and whites in the rural South attended separate churches and schools, and many black children's school attendance was limited by economic pressures and landlords' demands for their labor. Black families who lived in isolation from other African Americans probably felt excluded from the institutions that provided the basis for community life. In addition, some rural southerners did not attend church at all and may have been largely excluded from rural communities. In his 1936 study of two Georgia Black Belt counties, sociologist Arthur F. Raper found a decline in the influence of white churches in rural communities, largely because white landowners shifted their memberships and money to small town churches while white tenants and sharecroppers could not afford to support churches. On the other hand, he found that rural black churches were large and vibrant community centers, albeit impoverished ones. The fact that rural southerners saw church and school participation as markers of community membership suggests that these communities may not have been as open or inclusive as their stories might lead a listener to believe.[51]

Just as church and school could bind rural communities, so could race and ethnicity, as James Samuel's recollection suggests. In the rural South, whites and blacks often lived on the same farms or plantations or in close proximity; yet not all residents of the neighborhood were perceived as participating in community life in the same way. Certainly this was clear in the case of Opal Bateman's listing of white families when asked about the boundaries of community in Spring Creek, Texas. Blacks drew similar racial boundaries. When asked about life in her community in Chickasaw County, Mississippi, Minnie Wade Weston described a neighborhood knit together by mutual exchanges, exchanges confined to the black community. She explained: "One didn't have, the other one had. . . . That's the way they lived. And the children and all growed up together. Lovely. And I never heard, when I was a young girl, I never heard of anything but helping between the black people of that time. The biggest trouble that they had was among the white." To Weston, relations in the black community were harmonious while relations with white neighbors could be marked by conflict.[52]

Community relations between blacks and whites were not always contentious, however, particularly when relations between blacks and whites were based in black dependency. For example, black Arkansan Helen Howard recalled that her landlord's wife would bring food to sick tenants living and working on her property. Howard speculated that race relations in her community were pretty good because the only white family with whom blacks had contact was the landlord's family.[53]

Some black people seemed to see themselves as being part of two communities: one made up of African Americans and another that included whites who lived in close proximity. They might have felt most at home in the black community, but they might also consider themselves part of a larger geographically based community that included whites. Rev. W. C. Tims, an African American born in Claiborne Parish, Louisiana, described a community bounded by geographic and racial lines and centered in the church:

> It was a black community, all solid black community. Most of them were sharecropping. They were working the land for like halves or so much. It was a large black community. And then it would cross probably a white community, and then there would be another large black community. So you had many large black communities, and some of them were larger than others because of the way that blacks would own land and purchase land or help somebody save the land or bring others in to own land, to grow the community, and the church was located in the community.

Tims's community included black sharecropping families who aided one another, and the community was rooted in the church. Yet in another place in his narrative Tims described the distance between households in rural Louisiana and said, "This would take in a whole community. For instance, say probably five miles square you pretty well knew all of the farmers, all the white farmers, and all the children knew each other and they would be around each other, and this would be more or less the boundaries if they were going to be around the community going places."[54]

Black North Carolinian Bertha Todd also included whites in her description of the rural community where she grew up: "We were a pretty well-knit neighborhood, white and black. And there were whites who lived in the neighborhood and we would share foods, and in time of illness we would check on each other." She added that whites and blacks attended separate churches, but noted that whites from the neighborhood attended blacks' "barn parties"—dances in tobacco barns—although whites and blacks did not dance together. Nor is it likely that blacks attended dances organized by whites. These stories and many others suggest that racial divides created two communities for black people. They centered most of their social lives and their mutual aid networks within the black community, but they were also part of a larger community that included interactions with and dependence on whites. Perhaps, too, these stories indicate that rural communities were often more integrated than they appeared at first glance.[55]

Like black southerners, ethnic groups saw themselves as separate from native-born whites and formed relatively autonomous communities when their numbers were sufficiently large. For example, significant numbers of Norwegians, Czechs, and Germans migrated to central Texas in the late nineteenth and early twentieth centuries. Oris Pierson's parents came to Texas from Norway and farmed west of Clifton. He said, "I suppose that some people feel that the Norwegian community is a rather peculiar thing because when the Norwegians first came over here they were clannish. . . . They felt that it would be better if they remained just as a Norwegian group and didn't intermarry with anyone else." Mary Simcik described her central Texas community as including the people who went to the local Catholic church, a congregation dominated by Czech immigrants. To some extent, the "clannishness" of various ethnic communities in the South may have been born of necessity. While single immigrants or one immigrant family might have found reluctant acceptance into an existing rural community, rural blacks and whites might have greeted large numbers of immigrants with suspicion and distrust. Forming their own communities provided a comfortable way for immigrants to build a new life in a new land while maintaining many of their Old World traditions.[56]

Rural communities included men, women, and children, but as these stories suggest, it was women who did much of the work of maintaining community ties. Tending the sick and cooking for community gatherings would have fallen within the domain of women. So would much of the work involved in organizing school and community activities. Informal visiting among women built lines of communications among the community's members. In a sense, the meaning of community itself was gendered, with men and women playing different roles and expecting different returns from community membership.

Whatever geographic, institutional, racial, or ethnic boundaries defined community and whoever did the work of community building, rural southerners stoutly denied that socioeconomic differences excluded anyone from the community. White east Tennessean LaVerne Farmer told an interviewer, "If people around needed things, why they'd help each other out. But back then I don't recall anybody being much poorer than anybody else. They just shared what they had." As the daughter of a dairy farmer and creamery operator who was probably one of the more prosperous men in the community, Farmer perhaps had more to share than many, but socioeconomic barriers did not exist in her memories of community.[57]

Shirley Sherrod seemed more aware of socioeconomic differences, but she denied that they shaped relations among neighbors. Sherrod was one of five daughters of a landowning African American family in Baker County, Georgia. She grew up in an area called Hawkins Town, a black-owned community made up entirely of her extended family and a few of their agricultural laborers. Sherrod recalled the entire community pitching in together on each other's farms. "You know, if it was my father's time to harvest peanuts, then everybody'd just come and help him." She also remembered that the landless laborers who lived and worked on her parents' farm shared in the close-knit community:

> There was one family, the Williams family, was a female head of household. She had about nine children and they all grew up there on the farm. . . . They were laborers. But they were

also like family too. So it wasn't strictly a laborer relationship. They were also like family. In fact, the lady I told you about who had nine children, she attends our family reunion. We've collected money to make some renovations on the family reunion site this year and she donated just like all the rest of us. So they were more like family although they were not related to us. And it was the same way with others who lived on [the] farm.[58]

Shirley Sherrod was clearly conscious of the Williamses' status as laborers, but she maintained that the relationship between the two families "wasn't strictly" that of landowner and laborer. For the Sherrods and the Williamses, the ties of race were stronger than socioeconomic barriers, at least in Shirley's memory.

Whatever the boundaries of a particular community, southerners described rural communities as performing three functions. First, they provided the social center for rural families. Rev. W. E. Tims explained that in the rural black communities of Louisiana and Arkansas, people gathered informally for domino and baseball games or to swim or fish together in local ponds. People gathered to race horses and mules. Sometimes after cotton season was over, the community held dances with local musicians providing the music. Tims told his interviewer, "Those who engaged in the kind of activities that we were talking about, that gave you that kind of sense of pride and value." In other words, participating in the life of the community helped individuals feel that others in the community cared about them, that they were persons of worth. Such ties, he implies, were sustaining. Numerous narrators concurred with Tims that rural communities provided a social life and a sense of belonging. White Texan Opal Bateman fondly recalled that her community gathered at all-day singings and weeklong revivals at church. School plays and Christmas pageants provided another opportunity to congregate as did ice cream socials hosted by neighbors. Narrators also explained that simple visiting among neighbors was an important part of community life. White Mississippian Ruth Irwin recalled childhood life on her parents' plantation. She said, "When my mother saw somebody turn in our driveway she run put on a clean apron and she would go out to the gate and say, 'Oh, I'm so glad you've come.' And you didn't have to let people know you were coming. They knew you were coming to spend the day when you saw 'em drive in." When the interviewer suggested that people then were perhaps not as busy as today, Irwin replied, "I don't know what you'd call busy. My mother helped my father to milk 15 cows. She churned butter in a dasher churn for sale. After we got a separator to separate the cream, she sold cream. She sold 20 dozen eggs a week. She had three girls and she made all their clothes and one boy and she made his shirts. She made my father's shirts. She cooked for five day hands, two meals a day on workdays, five days a week. I reckon you'd call that work." In spite of her mother's heavy workload, Ruth Irwin remembered that visiting with neighbors assumed a high priority in daily life. Perhaps the arrival of company also provided Irwin's mother with much-needed rest.[59]

The social component of community life often blended with the second component: mutual aid. Indeed many historians have documented the way that mutual aid networks helped define the boundaries of community. Historian Jane Pedersen has argued that patterns of mutual aid may have operated to reduce conflict in rural communities and served as "a force for solidarity and harmony in the community. Alienating one's neighbors would have been expensive for the farmer who could not afford to hire a crew or buy the equipment to provide alternative help."[60]

Mutual aid often occupied the center of stories of rural community. For example, Black Arkansan Helen Howard, the daughter of a tenant farmer, explained that helping each other "was just a tradition and everybody fell in line with it and just kept up that tradition on down through." The tradition of mutual aid included the practice of sharing material resources. Myrtle Dodd reported that, when her Texas tenant farming family did not live on a farm that boasted an orchard, landowning neighbors with orchards shared their fruit. "I can remember . . . at Eddy the neighbors were the Mayberrys. . . . [W]hen they had excess garden stuff or when—they had a big orchard—when it came on [ripened], why, they were glad for my father and mother to take it."[61]

In addition to sharing material goods, community members also pooled their labor, both to maintain community institutions and to help individual farm families. White Texan Viola Anderson Bateman told an interviewer that one of the biggest social events of the year in her community of Spring Creek was the annual cemetery "working," when neighbors gathered to clean up the cemetery. Rural communities also gathered to make light work of large tasks. When asked about the thresher coming to her home farm as a child, white Texan Laura Bateman said, "I remember that when I was a kid because we always had to cook for them [the threshers], you know. It was quite a big day when we'd have to cook. . . . And the ladies would get together and cook that dinner. They'd swap out. If it was at my house today, they helped me. If it was over at their house tomorrow, I helped them. That's the way we did the work, swapped out." Black Georgian Roosevelt Cuffie talked about the way members of his community helped each other at hog killing time and other times of peak work, sharing the proceeds of that work. He explained, "So that was a great deal of unity. And everybody, in my opinion, got along very good. There wasn't a whole lot of misunderstanding." Alma Hale, a white landowning Texan, recalled that her own mother often looked after the children of the black widower who worked on Alma's father's rented farm. Mutual aid extended across class and sometimes racial lines for a variety of reasons. As was the case with John West, the Tennessee farmer who talked at length about his efforts to help others in chapter 1, many of the most prosperous assisted the less wealthy as both an act of charity and as a means of displaying their status and success. In addition, as historian Steven Hahn points out, members of the community strongly identified with each other, in spite of the divisions of class. Prosperous and struggling people coexisted in close proximity, a situation unlike the socioeconomically segregated neighborhoods of America's suburbs and cities. Simple contact may have minimized the lines between poor, middling, and wealthy rural people.[62]

Neighbors also helped families in crisis. They cared for the sick, tended fields for farmers who fell ill, and pitched in to assist neighbors who lost homes to fire or flood. Black Mississippian Amy Jones explained that in her childhood community "if something happen in your family—it didn't have to be death, just sick—people would come from miles bringing us food and stuff. . . . *Real* help each other [emphasis hers]. And I mean it wasn't a help each other talking about it; they would really come together. And it didn't have to be relatives to do that."[63]

A third function of rural communities was to provide social

control. Amy Jones explained that in her childhood community, the neighbors assisted with disciplining children. "If we did wrong, they would come whoop us. That's right. And you were scared . . . to tell your mama and your daddy you got a whooping because you were subject to getting another one. [laughter] That's true . . . but nowadys you can't do that." Fellow Mississippian Chris Young concurred:

> See, on church [days], they'd all meet up there, and she'd say, 'Mrs. Young, I saw your son at such and such a place doing such and such a thing, and I got on to him.' She'd [his mother] say, 'thank you.' And when you got home from church, she wanted to know why did that lady have to whoop you, or that man, what were you doing? . . . So that kept things in line. Now a kid go home and tell his mama, the teacher whooped me, the parents will go out there and want to kill the teacher. They didn't have that back there then.

White Texan Carl Neal lamented the loss of safety for children. "The neighbors looked after you just like they did their own kids if you happened to be over there. . . . You didn't worry about your kid talking to a stranger. They were perfectly all right. Nobody was going to harm a kid."[64]

Disciplining children was not the only form of social control practiced in rural communities, for they also disciplined adults. In efforts to force adults to conform to community norms, class emerged as a prominent force in determining who exercised the prerogative of enforcing community standards, who was a target of discipline, and the effectiveness of efforts at social control. White Tennessean Mary Evelyn Russell Lane explained that when one of her father's tenant farmers physically abused his children, her father ordered the abuser to stop and monitored his behavior thereafter. In this example, we see dimensions of the power conferred by Russell's standing as a landowner. The tenant had to bow to social control because of his economic dependence on Lane's father. Nonetheless, Russell was acting to enforce community standards of appropriate child discipline. Communities also worked together to uphold community values and norms when neighbors transgressed the boundaries of acceptable behavior. For example, black Mississippian Maurice Lucas maintained that in predominantly black communities like Mound Bayou and his own Renova, "if they had a black lady that was whoring around with white folk, they'd run her ass out of town. . . . They run several out of this community when we were little boys. . . . But that was pretty predominant in communities where they were all black communities like here and Mound Bayou. Black folks ain't going to put up with that mess. But we were the boss. We were in charge. Yeah, we were the majority owners. . . . That had to come to a screeching halt. . . . And most of it was done through the church in those days."[65] White North Carolinian T. H. Kilby also recalled that community members worked to enforce prevailing standards of behavior. He told an interviewer:

> In the community where I grew up in, I can hardly remember anybody ever having a conflict with a neighbor. I do remember one or two people that, maybe, got out in the community and tried to make a little liquor, and the rest, they wouldn't stand for that. And they'd report them up for something. And that's about the only thing, honestly, that I could ever think about a conflict. But the people, they loved each other, and the people got along real good. They just didn't have conflict like we do today. It's just a different world to live in. So that's about the extent of the conflicts. There just wasn't any. Maybe with the girls or the boys, a falling out over the boyfriend or the girlfriend sometimes, something like that. [Chuckles] But as far as parents getting along, everybody got along.[66]

Kilby admits to some conflict in his community—conflict based in competition among young people and conflict that arose when one neighbor reported another for breaking the law. Nonetheless, he minimizes this conflict in order to maintain his image of a community where "everybody got along."

Cracks in the Mythology of Rural Community

If these stories sound too good to be true to our ears, the oral histories themselves provide internal clues to unlocking the meaning of the mythology of harmonious rural communities. Astute interviewers sometimes question the mythology and force narrators to acknowledge that things were not always so harmonious in rural communities, as was the case with T. H. Kilby's statements. In other cases, the narrator will tell a story at another point in the interview that seems to contradict the sweeping generalizations he or she earlier made about life in rural neighborhoods.

For example, Black Mississippian Essie Mae Alexander told an interviewer that black families in her childhood community shared with each other. She said:

> That's one of the other ways that we survived. I can't say that we ever went hungry. . . . And my mother used to, they'd gather vegetables. . . . She just fixed a lot of food and everybody came and ate with us. And what we didn't have, maybe somebody else had. And one thing that most of 'em shared, we had milk cows. And when our cows would go dry . . . then someone else would share their milk and butter with us until our cows got back where they [were producing again]—and we did the same with them.[67]

Notice the romantic story of the helpful community. If the interviewer had left it at that, we would be left with an account much like those in other oral histories: everybody in the community shared what they had. But this interviewer probed further and asked Alexander if *all* the families in the community participated so willingly in this sharing of resources. Alexander then admitted that, indeed, there were a *few* people on the plantation who didn't participate in mutual aid activities. She explained that some extended family members who lived on the same plantation enjoyed more prosperity than her own family, and those relatives didn't share resources. But, she maintained, her mother still helped those family members if someone was sick. Here, Alexander is clearly indicating that not all families were at the same economic level and that they didn't all share resources. In fact, the families who had the most shared the least. Until pressed, she omitted this negative detail that would seem to undermine her account of the cooperative rural community. She also asserted that her mother was a selfless and caring woman who continued to share with even the most selfish community members.

Another rare admission that not all farm families participated in community mutual aid networks came from black Arkansan Cleaster Mitchell. She recalled that in her rural community,

> Some of them were selfish. They lived to themselves, and what they had was theirs. They didn't share nothing with anybody. Some of them was so selfish, they did not even share with their own families. . . . When you run up on somebody that was selfish and didn't share, nobody pointed him out and said he's a bad guy or he's this or that or the other. They just said, 'Don't bother Mr. whatever his name is. . . .' Because it always got around who shared and who didn't share, see. But if they had somebody in the community that did not share with their own family, other people shared with them. The church family shared with them.[68]

The existence of conflict and "selfishness" in the communities that Alexander and Mitchell remember does not necessarily indicate that rural communities were not tightly-knit, of course. As historian Orville Vernon Burton has observed, conflict could also "affirm and reveal community bonds." People who failed to share might be neighbors, but they were perpetually seen as outsiders by those who participated in the daily exchanges of resources and aid that marked true community membership.[69]

Black Mississippian Dorsey M. White gave one of the more nuanced descriptions of rural community found in this interview sample, and his testimony supports the idea that tight-knit communities could be drawn more closely together by defining themselves in contrast to neighbors who did not share their values. When asked about the community on the plantation where he grew up, White said,

> Well, you know, the black community on the plantation is I guess more or less like your regular society. You have people with the same type attitudes and desires and what have you. . . . [Y]ou have some people, they try to prosper and try to better their condition and you have some that just live and be more or less satisfied with whatever come their

way, but some people would try to improve their surround-
ings and some tried to raise the children and be good citizens or good neighbors, and some didn't care and just had
chaos like you know we still have today. . . . As far as I can
see, there was quite a bit of sharing. People would help each
other quite frequently. You tend to lean on your neighbors,
if he had something that you didn't have, you would share
and you could depend on them to help you through the hard
times. But as a result, no one had a lot to share, you know,
but they would share what they did have to a great extent.[70]

White's story indicates that shared values formed an important
marker of community membership. In his view, some people "try
to prosper" and thus are more a part of the community than those
who "just live and be more or less satisfied with whatever come their
way."

Stories about Community as Critiques
of Contemporary Life

As with stories about the mixed blessings wrought by technology
and about the way young people are raised today, rural narrators'
stories about community contain implicit and explicit critiques of
modern life. Of course, most of us tend to attribute a rosier glow to
memories embedded in our youth. Undoubtedly, a number of narrators were fondly remembering their childhood days, and many of
the community activities they extol are the types of activities children would remember with nostalgia: large gatherings featuring special foods like ice cream, opportunities to play with other children,
events that would provide breaks in the monotony of daily life on the
farm. Nonetheless, many of these narrators were not children during
the period they describe. Frances Podsednik and her husband were
adults struggling to establish a farm by 1910. Minnie Wade Weston
was born in 1905, Oris Pierson in 1899, and Mary Simcik in 1900,
so most of their stories occurred when they were adults. Essie Mae
Alexander was sharecropping well into the 1950s. Moreover, nostalgia itself is an expression of social critique. Historian Eric Foner
argues that "[A]s a wholesale rejection of the present, nostalgia can

serve as a powerful mode of protest."[71] Rural southerners lament that yesterday's communities are gone, leaving us to live among collections of indifferent and uninvolved neighbors. Black Mississippian Alice Giles noted that "people shared more. People's not like, peoples today not like they were then. . . . Everybody seemed like they were more lovely and kind then."[72]

Like all of us, rural southerners think they know what has gone wrong with modern society. The reasons they give for the decline of community tell us a great deal about their criticisms of modern life. For some, the problems grew from leaving the land and the new types of work in which rural people engaged. For example, Black Mississippian Ruthie Lee Jackson told an interviewer that blacks helped each other in the early part of the twentieth century "[m]uch more than they do now. . . . When we be farming, if we didn't get through with our crop, . . . some of our neighbors would come and make a round or two for us in our field. . . . They would come and help us get through. . . . Colored people was better than they is to one another now, and they would come and help us get through. . . . But now people don't pay you too much attention. They're not like that anymore because everybody's doing different work now and they don't have time." Black Alabaman Monroe Wood recalled the visiting patterns of his childhood:

> Now nobody visits nobody. They ain't got time to fool with you. . . . And people work twelve months a year now. You're in a public job, you're going to work twelve months a year. Back then, by the Fourth of July, we was done laying by, we didn't do nothing but fish and run up and down the road all summer. . . . We'd hunt in the winter time, and that's all, there was no job . . . until World War II come along . . . and everybody went to working day and night. . . . Used to be you didn't hear tell of nobody working at night, but now there's as many jobs run at night as there is in the daytime.

Jackson's and Wood's stories illustrate how leaving the land for off-farm jobs altered the rhythms of daily life in ways that profoundly reshaped the form and meaning of community.[73]

White Texan Carl Neal also believed the new rhythms created by off-farm jobs had brought about a loss of community. He lamented: "And that's when the neighbors meant something. They visited, they knew each other, they knew their problems and the good parts of their lives, and if a neighbor needed help, you went to help. You didn't go to make a dollar, you went to help the neighbor. For that part at least it was a far better time than now because people cared about people. They had time to care about people. We worked hard, but it was a laid back time of life. You didn't have all the stress that they have today and all the hustle and going."[74] Neal's complaints about the loss of community reflect several concerns. Off-farm jobs with their strict schedules left people with little time to nurture community ties. The stresses of modern life—"all the hustle and going"—robbed people of energy once devoted to visiting each other. But at least as destructive in Neal's mind was the growing materialism of the modern world—the desire to "make a dollar"—and the increasing lack of concern for others. In Neal's story, the determined individualism of the modern world undermined a sense of connection to one's fellow man.

For other narrators, the growing population of the countryside and the move to urban centers caused community decline. White Mississippian Ruth Irwin noted, "You know, it seemed to me we didn't have as many problems then. We wadn't [sic] so thickly populated in the country, and as the population grew thicker, the problems grew more. I don't understand that; they should have grown better. But we didn't have robbing and killing then like we do now. We heard about it in some big city off away from us. And when it did happen, it was . . . a distress and a disgrace that hurt everybody." A white Kentucky woman agreed: "I think you lose a lot of the identity of people who work in them [cities] and who trade in them because when you go into the stores, the larger chain stores and so forth, the clerks don't know you. I think we're all just human that we want somebody to wait on us that has known us all these years and help us to make selections and then to be friendly when you go in. A lot of the people now who work in stores, people who it's just a job to them . . . they really don't care about the public."[75]

An underlying theme in both Carl Neal's and Ruth Irwin's statements is the loss of familiarity. They longed to see familiar faces around them and to know "their problems and the good parts of their lives," in Neal's words. White Alabaman Kiffin Browning strikes the same note in his lament about the changes in the once-tiny town of Ashland, Alabama. He complained:

> It used to be just a big country town where farmers came and purchased their seed and feed and fertilizer. That was mostly what the businesses were around the square. Since that time, we have these sewing factories, and in later years, we've gotten a poultry packing plant. . . . That made a big difference. More people moved into town. . . . When I first moved here, I knew nearly everybody in Ashland. They're people in Ashland now that I don't know, never see, have no opportunity of ever knowing, because they come and go. . . . Schools and churches have changed because of that too.

Unfamiliar people had moved in, people whose parents and grand-parents had not been part of the community. Historian Paul K. Conkin has said that today's yearning for community is grounded in our uprooted pluralistic world. He goes on to argue that "In a dozen ways, diverse Americans are trying to regain, or reclaim, a village." Neal, Irwin, and Browning clearly would like to reclaim villages where all the faces were familiar and perhaps a world where they wielded some personal influence.[76]

Some narrators believed that a loss of shared values rooted in an evangelical Christian religious faith lay at the heart of the loss of community. Letha Anderson McCall, a white farm woman from North Carolina, recalled the importance of neighborly aid in helping her family move from one North Carolina county to another around 1918. The interviewer commented on this neighborliness and asked Mrs. McCall whether there was enough of that kind of neighborliness today. She replied, "No, that's why there's so much envy and strife among people. We're not neighborly enough. We're not Christian enough to reach out to help someone else. All for self."[77]

Some African Americans suggested that the vicissitudes of the Jim Crow system had actually drawn rural black communities closer together. Black Mississippi minister David C. Matthews reported, "During those days of struggle and poverty, the so-called black community was pretty close knit together. There were problems but they were closer together than they are now because we had to share. . . . We didn't have much but we didn't have to worry about anybody taking that little because nobody was taking from anybody." Solidarity within the black community was a key to surviving in the hostile world of the segregated South, but Matthews hints that black people may feel less need for that solidarity today.[78]

Many narrators, now elderly and in poor health, probably fear losing their independence and being forced to enter a health care facility. These concerns drive many to lament the loss of mutual aid networks that once cared for the sick and the elderly. For example, widowed African American Anna Bertha Pitts found herself living in a federally subsidized apartment complex for the elderly in Albany, Georgia, at the end of her life. Her only son had been stabbed to death in 1976. Her husband had died in 1965 after a lifetime of poorly paid work in chalk mines, leaving her with few resources. Pitts made her living as a farm laborer from the time of his death until her own retirement in the 1980s. Undoubtedly, she lived on a meager fixed income and concern about how she would fare as her health failed must have weighed heavily on her mind. Pitts complained,

> Folks were living more better back there than they is now. And they cared for one another. They loved one another better than they do now. If you got sick and up in age like I was, if somebody come along, "Miss Pitts, anything I can do?" If they stayed there all night, they going to stay there with you. But now, they'll come in. "How you doing?". . . You don't see them no more. That's been a great change made since then. . . . So sometime I think we need to go back and pick up some of that they left off.[79]

Pitts's lament is striking partly because of the things she does not mention. In the first half of the twentieth century, professional health care would have been largely unavailable to rural African Americans like Pitts (and to many whites), a situation in marked contrast to conditions today. She does not, however, mention professional health care. Pitts and many rural folks believed help should come attached to a human face they had known for years. Yet even in earlier times, people excluded from rural communities might have also been excluded from the community network of care.

Narrators' explanations for the decline of rural community life are striking for the reasons they omit. Most narrators cite only two larger economic or structural forces as eroding rural community: off-farm jobs and the increased commercialism of society as a whole. No one mentioned that mechanized farming with its use of expensive equipment made the sharing of farm equipment not only less necessary but also financially risky. After all, an inexperienced neighbor could seriously damage a combine or a tractor. In fact, many narrators praised the introduction of farm equipment for lightening the workload and increasing productivity. Perhaps they did not want to undermine that message by admitting that mechanization could have negative consequences for community. Narrators also did not mention that the advent of New Deal farm legislation and subsequent federal agricultural allotment programs, which often favored large farmers, created more competition among local farmers vying for larger allotments. This competition could undermine community ties. Indeed the very material progress that had improved the lives of rural southerners over the past half century had rendered the types of community ties of the early twentieth century less essential, but perhaps not surprisingly, no narrator made that connection. Instead rural people focus as much on sociocultural forces and individual failings and faults—greed, rampant individualism, loss of religious faith, urbanization, and new kinds of work—as on structural forces that are largely beyond individual control. They are willing to blame community decline on self-centered individuals or even a decline in societal values but not on impersonal technological or political forces or on material progress.

Conclusions

As these examples suggest, rural southerners recounting their lives at the end of the twentieth century constructed their stories about rural life around their notions about the flaws in contemporary life. Farm people who recounted their lives at the end of the twentieth century differed significantly from many romantic agrarian thinkers. Unlike the Southern Agrarians whose writings celebrated an idyllic (and largely nonexistent) prosperity among late-nineteenth-century southern yeomen farmers, oral history narrators acknowledged the material hardships of farm life in an earlier time.[80] They acknowledged many improvements in modern life, and they relished their improved standard of living. Nonetheless, they saw material progress and modernization as a mixed blessing—as a source of new problems and of declining social values as well as comfort and convenience. They constantly compared an impoverished but more wholesome "then" to a comfortable, affluent, and problematic "now." In part, they saw the decline of agriculture and increasing distance from life on the land as the origin of today's problems. They believed that living on the land had shaped a core of common values of hard work, self-sufficiency, and mutual aid, values that they feel are missing in today's society. Their recollections present yesterday's strong, hardworking communities of farm folk in sharp contrast to what they perceive as the disconnected neighborhoods of soft and materialistic young people in which their children and grandchildren live. To say that they idealize the past through the sentimental lens of old age is to dismiss their very real concerns and some valid observations. While they are grateful that their children and grandchildren did not have to struggle so much, they recognize that their own struggles shaped virtue and strength of character. Their stories turn again and again to hardship and outright suffering, and none expressed any interest in returning to an earlier time and an earlier standard of living. Still, they share a sense of loss. Narrators feared that modern America has lost a type of psychic strength, an emotional stamina that they believe allowed them to outlast hard times. Nowhere is this sense that "it's not like today" more pronounced than in their stories about the decline of community.

Scholars have long noted that the shift from an agrarian to an urban industrial society profoundly transformed relationships among individuals, forcing people to turn from face-to-face and largely informal patterns of interaction to predominantly anonymous contacts with strangers mediated through formal institutions.[81] For example, historian Thomas Bender has noted that in the nineteenth century, social analysts worried that modernity, urbanization, and capitalism were undermining community, an analytical trope that persists up to the present. Bender argues that many students of American life have erroneously read social change as community decline, ignoring evidence that traditional patterns of communal relations often persisted with modernization, albeit often in a changed form. Teasing out which came first—changes in rural community or larger cultural narratives about community decline—proves to be an impossible task. Nonetheless, rural southerners' stories about the idyllic communities of the early twentieth century suggest that they have absorbed some ideas from the community decline model as a means of explaining the transformations in their own lives.[82]

However, as Bender points out, communities did not break down; rather, they took on radically different meanings. Economist Bruce Gardner argues that in the aggregate, the quality of life in rural communities has actually improved, based on such measures as education, standard of living, incidence of poverty, and other indicators. Nonetheless, the composition of rural communities has changed; today's rural residents are less likely to be engaged in agriculture and less likely to have been born in the rural community in which they live. Institutions, often institutions run by governmental agencies or distant officials, have replaced mutual aid as assistance to those in need. In some cases, law enforcement and social service agencies have replaced the social control mechanisms of traditional rural communities. Turning to institutional mechanisms for help can be liberating for some community members—perhaps especially women, children, African Americans, and the poor. As intrusive as social welfare agencies can be, many people may find more personal freedom and privacy in aid from these agencies than in assistance from interfering neighbors—assistance that often is attached to the repressive constraints of community influence and patriarchal control. As Bender reminds us, "For the poor and weak in our society, the experience of community seldom has any significant connections with the levers of power. For American elites, however, power and community often overlap."[83]

Nonetheless the poor and weak joined the elites of rural neighborhoods in lamenting the loss of community, and they apparently do not believe the transmuted forms of community that have replaced traditional ones provide the same benefits. Narrators mourned the decline in their personal influence over community life, a pattern that suggests that most of the storytellers shared an attitude that the best way to obtain what you need from a "higher-up" is through a personal appeal or a relationship of patronage. Romanticizing mid-twentieth-century rural communities and especially community-based mutual aid networks could be a statement of preference for local control. By defining community in opposition to relationships based on competition or utility or those forged in the context of anonymous formal structures such as the capitalist marketplace or government agencies, narrators highlight the close personal ties of community. They can critique the liberal, industrial state without acknowledging the real limitations of their often insular, oppressive, and exclusive rural communities of yore.

Race shapes these stories about community in interesting ways. As previously indicated, there were racial differences in the way narrators defined community, with white people talking about "community" as universal even though they largely referred to a community of fellow whites, while black people described themselves as being part of two communities, one black and the other racially mixed. Black people offer one reason for community decline not posed by white narrators: the erosion of the solidarity-producing oppression of the Jim Crow system. Nonetheless, blacks and whites alike mythologize mid-twentieth-century rural enclaves, and they share similar critiques of modern life. The implication is that narrators share a broad consensus on what has been lost with the loss of a rural world.

In their laments about a lost world of idyllic close-knit communities, rural southerners express their sense of the costs exacted by the profound disruptions of economic transformation. Perhaps their laments are only more attenuated versions of the unease heard in many segments of American society today—a discomfort with a world where face-to-face interactions increasingly give way to anonymous encounters with strangers or with technology. Our reaction is not new; historians have long noted that economic changes and the stress of adjusting to new social realities can result in a longing for an earlier time.[84]

Because such regrets are not new, scholars may be tempted to dismiss these critiques of contemporary life as mere nostalgia. Yet in doing so, students of the past miss important evidence that will enhance our understanding of the impact of change on individuals, communities, and societies as a whole. Historians have sometimes

ignored the affective content in sources generated by ordinary people, focusing instead on "factual" content that can be verified by
comparisons with other sources. Nonetheless, affective content can
be verified, too, by looking for patterns in the stories told by particular groups of people. And affective content can be most revealing. I
would argue that we must take seriously these narrators' longing for
lost community because they are using these stories about the past
quite deliberately. Historian Michael Frisch has noted that the main
value of oral history is that it is a tool for examining "how people
make sense of their past, how they connect individual experience and
its social context, how the past becomes part of the present, and how
people use it to interpret their lives and the world around them."
Rural southerners are using their stories about past communities as a
means of understanding the world in which they live. These narrators
did not long for the "good old days." Almost none of them expressed
a desire to return to the past. Many explicitly stated they would not
want to return to those days when daily life was more uncertain and
less comfortable. Yet they feel that we have lost something.[85]

Rural southerners use their stories about the country communities of their childhoods and young-adult years in several ways.
First, the notion of strong rural communities is central to their own
identities as country people. Stories about community often emerged
without much prompting when narrators were asked about rural life.
The ready accessibility of memories about community suggests that
these stories had been told over and over and that they are central
to the narrator's sense of him- or herself. In other words, one of the
main threads binding together the community of memory of the rural
South is the idea of belonging to a tightly knit community, and a
central component of narrators' rural identities is the belief that they
were "good" community members.[86]

Second, narrators are unlikely to use their stories to openly critique the material or technological progress or government policies
that helped bring about the decline of community as they knew it.
Instead, they will blame the loss of community on changing patterns
of work, urbanization, declining community values, or on individual
failings. Scholar Naomi Norquay argues that since memories have
both personal and social dimensions, "forgettings work to make the
boundaries and demarcations of the dominant culture invisible." In

a culture that generally praises the economic and social "progress" of the rural South, criticizing the processes that brought about that progress may seem less than acceptable. As a result, narrators minimize the negative consequences of "progress" from their stories.[87]

The third way in which narrators use their memories of rural community is as the rubric for evaluating communities in contemporary life. Few believe the present measures up to the past. Recently a number of scholars, most notably Robert Putnam, have documented the decline of civic engagement and the resulting loss of social capital in American life over the past thirty years. Social capital, the kind of reciprocal obligations built up by participation in formal and informal mutual aid networks, provides people who participate in social networks with access to both human and material resources. Putnam argues that a decline in social capital, caused by less individual engagement with community life, leads to more social problems. To most of the narrators of oral history accounts about rural community, the work of Putnam and his colleagues would ring true. Rural southerners believe that things are a mess all over, and they are a mess because of the decline of community. They seem to be saying: if only we went back to a world more like it was "then," we would have fewer problems.[88]

Finally, I would like to suggest that for many rural southerners, telling stories about how the past was "not like today," is in part, a political act. The stories constitute an attempt to convince a younger generation that some facets of contemporary life need altering, that they need to return to a world where people shared an ethic of care and concern and a sense of responsibility for each other. It is hard to determine the extent to which narrators were conscious of using narratives as a force in creating the future. Nonetheless, older people often seem to use stories about the "good old days" as cautionary tales or sources of instruction. For example, sociologist Karen E. Fields found this to be the case when she interviewed her grandmother in order to write *Lemon Swamp*, a memoir of black life in the Jim Crow South. Fields later observed that in the course of the interviews, "Gram assigned me a part in a continuing guerrilla war in which memory is not only a source of information about the past but also a force in creating the future." Narrators' complaints that young people expected too many material possessions at an early age rested in concerns about waste and about the long-term economic health of individuals and the nation as a whole. Their concerns echo the issues raised by environmentalists and advocates of sustainability in agriculture and in land-use practices. Their laments about the loss of community and about the deplorable behavior of young people rest in concerns about rising rates of crime, teen pregnancy, and social instability, but they also offer suggestions about how to reform social institutions so they operate more humanely and effectively. In the end, I believe that rural southerners hope to convince the younger generation that some elements of older rural community life are worth reviving.[89]

Conclusion

Often when it comes, the end of cultivation is no louder than the tumbling of apples into crates in a cave-cool, cave-dark room, but the life lived in the wake of its disappearance is a break with a long history and the days that follow—as the worked and tended country disappears, along with its bales and stacks, rows and grids, the men and women moving among them—are different in intent and kind. It may take a while for the idea to die away—there may be a romanticized echo, in which farming's rewards are imagined more vividly than its costs—but its end is one of those times the whole pattern shakes and quivers and settles into new shapes and figures.

—Jane Brox, *Clearing Land:*
Legacies of the American Farm

What I remember redeems me. . . .

—Charles Wright, "Apologia Pro Vita Sua"

Rural southerners who told their life stories late in the twentieth century knew that a way of life was passing. The transformation of agriculture undermined farm people's ties to the past—indeed their very sense of themselves. Through their memory stories, they sought a kind of redemption, a restoration of a sense that their lives and their way of life had mattered. They described transformations in ways calculated to give meaning to their losses. Their stories reflect their struggles to define the significance of farming and rural life once it was transformed.

Farm people constructed a community of memory around particular remembered characteristics of life on the land: self-sufficiency, a rural work ethic, persistence through hard times, a commitment to mutual aid, an attachment to the land and the local community, and the relative equality of rural folk. By telling stories about the rural community of memory, farming people communicated a strong sense of what they shared and what made them different—even better—than folks who had not lived on the land. Their stories urged a younger generation not to dismiss the values shaped by life on the land.

Sharp class, generational, and racial divides marked rural southerners' descriptions of transformation and its meanings. Narrators who came of age before World War II saw mechanization as the principal agent of change, and they offered detailed descriptions of the ways that mechanization altered their daily lives and especially their work. They rarely remembered agribusiness, world commodities markets, or federal intervention as playing any role in transforming farming, in spite of the fact that these forces were already exerting influence in the interwar years. By contrast, narrators who came of age during and after World War II told a more complex and nuanced tale, lamenting the way that global competition, the power of agribusiness corporations, and pressures to make large capital investments conspired to make family farming less viable. They often criticized the federal government for implementing agricultural policies that undermined the financial health of family farms or for failing to take steps to assure the future security of those farms. The stories of African Americans, landowning and landless alike, were marked by similar generational divides, but African Americans also emphasized the insidious effects of institutionalized racial discrimination, which served to systematically push black farmers off the land.

Rural southerners also used their stories to critique modern life. Over and over, they insisted that "it was not like today," and they often found "today" lacking. Although narrators, particularly women, rejoiced in the material improvements in daily life, they lamented the crass materialism and deplorable behavior of the younger generation as well as the decline of strong rural communities, changes they blamed at least in part on the transformation of the countryside. Thus rural southerners used their stories about the past as cautionary tales for the young. Historian Iwona Irwin-Zarecka has noted, "at its most fundamental, much of memory work is done 'for posterity.' . . . A specific vision of the future frames the utilization of the past."[1] By telling idealized tales about strife-free rural communities of an earlier time, narrators asserted the importance of values they believed were being lost.

Rural people's stories about the past were not created in a vacuum, however. Subsequent experiences, shifts in the agricultural economy and federal policy, persistent racial discrimination, and even the influences of education and the mass media were all forces that continually shaped and reshaped narratives about rural change. The postwar generation's stories of transformation proved more complex, layered, and subtle than those of the prewar generation in part because their experiences were more complex, but also because the outside forces shaping their storytelling were more varied and complicated.

Narrators' stories about the transformation of the rural South give us a better understanding of the ways that the very meaning of farming changed over the course of the twentieth century. Early in the century, most rural people saw farming as a means—sometimes the only available means—of earning a living. Many also embraced farming as a way of life that offered a level of autonomy and economic security not offered by wage work. Yet farm life proved hard, especially during the prolonged agricultural depression of the interwar years. Many farm youth who came of age during the Great Depression—especially the children of the landless—could not wait to leave the land for better opportunities elsewhere. For example, Bill Lewellyn remembered bitter poverty, first on a tenant farm where he watched tuberculosis slowly rob his father of life and later on rented land where his grandparents eked out a living selling truck crops, eggs, and butter. His memory stories did not romanticize life on the land. Lewellyn seized on an opportunity created by wartime mobilization and took a manufacturing job that offered higher pay and more financial security. Lewellyn and many others of his generation may have missed life on the land—indeed, many of them farmed part-time in later life—but they preferred an easier livelihood.

By contrast, many narrators who came of age after the war, especially those who owned land, believed the postwar period had offered fresh opportunities for farmers. After the desperate poverty of the Great Depression and the shortages and rationing of World War II, agricultural experts promised a new level of prosperity to farmers who adopted modern methods of working the land. As Arkansas rice farmer Kenneth Gosney put it, "After World War II, a young person, if he had the ambition—everything was go [in farming]."[2] Like thousands of eager young farmers, Gosney embraced the advice of experts wholeheartedly, believing that they were at the forefront of a new era when American agriculture could benefit from adopting the business-like practices that had made American industry great.

As the industrial ideal for agriculture took hold in the postwar period, many farm people expected farming to offer them the same level of opportunities for financial success as other booming postwar industries. A new sense of farmer identity often accompanied these rising expectations. As historian David B. Danbom put it, "Material changes have been paralleled by changes in the habits of mind."[3] Shifts in the meaning of farming were accompanied by shifts in the class consciousness of farm people. Most people who managed to persist on the land after World War II embraced the promise of middle-class status, changing their farming and management practices in an attempt to enjoy such status. Farm people were profoundly ambivalent about the transformation of agriculture, and their stories illustrate the tension between farming as a way of life and farming as a business. The former choice might offer autonomy but also relegated farm families to a life lived on the margins of American society. While the latter was riskier, it promised the material and social benefits provided by middle-class status. The tensions were most apparent in stories told by farmers who had embraced industrial agriculture with limited success. They often called, perhaps futilely, for a return to an earlier style of farming. For example, African American Georgia farmer Woodrow Harper Sr. spent a lifetime struggling to succeed by specializing in soybean production. In 1987, he told historian Lu Ann Jones, "[D]iversified farming, the type of farming that we used to do, raising cotton and corn[,] needs to be revived . . . to make the livelihood better for the farmer."[4]

Yet even as farmers' perceptions of the meaning of farming changed, they clung to traditional agrarian ideology. Agrarianism—the belief that the independent, self-reliant family farm shaped virtuous citizens—permeated the stories that rural narrators told about life on the land. Their accounts are laced with assertions that family farming molded superior citizens and provided, in the words of historian Victor Davis Hanson, "the moral cement of the community."[5] They also believed that the traditional family farm, as it existed before the days of government intervention, powerful corporations, and global competition, could best integrate material prosperity with a healthy environment and society. Finally, they maintained a staunch belief that the local community provided the best mechanism for addressing social problems such as poverty, care for the elderly, and crime.

Studying the ways people use memory and connect individual memory to the larger past has the potential to provide scholars with new insights into the past. For example, this case study of the relationship between history and memory has the potential to illuminate one of the most puzzling aspects of late-twentieth-century agricultural history: why small farmers failed to organize effectively after World War II to counter the trend toward "bigness" in agriculture. The narratives examined here suggest several reasons. First, the stories farmers tell demonstrate the contingent nature of farmers' interest group formation. Anthropologist Miriam J. Wells argues that one factor that has historically undermined farmers' desire to organize was "the multiple and ambiguous pulls of socioeconomic status." People may hold more than one economic position simultaneously and their jobs may "endow them with objectively conflicting economic interests" that make it hard to identify with only one class or interest group. Moreover, she says, the noneconomic aspects of status, such as race, have become politicized and shape individuals' identification with particular interest groups.[6]

The reasons for southern farmers' failure to organize on a large scale in the postwar period are undoubtedly complex, but oral history narrators provide some tantalizing clues that support Wells's analysis. In the postwar period, in part thanks to the concerted educational efforts of creditors, agricultural experts, and agribusiness corporations, many farm people came to share the interests and ambitions of the larger middle class.[7] They wanted to build comfortable and attractive homes, drive late-model cars, take vacations to interesting locations, and send their children to college. Most believed their best hope to achieve these ambitions lay in embracing the tenets of industrial agriculture. They mechanized, specialized, and devoted most of their efforts to producing for the marketplace. They learned to negotiate the complexities of federal farm programs. They depended on bankers to provide the operating capital for industrial farming, even if it meant sacrificing some autonomy. They allied themselves with the cigarette manufacturers, poultry processors, and other power-ful corporations who purchased their products, believing such alli-ances were the key to farming success. Their ties to middle-class folks who were not farmers undercut their desire to organize as farmers. As political scientist Merle Black put it, "Once Southerners became middle class, or had the possibility of becoming middle class, popu-lism died."[8] For example, Tennessee farmer John West wanted to be respected by his local bank president (see chapter 1). Therefore he would have been reluctant to join in any organizational effort that might have undercut his ties to the bank president and jeopardized his access to loans in the future. To organize in ways that would have effectively combated their growing dependence on the federal government, bankers, and agribusiness firms might have been good for farmers as a group but might also have impaired their success individually. In short, the rational self-interest of many, perhaps most farmers, lay in *not* organizing.

In addition to farm people's identification with the larger middle class, racial differences among rural southerners also undermined their sense of shared interests. Racial discrimination persisted, leav-ing black farmers feeling as if they faced multiple enemies—federal bureaucrats, a discriminatory business community, and their fellow white farmers. As black Georgia farmer Woodrow Harper Sr. put it, "the big fish is eating up the little ones" (see chapter 1). In Harper's stories, the big fish in his community were white landowners. The small fish—landless black farmers—could not compete with white farmers' resources or their access to help from agribusiness firms and the federal government. Harper would have had trouble trust-ing any interracial farm organization to place the interests of small black farmers on the same plane with those of more powerful and larger white farmers. Black farmers, especially non-landowners, felt too marginalized and were too few to effectively organize.

The narratives provide insight into other factors that inhibited farmers' desire to organize. They often failed to resist the trend toward "bigness" because most did not recognize bigness as a threat until it was too late to counter the trend. Farmers like Kenneth Gosney bought into the idea that expansion and specialization were the keys to pros-perity. In the process, he and his fellow farmers became increasingly embedded in the global marketplace. This global agricultural econ-

omy undermined their ability to develop effective economic or political alternatives. Limiting productivity, cooperative marketing, and
other traditional strategies for farmer organizing would have proved
completely ineffective in improving farm prices by the late twentieth
century. Even those farmers who did organize failed to develop effective strategies. Resistant to radical solutions, farm organizations hired
lobbyists and filed class-action lawsuits, demonstrating their persistent
faith in using the system as a means of change.[9]

As their numbers dwindled, farmers felt increasingly powerless
to pressure elected officials on their own behalf. Narrators who had
tried working with farm organizations in failed attempts to lobby
Congress often expressed this sense of helplessness. Kate Graham's
sense of frustration after her testimony to a congressional committee
on behalf of WIFE was typical. "It just turned my thinking around
completely to see what they [legislators] were doing. And the sad
thing about it is, . . . they didn't care. You know they DID NOT care.
And they care even less now because there are fewer farmers."[10] Such
feelings of helplessness often led farmers to give up on efforts to organize or influence political leaders. French scholar Pierre Bourdieu has
noted that, "'Interest' or 'indifference' towards politics would be better understood if it were seen that the propensity to use a political
power . . . is commensurate with the reality of this power, or, in other
words, that indifference is only a manifestation of impotence."[11] In
the face of what philosopher Ronald Jager has called "the devouring
forces of industrial agriculture," many narrators felt powerless to
effect any change that would make agriculture a viable enterprise.[12]
As the oral history narrators suggest, farmers often cannot translate
the failure of the system into alternative visions of how agriculture
might work, and that inability to envision alternatives stymies their
ability to organize.

Another factor inhibiting the desire of farmers to organize is the
intense individualism that is a hallmark of modern American family
farming. Early-twentieth-century farmers may have shared a commitment to mutual aid that built community solidarity, a solidarity that
might facilitate organizing, but as farmers increasingly approached
farming as a business, they saw it as an entrepreneurial business
built by individuals or at least by individual families. Anthropologist
Kathryn Marie Dudley argues,

a cultural commitment to economic growth has instantiated a system of morality which requires a distinctive conception of the self: one that is held personally accountable for the consequences of economic risk-taking. This *entrepreneurial self*, I propose is the conceptual linchpin of capitalist culture. It facilitates a moral order that allows Americans to endow their lives with meaning, even as it undercuts collective resistance to the conditions that have made traditional ways of life increasingly hard to sustain.

In short, family farmers' commitment to independence comes at the expense of social solidarity and the ability to organize to pursue a common cause.[13] Instead of seeking to transform American society, many farmers have turned to small-scale and individual solutions such as farming for niche markets and selling directly to consumers.[14] In oral history narratives, this individualism often emerges in the silences and in the construction of individual identity. For example, John West's focus on himself as a self-made man illustrates this intense individualism. So does William Graham's frustration that his fellow Lee County, South Carolina, farmers would not join him in the American Agriculture Movement. He said, "If all the farmers had come together . . . , we wouldn't be in the situation we are in now, I don't believe." Perhaps Graham's neighbors feared that joining a farm protest organization would signal impending failure. Whatever their reasons for refusing to join, Graham believed that it was because his neighbors hoped to take advantage of his misfortune. He said, "A lot of these farmers that have quit in Lee County in the last few years—we couldn't get them to join with us. They really wanted us to go [out of business] so they could buy our land when we lost it." The Grahams' neighbors may have hoped to obtain his land, but for some the reality proved bleak. By the time I interviewed William Graham in 2002, many more Lee County farmers had given up the farming ghost. As Graham put it, "[They thought] the more land they could get, the more money there would be to make. It didn't work out that way. They lost it."[15]

Appendix One
Demographic Data

Table 1
Interviewees by Race and Sex

Sex	Number	Percentage	White	Percentage	Black	Percentage
Male	244	46	189	35.6	55	10.4
Female	287	54	210	39.5	77	14.5
Total	531	100	399	75	132	25

Note: There were 475 interviews or interview sets (two or more interviews with the same person(s) by the same interviewee(s)) and a total of 531 people interviewed.

Table 2
Interviews by State

State	Number of Interviewees	Percentage[*]
Alabama	60	13.0
Arkansas	14	3.0
Florida	3	<0.5
Georgia	25	5.3
Kentucky	3	<0.5
Louisiana	13	2.7
Maryland	1	<0.5
Mississippi	41	8.6
North Carolina	118	25.0
South Carolina	43	8.9
Tennessee	32	6.8
Texas	79	16.7
Virginia	35	7.4
West Virginia	2	<0.5
Unknown	6	<0.5

Note: There were 475 interviews or interview sets and a total of 531 people interviewed.

[*]Rounded to the nearest tenth; may not add up to 100 percent because of rounding.

Table 3
Interviews by Interview Purpose

Interview Purpose	Number of Interviewees	Percentage[*]
Black Life in the Jim Crow South	66	14.0
Civil Rights Movement	8	1.6
Southern Industrialization	51	10.8
Rural Life	315	66.2
Other	35	7.4

Note: There were 475 interviews or interview sets and a total of 531 people interviewed.

[*]Rounded to the nearest tenth; may not add up to 100 percent because of rounding.

Table 4
Interviewees by Decade of Birth[*]

Decade of Birth	Number of Interviewees	Percentage[#]
1870s	1	<0.2
1880s	7	1.5
1890s	33	6.9
1900s	89	18.7
1910s	103	21.7
1920s	88	18.5
1930s	25	5.3
1940s	4	<1
1950s	4	<1
Unknown[&]	121	25.5

Note: There were 475 interviews or interview sets and a total of 531 people interviewed.

[*]In many of the cases where two people were interviewed, the birthdate of only one was recorded. Therefore, this table reflects the birthdate of the first interviewee to state a birthdate. In almost every case, the second interviewee was born in the same decade.

[#]Rounded to the nearest tenth; may not add up to 100 percent because of rounding.

[&]Decade of birth difficult to estimate from context of interview but born before 1950.

Table 5
Landowning Status by Race

Landowning Status	Number	Percentage*	White	Percentage of Whites*	Black	Percentage of Blacks*
Non-landowner (day laborer, share-cropper, tenant, renter, farm manager)	97	20.4	44	12.6	54	43.5
Landowner	260	54.7	216	61.5	44	35.4
Lived in rural area, but primary source of income was off-farm job	19	4	15	4.3	4	3
Non-landowner advancing to landowner	17	3.6	14	4	3	2.4
Landowner becoming non-landowner	6	1.3	4	1.1	2	1.6
Landowner moving to off-farm work	6	1.3	5	1.4	1	0.8
Non-landowner moving to off-farm work	2	>0.4	2	0.6	0	0
Off-farm work moving to landownership	2	>0.4	2	0.6	0	0
Unknown	66	13.9	49	13.9	16	12.9
Total	475		351		124	

Note: There were 475 interviews or interview sets and a total of 531 people interviewed.

*Rounded to the nearest tenth; may not add up to 100 percent because of rounding.

Table 6
Education Level by Race

Education Level	Total	Percentage of Total*	White	Black
Elementary School	35	7.4	24	11
High School	97	20.4	72	25
Attended college	16	3.4	13	3
College graduate	62	13	46	16
Postgraduate work or degree	29	6.1	18	11
Vocational or technical school#	13	2.7	10	3
Unknown	223	46.9	168	55
Total	475		351	124

Note: There were 475 interviews or interview sets and a total of 531 people interviewed.

*Rounded to the nearest tenth; may not add up to 100 percent because of rounding.

#Including secretarial or business college, vocational training program, beauty school, non-degree nursing program, etc.

Appendix Two
List of Interviewees

Abbreviations

Education

E = elementary
HS = high school (attended and/or graduated)
AT = attended college
CG = college graduate
G = postgraduate work and/or degree
VT = vocational or technical school

Landowning Status

O = landowner
N = non-landowner (sharecropper, tenant, cash renter)
OF = living in country, but had off-farm job
N-O = non-landowning farmer who became landowning farmer
O-N = landowning farmer who became non-landowning farmer
OF-O = off-farm job, then landowning farmer
O-OF = landowning farmer who took off-farm job
N-OF = non-landowning farmer who took off-farm job

Last Name	First Name	State	Year of Interview	Sex	Race	Year of Birth	Landowning Status	Level of Education
Aaron	Junie Edna Kaylor	NC	1979	F	W	1904	O	unknown
Abernathy	Mr. and Mrs. Yates	NC	1984	M/F	W	unknown	O	unknown
Accardo	Paul	LA	1988	M	W	1906	O	unknown
Adams	Deola Mayberry	TX	1987	F	AA	1914	O	HS
Adams	Harry Singleton	NC	1979	M	W	unknown	O	unknown
Adams	Hubert	AL	1990	M	W	1913	N	unknown
Adamson	Mary Price	NC	1976	F	W	1909	O	CG
Alexander	Essie Mae	MS	1995	F	AA	1927	N	unknown
Alford	Lillian Jane	TX	1991	F	W	1908	O	HS
Allen	David	SC	1987	M	W	1923	N	CG
Anderson	Ernestine	TX	1999	F	AA	1927	N	CG
Anderson	G. W.	TX	1992	M	W	unknown	O	CG
Anderson	Oliver	TX	1992	M	W	1913	O	HS
Anderson	Walter and Adra	TN	1987	M/F	W	1911/1908	O	unknown
Andrews	Bertha	AL	1982	F	W	unknown	unknown	unknown
Andrews	John William	NC	1987	M	W	1919	O	HS
Andrews	Norbert King	NC	1985	M	W	1908	O	CG
Andrews	O. N.	AL	1988	M	W	1909	O	CG
Arbuckle	Marion D.	VA	1977/78	M	W	1886	O	HS
Ardoin	Leslie	LA	1988	M	W	unknown	O	unknown
Armstrong	Coy	NC	1985	M	W	unknown	unknown	unknown
Arnett	Irby	VA	1981	F	W	1916	O	VT
Austin	Eunice	NC	1980	F	W	1915	N	unknown
Avis	Annie Maud Knittel	TX	1991	F	W	1919	O	VT
Baber	Charles	VA	1978	M	W	unknown	unknown	unknown
Bailey	Charles	MS	1987	M	W	1919	O	HS
Bailey	Howard Taft	MS	1987	M	AA	1909	O	unknown
Baldwin	Curtis	NC	1978	M	AA	unknown	unknown	unknown

Last Name	First Name	State	Year of Interview	Sex	Race	Year of Birth	Landowning Status	Level of Education
Banks	Earl W.	MS	1975	M	AA	1905	O	G
Barbee	Annie Mack	NC	1979	F	AA	1913	N	unknown
Barger	Katherine	VA	1981	F	W	unknown	unknown	unknown
Barham	Lois	NC	1984	F	W	unknown	unknown	unknown
Barnes	Lavonia Jenkins	TX	1976	F	W	1906	OF	CG
Bateman	David	NC	1984	M	W	unknown	O	unknown
Bateman	Laura Belle Holley	TX	1994	F	W	1910 ca.	O	unknown
Bateman	Opal	TX	1993	F	W	1916	O	E
Bateman	Viola Anderson	TX	1992	F	W	1910	N	HS
Bedell	Dewey	AL	1988	M	AA	1907	O	unknown
Bedsole	J. T.	AL	1986	M	W	unknown	unknown	unknown
Bekkelund	Ima Hoppe	TX	1997	F	W	1921	N	HS
Bell	Sallie	AL	1992	F	AA	unknown	unknown	G
Bennett	Virginia	AL	1976	F	W	1920 ca.	O	unknown
Benson	Dick	GA	1987	M	W	1929	O	VT
Benton	Aubrey and Ina Bell	GA	1987	M/F	W	1912	N-O	E
Best	Rachel	NC	1986	F	W	unknown	O	unknown
Blackwell	Unita	MS	1977	F	AA	1933	N	HS
Blue	Mrs. Elvie	AL	1980	F	W	1919	OF	unknown
Bock	Rev. Warren	NC	1998	M	W	1938	OF	G
Boward	Ruby E.	VA	1977	F	W	unknown	unknown	unknown
Boyce	Lena	NC	1984	F	W	unknown	O	unknown
Bradford/Norwood	Nara/Elijah	MS	1987	F/M	W	1905/1902	O	E
Brantley	L. D.	AR	1987	M	W	1926	N-O	HS
Brookshire	unknown	KY	1982	F	W	unknown	O	CG
Browing	Kiffin	AL	1988	M	W	1916	OF	unknown
Brown	Frances Holmstrom	TX	1992	F	W	1909	O	HS
Brown/Legree	George L./Joseph P.	SC	1994	M	AA	1915 ca.	O	unknown

Last Name	First Name	State	Year of Interview	Sex	Race	Year of Birth	Landowning Status	Level of Education
Brown	Gertrude	NC	1978	F	W	unknown	unknown	unknown
Brown	Gordon	AR	1987	M	W	1903	O	CG
Brown	Hannah Hoff	TX	1976	F	W	1905	O	G
Brown	Howell	VA	2002	M	W	1930 ca.	O	unknown
Brown	Mamie	MS	1987	F	AA	1906	O	unknown
Brownell	Jim	VA	2002	M	W	1930 ca.	O	unknown
Broyles	Lizzie	TN	1975	F	W	1890	O	unknown
Buck	Gilbert	TX	1993	M	W	1936	OF	AT
Burt	Thomas	NC	1976	M	W	unknown	N	unknown
Bush	Mr. and Mrs. James B	VA	1977	M/F	W	1892	O	unknown
Busselman	Norman and Willie	VA	1986	M/F	W	1910	O	unknown
Butts	William A.	MS	1976	M	AA	1933	O	G
Byers	Sanford	GA	1987	M	W	1918	O	unknown
Campbell	Will D.	TN	1976	M	W	1924	O	G
Carden	Stella Foust	NC	1979	F	W	1907	N	unknown
Carroll	Dovie Lee and Etta	TX	1990	M/F	W	1902/1907	O	HS
Carter	Ethel H.	VA	1988	F	W	1920 ca.	O	unknown
Carter	Viola	GA	1994	F	AA	1921	N	E
Case	Mr. and Mrs. L. C., Jr.	NC	1994	M/F	W	1920 ca.	OF	unknown
Cash	Kline	SC	1997	M	W	1945 ca.	O	CG
Castleberry	Guy	GA	1987	M	W	1900	O-OF	unknown
Caufield	Alice Owens	TX	1993	F	AA	1907	N	AC
Caughron	Roy, Rex, and Kermit	TN	1987	M	W	1915 ca.	N	unknown
Cazalas	Sarah L. R.	AL	1984	F	W	1925	N	HS
Chapman	J. C. and Tiny	AL	1987	M/F	W	1914	O	unknown
Clark	Chester and Roxana	NC	1979	M/F	AA	unknown	N	unknown
Clark	French	TN	1994	F	W	1905	OF	HS
Clay	Marshall	NC	1979	M	W	unknown	N	unknown

Last Name	First Name	State	Year of Interview	Sex	Race	Year of Birth	Landowning Status	Level of Education
Clayborne	Sam F.	VA	1979	M	W	1886	O	unknown
Cleveland	Myrtle Spencer	SC	1979	F	W	1908	unknown	E
Coats	Danny	NC	1998	M	W	unknown	unknown	unknown
Cockerham	Lester and Marie	NC	1987	M/F	W	1905/1908	O	unknown
Colley	J. C. and Lizzie	AL	1987	M/F	W	1906/1905	O	unknown
Collier	Shirley	NC	1984	F	W	unknown	unknown	unknown
Colvard	Russell	NC	2000	M	W	1920 ca.	O	HS
Colvin	R. C.	MS	1987	M	W	1905	O	HS
Connell	Alton	GA	1987	M	W	1905	O	E
Cooper	Marguerite	TX	1977	F	W	1888	O	CG
Costan	John	NC	1984	M	W	unknown	unknown	unknown
Cotton	T. J.	NC	1977	M	W	1905	O	unknown
Cox	Pauline	NC	2002	F	AA	unknown	unknown	unknown
Crawford	Cecil and May	NC	1985	M/F	W	unknown	O	unknown
Crocker	Ethel	AL	1975	F	W	unknown	N	unknown
Crosby	Victor and Ruth	NC	1987	M/F	W	1919/1919	O	unknown
Crouse	Munsey and Waine	NC	1984	M/F	W	unknown	O	unknown
Crumpton	Eula	AL	1980	F	W	1915 ca.	O	HS
Crumpton	Gordon	AL	1980	M	W	1913	O	unknown
Cuffie	Roosevelt A.	GA	1994	M	AA	1926	O	HS
Culpepper	Ruth Rhodes	VA	1980	F	W	1899	O	HS
Cunningham	Tom B.	SC	1991	M	W	1923	O	HS
Daughtry	H. E.	NC	1984	M	W	unknown	O	CG
Daughtry	Robuck and Elizabeth	TX	1994	M/F	W	1908/1912	O	CG/CG
Davidson	Betty and Lloyd	NC	1979	F/M	W	1912/1913	O	unknown
Davis	Mrs. Dewey	AL	1986	F	W	unknown	OF	unknown
Davis	Ethel	TN	1994	F	W	1905	O	HS
Davis	Fredda	NC	1984	F	W	1892	O	unknown

Last Name	First Name	State	Year of Interview	Sex	Race	Year of Birth	Landowning Status	Level of Education
Davis	Lornie	AL	1976	F	AA	1904	OF	unknown
Davis	Otto and Pauline	SC	1987	M/F	W	1909/1911	O	unknown
Dawson	Joesph M.	TX	1971	M	W	1879	N	CG
Delasbour	Anna	LA	1988	F	AA	1903	N	E
DeLoach	Mrs. Quinnie Velma	AL	1980	F	W	1908	O	E
Delozier	Arthur	TN	1994	M	W	1902	O	HS
DeMent	J. M.	TX	1992	M	W	1913	O	AC
DeMent	Robert	TX	1993	M	W	1905 ca.	O	CG
Denning	Lamas and Janie	TX	1998	M/F	W	1920 ca.	O	HS
Diggs	Annie Mae	NC	2001	F	AA	unknown	O	unknown
Dodd	Myrtle I.	TX	1990	F	W	1905	N	CG
Downing	Avery R.	TX	1983	M	W	1913	O	G
Dreyer	Edna J.	TX	1997	F	W	1914	O	HS
Dryman	Mr. and Mrs. Hugh	NC	1984	M/F	W	unknown	O	unknown
Ducrest	Jesse	MS	1987	M	W	1925 ca.	OF-O	HS
Dugger	Roy M.	TX	1982	M	W	1925	N	G
Dumas	Bertha L.	AL	1976	F	W	unknown	unknown	unknown
Dunlap/Ross	Kathryn/Susie	NC	1975	F/F	AA	unknown	unknown	unknown
Durham	Flossie M.	NC	1976	F	W	1883	N	E
Durham	Frank	NC	1979	M	W	1905	N	E
Duty	Elaine	VA	1976	F	W	1915 ca.	O	AC
Dyke	Maude	WV	1981	F	W	1893 ca.	O	HS
Edwards	Zelphia	LA	1982	F	W	unknown	O	unknown
Elgin	Jimmy	NC	1978	M	W	unknown	unknown	unknown
Elliott	Mrs. W. D.	NC	1984	F	W	unknown	O	unknown
Elmore	George R.	NC	1974	M	W	1902	N-OF	CG
Emmons	Martha	TX	1985	F	W	1894	O	G
Engelbrecht	Ben and Earlien	TX	1997	M/F	W	1916/1918	O	HS

Last Name	First Name	State	Year of Interview	Sex	Race	Year of Birth	Landowning Status	Level of Education
Engelbrecht	Marvin	TX	1997	M	W	1920 ca.	O	HS
Ervin	Hassie R. W.	NC	2002	F	AA	unknown	unknown	unknown
Estes	Elizabeth W.	TX	1976	F	W	1908	O	VT
Evans	Anna	KY	1981	F	W	1900	O	AC
Evans	Dolly	AL	1975	F	W	1894	unknown	E
Evans	Rubie W.	TX	1990	F	AA	1915	O	G
Farmer	LaVerne	TN	1993	F	W	1931	O	G
Farrow	Mildred	AL	1987	F	W	1929	O-OF	HS
Felknor	Jessie F.	TN	1987	F	W	1911	O	HS
Fenner	Lillie Pierce	NC	1993	F	AA	1907	N	E
Fetner	Woodrow	AL	1987	M	W	1914	O-N	unknown
Fielder	Margaret N.	VA	1977	F	W	unknown	unknown	unknown
Finchum	Eva and Amos	TN	1987	F/M	W	unknown	O	unknown
Finley	Vesta	NC	1975	F	W	unknown	N	unknown
Fishburne	Elliott G.	VA	1977	M	W	unknown	unknown	unknown
Fleming	Murray	NC	1984	M	W	unknown	unknown	unknown
Floyd	John C.	AL	1984	M	W	1897	O-N	unknown
Folley	Della Inez	TX	1990	F	W	1908	O	AC
Forney	Myrtle	NC	1993	F	AA	1909	O	G
Foster	Jim and Virgie	NC	1987	M/F	W	1910/1915	O	unknown
Fouts	Mary	KY	1981	F	W	1909	O	unknown
Fox	Lillian	NC	1981	F	W	1910 ca.	O	E
Foy	James	AL	1988	M	W	1916	O	G
Freeman	Grace	SC	1983	F	W	unknown	unknown	unknown
Fuller	Thomas F.	NC	1975	M	W	1900 ca.	O	unknown
Gaddy	Carry H.	NC	2001	F	AA	1920 ca.	OF	unknown
Gambrell	Ida May	SC	2003	F	W	1907	N-O	E
Garber	Sallie Reed	VA	1977	F	W	unknown	unknown	unknown

Last Name	First Name	State	Year of Interview	Sex	Race	Year of Birth	Landowning Status	Level of Education
Gates	Pat	SC	1981	F	W	1920 ca.	O	HS
Gentry	Myrtle S.	SC	1979	F	W	unknown	N	unknown
George	Mrs. Leler	SC	1987	F	AA	1903	O	unknown
Gibbs	Marian G.	TX	1987	F	W	1919	O	CG
Gibson	O. C.	MS	1995	M	AA	1928	N	HS
Giles	Alice Owens	MS	1995	F	AA	1920	N	HS
Gilliam	Nell	VA	1988	F	W	1924	O	unknown
Gillis	John M.	NC	1984	M	W	unknown	unknown	unknown
Glenn	F. Berkeley	VA	1977	M	W	unknown	unknown	unknown
Glenn	Josephine	NC	1977	F	W	1907	N	HS
Godwin	John	NC	1984	M	W	unknown	unknown	unknown
Gosney	Jessie and Kenneth	AR	1987	F/M	W	1928	O	HS
Graham	Melvin	NC	1996	M	W	1924	O	AC
Graham	William and Kate	SC	2002	M/F	W	1928 ca.	O	CG
Gramling	Henry, II	SC	1997	M	W	1950 ca.	O	CG
Graves	Lonnie	TX	1991/1993	M	AA	1916	O	HS
Gray	Wardell	MS	1987	M	AA	1916	O	HS
Grier	Katie	NC	2001	F	AA	1925	N	VT
Griffin	A. C. and Grace	NC	1986	M/F	W	1908	O	HS
Guderian	Pearl	TX	1991	F	W	1905	O	HS
Guy	Katherine	TX	1993	F	AA	1915	N-O	HS
Hale	Alma	TX	1988	F	W	1902	O	CG
Hall	James	GA	1994	M	AA	1917	N	unknown
Hall	Joe C.	NC	1987	M	W	1910	N-O	HS
Hall	Ophelia	TX	1986	F	AA	1914	O	HS
Hall	Mrs. Pinkey	MS	1995	F	AA	1925 ca.	O	HS
Hamil	Howard	AL	1987	M	W	unknown	unknown	unknown
Hamilton	Lehon and Maxine	VA	2002	M/F	W	1930 ca.	O	unknown

Last Name	First Name	State	Year of Interview	Sex	Race	Year of Birth	Landowning Status	Level of Education
Hammond	Theo	NC	1981	F	W	1899	OF	CG
Hardin	Alice	SC	1980	F	W	1911	N	E
Harper	Woodrow	GA	1987	M	AA	1917	N-O	HS
Harrington	A. M.	SC	1987	M	W	unknown	O	unknown
Harrington	Edward and Mary E.	NC	1979	M/F	W	1913	O	unknown
Harris	Edna	NC	1987	F	W	1926	O	unknown
Harris	Gladys	NC	1979	F	W	unknown	unknown	unknown
Harris	Rev. John	LA	1988	M	W	1912	N	HS
Harris/Skinner	Virginia/Dorothy	SC	2001	F/F	W	1920/1914	O	VT
Hartsoe	Gwyn	NC	1999	M	W	1916	O-OF	HS
Hartsoe	Mae	NC	1999	F	W	1916	O-OF	HS
Harvell	Evelyn	SC	1980	F	W	unknown	unknown	unknown
Harwell	Rita	AL	1981	F	W	1914	N-O	HS
Hatch	Roy H.	TX	1973	M	W	1890	O	CG
Hayes	Maggie	AL	1977	F	W	1892	N	unknown
Head	A. L.	AL	1975	M	W	1884	N	CG
Heard	Estelle and John	AL	1987	F/M	AA	1926/1932	N	unknown
Herring	Harriet	NC	1976	F	W	1892	O	G
Hill	Frank	TN	1987	M	W	1913	O	unknown
Hill	Mary	NC	1979	F	W	1899	OF	unknown
Hobbs	Everett and Edna	TN	1994	M/F	W	1912/1912	O-OF	HS
Hodges	Estelle	NC	1979	F	W	unknown	unknown	unknown
Hold	Nancy	NC	1985	F	W	unknown	O	unknown
Holt	W. Bruce	NC	1985	M	W	unknown	O	unknown
Hooten	Henry and Lillian	AL	1994	M/F	AA	unknown	N	unknown
Horn	C. P.	AL	1988	M	W	1917	O	G
Howard	Helen	AR	1995	F	AA	1909	N	unknown
Howard	Sallie Mae	SC	1995	F	AA	unknown	N	unknown

Last Name	First Name	State	Year of Interview	Sex	Race	Year of Birth	Landowning Status	Level of Education
Howell	Elmin K.	TX	1980	M	W	1930	O	G
Hudson	Juanita and Mack	NC	1998	F/M	W	1928	O	unknown
Hunt	Catherine Pike	AL	1986	F	W	1920	OF	HS
Ingram	James	MS	1995	M	AA	1925	N	G
Inman	Chester F.	TN	1984	M	W	1911	O	HS
Irwin	Ruth	MS	1982	F	W	1905 ca.	O	unknown
Jackson	Irene	SC	2003	F	W	1910	O	E
Jackson	Lottie	GA	1981	F	W	1910 ca.	N	E
Jackson	Ruthie L.	MS	1995	F	AA	unknown	N	E
James	Herman	LA	1994	M	AA	unknown	N	unknown
Jefferson	Henrietta	FL	1994	F	AA	unknown	N	unknown
Jefferson	Vivian	AR	1982	F	W	1887	OF-O	CG
Jewell	Worth	AL	1982	M	W	1911	O	E
Johnson	Eunice	TX	1986	F	AA	1896	N	E
Johnson	Herbert	GA	1987	M	W	1914	O	unknown
Johnson	Maudie	MS	1995	F	AA	unknown	N	unknown
Johnson	Ruth S.	NC	1994	F	AA	1916	N-O	AC
Johnson	Vera	SC	1980	F	W	1913	N	E
Jones	Amy	TN	1995	F	AA	1932	N	unknown
Jones	Billy Lee	LA	1982	F	W	1910	O	unknown
Jones	Cora	TX	1988	F	AA	1905	OF	CG
Jones	Lillie	MS	1974	F	AA	1892	O	HS
Jones	Maggie	NC	1984	F	W	unknown	unknown	unknown
Jones	Otha	TN	1995	F	W	1932	N	VT
Jones	Peggy D.	TN	1994	F	W	1899	O	AC
Jones	Wilhelmina	AL	1994	F	AA	unknown	N	unknown
Keatts	Rowena	TX	1986	F	AA	1911	O	G
Kennedy	Annie	AL	1987	F	W	1906	unknown	unknown

Last Name	First Name	State	Year of Interview	Sex	Race	Year of Birth	Landowning Status	Level of Education
Kilby	T. H.	NC	1987	M	W	1912	O	unknown
Killian/Bolick	Kathryn/Blanche	NC	1989	F/F	W	1907/1916	O	E
Kimbrough	Lorene	TN	2001	F	W	1921	O	AC
Kirby	Money and Anne	AR	1995	M/F	AA	1914	O	CG
Kirk	Bobby	NC	1985	M	W	unknown	O	unknown
Kirk	Maybelle	NC	1985	F	W	unknown	O	unknown
Kirk	Robert	NC	1985	M	W	unknown	O	unknown
Knight	Thomas	MS	1992	M	AA	1920	O	HS
Kuykendall	Leota	TX	1992	F	W	1936	O	HS
Lane	Clyde and Carolyn	TN	1987	M/F	W	1908	O	unknown
Lane	Mary Evelyn	TN	1994	F	W	1912	O	CG
Laney	John B.	MS	1987	M	W	1918	O	HS
Langley	Nellie	NC	1986	F	W	1919	O	HS
Lasseter	Elizabeth	AL	1976	F	W	1915 ca.	N-O	unknown
Lawrimore	Rufus B.	SC	1987	M	W	1908	O	unknown
Lawson	John and Hettie	TN	1993	M/F	W	1898/1901	O	HS
Laycock	Curtis and Betty	VA	2002	M/F	W	1930 ca.	O	unknown
Lee	Korola	TN	1994	F	W	1912	O	CG
Legnon	Lena Porrier	LA	1987	F	W	1910 ca.	O	VT
Lenius	Jane	AR	1987	F	W	1916	O	AC
Levy	Moses	SC	1995	M	AA	1918	O	HS
Lewellyn	Bill and Evelyn	TN	1993	M/F	W	1921/1924	OF	HS
Lewis	James and Marion	NC	1993	M/F	W	1920	O	CG
Lewis	Ralph	TN	1987	M	W	1920 ca.	O	HS
Linam	Raymond	TX	1975	M	W	1905	N	VT
Lincecum	Charlie	TX	1992	M	AA	1909	N	unknown
Little	Arthur	NC	1979	M	W	1908	O	CG
Little	John	NC	1998	M	W	1928	O	HS

Last Name	First Name	State	Year of Interview	Sex	Race	Year of Birth	Landowning Status	Level of Education
Little	Orry	MS	1982	F	W	1905 ca.	O	unknown
Lloyd	Asbury	VA	2002	M	W	1930 ca.	O	unknown
Lloyd	Carolyn Shotts	NC	1985	F	W	unknown	O	unknown
London	John	NC	1978	M	W	unknown	unknown	unknown
London	Marie	TX	1992	F	AA	1896	O-N	HS
Loth	John E.	VA	1976	M	W	unknown	unknown	unknown
Love	Mabel	TN	1994	F	W	1910	N-O	HS
Lowder	Clayton	SC	1987	M	W	1914	O	unknown
Lowder	Kathy	SC	1987	F	W	1945	O	unknown
Lowery	Ken	VA	2002	M	W	1930 ca.	O	unknown
Lucas	Henry	NC	1984	M	W	unknown	O	unknown
Lucas	Maurice	MS	1995	M	AA	1950	O	CG
Lucas	Willie Ann	AR	1995	F	AA	1915 ca.	unknown	CG
Lyall	Dema	NC	1984	F	W	1920 ca.	O	HS
Lyons	Theresa	MS	1995	F	AA	1920 ca.	N	AC
Malone	Tom	AR	1995	M	AA	1914	O	unknown
Malone	Vera	TX	1975	F	AA	1902	O	CG
Mangrum	J. B.	AL	1984	M	AA	1916	N	HS
Manning	Ruth	TX	1987	F	AA	1909	O	HS
Marion	Houston	VA	1977	M	W	unknown	unknown	unknown
Marshall	Amy	TX	1992	F	W	1898	O-N	HS
Massirer	Agnes	TX	1997	F	W	1909	O	E
Massirer	Van Doren	TX	1998	M	W	1936	O	G
Matthews	David	MS	1995	M	AA	1920	N	G
Matthews	Watkins	TX	1979	M	W	unknown	unknown	CG
Matthies	Howard and Olefa	TX	1991	M/F	W	1912/1912	O	CG
Mayberry	Louie	TX	1987	M	AA	1907	N	HS
McBrayer	Ruth H.	SC	1998	F	W	1912	O	AC

Last Name	First Name	State	Year of Interview	Sex	Race	Year of Birth	Landowning Status	Level of Education
McCall	Letha	NC	1982	F	W	1890	O	HS
McCann	Beatrice	VA	1980	F	W	1900 ca.	O	HS
McChesney	John M., Jr.	VA	1983	M	W	1908	unknown	unknown
McCray	Josephine	SC	1995	F	AA	unknown	unknown	unknown
McDaniel	D. Y.	TX	1975	M	W	1898	O	G
McGee	Dean	LA	1987	M	W	1923	O	HS
McIntyre	Virginia	LA	1982	F	W	1918 ca.	O	CG
McMillon	Salina	NC	1976	F	AA	unknown	N	unknown
McMinn	Roger	AL	1980	M	W	unknown	unknown	unknown
Meyers	Flake and Nellie	NC	1979	M/F	W	unknown	unknown	unknown
Miller	Dora	NC	1979	F	W	unknown	O	CG
Miller	John C. and Virginia	NC	2000	M/F	AA	1923	O	CG
Minchew	Edna	GA	1987	F	W	1912	unknown	unknown
Mire	John	LA	1987	M	W	1930 ca.	N	CG
Mitchell	Alma	VA	1995	F	AA	1930 ca.	N	unknown
Mitchell	Cleaster	AR	1995	M	AA	1922	OF	unknown
Moen	Ollie Mae	TX	1986	M	W	1910	N	HS
Moody	Edgar and Lorene	MS	1987	M/F	W	1911	N	unknown
Moore	Bill	NC	1984	M	W	unknown	unknown	unknown
Moore	Joan	VA	2002	F	W	ca. 1955	O	unknown
Morgan	Jane	MS	1980	F	W	1910 ca.	O	unknown
Morman	Sue	unkn.	1982	F	W	unknown	O	HS
Morris	Walter	AL	1987	M	W	1912	O	unknown
Morrison	Alvin	NC	1984	M	W	unknown	O	unknown
Moseley	Ora Nell	TX	1992	F	W	1926	O	VT
Moser	Dolly	NC	1979	F	W	1902	O	unknown
Mount	Grace	AL	1990	F	W	unknown	unknown	unknown
Murray	Lurline Stokes	SC	1987	F	W	1915	O	unknown

Last Name	First Name	State	Year of Interview	Sex	Race	Year of Birth	Landowning Status	Level of Education
Murray	Nathan	NC	1984	M	W	unknown	O	unknown
Nalls	Mable	AL	1976	F	AA	1915	N	unknown
Neal	Carl	TX	1993	M	W	1921	N	HS
Neal	Dora	SC	1982	F	W	1897	O	HS
Nelson	Hautie	TN	1982	F	W	1916 ca.	O	HS
Nelson	Margaret	SC	1995	F	AA	1908	N	unknown
Nesbit	Louise	SC	1994	F	AA	unknown	unknown	unknown
Newman	Betty	unkn.	1981	F	W	unknown	O	unknown
Nixon	Irene	GA	1981	F	W	1890 ca.	N	E
Norman	Icy	NC	1980	F	W	1911	N	E
Padgett	Everett	SC	1980	M	W	unknown	unknown	unknown
Padgett	Mary Elizabeth	SC	1980	F	W	unknown	N	unknown
Pardise	Emphel	AL	1984	M	AA	unknown	O	unknown
Parker	Jonah	NC	1987	M	W	1927	O	unknown
Parrish	Keith and Martha	NC	1998	M/F	W	1950 ca.	O	CG
Patout	William	LA	1987	M	W	1908	O	CG
Patterson	T. A.	TX	1975	M	W	1906	O	G
Patterson	Vanona	NC	1987	F	W	1891	O	unknown
Pender	Bessie	MD	1986	F	W	1919	N-O	HS
Pettigrew/Bowman	Donald/Wilbert	LA	1988	M/M	W	1904	OF	unknown
Phelps	Frances	AL	1984	F	W	1909	N-OF	unknown
Phillips	Henrietta	NC	1981	F	W	unknown	OF	HS
Pickford	Herbert A.	VA	1981	M	W	1907	unknown	unknown
Pierson	Oris	TX	1972	M	W	1899	O	AC
Pitts	Anna B.	GA	1994	F	AA	1913	N	unknown
Player	C.B., Jr.	SC	1987	M	W	1926	O	unknown
Pointer	A. Elizabeth	AL	1994	F	AA	unknown	N	unknown
Poland	Curtis	VA	2002	M	W	1930 ca.	O	unknown

Last Name	First Name	State	Year of Interview	Sex	Race	Year of Birth	Landowning Status	Level of Education
Poole	Lorene	SC	1995	F	AA	unknown	unknown	unknown
Porter	Virginia	MS	1987	F	AA	1900	N	E
Posednik	Frances	TX	1969	F	W	1890 ca.	N-O	E
Potts	Edwin	VA	2002	M	W	1930 ca.	O	unknown
Price	Lillie	NC	1985	F	W	1898	O	HS
Price	Pauline	NC	1998	F	W	1903	O	AC
Quinn	Eldred and Mary	SC	2000	M/F	W	1921	N	CG
Ratliff	Coria	VA	1982	F	W	unknown	O	unknown
Redmond	Virgie St. John	NC	1987	F	W	1919	O	unknown
Reed	Willie	MS	1995	M	AA	unknown	unknown	unknown
Reeves	Charles	GA	1986	M	W	unknown	unknown	unknown
Reyer	Joe	MS	1974	M	W	1900 ca.	N	unknown
Richburg	Joesph	SC	1995	M	AA	unknown	unknown	unknown
Richter	Donald and Wilma	TX	1998	M/F	W	1924/1929	O	CG
Ridge	Albert	TN	1994	M	W	1912 ca.	N	HS
Rivers	Mrs. Marion Byrd	SC	1987	F	AA	1910	O	unknown
Roberts	James and Gerti	NC	1987	M/F	W	1923/1915	O	unknown
Robinson	James W.	MS	1995	M	AA	1920	O	HS
Rogers	Dixie	VA	1977	F	W	1893	unknown	unknown
Rolling	Susie	MS	1995	F	AA	unknown	unknown	unknown
Rucker	William	GA	1987	M	AA	1913	O	HS
Rutherford	Wilson	TX	1974	M	W	1918	O	CG
Samuel	James	NC	1996	M	AA	1930 ca.	N	CG
Sanders	Albert	SC	1980	M	W	1900 ca.	N	G
Sarten	Della	TN	1987	F	W	1901	O	HS
Scoggins	Lillie	GA	1987	F	W	1921	O	unknown
Searles	Clarence	GA	1994	M	AA	1915	O	CG
Sellers	Etta	SC	1982	F	W	1890 ca.	O	CG

Last Name	First Name	State	Year of Interview	Sex	Race	Year of Birth	Landowning Status	Level of Education
Shepherd	Grady	NC	1987	M	W	1911	O	unknown
Sherrod	Shirley	GA	1994	F	AA	1947	O	CG
Shipp	Mary	GA	1994	F	AA	1927	O	G
Shockley	Ethel	NC	1977	F	W	1902	O	E
Shute	John R.	NC	1982	M	W	unknown	N	unknown
Simcik	Mary	TX	1974	F	W	1900	O	E
Simmons	Essie	AR	1982	F	W	1901 ca.	O	AC
Simmons	Kate	TN	1994	F	W	1913	O	HS
Simmons	Ralph	NC	1977	M	W	unknown	O	unknown
Simrall	Mrs. B. N.	MS	1982	F	W	1900 ca.	unknown	CG
Singleton	Gordon	TX	1973	M	W	1890	O	G
Smith	Ann	NC	1977	F	W	1902	O	HS
Smith	Sanford	SC	1997	M	W	1930 ca.	O	CG
Snipes	Charles	NC	1985	M	W	unknown	unknown	unknown
South	Dianne	AL	1980	F	W	unknown	unknown	unknown
Sowell	Walter	AL	1986	M	W	unknown	unknown	unknown
Speed	Cornelius	FL	1994	M	AA	unknown	N	unknown
Spencer	Robert J.	TN	1995	M	AA	1910 ca.	O	unknown
Spring	Jimmy	VA	2002	M	W	unknown	O	unknown
Springer	R. A.	TX	1972	M	W	1905	O	G
Stafford	Bessie	TX	1987	F	AA	unknown	O	CG
Stevenson	J. Robert	AL	1988	M	W	1926	N-O	CG
Stewart	Ada Mae	GA	1994	F	AA	unknown	unknown	unknown
Stowers	Henry	VA	2002	M	W	unknown	O	unknown
Studivant	Lenora	VA	1995	F	AA	1920	O	HS
Sullivan	Phyllis	WV	1980	F	W	1940 ca.	unknown	HS
Summers	Ray	TX	1980	M	W	1910	N	G
Sumner	Ollie	AL	1976	M	W	1896	N	unknown

Last Name	First Name	State	Year of Interview	Sex	Race	Year of Birth	Landowning Status	Level of Education
Symington	Mrs. J. H.	VA	2002	F	W	unknown	O	unknown
Taylor	Julia	MS	1995	F	AA	unknown	unknown	unknown
Taylor	Lovell	AL	1994	M	AA	1923	N	HS
Teer	Mike	NC	1985	M	W	unknown	O	unknown
Temple	Effie	TN	1987	F	W	unknown	O	unknown
Tensley	Rosa	AL	1980	F	AA	1880	O-N	unknown
Thornton	Clara	AL	1980	F	W	1905	O	unknown
Thorp	Mary	AL	1984	F	W	1896	N-O	unknown
Tillery	Roy Lee	NC	1994	M	AA	1915 ca.	N	unknown
Tims	Rev. W. C.	AR	1995	M	AA	1922	O	G
Todd	Bertha	NC	1994	F	AA	unknown	O-OF	CG
Trotter	Joe	TX	1993	M	AA	1896	N	E
Tucker	B. T.	TX	1993	M	AA	1918	O	E
Tucker	Edith	AL	1976	F	W	1910 ca.	N	unknown
Tucker	Fred	TX	1993	M	AA	1918	O	E
Tucker	Lizzie	TX	1993	F	AA	1918	O	E
Tucker	Samuel	TX	1993	M	AA	1920	O	E
Waggoner	J. T., Sr.	AL	1982	M	W	1907	O	CG
Walker	L. D. and Lula	AL	1987	M/F	W	1900/1901	OF	unknown
Ward	Alleyne	TX	1983	F	W	1908 ca.	O	VT
Ward	Lee	AL	1980	M	W	1927	O-N	CG
Warner	Anna Mae	TX	1976	F	W	1890	O	HS
Watkins	Jurl	GA	1994	F	AA	1932	O	G
Watson	Ester	NC	1992	F	AA	unknown	unknown	unknown
Watson/Martin	Mary/Lillian	MS	1987	F/F	W	1905 ca.	N-O	HS
Weathersbee	Susie	NC	1993	F	AA	unknown	N	unknown
Webb	Ann	AR	1982	F	W	unknown	O	unknown
Webster	Eugene	TX	1993	M	AA	1909	N	HS

Last Name	First Name	State	Year of Interview	Sex	Race	Year of Birth	Landowning Status	Level of Education
Webster	Fred	AL	1984	M	W	1900 ca.	O	CG
Weir	Bernice	TX	1990	F	W	1900	O	HS
Welborn	S. L.	GA	1987	M	W	1912	N	HS
West	John and Martha Alice	TN	1993	M/F	W	1912	O	HS
Weston	Minnie Wade	MS	1995	F	AA	1905	N	unknown
White	Bernice	MS	1995	F	AA	unknown	N	unknown
White	Dorsey	MS	1995	M	AA	1935	N	CG
White	Wallace	NC	1986	M	AA	1913	O	unknown
Whitesell	Emma	NC	1977	F	W	1919	O	unknown
Wigley	Mabry	MS	1987	M	W	1908	N-O	E
Wilborn	Isaac	SC	1994	M	AA	unknown	N	unknown
Williams	Barbara	TX	1998	F	AA	1924 ca.	N	CG
Williams	Grover	TX	1992	M	AA	1929	O	HS
Williams	Leola	GA	1984	F	AA	1919	N	unknown
Williamson	Wilma	TN	1994	F	W	1915	O	HS
Wills	Hubert and Almyra	NC	1993	M/F	AA	1920 ca.	unknown	VT
Wilson	Lucy	NC	1982	F	AA	1930 ca.	unknown	VT
Wimberley	Robert	AL	1984	M	W	unknown	unknown	unknown
Winskie	Dent and Annalee	GA	1987	M/F	W	1912	O	unknown
Wood	Flossie and Monroe	AL	1987	F/M	W	1920	N	unknown
Woodard	Henry	MS	1987	M	AA	unknown	N	unknown
Wright	Robbie	SC	1994	M	AA	unknown	unknown	unknown
Young	Archie	FL	1988	M	W	1918	O	HS
Young	Chris	MS	1995	M	AA	1927	N	CG
Young	Kenneth	AL	1994	M	AA	unknown	O	CG
Young	Samuel	SC	1995	M	AA	unknown	N	unknown

Appendix Three
Interviews

Archives and Private Collections

Auburn University

American Folklore and Oral History Collection

Adams, Hubert. Interviewed by Tripp Haston. February 24, 1990, Phenix City, Alabama.

Andrews, O. N. Interviewed by Jill Nordwall. February 24, 1988, Auburn, Alabama.

Bedell, Dewey. Interviewed by John Biblis. March 5, 1988, Auburn, Alabama.

Bedsole, J. T. Interviewed by Charles Elmore. March 10, 1986, Malvern, Alabama.

Blue, Mrs. Elvie. Interviewed by Beth Dees. February 18, 1980, Alabama.

Blue, Mrs. Elvie. Interviewed by Bruce Powell. February 27, 1980, Alabama.

Cazalas, Sarah Louise Reynolds. Interviewed by Glenn R. Adwell. February 25, 1984, Birmingham, Alabama.

Crumpton, Eula. Interviewed by Ann Weddington. February 26, 1980, Opelika, Alabama.

Crumpton, Gordon. Interviewed by Louise Bailey. February 18, 1980, Opelika, Alabama.

Davis, Mrs. Dewey. Interviewed by Michelle T. Doty. March 5, 1986, Opelika, Alabama.

DeLoach, Mrs. Quinnie Velma. Interviewed by Linda M. Sommer. February 18, 1980, Opelika, Alabama.

Floyd, John C. Interviewed by David Pullen. February 19, 1984, Mexia, Alabama.

Foy, James E. V. Interviewed by John R. Chaney. February 24, 1988, Auburn, Alabama.

Gilliam, Nell. Interviewed by Karen Moran. February 20, 1988, Manville, Virginia.

Hunt, Catherine Pike. Interviewed by Sandra Appel. February 15, 1986, Waverly, Alabama.

Inman, Chester Flournoy. Interviewed by Charles R. Clifton. February 26, 1984, Lawrenceburg, Tennessee.

Jewell, Worth. Interviewed by Kevin Price. February 18, 1982, Opelika, Alabama.

Johnson, Vera. Interviewed by Fred E. Hembree. York County, South Carolina, August 31, 1980.

Mangrum, J. B. Interviewed by Jeffrey P. Jones. May 15, 1984, Little Texas, Alabama.

McMinn, Roger. Interviewed by L. Barber. February 29, 1980, Alabama.

Mount, Grace Gamble. Interviewed by Scott B. Smith. February 16, 1990, Alabama.

Nalls, Mabel. Interviewed by Earl Dupass. May 10, 1976, Birmingham, Alabama.

Paradise, Emphel W. Interviewed by Carolyn Reed. February 19, 1984, Lochapoka, Alabama.

Phelps, Frances Read. Interviewed by Lawrence R. Phelps. February 26, 1984, Greenville, Alabama.

Reeves, Charles. Interviewed by Rita Reeves. March 6, 1986, Americus, Georgia.

South, Dianne. Interviewed by Valerie Williams. February 28, 1980, Alabama.

Sowell, Walter F. Interviewed by James D. Packard. February 24, 1986, Auburn, Alabama.

Stevenson, J. Robert. Interviewed by Thomas J. Moore. March 3, 1988, Auburn, Alabama.

Tensley, Rosa McCowan [Mrs. Eula Mae Grimes also present]. Interviewed by Stephen C. Harvey. February 27, 1980, Notasulga, Alabama.

Thornton, Clara Mozelle. Interviewed by Jim Platt. March 23, 1980, Alabama.

Thorp, Mary. Interviewed by Linda Morgan. February 26, 1984, Auburn, Alabama.

Waggoner, J. T. Sr. Interviewed by Mark Waggoner. January 22, 1982, Jasper, Alabama.

Ward, Lee. Interviewed by Joel Alvis. February 15, 1980, Alabama.

Webster, Fred. Interviewed by Gerald Born. November 4, 1984, Berry, Alabama.

Wimberley, Robert Lee. Interviewed by Michael Mosley. March 3, 1984, Lush, Alabama.

Young, Archie Roscoe. Interviewed by Leslie Young. February 27, 1988, Miami, Florida.

Pamela Grundy Oral History Collection

Browing, Kiffin. Interviewed by Pamela Grundy. May 3, 1988, Ashland, Alabama.

Chapman, J. C. and Tiny. Interviewed by Pamela Grundy. June 3, 1987, Shiloh, Alabama.

Colley, J. C. and Lizzie. Interviewed by Pamela Grundy. June 2, 1987, Mountain, Alabama.

Farrow, Mildred. Interviewed by Pamela Grundy. July 24, 1987, Cragford, Alabama.

Fetner, Woodrow. Interviewed by Pamela Grundy. August 24, 1987, Cragford, Alabama.

Hamil, Howard. Interviewed by Pamela Grundy. May 27, 1987, Mellow Valley, Alabama.

Heard, Estelle and John. Interviewed by Pamela Grundy. October 17, 1987, Delta, Alabama.

Horn, C. P. Interviewed by Pamela Grundy. February 24, 1988, Ashland, Alabama.

Kennedy, Annie Maude. Interviewed by Pamela Grundy. May 26, 1987, Mountain, Alabama.

Morris, Walter Roland Shine. Interviewed by Pamela Grundy. September 1, 1987, Cragford, Alabama.

Walker, L. D. and Lula. Interviewed by Pamela Grundy. June 23, 1987, Cragford, Alabama.

Wood, Flossie and Monroe. Interviewed by Pamela Grundy. May 28, 1987, Delta, Alabama.

Author's Collection

Cash, Kline. Interviewed by Melissa Walker. October 4, 1997, Chesnee, South Carolina.

Gambrell, Ida May. Interviewed by Kristin Oates. Undated ca. 2003, Honea Path, South Carolina, copy of tape in author's possession.

Graham, William and Kate [pseudonym]. Interviewed by Melissa Walker. April 30, 2002, Asheville, North Carolina.

Gramling, Henry II. Interviewed by Melissa Walker. October 10, 1997, Gramling, South Carolina.

Harris, Virginia and Dorothy Skinner. Interviewed by Melissa Walker. May 31, 2001, Spartanburg, South Carolina.

Jackson, Irene. Interviewed by Kristen Arthur. Undated ca. March 2003, Spartanburg, South Carolina, copy of transcript in author's possession.

Kimbrough, Lorene. Interviewed by Melissa Walker. August 15, 2001, Maryville, Tennessee.

McBrayer, Ruth Hatchette. Interviewed by Melissa Walker. August 20, 1998, Chesnee, South Carolina.

Ridge, Albert. Interviewed by Melissa Walker. July 19, 1994, Loudon, Tennessee.

Smith, Sanford N. Interviewed by Melissa Walker. September 17, 1997, Spartanburg, South Carolina.

Baylor University
Texas Collection

Alford, Lillian Jane. *The Oral Memoirs of Lillian Jane Alford.* Interviewed by Anne Radford Phillips. December 5, 1991, Burton, Texas.

Avis, Annie Maud Knittel. *The Oral Memoirs of Annie Maud Knittel Avis.* Interviewed by Anne Radford Phillips. November 11 and December 5, 1991, Burton, Texas.

Barnes, Lavonia Jenkins. *The Oral Memoirs of Lavonia Jenkins Barnes.* Interviewed by Pamela B. Crow on three occasions from March 8 to 22, 1976, Waco, Texas.

Cooper, Marguerite. *The Oral Memoirs of Marguerite Cooper.* Interviewed by Kay Clifton. March 25, 1977, Waco, Texas.

Daughtrey, Elizabeth Stevenson and Elisha Robuck. *The Oral Memoirs of Elizabeth Stevenson and Elisha Robuck Daughtrey.* Interviewed by Jaclyn Jeffrey. December 6, 1994, Del Rio, Texas.

Dawson, Joseph Martin. *The Oral Memoirs of Joseph Martin Dawson.* Interviewed by Thomas L. Carlton. January 18 and February 17, 1971, Corsicana, Texas.

Dawson, Joseph Martin. *The Oral Memoirs of Joseph Martin Dawson.* Interviewed by Rufus D. Spain on three occasions from April 2 to May 24, 1971, Waco, Texas.

Dodd, Myrtle Irene Calvert. *The Oral Memoirs of Myrtle Irene Calvert Dodd.* Interviewed by Rebecca Sharpless on four occasions from August 14 to September 19, 1990, Waco, Texas.

Downing, Avery R. *The Oral Memoirs of Avery R. Dodd.* Interviewed by James M. Sorelle and Thomas L. Charlton. August 23 and 25, 1983, Waco, Texas.

Dugger, Roy M. *The Oral Memoirs of Roy M. Drugger.* Interviewed by Thomas L. Charlton on three occasions from June 8 to June 29, 1982, Waco, Texas.

Emmons, Martha. *The Oral Memoirs of Martha Emmons.* Interviewed by Rebecca S. Jimenez on three occasions from August 29 to September 19, 1985, Waco, Texas.

Estes, Elizabeth Williams. *The Oral Memoirs of Elizabeth Williams Estes.* Interviewed by Margaret Mills. May 5 and June 4, 1976, Waco, Texas.

Hale, Alma Stewart. *The Oral Memoirs of Alma Stewart Hale.* Interviewed by Doni Van Ryswyk on eight occasions from January 27 to March 28, 1988, Waco, Texas.

Hatch, Roy H. *The Oral Memoirs of Roy H. Hatch.* Interviewed by Thomas L. Charlton on three occasions from March 6 to May 3, 1973, Waco, Texas.

Howell, Elmin Kimboll Jr. *The Oral Memoirs of Elmin Kimball Howell Jr.* Interviewed by William Lee Pitts. May 20, 1980, Waco, Texas.

Malone, Vera. *The Oral Memoirs of Vera Malone.* Interviewed by LaWanda Ball. December 5, 1975, Waco, Texas.

Matthews, Watkins Reynolds. *The Oral Memoirs of Watkins Reynolds Matthews.* Interviewed by Thomas L. Charlton and Tom Z. Parish. November 5, 1979, Throckmorton, Texas.

McDaniel, Douthit Young. *The Oral Memoirs of D. Y. McDaniel.* Interviewed by Thomas L. Charlton on eight occasions from May 15 to June 24, 1975, Waco, Texas.

Moen, Ollie Mae Allison. *The Oral Memoirs of Ollie Mae Allison Moen.* Interviewed by Jaclyn Jeffrey on eight occasions from May 29 to July 30, 1986, Waco, Texas.

Moseley, Ora Nell Wehring. *The Oral Memoirs of Ora Nell Wehring Moseley.* Interviewed by Lois E. Myers. January 22, 1992, Burton, Texas.

Neal, Carl. *The Oral Memoirs of Carl Neal.* Interviewed by Lois E. Myers. February 4 and 11, 1993, McLennan County, Texas.

Patterson, Dr. Thomas Armour. *The Oral Memoirs of Thomas Armour Patterson.* Interviewed by Thomas L. Charlton on five occasions from August 18, 1971, to November 8, 1976, Texas.

Pierson, Oris. *The Oral Memoirs of Oris Pierson.* Interviewed by Suzanne Olsen. November 2 and 29, 1972, Clifton, Texas.

Podsednik, Frances Bartek. *The Oral Memoirs of Frances Bartek Podsednik.* Interviewed by Rev. Henry Apperson. September 25, 1969, West, Texas.

Rutherford, Wilson M. *The Oral Memoirs of Wilson M. Rutherford.* Interviewed by Robert Meyers. April 5 and 6, 1974, El Campo, Texas.

Simcik, Mary Hanak. *The Oral Memoirs of Mary Hanak Simcik.* Interviewed by LaWanda Ball. November 24, 1974, Waco, Texas.

Singleton, Dr. Gordon G. *The Oral Memoirs of Dr. Gordon G. Singleton.* Interviewed by Rufus B. Spain on thirteen occasions from August 15, 1973, to March 25, 1974, Waco, Texas.

Springer, R. A. *The Oral Memoirs of R. A. Springer.* Interviewed by Thomas L. Charlton with Rufus B. Spain on three occasions from August 6, 1971, to August 4, 1972, Dallas, Texas.

Summers, Ray. *The Oral Memoirs of Ray Summers.* Interviewed by Daniel B. McGee on ten occasions from August 11 through 29, 1980, Waco, Texas.

Ward, Alleyne Holliman. *The Oral Memoirs of Alleyne Holliman Ward.* Interviewed by Patricia Wallace. July 2, 1983, Houston, Texas.

Warner, Anna Mae Bell. *The Oral Memoirs of Anna Mae Bell Warner.*

Interviewed by LaWanda Ball. February 13 and 16, 1976, Waco, Texas.

Weir, Bernice Porter Bostwick. *The Oral Memoirs of Bernice Porter Bostwick Weir*. Interviewed by Rebecca Sharpless on four occasions from July 9, 1990, to August 6, 1990, McLennan County, Texas.

Institute for Oral History

Adams, Deola Mayberry. Interviewed by Rebecca Sharpless. August 4, 1987, Gatesville, Texas.

Anderson, Ernestine G. [joined by Mrs. H. P. Williams]. Interviewed by Lois Myers. February 17, and March 30, 1999, Riesel, Texas.

Anderson, G. W. Interviewed by Sharon Siske. June 28, 1992, Meridian, Texas.

Anderson, Oliver. Interviewed by Sharon Siske. June 28, 1992, Meridian, Texas.

Bateman, Laura Belle Holley. Interviewed by Sharon Siske Crunk. January 20, 1994, Meridian, Texas.

Bateman, Opal. Interviewed by Sharon Siske Crunk. March 12, 1993, Iredell, Texas.

Bateman, Viola Anderson. Interviewed by Sharon Siske. July 5, 1992, Clifton, Texas.

Bekkelund, Ima Hoppe. Interviewed by Lois E. Myers. February 25, 1997, Woodway, Texas.

Brown, Frances Homstrom. Interviewed by Anne Radford Phillips. January 29, 1992, Jonah, Texas.

Brown, Hannah Pauline Hoff. Interviewed by LaWanda Ball. April 23, 1976, Waco, Texas.

Buck, Gilbert. Interviewed by Dan K. Utley. June 28 and July 1, 1993, Burton, Texas.

Carroll, Dovie Lee and Etta Lillian Hardy. Interviewed by Rebecca Sharpless on seven occasions from September 21, 1990, to July 11, 1991, Waxahachie, Texas.

Caufield, Alice Owens. Interviewed by Rebecca Sharpless on eight occasions between January 20 and April 21, 1993, Waco, Texas.

DeMent, J. M. Interviewed by Dan K. Utley. August 13, 1992, Pasadena, Texas.

DeMent, Robert. Interviewed by Dan K. Utley. June 28, 1993 and July 1, 1993, Burton, Texas.

Dreyer, Edna Jaeckle. Interviewed by Lois E. Myers. May 21, 1997, Gatesville, Texas.

Engelbrecht, Benjamin Franklin and Earlien Freyer Engelbrecht. Interviewed by Rebecca Sharpless on four occasions from February 13, 1997, to April 22, 1997, Crawford, Texas.

Engelbrecht, Marvin. Interviewed by Jaclyn Jeffrey. March 11, 1997, Crawford, Texas.

Evans, Rubie Williams. Interviewed by Rebecca Sharpless on August 3 and 16, 1990, Waco, Texas.

Folley, Della Inez. Interviewed by Rebecca Sharpless on four occasions from September 4, 1990, to October 17, 1990, Mart, Texas.

Gibbs, Marian G. Interviewed by Jay M. Butler. August 1987, Waco, Texas.

Graves, Lonnie. Interviewed by Anne Radford Phillips. October 10, 1991, Satin, Texas.

Graves, Lonnie. Interviewed by Jay M. Butler. June 30, 1993, Satin, Texas.

Guderian, Pearl Elizabeth Wynn. Interviewed by Anne Radford Phillips. December 7, 1991.

Guy, Katherine. Interviewed by Jay M. Butler. July 28, 1993, Satin, Texas.

Hall, Ophelia Mae Mayberry. Interviewed by Rebecca Sharpless on May 26 and June 10, 1986, Gatesville, Texas.

Johnson, Eunice Brown. Interviewed by Rebecca Sharpless. July 31, 1986, and April 14, 1987, Gatesville, Texas.

Jones, Cora Lee McCall. Interviewed by Doni Van Ryswyk on nine occasions from January 25, 1988, to May 4, 1988, Waco, Texas.

Keatts, Rowena Weatherly. Interviewed by Rebecca Sharpless on five occasions from May 5, 1986, to April 15, 1987, Waco, Texas.

Kuykendall, Leota Wagner. Interviewed by Anne Radford Philips on three occasions from February 20, 1992, to March 23, 1992, Waco, Texas.

Linam, R. H. Interviewed by Thomas L. Charlton on five occasions from April 9, 1975, to July 13, 1976, Waco, Texas.

Lincecum, Charlie and Grover Williams. Interviewed by Dan K. Utley. August 28, 1992, Lee County, Texas.

London, Marie. Interviewed by Anne R. Phillips and Jacquelyn Johnson. April 2, 1992, Waco, Texas.

Manning, Ruth Weatherly. Interviewed by Rebecca Sharpless. April 25, 1987, Gatesville, Texas.

Marshall, Amy Stella Barrington. Interviewed by Anne Radford Phillips. January 22, 1992, Weir, Texas.

Massirer, Agnes. Interviewed by Lois E. Myers. April 11, 1997, Crawford, Texas.

Massirer, Van Doren. Interviewed by Lois E. Myers. January 9, 1998, Crawford, Texas.

Matthies, Howard and Olefa Koerth. Interviewed by Thomas L. Charlton, Dan K. Utley, and Deb Hoskins on four occasions from December 20, 1991, to October 29, 1992, Burton, Texas.

Mayberry, Louie Edward. Interviewed by Rebecca Sharpless. March 19, 1987, Goliad, Texas.

Richter, Donald and Wilma. Interviewed by Lois E. Myers. September 8, 1998, Leroy, Texas.

Stafford, Bessie Lee Barrens. Interviewed by Rebecca Sharpless. May 7, 1987, Waco, Texas.

Trotter, Joe C. Interviewed by Jay M. Butler. June 30, 1993, Satin Texas.

Tucker, B. T. Interviewed by Jay M. Butler. August 20, 1993, Tucker Bottom, Texas.

Tucker, Fred Douglas. Interviewed by Jay M. Butler. August 26, 1993, Waco, Texas.

Tucker, Lizzie M. Interviewed by Jay M. Butler. August 20, 1993, Waco, Texas.

Tucker, Samuel. Interviewed by Jay M. Butler. August 20, 1993, Waco, Texas.

Webster, Eugene. Interviewed by Jay M. Butler. July 8, 1993, Downsville, Texas.

Williams, Barbara Hamilton. Interviewed by Lois E. Myers. April 21, 1998, Waco, Texas.

Williams, Grover L. Sr. Interviewed by Dan K. Utley on five occasions between Nov. 25, 1991, and June 12, 1992, Burton, Texas.

Duke University

Behind the Veil Collection, Center for Documentary Studies

Alexander, Essie Mae. Interviewed by Paul Ortiz. August 10, 1995, Greenwood, Mississippi, Box UT5, Tray C.

Brown, George L and Joseph Prince Legree. Interviewed by Sally Graham and Tunga White. August 10 and 11, 1994, St. Helena Island, South Carolina, Box UT11, Tray B.

Carter, Viola. Interviewed by Charles H. Houston Jr. June 24, 1994, Albany, Georgia, Box UT1, Tray A.

Cuffie, Roosevelt A. Interviewed by Tunga White. June 29, 1994, Sylvester, Georgia, Box UT1, Tray A.

Fenner, Lillie Pierce. Interviewed by Chris Stewart. June 26, 1993, Halifax, North Carolina, Box UT4, Tray D.

Forney, Myrtle. Interviewed by Karen Ferguson. June 23, 1993, Whitakers, North Carolina, Box UT4, Tray D.

Gibson, O. C. Interviewed by Paul Ortiz. July 31, 1995, Greenwood, Mississippi, Box UT5, Tray D.

Giles, Alice. Interviewed by Paul Ortiz. August 8, 1995, Indianola, Mississippi, Box UT5, Tray D.

Hall, James and Lolly. Interviewed by Gregory Hunter. June 17, 1994, Sylvester, Georgia, Box UT1, Tray B.

Hooten, Henry and Lillian. Interviewed by Paul Ortiz. July 11, 1994, Tuskegee, Alabama, Box UT12, Tray C.

Howard, Helen. Interviewed by Doris G. Dixon. July 19, 1995, Cotton Plant, Arkansas, Box UT1, Tray D.

Howard, Sallie Mae. Interviewed by Kisha Turner. June 28, 1995, South Carolina, Box UT11, Tray D.

Ingram, James. Interviewed by Doris G. Dixon. August 8, 1995, Yazoo City, Mississippi, Box UT5, Tray D.

Jackson, Ruthie L. Interviewed by Mausiki Stacey Scales. August 10, 1995, Itta Bena, Mississippi, Box UT5, Tray D.

James, Herman Joseph Sr. Interviewed by Kate Ellis. August 3, 1994, New Iberia, Louisiana, Box UT 8, Tray C.

Jefferson, Henrietta. Interviewed by Stacey Scales and Tywanna Whorley. August 8, 1994, Tallahassee, Florida, Box UT12, Tray B.

Johnson, Maudie Moore. Interviewed by Doris Dixon. August 4, 1995, Greenwood, Mississippi, Box UT5, Tray D.

Johnson, Ruth Stewart. Interviewed by Rhonda Mawhood. ca. 1994, Tillery, North Carolina, Box UT5, Tray A.

Jones, Amy. Interviewed by Mausiki Scales. June 28, 1995, Memphis, Tennessee, Box UT6, Tray D.

Jones, Otha B. Strong. Interviewed by Laurie Green. August 8, 1995, Memphis, Tennessee, Box UT7, Tray A.

Jones, Wilhelmina R. Interviewed by Paul Ortiz. ca. 1994, Tuskegee, Alabama, Box UT12, Tray D.

Kirby, Money Alain and Anne Oda. Interviewed by Mausiki Stacey Scales. July 13, 1995, Magnolia, Arkansas, Box UT2, Tray A.

Levy, Moses. Interviewed by Kisha Turner and Blair Murphy. June 29, 1995, South Carolina, Box UT 11, Tray D.

Lewis, James and Marion. Interviewed by Karen Ferguson. July 29, 1993, Havelock, North Carolina, Box UT8, Tray A.

Lucas, Maurice. Interviewed by Mausiki Scales. August 7, 1995, Renova, Mississippi, Box UT5, Tray D.

Lucas, Willie Ann. Interviewed by Paul Ortiz. July 7, 1995, Brinkley, Arkansas, Box UT2, Tray A.

Lyons, Theresa Cameron. Interviewed by Leslie Brown. August 16, 1995, Durham, North Carolina, Box UT4, Tray B.

Malone, Tom. Interviewed by Doris Dixon. Undated ca. 1995, Cotton Plant, Arkansas, Box UT2, Tray A.

Matthews, David. Interviewed by Paul Ortiz. ca. 1995, Mississippi, Box UT5, Tray D.

McCray, Josephine Dickey. Interviewed by Mary Hebert. June 27, 1995, South Carolina, Box UT11, Tray D.

Mitchell, Alma. Interviewed by Mary Hebert. July 20, 1995, Norfolk, Virginia, Box UT10, Tray C.

Mitchell, Cleaster. Interviewed by Paul Ortiz. July 16, 1995, Brinkley, Arkansas, Box UT2, Tray A.

Nelson, Margaret Christine. Interviewed by Mary Hebert. July 5, 1995, Summerton, South Carolina, Box UT11, Tray D.

Nesbit, Louise. Interviewed by Sally S. Graham. August 13, 1994, Pawley's Island, South Carolina, Box UT11, Tray C.

Pitts, Anna B. Interviewed by Charles H. Houston Jr. June 25, 1994, Albany, Georgia, Box UT1, Tray C.

Pointer, A. Elizabeth Harris. Interviewed by Paul Ortiz. July 22 and 24, 1994, Tuskegee, Alabama, Box UT12, Tray D.

Poole, Lorene. Interviewed by Blair Murphy and Kisha Turner. ca. 1995, Summerton, South Carolina, Box UT11, Tray D.

Reed, Willie. Interviewed by Paul Ortiz. August 2, 1995, Indianola, Mississippi, Box UT6, Tray A.

Richburg, Joseph. Interviewed by Mary Hebert. June 26, 1995, South Carolina, Box UT12, Tray A.

Robinson, James W. Interviewed by Stacey Scales. August 10, 1995, Greenwood, Mississippi, Box UT6, Tray A.

Rolling, Susie. Interviewed by Mausiki Scales. ca. 1995, LeFlore County, Mississippi, Box UT6, Tray A.

Searles, Clarence Arthur. Interviewed by Gregory Hunter. 1994, Albany, Georgia, Box UT1, Tray C.

Sherrod, Shirley Miller. Interviewed by Charles H. Houston Jr. June 30, 1994, Albany, Georgia, Box UT1, Tray C.

Shipp, Mary. Interviewed by Tunga White. June 28, 1994, Sylvester, Georgia, Box UT1, Tray C.

Speed, Cornelius. Interviewed by Paul Ortiz. July 27 and August 3, 1994, Tallahassee, Florida, Box UT12, Tray C.

Spencer, Robert Jefferson. Interviewed by Mausiki Stacey Scales. June 20, 1995, Memphis, Tennessee, Box UT7, Tray A.

Stewart, Ada Mae. Interviewed by Tunga White. July 6, 1994, Moultrie, Georgia, Box UT1, Tray C.

Studivant, Lenora. Interviewed by Kisha Turner. August 8, 1995, Norfolk, Virginia, Box UT10, Tray C.

Taylor, Julia. Interviewed by Paul Ortiz. ca. 1995, LeFlore County, Mississippi, Box UT6, Tray A.

Taylor, Lovell. Interviewed by Paul Ortiz. June 28, 1994, Birmingham, Alabama, Box UT2, Tray D.

Tillery, Roy Lee. Interviewed by Leslie Brown. ca. 1994, Enfield, North Carolina, Box UT5, Tray B.

Tims, Rev. W. C. Interviewed by Paul Ortiz. July 20, 1995, Magnolia, Arkansas, Box UT2, Tray A.

Todd, Bertha. Interviewed by Sonya Ramsey. ca. 1994, Wilmington, North Carolina, Box UT13, Tray D.

Watkins, Jurl Lee. Interviewed by Gregory Hunter. June 28, 1994, Sylvester, Georgia, Box UT1, Tray C.

Weathersbee, Susie. Interviewed by Leslie Brown. June 30, 1993, Halifax, North Carolina, Box UT5, Tray B.

Weston, Minnie Wade. Interviewed by Paul Ortiz. August 8, 1995, Moorehead, Mississippi, Box UT6, Tray A.

White, Bernice. Interviewed by Paul Ortiz. ca. 1995, LeFlore County, Mississippi, Box UT6, Tray A.

White, Dorsey M. Interviewed by Paul Ortiz. August 3, 1995, Indianola, Mississippi, Box UT6, Tray B.

Wilborn, Isaac. Interviewed by Tunga White. August 12, 1994, Hilton Head, South Carolina, Box UT11, Tray C.

Williams, Leola D. Interviewed by Charles H. Houston Jr. June 28, 1994, Albany, Georgia, Box UT1, Tray C.

Wills, Hubert R. and Almyra P. Interviewed by Rhonda Mawhood. June 30, 1993, Whitakers, North Carolina, Box UT5, Tray C.

Wright, Robbie Louise. Interviewed by Tunga White. August 6, 1994, Beaufort, South Carolina, Box UT11, Tray C.

Young, Chris Sr. Interviewed by Doris Dixon. ca. 1995, LeFlore County, Mississippi, Box UT6, Tray B.

Young, Kenneth B. Interviewed by Paul Ortiz. July 12, 1994, Tuskegee, Alabama, Box UT13, Tray A.

Young, Samuel. Interviewed by Mark Hebert. ca. 1995, Clarendon County, South Carolina, Box UT 12, Tray A.

East Tennessee State University, Johnson City, Tennessee
Charles Gunter Collection, Archives of Appalachia

Broyles, Lizzie. Interviewed by Lon Broyles. November 16, 1975, Limestone, Tennessee. CG, 3A.

Lawson-McGhee Library, Knoxville, Tennessee
McClung Historical Collection

Clark, French. Interviewed by Melissa Walker. July 22, 1994, Maryville, Tennessee.

Davis, Ethel [pseudonym]. Interviewed by Melissa Walker. July 19, 1994, Loudon County, Tennessee.

Delozier, Arthur [pseudonym]. Interviewed by Melissa Walker. July 24, 1994, Lenoir City, Tennessee.

Farmer, LaVerne. Interviewed by Melissa Walker. August 9, 1993, Maryville, Tennessee.

Hobbs, Everett and Irma [pseudonym]. Interviewed by Melissa Walker, July 19, 1994. Philadelphia, Tennessee.

Jones, Peggy Delozier [pseudonym]. Interviewed by Melissa Walker, July 21, 1994. Philadelphia, Tennessee.

Lane, Mary Evelyn Russell. Interviewed by Melissa Walker, August 8, 1994. Maryville, Tennessee.

Lawson, John Oliver and Hettie. Interviewed by Melissa Walker, August 16, 1993. Alcoa, Tennessee.

Lee, Korola Neville. Interviewed by Melissa Walker, August 10, 1994. Friendsville, Tennessee.

Lewellyn, Bill and Evelyn. Interviewed by Melissa Walker, August 10, 1993. Greenback, Tennessee.

Love, Mabel [pseudonym]. Interviewed by Melissa Walker. July 19, 1994, Loudon County, Tennessee.

Simmons, Kate [pseudonym]. Interviewed by Melissa Walker, August 5, 1994. Loudon, Tennessee.

West, John and Martha Alice. Interviewed by Melissa Walker, August 12, 1993. Friendsville, Tennessee.

Williamson, Wilma Cope. Interviewed by Melissa Walker, July 18, 1994. Maryville, Tennessee.

Library of Virginia, Richmond, Virginia

Waynesboro Oral Histories

Arbuckle, Marion D. Interviewed by Caroline Baum and Kitty Wiggins. August 30, 1977, and March 9, 1978, Waynesboro, Virginia.

Baber, Charles William. Interviewed by Caroline Baum and Kitty Wiggins. March 2, 1978, Waynesboro, Virginia.

Barger, Katherine. Interviewed by Fred Cook. April 1981, Waynesboro, Virginia.

Boward, Ruby E. Interviewed by Barbara Neet and Anne Kidd. April 21, 197?, (ca. 1977), Waynesboro, Virginia.

Bush, Mr. and Mrs. James B. Interviewed by Caroline Baum and Kitty Wiggins. January 18, 1977, Waynesboro, Virginia.

Clayborne, Sam F. Interviewed by Howard Clayborne. March 5, 1979, Waynesboro, Virginia.

Culpepper, Ruth Rhodes. Interviewed by Caroline Baum and Kitty Wiggins. June 24, 1980, Waynesboro, Virginia.

Diggs, Mealie. Interviewed by unnamed person. Undated ca. 1996, Waynesboro, Virginia.

Fielder, Margaret Noland. Interviewed by Caroline Baum and Kitty Wiggins. May 19, 1977, Waynesboro, Virginia.

Fishburne, Elliott G. Interviewed by Barbara Neet. August 4, 1977, Waynesboro, Virginia.

Garber, Sallie Reed. Interviewed by Will Cockrell. April 2, 1977, Waynesboro, Virginia.

Glenn, F. Berkeley. Interviewed by Caroline Baum and Kitty Wiggins. March 3, 1977, Waynesboro, Virginia.

Loth, John Ellison. Interviewed by Caroline Baum and Kitty Wiggins. November 18, 1976, Waynesboro, Virginia.

Marion, Houston Briscoe. Interviewed by Caroline Baum and Kitty Wiggins. May 5, 1977, Waynesboro, Virginia.

McChesney, John M. Jr. Interviewed by Caroline Baum and Kitty Wiggins. November 2, 1983, Waynesboro, Virginia.

Pickford, Herbert A. Interviewed by Caroline Baum and Kitty Wiggins. November 16, 1981, Waynesboro, Virginia.

Rogers, Dixie Virginia Lambert. Interviewed by Caroline Baum and Kitty Wiggins. February 8, 1977, Waynesboro, Virginia.

Smithsonian Institution, Washington, D.C.

Oral History of Southern Agriculture, Behring Center, National Museum of American History

Accardo, Paul. Interviewed by Lu Ann Jones. June 3, 1988, Patterson, Louisiana.

Allen, David. Interviewed by Lu Ann Jones. January 15, 1987, and July 3, 1989, Hartsville, South Carolina.

Anderson, Walter and Adra. Interviewed by Lu Ann Jones. May 3, 1987, Corryton, Tennessee.

Andrews, John William. Interviewed by Lu Ann Jones. May 20, 1987, Boomer, North Carolina.

Ardoin, Leslie. Interviewed by Lu Ann Jones. May 16, 1988, Mamou, Louisiana.

Bailey, Charles. Interviewed by Lu Ann Jones. October 9, 1987, Tunica, Mississippi.

Bailey, Howard Taft. Interviewed by Lu Ann Jones. October 16, 1987, Holmes County, Mississippi.

Benson, Dick. Interviewed by Lu Ann Jones. January 28, 1987, Tifton, Georgia.

Benton, Aubrey and Ina Bell. Interviewed by Lu Ann Jones. April 28, 1987, Commerce, Georgia.

Bradford, Nara and Elijah Norwood. Interviewed by Lu Ann Jones. October 28, 1987, Hattiesburg, Mississippi.

Brantley, L. D. Interviewed by Lu Ann Jones. September 30, 1987, Coy, Arkansas.

Brown, Gordon. Interviewed by Lu Ann Jones. September 22, 1987, Scott, Arkansas.

Brown, Mamie. Interviewed by Lu Ann Jones. October 23, 1987, Belzoni, Mississippi.

Busselman, Norman and Willie. Interviewed by Lu Ann Jones. December 15, 1986, Suffolk, Virginia.

Byers, Sanford. Interviewed by Lu Ann Jones. April 20 and 23, 1987, Gainesville, Georgia.

Carter, Ethel H. and Charlotte Haransky. Interviewed by Lu Ann Jones. September 22, 1988, Ringgold, Virginia.

Castleberry, Guy. Interviewed by Lu Ann Jones. April 24, 1987, Gainesville, Georgia.

Caughron, Kermit, Rex, and Roy. Interviewed by Lu Ann Jones. May 9, 1987, Cades Cove, Tennessee.

Cockerham, Lester and Marie. Interviewed by Lu Ann Jones. May 21, 1987, Roaring River, North Carolina.

Colvin, R. C. Interviewed by Lu Ann Jones. October 22, 1987, Greenwood, Mississippi.

Connell, Alton. Interviewed by Lu Ann Jones. January 29, 1987, Lenox, Georgia.

Crosby, Victor and Ruth. Interviewed by Lu Ann Jones. May 13, 1987, Harmony, North Carolina.

Cunningham, Tom B. Interviewed by Lu Ann Jones. January 17, 1991, Darlington, South Carolina.

Davis, Fredda. Interviewed by Lu Ann Jones. May 26, 1987, Laurel Springs, North Carolina.

Davis, Otto and Pauline. Interviewed by Lu Ann Jones. January 8, 1987, Darlington, South Carolina.

Delasbour, Anna. Interviewed by Lu Ann Jones. June 2, 1988, Franklin, Louisiana.

Ducrest, Jesse. Interviewed by Lu Ann Jones. October 19, 1987, Belzoni, Mississippi.

Felknor, Jessie Franklin. Interviewed by Lu Ann Jones. May 2 and 7, 1987, White Pine, Tennessee.

Finchum, Eva and Amos. Interviewed by Lu Ann Jones. April 30, 1987, Sevierville, Tennessee.

Foster, Jim and Virgie. Interviewed by Lu Ann Jones. May 19, 1987, Millers Creek, North Carolina.

George, Mrs. Leler and family. Interviewed by Lu Ann Jones. July 4, 1989, Bishopville, South Carolina.

Gosney, Jessie and Kenneth. Interviewed by Lu Ann Jones. October 1, 1987, Carlisle, Arkansas.

Gray, Wardell. Interviewed by Lu Ann Jones. October 27, 1987, Carson, Mississippi.

Griffin, A. C. and Grace. Interviewed by Lu Ann Jones. December 8 and 10, 1986, Edenton, North Carolina.

Hall, Joe C. Interviewed by Lu Ann Jones. December 11, 1986, Edenton, North Carolina.

Harper, Woodrow Sr. Interviewed by Lu Ann Jones. April 17, 1987, Hartwell, Georgia.

Harrington, A. M. Interviewed by Lu Ann Jones. January 16, 1987, Florence, South Carolina.

Harris, Edna. Interviewed by Lu Ann Jones. May 15 and 16, 1987, Harmony, North Carolina.

Harris, Reverend John. Interviewed by Lu Ann Jones. May 28, 1988, Franklin, Louisiana.

Hill, Frank. Interviewed by Lu Ann Jones. May 4, 1987. Knoxville, Tennessee.

Johnson, Herbert. Interviewed by Lu Ann Jones, January 29, 1987, Tifton, Georgia.

Kilby, T. H. Interviewed by Lu Ann Jones. May 19, 1987, North Wilkesboro, North Carolina.

Lane, Clyde and Carolyn. Interviewed by Lu Ann Jones. May 5, 1987, Maryville, Tennessee.

Laney, John B., Jr. Interviewed by Lu Ann Jones, October 9, 1987, Lyon, Mississippi.

Langley, Nellie Stancil. Interviewed by Lu Ann Jones. December 5, 1986, Stantonsburg, North Carolina.

Lawrimore, Rufus B. Interviewed by Lu Ann Jones. January 5, 1987, Hemingway, South Carolina.

Legnon, Lena Porrier. Interviewed by Lu Ann Jones. May 30, 1988, Jeanerette, Louisiana.

Lenius, Jane. Inteviewed by Lu Ann Jones. September 24, 1987, Stuttgart, Arkansas.

Lewis, Ralph. Interviewed by Lu Ann Jones. May 2, 1987, White Pine, Tennessee.

Lowder, Clayton. Interviewed by Lu Ann Jones. January 14, 1987, Sumter, South Carolina.

Lowder, Kathy. Interviewed by Lu Ann Jones. January 7, 1987, Sumter, South Carolina.

McGee, Dean. Interviewed by Lu Ann Jones. May 12, 1988, Church Point, Louisiana.

Minchew, Edna. Interviewed by Lu Ann Jones. January 21, 1987, Wray, Georgia.

Mire, John. Interviewed by Lu Ann Jones. May 11, 1988, Ville Platt, Louisiana.

Moody, Edgar and Lorene. Interviewed by Lu Ann Jones. October 21, 1987, Hollandale, Mississippi.

Parker, Jonah. Interviewed by Lu Ann Jones. May 18, 1987, Moravian Falls, North Carolina.

Patout, William. Interviewed by Lu Ann Jones. May 26, 1988, New Iberia, Louisiana.

Patterson, Vanona. Interviewed by Lu Ann Jones. May 13, 1987, Hiddenite, North Carolina.

Pender, Bessie. Interviewed by Lu Ann Jones. December, 30, 1986, Maryland.

Pettigrew, Donald and Wilbert Bowman. Interviewed by Lu Ann Jones. May 5, 1988, Iowa, Louisiana.

Player, C. B., Jr. Interviewed by Lu Ann Jones. January 12, 1987, Bishopville, South Carolina.

Porter, Virginia. Interviewed by Lu Ann Jones, October 23, 1987, Belzoni, Mississippi.

Rivers, Mrs. Marion Byrd. Interviewed by Lu Ann Jones. January 13, 1987, Lamar, South Carolina.

Roberts, James and Gerti. Interviewed by Lu Ann Jones. May 21, 1987, Roaring River, North Carolina.

Rucker, William. Interviewed by Lu Ann Jones. April 16, 1987, Elberton, Georgia.

Sarten, Della. Interviewed by Lu Ann Jones. May 1, 1987, Sevierville, Tennessee.

Scoggins, Lillie. Interviewed by Lu Ann Jones. January 31, 1987, Ashburn, Georgia.

Shepherd, Grady. Interviewed by Lu Ann Jones. May 27, 1987, Lansing, North Carolina.

Temple, Effie. Interviewed by Lu Ann Jones. May 8, 1987, Sevierville, Tennessee.

Watson, Mary and Lillian Martin. Interviewed by Lu Ann Jones. October 18, 1987, Belzoni, Mississippi.

Welborn, S. L. Interviewed by Lu Ann Jones. April 27, 1987, Jefferson, Georgia.

White, Wallace. Interviewed by Lu Ann Jones. December 11, 1986, Edenton, North Carolina.

Wigley, Mabry. Interviewed by Lu Ann Jones. October 19, 1987, Hollandale, Mississippi.

Winskie, Dent and Annalee. Interviewed by Lu Ann Jones. January 23, 1987, Dent, Georgia.

Woodard, Henry. Interviewed by Lu Ann Jones. October 5, 1987, Tunica, Mississippi.

Spartanburg County Public Library, Spartanburg, South Carolina
Kennedy Local History Collection

Quinn, Eldred and Mary. Interviewed by Melissa Walker. October 18, 2000, Spartanburg, South Carolina.

University of Alabama at Birmingham

Bennett, Virginia. Interviewed by Cynthia Williams. May 14, 1976, Alabama.

Crocker, Ethel. Interviewed by Ann McIntosh. September 10, 1975, Alabama.

Davis, Lornie. Interviewed by Alice Rambo. April 30, 1976, Alabama.

Dumas, Bertha L. Interviewed by Wanda S. Willingham. May 1, 1976, Birmingham, Alabama.

Evans, Dolly. Interviewed by Marilyn Jones. Spring 1975, Liberty Hill, Alabama.

Hayes, Maggie Lee Davis. Interviewed by Sandra B. Prater. January 22, 1977, Vernon, Alabama.

Head, A. L. Interviewed by Donnie Breaseale. October 26 and November 18, 1975, Blountville, Alabama.

Lasseter, Elizabeth Harden. Interviewed by Milton E. Turner. May 8, 1976, Gadsden, Alabama.

Sumner, Ollie. Interviewed by Billy Raper. February 18, 1976, Alabama.

Tucker, Edith. Interviewed by Becky Zins. May 5, 1976, Birmingham, Alabama.

University of North Carolina at Chapel Hill
Southern Oral History Project, #4007
Southern Historical Collection, Wilson Library

Aaron, Junie Edna Kaylor. Interviewed by Jacquelyn Hall. December 12, 1979, Conover, North Carolina. #H-106.

Abernathy, Mr. and Mrs.Yates. Interviewed by Harry Wilson and Gordon McDaniel. August 23, 1984, Vale, North Carolina. #D-1.

Adams, Harry Singleton. Interviewed by Allen Tullos. February 28, 1979, Burlington, North Carolina. #H-9.

Adamson, Mary Price. Interviewed by Mary Frederickson. April 19, 1976, Oakland, California. #G-1.

Andrews, Norbert King. Interviewed by Marilyn T. Grunkemeyer. October 22 and November 18, 1985, Orange County, North Carolina. #K-1.

Armstrong, Coy. Interviewed by Mary L. Dexter. October 16, 1985, Mebane, North Carolina. #K-2.

Austin, Eunice. Interviewed by Jacquelyn Hall. July 2, 1980, Newton, North Carolina. #H-107.

Baldwin, Curtis. Interviewed by Robert Jeffrey. November 1 and December 9, 1978, Bynum, North Carolina. #H-61.

Barbee, Annie Mack. Interviewed by Beverly W. Jones. May 28, 1979, Durham, North Carolina. #H-190.

Barham, Lois. Interviewed by Lorrie Constantinos. October 15, 1984, Wake County, North Carolina. #D-2.

Bateman, David. Interviewed by Larry Johnson. Undated ca. 1984, Tyner, North Carolina. #D-3.

Best, Rachel. Interviewed by Lynn Hudson. October 26, 1985, Cane Creek, North Carolina. #K-3.

Best, Rachel. Interviewed by Misti Turbeville. August 12, 1986, Orange County, North Carolina. #K-4.

Bock, Rev. Warren. Interviewed by Lu Ann Jones and Charles D. Thompson. July 21, 1998, Benson, North Carolina. #K-225.

Boyce, Lena. Interviewed by Sue Beal. October 16, 1984, Rehobeth, North Carolina, #D-5.

Brown, Gertrude [pseudonym]. Interviewed by James Leloudis and Mary Murphy. November 14, 1978, Bynum, North Carolina.

Burt, Thomas. Interviewed by Glenn Henson. October 26, 1976, Creedmoor, North Carolina. #H-194.

Carden, Stella Foust. Interviewed by Mary Murphy. April 25, 1979, Burlington, North Carolina. #H-14.

Case, Mr. and Mrs. L. C., Jr. Interviewed by Bonnie Bishop. June 19, 1984, North Carolina. #D-6.

Clark, Chester and Roxanna. Interviewed by unnamed interviewer. January 5 and January 26 and June 8, 1979, Durham, North Carolina. #H-197.

Clay, Marshall Haywood. Interviewed by Patty Dilley. August 13, 1979, Newton, North Carolina. #H-114.

Cleveland, Myrtle Spencer. Interviewed by Allen Tullos. October 22, 1979, Greenville, South Carolina. #H-238.

Coats, Danny Wade. Interviewed by Lu Ann Jones. July 26, 1998, Coats, North Carolina. #K-226.

Collier, Shirley. Interviewed by Renate Dahlin. June 4, 1984, Fayetteville, North Carolina. #D-8.

Costan, John. Interviewed by Larry Johnson. June 22, 1984, Albermarle County, North Carolina. #D-9.

Cotton, T. J. Interviewed by Rosemarie Hester. June 17, 1977, Badin, North Carolina. #H-4.

Crawford, Cecil and May. Interviewed by Laura Edwards. October 10, 1985, Orange County, North Carolina. #K-5.

Crouse, Munsey and Waine. Interviewed by Una Edwards. October 3, 1984, Allegheny County, North Carolina. #D-10.

Daughtry, H. E. Interviewed by Larry Johnson. Undated ca. 1984, Albermarle County, North Carolina. #D-11.

Davidson, Betty and Lloyd. Interviewed by Allen Tullos. February 2 and 15, 1979, Burlington, North Carolina. #H-19.

Davis, Fredda. Interviewed by Ruth Dasmann. September 26, 1984, North Carolina. #D-12.

Denning, Lamas and Janie. Interviewed by Lu Ann Jones and Charlie Thompson. July 14, 1998, Benson, North Carolina. #K-227.

Dryman, Mr. and Mrs. Hugh. Interviewed by Bonnie Bishop. June 18, 1984, Haywood County, North Carolina. #D-13.

Durham, Flossie Moore. Interviewed by Mary Frederickson and Brent Glass. September 2, 1976, Bynum, North Carolina. #H-66.

Durham, Frank Sidney. Interviewed by Douglas DeNatale. September 10 and 17, 1979, Bynum, North Carolina. #H-67.

Duty, Elaine Tiller. Interviewed by Ronald Eller. January 30, 1976, Abingdon, Virginia. #B-18.

Elgin, Jimmy. Interviewed by Marcella Groon on two occasions undated Winter 1978, Bynum, North Carolina. #H-69, 70.

Elliott, Mrs. W. D. Interviewed by Larry Johnson. Undated ca. 1984, Tyner, North Carolina. #D-15.

Elmore, George R. Interviewed by Hugh P. Brinton. May 15, 1974, Durham, North Carolina. #H-265.

Elmore, George R. Interviewed by Brent Glass. March 11, 1976, Durham, North Carolina. #H-266.

Finley, Vesta. Interviewed by Mary Frederickson and Marion Roydhouse. July 22, 1975, Marion, North Carolina. #H-267.

Fleming, Murray. Interviewed by Tom Candy. August 1, 1984, Scotland Neck, North Carolina. #D-16.

Fuller, Thomas F. Interviewed by Brent Glass. October 9, 1975, Mapleville, North Carolina. #H-269.

Gentry, Myrtle Shelton. Interviewed by Allen Tullos. November 9, 1979, Greenville, South Carolina. #H-246.

Gillis, John McNatt. Interviewed by Lane Hudson. Undated ca. 1984, North Carolina. #D-18.

Glenn, Mrs. Howard (Josephine K. Rogers). Interviewed by Cliff Kuhn. June 27, 1977, Burlington, North Carolina. #H-22.

Godwin, John. Interviewed by Renate Dahlin. June 27, 1984, Pembroke, North Carolina. #D-19.

Hardin, Alice Evelyn Grogan. Interviewed by Allen Tullos. May 2, 1980, Greenville, South Carolina. #H-248.

Harrington, Edward and Mary Estelle Terry. Interviewed by Mary Murphy. February 28, 1979, Burlington, North Carolina. #H-25.

Harris, Gladys Florence Bumgardner. Interviewed by Patty Dilley. Undated August 1979, Hickory, North Carolina. #H-124.

Harvell, Evelyn Gosnell. Interviewed by Allen Tullos. May 27, 1980, Greenville, South Carolina. #H-250.

Herring, Harriet. Interviewed by Mary Frederickson and Nevin Brown. February 5, 1976, location unknown. #G-27.

Hill, Mary [pseudonym]. Interviewed by Allen Tullos. March 29, April 3, July 21, and August 10, 1979, Burlington, North Carolina. #G-27.

Hodges, Estelle. Interviewed by unnamed interviewer. May 23, 1979, Durham, North Carolina. #H-204.

Holt, Nancy. Interviewed by Frances E. Webb. October 27, 1985, Orange County, North Carolina. #K-10.

Holt, W. Bruce. Interviewed by Steven J. Henegar. October 27, 1985, Orange County, North Carolina. #K-9.

Hudson, Juanita O. and Mack Reid. Interviewed by Lu Ann Jones and Charlie Thompson. July 8, 1998, Benson, North Carolina. #K-229.

Jones, Maggie. Interviewed by Una Edwards. October 21, 1984, Allegheny County, North Carolina. #D-21.

Killian, Kathryn Settlemyre and Blanche Settlemyre Bolick. Interviewed by Jacquelyn Hall. December 12, 1979, Newton, North Carolina. #H-131.

Kirk, Bobby. Interviewed by unnamed interviewer. Undated ca. 1985, Orange County, North Carolina. #K-13.

Kirk, Maybelle Snipes. Interviewed by Lynn Haessly. November 18, 1985, Orange County, North Carolina. #K-14.

Kirk, Robert L. Interviewed by Lynn Haessly. November 2, 1985, Orange County, North Carolina. #K-15.

Little, Arthur. Interviewed by Jacquelyn Hall. December 14, 1979, Newton, North Carolina. #H-132.

Lloyd, Carolyn Shotts. Interviewed by Angie Carter. October 28 and November 18, 1985, Chapel Hill, North Carolina. #K-17.

London, John. Interviewed by Gary Freeze. November 2, 1978, Pittsboro, North Carolina. #H-91.

Lucas, Henry P. Interviewed by Cathy Johnson. November 9, 1984, Sampson County, North Carolina. #D-24.

Lyall, Dema Reeves. Interviewed by Ruth Dasmann. September 5, 1984, Ashe County, North Carolina. #D-25.

McMillon, Salina. Interviewed by unnamed interviewer. October 25, 1976, Durham, North Carolina. #H-208.

Meyers, Flake and Nellie. Interviewed by Patty Dilley. August 11, 1979, Hickory, North Carolina. #H-133.

Miller, Dora Scott. Interviewed by Beverly Jones. June 6, 1979, Durham, North Carolina. #H-211.

Moore, Bill. Interviewed by Bonnie Bishop. August 1, 1984, Haywood County, North Carolina. #D-27.

Morrison, Alvin. Interviewed by Robert M. Rhodes. October 23, 1984, Iredell County, North Carolina. #D-20.

Moser, Dolly. Interviewed by Jacquelyn Hall. December 13, 1979, Hickory, North Carolina. #H-134.

Murray, Nathan. Interviewed by Cathy Johnson. June 14, 1984, Duplin County, North Carolina. #D-30.

Padgett, Everett. Interviewed by Allen Tullos. May 28, 1980, Greenville, South Carolina. #H-256.

Padgett, Mary Elizabeth Robertson. Interviewed by Allen Tullos. May 28, 1980, Greenville, South Carolina. #H-255.

Parrish, Keith and Martha T. Interviewed by Lu Ann Jones and Charlie Thompson. July 8, 1998, Benson, North Carolina. #K-230

Price, Lillie Morris. Interviewed by Mary Frederickson and Marion Roydhouse. July 22, 1975, Asheville, North Carolina. #H-283.

Ross, Susan and Kathryn Dunlap [pseudonyms]. Interviewed by George W. McDaniel. June 6, 1975, Durham, North Carolina.

Sanders, Albert N. Interviewed by Allen Tullos. May 30, 1980, Greenville, South Carolina. #H-256.

Shockley, Ethel Bowman. Interviewed by Cliff Kuhn. June 24, 1977, Burlington, North Carolina. #H-45.

Shute, John Raymond, Jr. Interviewed by Wayne Durrill. June 25, 1982, Monroe, North Carolina. #B-54.

Simmons, Ralph B. Interviewed by Patty Dilley. Undated month, Summer 1977, Conover, North Carolina. #H-145.

Smith, Ann [pseudonym]. Interviewed by Cliff Kuhn. June 29, 1977, location unknown.

Snipes, Charles. Interviewed by Al Carolonza. November 5, 1985, North Carolina. #K-23.

Teer, Mike. Interviewed by Karl Campbell. Undated ca. 1985, Orange County, North Carolina. #K-25.

Whitesell, Emma. Interviewed by Cliff Kuhn. June 27, 1977, Burlington, North Carolina. #H-57.

University of North Carolina at Charlotte, Special Collections Unit, J. Murrey Library, Transcripts available online at <http://newsouthvoices.uncc.edu/>.

Cox, Pauline. Interviewed by unnamed person. January 23, 2002, location unknown.

Diggs, Annie May. Interviewed by Melvin Young. October 30, 2001, Charlotte, North Carolina.

Ervin, Hassie Roulette Williams. Interviewed by Jasmine Gaither. January 10, 2001, location unknown.

Gaddy, Carry Harrison. Interviewed by Jamel Funderburk. October 29, 2001, location unknown.

Graham, Melvin. Interviewed by Mary Kratt. May 21, 1996, Charlotte, North Carolina.

Grier, Katie. Interviewed by Tameka Crosby. October 27, 2001, Charlotte, North Carolina.

Samuel, Reverend James. Interviewed by Vickie Crawford. August 6, 1996, Charlotte, North Carolina.

Watson, Ester. Interviewed by Shonda Watson. July 29, 1992, Charlotte, North Carolina.

University of Southern Mississippi

Mississippi Oral History Program

Banks, Earl W. Interviewed by Mike Garvey. August 26, 1975, Jackson, Mississippi. Transcript available online at <http://anna.lib.usm.edu/~spcol/crda/oh/ohbankseb.html>.

Blackwell, Unita. Interviewed by Mike Garvey. April 21, 1977, Mayersville, Mississippi. Transcript available online at <http://www.lib.usm.edu/~spcol/crda/oh/blackwelltrans.htm>.

Butts, Dr. William A. Interviewed by Orley B. Caudill. March 3, 1976, Mississippi. Transcript available online at <http://anna.lib.usm.edu/%7Espcol/crda/oh/ohbuttswb.html>.

Campbell, Will D. Interviewed by Orley B. Caudill. June 8, 1976, Mt. Juliet, Tennessee. Transcript available online at <http://anna.lib.usm.edu/%7Espcol/crda/oh/campbelltrans.htm>.

Hall, Mrs. Pinkey. Interviewed by Kim Adams. December 13, 1995, transcript available online at <http://www.lib.usm.edu/~spcol/crda/oh/hall-trans/htm>.

Jones, Lillie. Interviewed by Mike Garvey. December 11, 1974, Philadelphia, Mississippi. Transcript available online at <http://ann.lib.usm.edu/%7Espcol/crda/oh/ohjoneslb.html>.

Knight, Thomas Sr. Interviewed by Charles Bolton. February 7, 1992, Hattiesburg, Mississippi. Transcript available online at <http://anna.lib.usm.edu/%7Espcol/crda/oh/ohknighttb.html>.

Reyer, Joe. Interviewed by Michael Garvey. August 23, 1974, Mississippi. Transcript available online at <http://anna.lib.usm.edu/%7Espcol/crda/oh/ohreyerjb.html>.

Winthrop University

Extension Homemakers Oral History Project, Archives and Special Collections, Dacus Library

Andrews, Bertha. Interviewed by [unknown first name] Langley. March 30, 1982, Alabama.

Arnett, Irby. Interviewed by Dean Reaves. November 4, 1981. Abingdon, Virginia.

Bell, Sallie. Interviewed by Mildred M. Ennis. April 2, 1982, Livingston, Alabama.

Brookshire, [unknown first name]. Interviewed by Mabel Bartram. Undated ca. 1982, Kentucky.

Clause, Irene. Autobiographical Tape. Undated ca. 1982, location unknown.

Edwards, Zelphia. Interviewed by Rebecca Fortenberry. Undated ca. 1982, Louisiana.

Evans, Anna. Interviewed by Mabel Bertram. September 11, 1981, Glasgow, Kentucky.

Fouts, Mary. Interviewed by Mabel Bartram. November 7, 1981, London, Kentucky.

Gates, Pat. Interviewed by Bea Cochran. Unspecified date, 1981, South Carolina.

Hammond, Theo. Interviewed by Virginia Bailey Harris. September 3, 1981, Columbus, North Carolina.

Harwell, Rita. Interviewed by Opal Price. March 15, year unclear, ca. 1981, Georgallen, Alabama.

Irwin, Ruth. Interviewed by Mrs. E. R. McKnight. April 1982, Mississippi.

Jefferson, Vivian. Interviewed by Katherine Skelton. April 13, 1982, Bentonville, Arkansas.

Jones, Billy Lee. Interviewed by Doris Ashley. May 10, 1982, West Monroe, Louisiana.

Little, Orry. Interviewed by Mrs. Harris Carmichael. May 14, 1982, Grenada, Mississippi.

McCall, Letha Anderson. Interviewed by Virginia Bailey Harris. March 18, 1982, Richmond County, North Carolina.

McCann, Beatrice. Interviewed by Margaret McKenzie. August 19, no year, ca. 1980, Roanoke, Virginia.

McIntyre, Virginia. Interviewed by Doris Ashley. May 3, 1982, Franklin Parish, Louisiana.

Morgan, Jane. Interviewed by Mrs. Harris Carmichael. No date, ca. 1980, Mississippi.

Mornan, Sue. Interviewed by Jennie Moon. April 12, 1982, unspecified southern state.

Neal, Dora. Interviewed by Susan Ghent. November 11, 1982, South Carolina.

Nelson, Hautie. Interviewed by Alpha Worrell. Undated, circa 1982, unspecified town in west Tennessee.

Newman, Betty. Interviewed by McKnight. Undated ca. 1981, unspecified southern state.

Phillips, Henrietta. Interviewed by Virginia Bailey Harris. November 27, 1981, Whiteville, North Carolina.

Ratliff, Coria. Interviewed by Mrs. Dean Reeves. Undated, ca. 1982, Little Prater, Grundy County, Virginia.

Sellers, Etta Sue. Interviewed by Bea Cochran. May 13, 1982, Clinton, South Carolina.

Simmons, Essie. Interviewed by M. Houser. April 19, 1982, Mulberry, Arkansas.

Simrall, Mrs. B. N., Sr. Interviewed by Mrs. E. R. McKnight. April 1982, Mississippi.

Sullivan, Phyllis. Interviewed by Margaret McKenzie. Undated, ca. 1980, Sandyville, West Virginia.

Webb, Ann. Interviewed by unnamed interviewer. April 28, 1982, Lowell, Arkansas.

Wilson, Lucy. Interviewed by Virginia Harris. Undated circa 1982, Cumberland County, North Carolina.

Other Oral Histories

Freeman, Grace. Interviewed by Ron Chepesiuk. February 20, 1983, South Carolina.

Published Interviews

Cooper, Leland R. and Mary Lee, eds. *The People of the New River: Oral Histories from the Ashe, Allegheny, and Watauga Counties of North Carolina* (Jefferson, N.C.: McFarland and Co., Publishers, 2001).
Russell Colvard
Gwyn and Mae Hartsoe
John Little
John C. and Virginia Miller
Pauline Price

Jones, Lu Ann, ed. "'God Giveth the Increase': Lurline Stokes Murray's Narrative of Farming and Faith," *Southern Cultures* 8 (2002): 106–21.

Jones, Lu Ann, ed. "'Mama Learned Us to Work': An Oral History of Virgie St. John Redmond," *Oral History Review* 17 (1989): 63–90.

Murphy, Mary, ed. "'I Give the Best Part of My Life to the Mill': An Oral History of Icy Norman," in *Women's Oral History: The Frontiers Reader*, ed. Susan H. Armitage et al. (Lincoln and London: University of Nebraska Press), 125–44.

Sherry Thomas, ed. *We Didn't Have Much, But We Sure Had Plenty: Rural Women in Their Own Words* (New York: Anchor Books), 1981.
    Maude Hunter Dyke
    Lillian Fox
    Lottie Jackson
    Irene Nixon

Weiss, Allison, ed. *It's Just a Way of Life: Reminiscing about the Family Farm* (Sterling, Va.: Loudon Heritage Farm Museum, 2002).
    Howell Brown
    Jim Brownell
    Lehon Hamilton
    Maxine Hamilton
    Curtis and Betty Laycock
    Asbury Lloyd
    Ken Lowery
    Joan Moore
    Curtis Poland
    Edwin Otts
    Jimmy Spring
    Henry Stowers
    Mrs. J. H. Symington

Notes

Abbreviations

AFOHC	American Folklore and Oral History Collection, Auburn University, Auburn, Alabama
BTV	Behind the Veil Collection, Center for Documentary Studies, Duke University, Durham, North Carolina
EHOHP	Extension Homemakers Oral History Project, Archives and Special Collections, Dacus Library, Winthrop University, Rock Hill, South Carolina
IOH	Institute for Oral History, Baylor University, Waco, Texas
LOV	Waynesboro Oral Histories, Library of Virginia, Richmond, Virginia
MHC	McClung Historical Collection, Lawson-McGhee Library, Knoxville, Tennessee
MOHP	Mississippi Oral History Program, University of Southern Mississippi, Hattiesburg, Mississippi
OHSA	Oral History of Southern Agriculture, Behring Center, National Museum of American History, Smithsonian Institution, Washington, D.C.
PGOH	Pamela Grundy Oral History Collection, Auburn University, Auburn, Alabama
SOHP	Southern Oral History Project, #4007, Southern Historical Collection, Wilson Library, University of North Carolina at Chapel Hill
TC	Texas Collection, Baylor University, Waco, Texas
UAB	University of Alabama at Birmingham

Introduction

1. Leota Wagner Kuykendall, interview by Anne Radford Philips, on three occasions from February 20, 1992, to March 23, 1992, Waco, Tex., IOH.

2. David Blight, "Southerners Don't Lie, They Just Remember Big," in *Where These Memories Grow: History, Memory, and Southern Identity*, ed. W. Fitzhugh Brundage (Chapel Hill: University of North Carolina Press, 2000), 347–54, quote on 349.

3. Alessandro Portelli, *The Battle of Valle Giulia: Oral History and the Art of Dialogue* (Madison: University of Wisconsin Press, 1997), 80.

4. John Crowe Ransom, "Reconstructed but Unregenerate," in *I'll Take My Stand: The South and the Agrarian Tradition*, by Twelve Southerners (Baton Rouge: Louisiana State University Press, 1977 edition of 1930 original), 6.

5. David Anderson, "Down Memory Lane: Nostalgia for the Old South in Post–Civil War Plantation Reminiscences," *Journal of Southern History* 71 (2005): 104–36, quotes on 108 and 109.

6. Dan T. Carter, "Scattered Pieces: Living and Writing Southern History," in *Shapers of Southern History: Autobiographical Reflections*, ed. John B. Boles (Athens and London: University Press of Georgia, 2004): 115–36, quote on 115.

7. David Blight, *Beyond the Battlefield: Race, Memory, and the American Civil War* (Amherst: University of Massachusetts Press, 2002).

8. Robert N. Bellah et al., *Habits of the Heart: Commitment and Individualism in American Life* (New York: Harper and Row Publishers, 1985), 153.

9. Edward Ayers, "Memory and the South," *Southern Cultures* 2 (1995): 5–8.

10. Pierre Bourdieu, *Distinction: A Social Critique of the Judgment of Taste*, trans. Richard Nice (London: Routledge and Kegan Paul, 1979, trans. 1984), 455.

11. Scott G. McNall, *The Road to Rebellion: Class Formation and Kansas Populism, 1865–1900* (Chicago: University of Chicago Press, 1988), 8–9.

12. Ibid., 9.

13. Susan Engel, *Context is Everything: The Nature of Memory* (New York: W. H. Freeman and Company, 1999), 159.

14. For a detailed discussion of the scholarship on collective memory, see the bibliographic essay.

15. Among the few historians who use oral history narratives to examine the way ordinary people articulate and use collective memory are John Bodnar, "Power and Memory in Oral History: Workers and Managers at Studebaker," in *Memory and American History*, ed. David Thelen (Bloomington: Indiana University Press, 1989), 72–92; and Sherry Lee Linkon and John Russo, *Steeltown U.S.A.: Work and Memory in Youngstown* (Lawrence: University Press of Kansas, 2002). Most such work has focused on the urban working class.

16. Valerie Raleigh Yow, *Recording Oral History: A Guide for the Humanities and Social Sciences*, 2nd ed. (New York: AltaMira Press, 2005): 52–53, 57.

17. Michael Frisch, *A Shared Authority: Essays on the Craft and Meaning of Oral and Public History* (Albany: State University of New York Press, 1990), 61.

18. Alessandro Portelli, *The Battle of Valle Giulia: Oral History and the Art of Dialogue* (Madison: University of Wisconsin Press, 1997), 57. Susan A. Crane makes a similar argument in "Writing the Individual Back into Collective Memory," *American Historical Review* 102.5 (December 1997): 1372–85.

19. Portelli, *Battle of Valle Giulia*, 157.

20. Steven Reschly, personal communication with author, April 10, 2004, copy in author's possession.

21. John Bodnar, *Remaking America: Public Memory, Commemoration, and Patriotism in the Twentieth Century* (Princeton: Princeton University Press, 1992), 17. I am indebted to Ted Ownby for an email conversation about the minefield of using memory to articulate theories of dominance and resistance. Ted Ownby, personal communication with author, March 15, 2004, copy in author's possession.

22. See the bibliographic essay for more on the social scientists who studied the rural South.

23. 1920 figures are from Gavin Wright, *Old South, New South: Revolutions in the Southern Economy since the Civil War* (Baton Rouge: Louisiana State University Press, 1986), 121.

24. I am grateful to historian Lu Ann Jones for her careful reading of chapter 1 and her thoughts on my reading of the Woodrow Harper Sr. interview. This quotation comes from author's personal email communication with Lu Ann Jones, July 1, 2005, copy in author's possession.

25. See for example, Irene Clause, autobiographical tape, undated ca. 1982, location unknown, EHOHP.

26. Jane Addams, *The Long Road of Women's Memory* (Chicago and Urbana: University of Illinois Press, 2002 reprint of 1916 edition), 7.

27. Elizabeth Tonkin, *Narrating Our Pasts: The Social Construction of Oral History* (Cambridge: Cambridge University Press, 1992), 9.

28. George Lipsitz, *Time Passages: Collective Memory and American Popular Culture* (Minneapolis: University of Minnesota Press, 1990), 213.

29. Alessandro Portelli, *The Death of Luigi Trastulli and Other Stories: Form and Meaning in Oral History* (Albany: State University of New York Press, 1991), 25.

30. Mary Fouts, interview by Mabel Bartram, November 7, 1981, London, Ky., EHOHP.

31. See the bibliographic essay for an extensive discussion of works on the transformation of southern agriculture.

32. David B. Danbom, *Born in the Country: A History of Rural America* (Baltimore: Johns Hopkins University Press, 1995), 127.

33. R. Douglas Hurt, *Problems of Plenty: The American Farmer in the Twentieth Century* (Chicago: Ivan R. Dee, 2002), 5–6.

34. Pete Daniel, *Breaking the Land: The Transformation of Cotton, Tobacco, and Rice Cultures since* 1880 (Urbana: University of Illinois Press, 1980), 31; Danbom, *Born in the Country*, 127.

35. Peter A. Coclanis, "The Paths before Us/U.S.: Tracking the Economic Divergence of North and South," in *The South, the Nation, and the World: Perspectives on Southern Economic Development*, ed. David L. Carlton and Peter A. Coclanis (Charlottesville and London: University of Virginia Press, 2003), 12–23, quote on 22.

36. Scott J. Peters and Paul A. Morgan, "The Country Life Commission: Reconsidering a Milestone in American Agricultural History," *Agricultural History* 78 (Summer 2004): 289–316, quote on 312.

37. Danbom, *Born in the Country*, 127–29; Pete Daniel, *Standing at the Crossroads: Southern Life in the Twentieth Century* (New York: Hill and Wang, 1986), 10–12; Daniel, *Breaking the Land*, 13.

38. Danbom, *Born in the Country*, 179–80; Wright, *Old South, New South*, 198.

39. Figures compiled from *Census of Agriculture, 1925*, pt. 2, pp. 736–45; Danbom, *Born in the Country*, 186.

40. Danbom, *Born in the Country*, 188, 193; U.S. Department of Agriculture, *Yearbook of Agriculture 1922*, 1002.

41. Danbom, *Born in the Country*, 127–29; Daniel, *Breaking the Land*, 139–41; *United States Census of Agriculture, 1930*, vol. 2, part 2, compiled from pp. 870–84, 470–75; Jacqueline Jones, *The Dispossessed: America's Underclass from the Civil War to the Present* (New York: Basic Books, 1992), 82–83, 96.

42. Hurt, *Problems of Plenty*, 63, 43.

43. Wright, *Old South, New South*, 228–31, 235; Danbom, *Born in the Country*, 213–15.

44. Wright, *Old South, New South*, 236, 252.

45. Pete Daniel, *Lost Revolutions: The South in the 1950s* (Chapel Hill: University of North Carolina Press, 2000), 9.

46. Wright, *Old South, New South*, 241.

47. Donald Holley, *The Second Great Emancipation: The Mechanical Cotton Picker, Black Migration, and How They Shaped the Modern South* (Fayetteville: University of Arkansas Press, 2000), 98.

48. Danbom, *Born in the Country*, 234–37.

49. Bruce L. Gardner, *American Agriculture in the Twentieth Century: How It Flourished and What It Cost* (Cambridge and London: Harvard University Press, 2002), 16–17.

50. Wright, *Old South, New South*, 248; Danbom, *Born in the Country*, 238; Jacqueline Jones, *Labor of Love, Labor of Sorrow: Black Women, Work, and the Family from Slavery to the Present* (New York: Vintage, 1985), 260–62.

51. I am grateful to Mark Schultz for hammering this point into my brain. See Schultz, personal correspondence with the author, September 2005, and Mark Schultz, *The Rural Face of White Supremacy: Beyond Jim Crow* (Urbana and Chicago: University of Illinois Press, 2005), 205–23.

52. Barry J. Barnett, "The U.S. Farm Financial Crisis of the 1980s," in *Fighting for the Farm: Rural America Transformed*, ed. Jane Adams (Philadelphia: University of Pennsylvania Press, 2003), 160–71, quote on 166.

53. Ibid., 167–68.

54. Gardner, *American Agriculture in the Twentieth Century*, 340.

55. Roger Thurow, "Black Farmers Hit the Road to Confront a 'Cycle of Racism,'" *Wall Street Journal*, May 1, 1998, p. 1; Armando Villafranca, "Too Little, Too Late: Black Farmers' Discrimination Settlement May Not Ease Years of Pain," *Houston Chronicle*, December 5, 1999, p. A1; Michael Fletcher, "Black Farmers' Awards May Top $1 Billion," *Washington Post*, October 16, 2000.

56. Catherine McNicol Stock, *Rural Radicals: Righteous Rage in the American Grain* (Ithaca: Cornell University Press, 1996), 16; William P. Browne, "Benign Public Policies, Malignant Consequences, and the Demise of African American Agriculture," in *African American Life in the Rural South, 1900–1950*, ed. R. Douglas Hurt (Columbia and London: University of Missouri Press, 2003), 129–51, quote on 135.

Chapter One. Three Southern
Farmers Tell Their Stories

1. Unless otherwise indicated, all quotes and information on McBrayer are drawn from Ruth Hatchette McBrayer, interview by Melissa Walker, August 20, 1998, Chesnee, S.C., tape and transcript in author's possession. An edited version of the interview has been published in Melissa Walker, ed., *Country Women Cope with Hard Times: A Collection of Oral Histories* (Columbia: University of South Carolina Press, 2004), 135–48.

2. Unless otherwise indicated all quotes from Woodrow Harper Sr. and details about his life come from Woodrow Harper Sr., interview by Lu Ann Jones, April 17, 1987, Hartwell, Ga., OHSA.

3. Unless otherwise indicated, this and all other subsequent information on the life of John West and all quotes are drawn from John and Martha Alice West, interview by Melissa Walker, August 12, 1993, Friendsville, Tenn., MHC. Martha Alice West's portion of the interview has been published in Walker, ed., *Country Women Cope with Hard Times*, 132–34.

4. Joseph E. Davis, ed., *Stories of Change: Narrative and Social Movements* (Albany: State University of New York Press, 2002), 20.

5. Margaret R. Somers, "The Narrative Construction of Identity: A Relational and Network Approach," *Theory and Society* 23 (1994): 605–49, quote on 616.

6. West interview.

7. Statistics compiled from Bureau of the Census and USDA, *Census of Agriculture, 1945,* v. I, pt. 20, Statistics for Counties, pp. 12, 19, 135.

8. For more on nineteenth-century conceptions of manhood among yeoman farmers, see Stephanie McCurry, *Masters of Small Worlds: Yeoman Households, Gender Relations, and the Political Culture of the Antebellum South Carolina Low Country* (New York: Oxford University Press, 1995).

9. Mary Evelyn Lane, interview by Melissa Walker, August 8, 1994, Maryville, Tenn.; French Clark, interview by Melissa Walker, July 22, 1994, Maryville, Tenn.; both in MHC.

10. See Ronald J. Grele, "Riffs and Improvisation: An Interview with Studs Terkel," in *Envelopes of Sound: The Art of Oral History,* 2nd ed., rev., ed. Ronald J. Grele (New York: Praeger, 1991), 10–49.

11. McBrayer interview.

12. For more on peach farming, see Melissa Walker, *All We Knew Was to Farm: Rural Women in the Upcountry South, 1919–1941* (Baltimore: Johns Hopkins University Press, 2000), chapter 7.

13. "Hatchette Dies of Pistol Wound," *Spartanburg Herald,* May 29, 1947, and Vernon E. Hatchette obituary, *Spartanburg Herald,* May 30, 1947.

14. On distinctive characteristics of women's autobiographical narratives, see Susan Stanford Friedman, "Women's Autobiographical Selves: Theory and Practice," in *The Private Self: Theory and Practice of Women's Autobiographical Writings,* ed, Shari Bentsock (Chapel Hill: University of North Carolina Press, 1988), 34–62; and Bella Brodski and Celeste Schenck, eds., *Life/Lines: Theorizing Women's Autobiography* (Ithaca, New York: Cornell University Press, 1988).

15. See Kline Cash, interview by Melissa Walker, October 4, 1997, Chesnee, S.C., tape and notes in author's possession; Henry Gramling II, interview by Melissa Walker, October 10, 1997, Gramling, S.C., tape and notes in author's possession.

16. Harper interview.

17. Statistics drawn from the Historical Census Data Browser, available online at <http://fisher.lib.virginia.edu/cgi-local/censusbin/census/census.pl>.

18. For more information, see "Hartwell Dam and Lake," U.S. Army Corps of Engineers, Savannah District, home page, available online at <http://www.sas.usace.army.mil/srl/history.htm>.

19. 1950 figures from Historical Census Data Browser, available online at <http://fisher.lib.virginia.edu/cgi-local/censusbin/census/census.pl>.

20. Michael Fletcher, "Black Farmers' Awards May Top $1 Billion," *Washington Post*, October 16, 2000.

Chapter Two. Rural Southerners and the Community of Memory

1. Susie Weathersbee, interview by Leslie Brown, June 30, 1993, Halifax, N.C., in the Behind the Veil Collection, Box UT5, Tray B, BTV; Arthur Little, interview by Jacquelyn Hall, December 14, 1979, Newton, N.C., SOHP.

2. Sherry Lee Linkon and John Russo, *Steeltown U.S.A.: Work and Memory in Youngstown* (Lawrence: University Press of Kansas, 2002), 3; Robert N. Bellah et al., *Habits of the Heart: Commitment and Individualism in American Life* (New York: Harper and Row, Publishers, 1985), 153.

3. David Jacobson, *Place and Belonging in America* (Baltimore and London: Johns Hopkins University Press, 2002); Twelve Southerners, *I'll Take My Stand: The South and the Agrarian Tradition* (Baton Rouge: Louisiana State University Press, 1977 reprint of 1930 edition); David B. Danbom, "Romantic Agrarianism in Twentieth Century America," *Agricultural History* 65 (1991): 1–12. For more on Jeffersonian agrarianism, see Drew McCoy, *Elusive Republic: Political Economy in Jeffersonian America* (New York: W. W. Norton, 1980); Roger G. Kennedy, *Mr. Kennedy's Lost Cause: Land, Farmers, Slavery, and the Louisiana Purchase* (New York: Oxford University Press, 2003).

4. Alessandro Portelli, *The Battle of Valle Giulia: Oral History and the Art of Dialogue* (Madison: University of Wisconsin Press, 1997), 153.

5. John West and Martha Alice West, interview by author, August 12, 1993, Friendsville, Tenn., MHC.

6. Twelve Southerners, *I'll Take My Stand*. On self-sufficiency, see especially Andrew Nelson Lytle's essay "The Hind Tit," 208.

7. Mrs. Pinkey Hall, interview by Kim Adams, December 13, 1995, location unknown, MOHP, transcript available online at <http://www.lib.usm.edu/~spcol/crda/oh/halltrans/htm>, 2.

8. Pierre Bourdieu, *Distinction: A Social Critique of the Judgement of Taste*, trans. Richard Nice (London: Routledge and Kegan Paul, 1979, trans. 1984), 197.

9. Frances Read Phelps, interview by Lawrence R. Phelps, February 26, 1984, Greenville, Ala., AFOHC; Irene Jackson, interview by Kristen Arthur, undated ca. March 2003, Spartanburg, S.C., copy of transcript in author's possession.

10. Ted Ownby, *American Dreams in Mississippi: Consumers, Poverty, and Culture, 1830–1998* (Chapel Hill: University of North Carolina Press, 1999), 25–31, 67–68, 98–103.

11. "The Relation between the Ability to Pay and the Standard of Living among Farmers," USDA Bulletin No. 1832 (Washington, D.C.: Government Printing Office, January 1926), 8–9.

12. Rosa McCowan Tensley, interview by Stephen C. Harvey, February 27, 1980, Notasulga, Ala., AFOHC.

13. Lu Ann Jones, "'God Giveth the Increase': Lurline Stokes Murray's Narrative of Farming and Faith," *Southern Cultures* 8 (2002): 106–21, quote from 111.

14. Elizabeth Harden Lasseter, interview by Milton E. Turner, May 8, 1976, Gadsden, Ala., Special Collections, UAB; Jurl Lee Watkins, interview by Gregory Hunter, June 28, 1994, Sylvester, Ga., BTV, Box UT1, Tray C.

15. Irene Jackson interview.

16. Flossie and Monroe Wood, interview by Pamela Grundy, May 28, 1987, Delta, Ala., PGOH.

17. Virginia Harris and Dorothy Skinner, interview by Melissa Walker, May 31, 2001, Spartanburg, S.C., tape and transcript in author's possession.

18. Worth Jewell, interview by Kevin Price, February 18, 1982, Opelika, Ala., AFOHC; [Ann Smith], interview by Cliff Kuhn, June 29, 1977, location unknown, SOHP; John West interview.

19. Sociologist Max Weber first explored the idea of the Protestant work ethic in his book, *The Protestant Ethic and the Spirit of Capitalism*. See the Stephen Kalberg translation (Chicago: Fitzroy Dearborn Publishers, 2001).

20. Carl R. Osthaus, "The Work Ethic of the Plain Folk: Labor and Religion in the Old South," *Journal of Southern History* 70:4 (November 2004): 745–82, quote on 756.

21. Ora Nell Wehring Moseley, *Oral Memoirs of Ora Nell Wehring Moseley* (interview by Lois E. Myers, January 22, 1992, Burton, Tex.), TC. For more on the nature of the work ethic, particularly among working-class people, see Weber, *Protestant Ethic and the Spirit of Capitalism*; Richard Sennett, *The Corrosion of Character: The Personal Consequences of Work in the New Capitalism* (New York and London: W. W. Norton & Company, 1998), especially 98–100; Michele Lamont, *The Dignity of the Working Man: Morality and the Boundaries of Race, Class, and Immigration* (New York and Cambridge: Russell Sage Foundation and Harvard University Press, 2000), especially 24–26.

22. Mealie Diggs, interview by unnamed person, undated ca. 1996, Waynesboro, Va., LOV.

23. Dema Reeves Lyall, interview by Ruth Dasmann, September 5, 1984, Ashe County, N.C., SOHP.

24. Jurl Lee Watkins, interview by Gregory Hunter, June 28, 1994, Sylvester, Ga., BTV, Box UT1, Tray C.

25. R. H. Linam, *Oral Memoirs of R. H. Linam* (interview by Thomas L. Charlton, on five occasions from April 9, 1975, to July 13, 1976, Waco, Tex.), TC.

26. Elmin Kimboll Howell Jr., *Oral Memoirs of Elmin Kimboll Howell Jr.* (interview by William Lee Pitts, May 20, 1980, Waco, Tex., TC).

27. Brooks quoted in Thordis Simonsen, ed., *You May Plow Here: The Narrative of Sara Brooks* (New York: W.W. Norton & Co., 1986), 49.

28. Dovie Lee and Etta Lillian Hardy Carroll, interview by Rebecca Sharpless on seven occasions from September 21, 1990, to July 11, 1991, Waxahachie, Tex., IOH.

29. Estelle and John Heard, interview by Pamela Grundy, October 17, 1987, Delta, Ala., PGOH.

30. John West interview.

31. Ray Summers, *Oral Memoirs of Ray Summers* (interview by Daniel B. McGee, on ten occasions from August 11 through August 29, 1980, Waco, Tex.), TC; Rita Harwell, interview by Opal Price, March 15, year unclear, ca. 1981, Georgallen, Ala., EHOHP.

32. Woodrow Fetner, interview by Pamela Grundy, August 24, 1987, Cragford, Ala., PGOH; Howard and Olefa Koerth Matthies, interview by Thomas L. Charlton, Dan K. Utley, and Deb Hoskins, on four occasions from December 20, 1991, to October 29, 1992, Burton, Tex., IOH.

33. Dr. William A. Butts, interview by Orley B. Caudill, March 3, 1976, location unknown, MOHP, transcript available online at <http://anna.lib.usm.edu/%7Espcol/crda/oh/ohbuttswb.html>.

34. Irene Clause, interview by unnamed person, undated ca. 1982, EHOHP.

35. [Unknown First Name] Brookshire, interview by Mabel Bartram, undated ca. 1982, Ky., EHOHP.

36. Robert N. Bellah et al., *Habits of the Heart: Commitment and Individualism in American Life* (New York: Harper and Row Publishers, 1985), 56.

37. Helen Howard, interview by Doris G. Dixon, July 19, 1995, Cotton Plant, Ark., BTV, Box UT1, Tray D.

38. Howard and Olefa Koerth Matthies interview.

39. Robert S. Weise, "Isolation and Southern Rural Poverty: Civic Society in the 'Problem' South," unpublished paper presented at the Southern Historical Association Annual Meeting, New Orleans, Louisiana, November 2001, p. 11, copy in author's possession.

40. Robert D. Putnam, *Bowling Alone: The Collapse and Revival of American Community* (New York: Simon and Schuster, 2000), 21.

41. Dean McGee, interview by Lu Ann Jones, undated ca. 1987, Church Point, La., OHSA.

42. Douglas Harper, *Changing Works: Visions of a Lost Agriculture* (Chicago: University of Chicago Press, 2001), 180.

43. Jones, "'God Giveth the Increase.'"

44. Carroll interview.

45. Putnam, *Bowling Alone*, 318.

46. Benjamin Franklin and Earlien Freyer Engelbrecht, interview by Rebecca Sharpless, on four occasions from February 13, 1997, to April 22, 1997, Crawford, Tex., IOH; LaVerne Farmer, interview by Melissa Walker, August 9, 1993, Maryville, Tenn., MHC; Della Inez Folley, interview by Rebecca Sharpless, on four occasions from September 4, 1990, to October 17, 1990, Mart, Tex., IOH; Dovie Lee and Etta Lillian Hardy Carroll, interview by Rebecca Sharpless, on seven occasions from September 21, 1990, to July 11, 1991, Waxahachie, Tex., IOH.

47. Nancy Holt, interview by Frances E. Webb, October 27, 1985, Orange County, N.C., SOHP; Edna Harris, interview by Lu Ann Jones, May 15 and 16, 1987, Harmony, N.C., OHSA.

48. Mrs. Leler George and family, interview by Lu Ann Jones, July 4, 1989, Bishopville, S.C., OHSA.

49. See Walker, *All We Knew Was to Farm*, 26–29.

50. Historian Janette Thomas Greenwood notes that urban, middle-class black people in Charlotte, North Carolina, coined the term "better class" to describe themselves. See *Bittersweet Legacy: The Black and White Better Classes in Charlotte, 1850–1910* (Chapel Hill: University of North Carolina Press, 1994).

51. For a discussion of African American class definitions, particularly among working-class blacks, see Robin D. G. Kelley, *Race Rebels: Culture, Politics, and the Working Class* (New York: Free Press, 1994), especially chapters 1 and 2.

52. [Ethel Davis], interview by Melissa Walker, July 19, 1994, Loudon County, Tenn., MHC; Betty Newman, interview by [unknown first name] McKnight, undated ca. 1981, EHOHP; Wilma Williamson, interview by Melissa Walker, July 18, 1996, Maryville, Tenn., MHC; LaVerne Farmer interview.

53. Billy Lee Jones, interview by Doris Ashley, May 10, 1982, West Monroe, La., EHOHP; Dovie and Etta Carroll interview.

54. Eldred and Mary Quinn, interview by Melissa Walker, October 18, 2000, Spartanburg, S.C., tape and transcript in author's collection; transcript in Kennedy Local History Collection, Spartanburg County Public Library.

55. [Ethel Davis] interview; Betty Newman interview.

56. Eldred and Mary Quinn interview.

57. Bill Lewellyn, interview by Melissa Walker, August 10, 1993, Greenback, Tenn., MHC.

58. Pat Gates, interview by Bea Cochran, unspecified date, 1981, South Carolina, EHOHP.

59. Myrtle Irene Calvert Dodd, interview by Rebecca Sharpless, on four occasions from August 14 to September 19, 1990, in Waco, Tex., TC.

60. Carl Neal, interview by Lois E. Myers, February 4 and 11, 1993, McLennan County, Tex., TC.

61. Rosa Tensley interview.

62. Cleaster Mitchell, interview by Paul Ortiz, July 16, 1995, Brinkley, Ark., BTV, Box UT2, Tray A.

63. Vera Malone, *Oral Memoirs of Vera Malone* (interview by LaWanda Ball, December 5, 1975, Waco, Tex.), TC.

64. Lonnie Graves, interview by Jay M. Butler, June 30, 1993, Satin, Tex., IOH.

65. Kenneth B. Young, interview by Paul Ortiz, July 12, 1994, Tuskegee, Ala., BTV, Box UT13, Tray A.

66. For more on the historically conditioned nature of oral history field-work, see Alessandro Portelli, *Death of Luigi Trastulli and Other Stories: Form and Meaning in Oral History* (Albany: State University of New York Press, 1991), 34.

67. Will D. Campbell, interview by Orley B. Caudill, June 8, 1976, Mt. Juliet, Tenn., MOHP, transcript available online at <http://anna.lib.usm.edu/%7Espcol/crda/oh/campbelltrans.htm>.

68. Ibid.

69. Grover L. Williams Sr., interview by Dan K. Utley, on five occasions between November 25, 1991, and June 12, 1992, Burton, Tex., IOH; J. C. and Tiny Chapman, interview by Pamela Grundy, June 3, 1987, Shiloh, Ala., PGOH.

70. Dovie Lee and Etta Lillian Hardy Carroll interviews.

71. Edward and Mary Estelle Terry Harrington, interview by Mary Murphy, February 28, 1979, Burlington, N.C., SOHP.

72. Flossie and Monroe Wood, interview by Pamela Grundy, May 28, 1987, Delta, Ala., PGOH.

73. Virginia Harris and Dorothy Skinner and interview.

74. Norbert King Andrews, interview by Marilyn T. Grunkemeyer, October 22, 1985, Orange County, N.C., SOHP.

75. Virginia Harris and Dorothy Skinner interview; [William and Kate Graham], interview by Melissa Walker, April 30, 2002, Asheville, N.C., tape and transcript in author's possession.

76. Thomas Armour Patterson, *Oral Memoirs of Thomas Armour Patterson* (interview by Thomas L. Charlton, on five occasions from August 18, 1971, to November 8, 1976), TC.

77. Bill Lewellyn interview.

Chapter Three. Memory and the Nature of Transformation

1. John and Martha Alice West, interview by Melissa Walker, August 12, 1993, Friendsville, Tenn., MHC.

2. Deola Mayberry Adams, interview by Rebecca Sharpless, August 4, 1987, Gatesville, Tex., IOH.

3. A. L. Head, interview by Donnie Breaseale, October 26 and November 18, 1975, Blountville, Ala., Special Collections, UAB.

4. Ruth Irwin, interview by Mrs. E. R. McKnight, April 1982, Miss., EHOHP.

5. J. D. Hamrick to Henry A. Wallace, August 28, 1933, Record Group (RG) 145, General Records of the Agricultural Adjustment Administration and Agricultural Adjustment Agency, Subject Correspondence 1933–1935, National Archives and Records Administration, College Park, Md.

6. For similar letters, see Newton Smith to Secretary of Agriculture, July 3, 1933; William P. Iney to Cotton Section, AAA; L. D. Ridlehoover to Henry A. Wallace, July 3, 1933, all in RG 145 (see note 5); M. Walter Thomas, "The Voice of the Farmer," *Progressive Farmer*, October 1937, 10; Herman Brown, "Free for All," *Southern Agriculturist*, March 1939, 14; E. L. Parish, "Free for All," *Southern Agriculturist*, January 1966, 32.

7. Mrs. H. M. C., "The Voice of the Farm," *Progressive Farmer*, February 1940, 58. Mrs. H. M. C.'s poignant letter sparked dozens of replies from other readers over the next four issues. Some readers were sympathetic to her plight, but many others missed her point about the unintended consequences of government policies, instead chiding her for criticizing crop reduction programs that were intended to help the farmer, for interfering in her son's decision making, and for unrealistic expectations of farm life. For the answers to Mrs. H. M. C., see "The Voice of the Farm" column in the March, April, and May 1940 issues of the magazine.

8. Arthur F. Raper, *Tenants of the Almighty* (New York: The MacMillan Company, 1943), 322, 331.

9. John Little quoted in Leland R. Cooper and Mary Lee Cooper, eds., *The People of the New River: Oral Histories from the Ashe, Alleghany and Watauga Counties of North Carolina* (Jefferson, N.C.: McFarland & Company, Inc., Publishers, 2001), 203.

10. Lu Ann Jones, "'God Giveth the Increase': Lurline Stokes Murray's Narrative of Farming and Faith," *Southern Cultures* 8 (2002): 106–21, quote on 110.

11. Cooper and Cooper, *People of the New River*, 195–203, quote on 198.

12. David Matthews, interview by Paul Ortiz, ca. 1995, Miss., BTV, Box UT5, Tray D.

13. Eldred and Mary Quinn, interview by Melissa Walker, October 18, 2000, Spartanburg, S.C., tape and transcript in author's collection; transcript in Kennedy Local History Collection, Spartanburg County Public Library.

14. Tom B. Cunningham, interview by Lu Ann Jones, January 17, 1991, Darlington, S.C., OHSA.

15. Marvin Engelbrecht, interview by Jaclyn Jeffrey, March 11, 1997, Crawford, Tex., IOH.

16. Tom B. Cunningham interview.

17. Dema Reeves Lyall, interview by Ruth Dasmann, September 5, 1984, Ashe County, N.C., SOHP.

18. Mike Teer, interview by Karl Campbell, undated ca. 1985, Orange County, N.C., SOHP.

19. Virginia McIntyre, interview by Doris Ashley, May 3, 1982, Franklin Parish, La., EHOHP.

20. Tom B. Cunningham interview.

21. Lamas and Janie Denning, interview by Lu Ann Jones and Charlie Thompson, July 14, 1998, Benson, N.C., SOHP.

22. A. C. and Grace Griffin, interview by Lu Ann Jones, December 11, 1986, Edenton, N.C., OHSA.

23. Norbert King Andrews, interview by Marilyn T. Grunkemeyer, October 22 and November 18, 1985, Orange County, N.C., SOHP.

24. Allison Weiss, ed., *It's Just a Way of Life: Reminiscing about the Family Farm* (Sterling, Va.: Loudon Heritage Farm Museum, 2002), 35.

25. Ibid., 127.

26. Kenneth Gosney, interview by Lu Ann Jones, October 1, 1987, Carlisle, Ark., OHSA.

27. Eldred and Mary Quinn interview.

28. Grover L. Williams Sr., interview by Dan K. Utley, November 25, 1991, Burton, Tex., TC.

29. J. Robert Stevenson, interview by Thomas J. Moore, March 3, 1988, Auburn, Ala., AFOHC.

30. Weiss, *It's Just a Way of Life*, p. 138.

31. Ibid., 32.

32. Van Doren Massirer, interview by Lois E. Myers, January 9, 1998, Crawford, Tex., IOH.

33. Cooper and Cooper, *People of the New River*, 28–35, quote on 32.

34. Otto and Pauline Davis, interview by Lu Ann Jones, January 8, 1987, Darlington, S.C., OHSA.

35. [William and Kate Graham], interview by Melissa Walker, April 30, 2002, Asheville, N.C., tape and transcript in author's possession.

36. Nathan Murray, interview by Cathy Johnson, June 14, 1984, Duplin County, N.C., SOHP.

37. Dick Benson, interview by Lu Ann Jones, undated ca. 1987, Tifton, Ga., OHSA.

38. Brian Donahue, "Review of *Larding the Lean Earth: Soil and Society in Nineteenth-Century America,* by Steven Stoll," *Journal of Southern History* (September 2003): 637.

39. For more on attitudes toward consumption and debt, see Ted Ownby,

American Dreams in Mississippi: Consumers, Poverty, and Culture, 1830–1998 (Chapel Hill: University of North Carolina Press, 1999), 20–22, 67–78.

40. Anthropologist Kathryn Marie Dudley found similar responses in her ethnographic study of one Midwestern farming community hit hard by the farm crisis of the 1980s. See Katherine Marie Dudley, "The Entrepreneurial Self: Identity and Morality in a Midwestern Farming Community," *in Fighting for the Farm: Rural America Transformed*, ed. Jane Adams (Philadelphia: University of Pennsylvania Press, 2003), 175–91.

Chapter Four. Memory and the Meaning of Change

1. Howard Taft Bailey, interview by Lu Ann Jones, October 16, 1987, Holmes County, Miss., OHSA.

2. Ethel H. Carter and Charlotte Haransky, interview by Lu Ann Jones, September 22, 1988, Ringgold, Va., OHSA.

3. [Mabel Love], interview by Melissa Walker, July 19, 1994, Loudon County, Tenn., MHC.

4. Zelphia Edwards, interview by Rebecca Fortenberry, undated, ca. 1982, Louisiana, EHOHP.

5. Mary Fouts, interview by Mabel Bartram, November 7, 1981, London, Ky., EHOHP.

6. Leota Wagner Kuykendall, interview by Anne Radford Philips, on three occasions from Feb. 20, 1992, to March 23, 1992, Waco, Tex., IOH.

7. Lena Boyce, interview by Sue Beal, October 16, 1984, Rehobeth, N.C., SOHP.

8. Amy Jones, interview by Mausiki Scales, June 28, 1995, Memphis, Tenn., BTV, Box UT6, Tray D. For a similar view, see Otha B. Strong Jones, interview by Laurie Green, August 8, 1995, Memphis, Tenn., BTV, Box UT7, Tray A.

9. Theresa Cameron Lyons, interview by Leslie Brown, August 16, 1995, Durham, N.C., BTV, Box UT4, Tray B.

10. Viola Carter, interview by Charles H. Houston Jr., June 24, 1994, Albany, Ga., BTV, Box UT1, Tray A.

11. L. D. and Lula Walker, interview by Pamela Grundy, June 23, 1987, Cragford, Ala., PGOH.

12. J. C. and Lizzie Colley, interview by Pamela Grundy, June 2, 1987, Mountain, Ala., PGOH.

13. Lottie Jackson, interview by Sherry Thomas, in Sherry Thomas, ed., *We Didn't Have Much, But We Sure Had Plenty: Rural Women in Their Own Words* (New York: Anchor Books, 1981), 99–108, quote on 100.

14. Dema Reeves Lyall, interview by Ruth Dasmann, September 5, 1984, Ashe County, N.C., SOHP.

15. Fredda Davis, interview by Ruth Dasmann, September 26, 1984, N.C., SOHP.

16. Dema Lyall interview.

17. Essie Mae Alexander, interview by Paul Ortiz, August 10, 1995, Greenwood, Miss., BTV, Box UT5, Tray C. See also Helen Howard, interview by Doris G. Dixon, July 19, 1995, Cotton Plant, Ark., BTV, Box UT1, Tray D.

18. Howard Taft Bailey interview.

19. Maurice Lucas, interview by Mausiki Scales, August 7, 1995, Renova, Miss., BTV, Box UT5, Tray D.

20. Clayon Lowder, interview by Lu Ann Jones, January 14, 1987, Sumter, S.C., OHSA.

21. Tom B. Cunningham, interview by Lu Ann Jones, January 17, 1991, Darlington, S.C., OHSA.

22. A. C. and Grace Griffin, interview by Lu Ann Jones, December 8 and 10, 1986, Edenton, N.C., OHSA.

23. John B. Laney Jr., interview by Lu Ann Jones, undated ca. 1987, Lyon, Miss., OHSA.

24. See for example, Pete Daniel, *Breaking the Land: The Transformation of Cotton, Tobacco, and Rice Cultures since 1800,* Illini Books ed. (Urbana and Chicago: University of Illinois Press, 1986), 98–105.

25. Minnie Adcock to Franklin Roosevelt, December 2, 1938, RG 96, Records of the Farmer's Home Administration, correspondence relating to compliance, 1935–1942, National Archives and Records Administration, College Park, Md.

26. L. D. Brantley, interview by Lu Ann Jones, undated ca. 1987, Ark., OHSA.

27. John William Andrews, interview by Lu Ann Jones, May 20, 1987, Boomer, N.C., OHSA.

28. Tom B. Cunningham interview.

29. John Bodnar, "Power and Memory in Oral History: Workers and Managers at Studebaker," in *Memory and American History,* ed. David Thelen (Bloomington: Indiana University Press, 1989), 90.

30. Avery R. Downing, *Oral Memoirs of Avery R. Downing* (interview by James M. Sorelle and Thomas L. Charlton, August 23 and 25, 1983, Waco, Tex.), TC.

31. Alice Evelyn Grogan Hardin, interview by Allen Tullos, May 2, 1980, Greenville, S.C., SOHP.

32. Edward and Mary Estelle Terry Harrington, interview by Mary Murphy, February 28, 1979, Burlington, N.C., SOHP.

33. C. P. Horn, interview by Pamela Grundy, February 24, 1988, Ashland, Ala., PGOH.

34. Douthit Young McDaniel, *Oral Memoirs of Douthit Young*

McDaniel (interview by Thomas L. Charlton, on eight occasions from May 15 to June 24, 1975, Waco, Tex.), TC.

35. Opal Bateman, interview by Sharon Siske Crunk, March 12, 1993, Iredell, Tex., IOH.

36. Allison Weiss, ed. *It's Just a Way of Life: Reminiscing About the Family Farm* (Sterling, Va.: Loudon Heritage Farm Museum, 2002), 129–30.

37. Arthur G. Neal, *National Trauma and Collective Memory: Major Events in the American Century* (Armonk, N.Y. and London: M. E. Sharpe, 1998), 58.

38. O. C. Gibson, interview by Paul Ortiz, July 31, 1995, Greenwood, Miss., BTV, Box UT5, Tray D.

39. Mary Shipp, interview by Tunga White, June 28, 1994, Sylvester, Ga., BTV, Box UT1, Tray C.

40. William Rucker, interview by Lu Ann Jones, undated ca. 1987, Elberton, Ga., OHSA.

41. Ophelia Mae Mayberry Hall, interview by Rebecca Sharpless, on May 26 and June 10, 1986, Gatesville, Tex., IOH.

42. Ray Stannard Baker, *Following the Color Line: American Negro Citizenship in the Progressive Era* (New York: Harper & Row, 1964 reprint of 1908 edition), 101.

43. Eugene Webster, interview by Jay M. Tucker, July 8, 1993, Downsville, Tex., IOH.

44. Valerie Grim, "From the Yazoo Mississippi Delta to the Urban Communities of the Midwest," in *Women's Oral History: The Frontiers Reader,* ed. Susan H. Armitage et al. (Lincoln and London: University of Nebraska Press, 2002), 272–92, quotes on 273. Grim's study of black women who left the Mississippi Delta for Midwestern cities found that they left for improved economic opportunities and for better social, cultural, and educational opportunities for their children. They liked the political voice black people had in the North. They also left to get away from racial violence.

45. Ibid., 276.

46. William Rucker interview.

47. James Hall, interview by Gregory Hunter, June 17, 1994, Sylvester, Ga., BTV, Box UT1, Tray B.

48. Mary Shipp interview.

49. James and Marion Lewis, interview by Karen Ferguson, July 29, 1993, Havelock, N.C., BTV, Box UT8, Tray A.

50. Opinion accepting consent decree by Paul Friedman, Judge in U.S. District Court for the District of Columbia, in *Timothy v. Pigford, et al., plantiffs v. Dan Glickman, Secretary, USDA, defendant and Cecil Brewington, et al., plantiffs v. Daniel R. Glickman, defendant, April 14, 1999,* text available online at <http://www.dcd.uscourts.gov/Opinions/1999/Friedman/97–

1978g.pdf>. For USDA's public statements about the case, see <http://www. usda.gov/da/consentsum.htm>.

51. William Rucker interview.

52. Howard Taft Bailey interview.

53. A. C. and Grace Griffin interview.

54. Weiss, ed., *It's Just a Way of Life*, 126.

55. Charles Bailey, interview by Lu Ann Jones, October 9, 1987, Tunica, Miss., OHSA.

56. Weiss, *It's Just a Way of Life*, 82.

57. Jessie and Kenneth Gosney, interview by Lu Ann Jones, October 1, 1987, Carlisle, Ark., OHSA.

58. See "Women in Farm Economics home page," <www.wifeline. com>, undated web page.

59. [William and Kate Graham], interview by Melissa Walker, April 30, 2002, Asheville, N.C., tape and transcript in author's possession.

60. Catherine McNicol Stock, *Rural Radicals: Righteous Rage in the American Grain* (Ithaca: Cornell University Press, 1996), 10.

61. R. Douglas Hurt, *Problems of Plenty: The American Farmer in the Twentieth Century* (Chicago: Ivan R. Dee, 2002), 152, 158.

62. Robert N. Bellah et al., *Habits of the Heart: Commitment and Individualism in American Life* (New York: Harper and Row Publishers, 1985), 22.

63. Iwona Irwin-Zarecka, *Frames of Remembrances: The Dynamics of Collective Memory* (New Brunswick: Transaction Publishers, 1994), 53.

64. Maurice Halbwachs, edited, translated and introduction by Lewis A. Coser, *On Collective Memory* (Chicago: University of Chicago Press, 1992), 51. Halbwachs said, "People of the past, whose life and actions are now immobilized in a clearly defined framework, may have once expressed good or bad intentions in relation to us, but we now expect nothing from them: they evoke in us neither uncertainty, rivalry, nor envy. We cannot love them nor can we detest them" (p. 51).

65. Michael Frisch, *A Shared Authority: Essays on the Craft and Meaning of Oral and Public History* (Albany: State University of New York Press, 1990), 12.

66. Lizabeth Cohen, *A Consumers' Republic: The Politics of Mass Consumption in Postwar America* (New York: Vintage Books, 2003), 152–65, quote on 152.

67. It is difficult to obtain a clear picture of the educational levels of narrators in this sample because the educational level of roughly half is unknown. Roughly half of the narrators born before 1920 can be verified as having at least attended high school; only about 40 percent of those born after 1920 can be verified as having at least some high school education. See Appendix.

68. Alessandro Portelli, *The Death of Luigi Trastulli and Other Stories: Form and Meaning in Oral History* (Albany: State University of New York Press, 1991), 15.

Chapter Five. The Present Shapes
Stories about the Past

1. Ted Ownby, *American Dreams in Mississippi: Consumers, Poverty, and Culture, 1830–1998* (Chapel Hill: University of North Carolina Press, 1999), 161.

2. David Thelen, ed., *Memory and American History* (Bloomington: Indiana University Press, 1989), ix, xi.

3. Karen Brodkin Sacks, "What's a Life Story Got to Do With It?," in *Interpreting Women's Lives: Feminist Theory and Personal Narratives*, ed. Joy Webster Barbre et al. (Bloomington: Indiana University Press, 1989), 85–95.

4. Sociologist Richard Sennett documents similar concerns among working-class men in late-twentieth-century American cities. See *The Corrosion of Character: The Personal Consequences of Work in the New Capitalism* (New York and London: W. W. Norton & Company, 1998).

5. Joyce E. Chaplin, *An Anxious Pursuit: Agricultural Innovation and Modernity in the Lower South, 1730–1815* (Chapel Hill: University of North Carolina Press, 1993), chapter 2.

6. Orville Vernon Burton, *In My Father's House Are Many Mansions: Family and Community in Edgefield, South Carolina* (Chapel Hill: University of North Carolina Press, 1985), 76.

7. Twelve Southerners, *I'll Take My Stand: The South and the Agrarian Tradition* (Baton Rouge: Louisiana State University Press, 1977 reprint of 1930 edition).

8. See bibliographic essay for scholarship on rural community.

9. Jacquelyn Dowd Hall, "'You Must Remember This': Autobiography as Social Critique," *Journal of American History* 85 (1998): 440.

10. L. D. and Lula Walker, interview by Pamela Grundy, June 23, 1987, Cragford, Ala., PGOH.

11. Mr. and Mrs. Yates Abernathy, interview by Harry Wilson and Gordon McDaniel, August 23, 1984, Vale, N.C., SOHP.

12. Fredda Davis, interview by Ruth Dasmann, September 26, 1984, N.C., SOHP.

13. Lena Boyce, interview by Sue Beal, October 16, 1984, Rehobeth, N.C., SOHP.

14. Will D. Campbell, interview by Orley B. Caudill, June 8, 1976, Mt. Juliet, Tenn., MOHP, transcript available online at <http://anna.lib.usm.edu/%7Espcol/crda/oh/campbelltrans.htm>, 7–8.

15. Bill Moore, interview by Bonnie Bishop, August 1, 1984, Haywood County, N.C., SOHP.

16. Mr. and Mrs. Yates Abernathy interview.

17. Jim and Virgie Foster, interview by Lu Ann Jones, May 19, 1987, Millers Creek, N.C., OHSA.

18. David Bateman, interview by Larry Johnson, undated ca. 1984, Tyner, N.C., SOHP.

19. Nellie Stancil Langley, interview by Lu Ann Jones, December 5, 1986, Stantonsburg, N.C., OHSA.

20. Anna Evans, interview by Mabel Bertram, September 11, 1981, Glasgow, Ky., EHOHP.

21. Eva Finchum, interview by Lu Ann Jones, April 30, 1987, Sevierville, Tenn., OHSA.

22. Letha Anderson McCall, interview by Virginia Bailey Harris, March 18, 1982, Richmond County, N.C., EHOHP.

23. Carl Neal, *Oral Memoirs of Carl Neal* (interview by Lois E. Myers on February 4 and 11, 1993, McLennan County, Tex.), TC.

24. Dovie Lee and Etta Lillian Hardy Carroll, interview by Rebecca Sharpless, on seven occasions from September 21, 1990, to July 11, 1991, Waxahachie, Tex., IOH.

25. Mr. and Mrs. Yates Abernathy interview.

26. Frances Bartek Podsednik, *Oral Memoirs of Frances Bartek Podsednik* (interview by Henry Apperson, September 25, 1969, West, Tex.), TC.

27. Eunice Brown Johnson, interview by Rebecca Sharpless, July 31, 1986, and April 14, 1987, Gatesville, Tex., IOH.

28. Lottie Jackson, interview by Sherry Thomas, in Sherry Thomas, ed., *We Didn't Have Much, But We Sure Had Plenty: Rural Women in Their Own Words* (New York: Anchor Books, 1981), 99–108, quote on 103.

29. Orry Little, interview by Mrs. Harris Carmichael, May 14, 1982, Grenada, Miss., EHOHP.

30. Mary Hanak Simcik, *Oral Memoirs of Mary Hanak Simcik* (interview by LaWanda Ball, November 24, 1974, Waco, Tex.), TC.

31. Robert Jefferson Spencer, interview by Mausiki Stacey Scales, June 20, 1995, Memphis, Tenn., BTV, Box UT7, Tray A.

32. Dovie Lee and Etta Lillian Hardy Carroll interviews.

33. Chris Young Sr., interview by Doris Dixon, ca. 1995, LeFlore County, Miss., BTV, Box UT6, Tray B.

34. Anna B. Pitts, interview by Charles H. Houston Jr., June 25, 1994, Albany, Ga., BTV, box UT1, Tray C.

35. Tom Malone, interview by Doris Dixon, undated ca. 1995, Cotton Plant, Ark., BTV, Box UT2, Tray A.

36. Ruth Irwin, interview by Mrs. E. R. McKnight, April 1982, Miss., EHOHP.

37. Irene Clause, autobiographical tape, undated ca. 1982, EHOHP.

38. Leland R. Cooper and Mary Lee Cooper, eds., *The People of the New River: Oral Histories from the Ashe, Alleghany and Watauga Counties of North Carolina* (Jefferson, North Carolina: McFarland & Company, Inc., Publishers, 2001), 143.

39. For only one example, see Allan Kulikoff's account of parental responses to the growing independence of their teenaged children in the wake of the British enclosure movement of the seventeenth century. See Kulikoff, *From British Peasants to Colonial American Farmers* (Chapel Hill: University of North Carolina Press, 2000), 30–32.

40. Cora Lee McCall Jones, *Oral Memoirs of Cora Lee McCall Jones* (interview by Doni Van Ryswyk, on nine occasions from January 25, 1988, to May 4, 1988, Waco, Tex.), TC.

41. Roy Rosenzweig and David Thelen, *The Presence of the Past: Popular Uses of History in American Life* (New York: Columbia University Press, 1998), 134–37.

42. Anna B. Pitts interview.

43. Jurl Lee Watkins, interview by Gregory Hunter, June 28, 1994, Sylvester, Ga., BTV, Box UT1, Tray C.

44. Minnie Wade Weston, interview by Paul Ortiz, August 8, 1995, Moorehead, Miss., BTV, Box UT6, Tray A.

45. Burton, *In My Father's House Are Many Mansions*, 314.

46. Cornelia Butler Flora, et al., *Rural Communities: Legacy and Change* (Boulder, Co.: Westview Press, 1992), 14, 65.

47. Steven Hahn, *A Nation under Our Feet: Black Political Struggles in the Rural South from Slavery to the Great Migration* (Cambridge, Mass.: Harvard University Press, 2003), 33.

48. Opal Bateman, interview by Sharon Siske Crunk, March 12, 1993, Iredell, Tex., IOH.

49. For more on the role of black churches in rural communities, see Lois E. Myers and Rebecca Sharpless, "'Of the Least and the Most': The African American Rural Church," in *African American Life in the Rural South: 1900–1950,* ed. R. Douglas Hurt (Columbia and London: University of Missouri Press, 2003), 54–80.

50. Reverend James Samuel, interview by Vickie Crawford, August 6, 1996, New South Voices Oral History Project, J. Murrey Atkins Library, University of North Carolina at Charlotte, available online at <http://newsouthvoices.uncc.edu/>.

51. Jane Marie Pederson, *Between Memory and Reality: Family and Community in Rural Wisconsin, 1870–1970* (Madison: University of Wisconsin Press, 1992), 91, 138; Arthur F. Raper, *Preface to Peasantry: A Tale of Two Black Belt Counties* (Chapel Hill: University of North Carolina Press, 1936), 354–59.

52. Minnie Wade Weston interview.

53. Helen Howard, interview by Doris G. Dixon, July 19, 1995, Cotton Plant, Ark., BTV, Box UT1, Tray D.

54. Rev. W. C. Tims, interview by Paul Ortiz, July 20, 1995, Magnolia, Ark., BTV, Box UT2, Tray A.

55. Bertha Todd, interview by Sonya Ramsey, ca. 1994, Wilmington, N.C., BTV, Box UT13, Tray D.

56. Oris Pierson, *Oral Memoirs of Oris Pierson* (interview by Suzanne Olsen, November 2 and 29, 1972, Clifton, Tex.), TC; *Oral Memoirs of Mary Hanak Simcik*.

57. LaVerne Farmer, interview by Melissa Walker, August 9, 1993, Maryville, Tenn., MHC.

58. Shirley Miller Sherrod, interview by Charles H. Houston Jr., June 30, 1994, Albany, Ga., BTV, Box UT1, Tray C.

59. Rev. W. C. Tims interview; Opal Bateman interview; Ruth Irwin, interview by Mrs. E. R. McKnight, April 1982, Miss., EHOHP. See also Oliver Anderson, interview by Sharon Siske, June 28, 1992, Meridian, Tex., IOH.

60. Pedersen, *Between Memory and Reality*, 154.

61. Helen Howard, interview by Doris G. Dixon, July 19, 1995, Cotton Plant, Ark., BTV, Box UT1, Tray D; Myrtle Irene Calvert Dodd, *Oral Memoirs of Myrtle Calvert Dodd* (interview by Rebecca Sharpless, on four occasions from August 14 to September 19, 1990, in Waco, Tex.), TC.

62. Viola Anderson Bateman, interview by Sharon Siske, July 5, 1992, Clifton, Tex., IOH; Laura Belle Holley Bateman, interview by Sharon Siske Crunk, January 20, 1994, Meridian, Tex., IOH; Roosevelt A. Cuffie, interview by Tunga White, June 29, 1994, Sylvester, Ga., BTV, Box UT1, Tray A, IOH; Alma Stewart Hale, *Oral Memoirs of Alma Stewart Hale* (interview by Doni Van Ryswyk, on eight occasions from January 27 to March 28, 1988, in Waco, Tex.), TC; Hahn, *A Nation under Our Feet*, 33.

63. Amy Jones, interview by Mausiki Scales, June 28, 1995, Memphis, Tenn., BTV, Box UT6, Tray D.

64. Amy Jones interview; Chris Young Sr., interview by Doris Dixon, ca. 1995, LeFlore County, Miss., BTV, Box UT6, Tray B; *Oral Memoirs of Carl Neal*.

65. Mary Evelyn Lane, interview by Melissa Walker, August 8, 1994, Maryville, Tenn., MHC; Maurice Lucas, interview by Mausiki Scales, August 7, 1995, Renova, Miss., BTV, Box UT5, Tray D.

66. T. H. Kilby, interview by Lu Ann Jones, May 19, 1987, North Wilkesboro, N.C., OHSA.

67. Essie Mae Alexander, interview by Paul Ortiz, August 10, 1995, Greenwood, Miss., BTV, Box UT5, Tray C.

68. Cleaster Mitchell, interview by Paul Ortiz, July 16, 1995, Brinkley, Ark., BTV, Box UT2, Tray A.

69. Orville Vernon Burton, "Reaping What We Sow: Community and Rural History," *Agricultural History* 76 (Fall 2002): 642.

70. Dorsey M. White, interview by Paul Ortiz, August 3, 1995, Indianola, Miss., BTV, Box UT6, Tray B.

71. Eric Foner, "The Russians Write a New History," in *Who Owns History? Rethinking the Past in a Changing World* (New York: Hill and Wang, 2002), 75–87.

72. Alice Giles, interview by Paul Ortiz, August 8, 1995, Indianola, Miss., BTV, Box UT5, Tray D.

73. Ruthie L. Jackson, interview by Mausiki Stacey Scales, August 10, 1995, Itta Bena, Miss., BTV, Box UT5, Tray D; Flossie and Monroe Wood, interview by Pamela Grundy, May 28, 1987, Delta, Ala., PGOH.

74. *Oral Memoirs of Carl Neal.*

75. Ruth Irwin, interview by Mrs. E. R. McKnight, April 1982, Miss., EHOHP; [Unknown First Name] Brookshire, interview by Mabel Bartram, undated ca. 1982, Ky., EHOHP.

76. Kiffin Browing, interview by Pamela Grundy, May 3, 1988, Ashland, Ala., PGOH; Paul K. Conkin, *A Requiem for the American Village* (Lanham, Md.: Rowman and Littlefield Publishers, Inc., 2000), 99.

77. Letha Anderson McCall, interview by Virginia Bailey Harris, March 18, 1982, Richmond County, N.C., EHOHP.

78. David Matthews, interview by Paul Ortiz, ca. 1995, Miss., BTV, Box UT5, Tray D. Historian James C. Cobb and memoirist Henry Louis Gates have also noted that the end of segregation led many rural southern blacks to feel a loss of community. See James C. Cobb, *Redefining Southern Culture: Mind and Identity in the Modern South* (Athens: University of Georgia Press, 1999), 132 and Henry Louis Gates, *Colored People: A Memoir* (New York: Vintage Books, 1995).

79. Anna B. Pitts, interview by Charles H. Houston Jr., June 25, 1994, Albany, Ga., BTV, Box UT1, Tray C.

80. See for example, Herman Clarence Nixon, "Whither Southern Economy?" (pp. 176–200) and Andrew Nelson Lytle, "The Hind Tit," (pp. 216–34) both in Twelve Southerners, *I'll Take My Stand.*

81. Ferdinand Tonnies, translated and edited by Charles P. Loomis, *Community and Society (Gemeinschaft und Gesellschaft)* (Lansing: Michigan State University Press, 1957); Max Weber, translated by A. M. Henderson and Talcott Parsons, edited and with an introduction by Talcott Parsons, *The Theory of Social and Economic Organizations* (New York: The Free Press, 1947); Emile Durkheim, translated by George Simpson, *The Division of Labor in Society* (New York: The Free Press, 1933). See also Douglas Harper, *Changing Works: Visions of a Lost Agriculture* (Chicago: University of Chicago Press, 2001), 47.

82. Thomas Bender, *Community and Social Change in America* (New Brunswick, N.J.: Rutgers University Press, 1978), especially 3–4, 46.

83. Bender, *Community and Social Change in America*, 110, quote on 149; Bruce L. Gardner, *American Agriculture in the Twentieth Century: How It Flourished and What It Cost* (Cambridge and London: Harvard University Press, 2002), chapter 4, esp. 127.

84. See for example, Kulikoff, *From British Peasants to Colonial American Farmers*, 16, 30; Burton, *In My Father's House Are Many Mansions*, 76.

85. Michael Frisch, *A Shared Authority: Essays on the Craft and Meaning of Oral and Public History* (Albany: State University of New York Press, 1990), 188.

86. Harper, *Changing Works*, 180.

87. Naomi Norquay, "Identity and Forgetting," *The Oral History Review* 26 (Winter 1999): 9.

88. Robert D. Putnam, *Bowling Alone: The Collapse and Revival of American Community* (New York: Simon and Schuster, 2000), especially 20–21; Naomi Norquay, "Identity and Forgetting," 1; Hall, "You Must Remember This," 440. Norquay also argues that "What is worth remembering . . . can be determined and regulated by larger social forces" (p. 1).

89. Karen E. Fields, "What One Cannot Remember Mistakenly," in *Memory and History: Essays on Recalling and Interpreting Experience*, ed. Jaclyn Jeffrey and Glenace Edwall (New York: University Press of America, 1994), 102.

Conclusion

Epigraphs: Jane Brox, *Clearing Land: Legacies of the American Farm* (New York: North Point Press, 2004), 19; and Charles Wright, "Apologia Pro Vita Sua," *Negative Blue* (New York: Farrar, Strauss and Giroux, 2000), 83.

1. Iwona Irwin-Zarecka, *Frames of Remembrances: The Dynamics of Collective Memory* (New Brunswick: Transaction Publishers, 1994), 101.

2. Jessie and Kenneth Gosney, interview by Lu Ann Jones, October 1, 1987, Carlisle, Ark., OHSA.

3. David B. Danbom, "Romantic Agrarianism in Twentieth Century America," *Agricultural History* 65 (1991): 1–12, quote on 8.

4. Woodrow Harper Sr., interview by Lu Ann Jones, April 17, 1987, Hartwell, Ga., OHSA.

5. Victor Davis Hanson, "Agricultural Equilibrium, Ancient and Modern," *The Journal of the Historical Society* 1.1 (2000): 101–35.

6. Miriam J. Wells, "The Contingent Creation of Rural Interest Groups," in *Figthing for the Farm: Rural America Transformed*, ed. Jane Adams (Philadelphia: University of Pennsylvania Press, 2003), 96–110,

quote on 98. Historian Catherine McNicol Stock has argued that rural producer radicalism persisted after the defeat of the nineteenth-century Populist/Democratic coalition in 1896, but that such radicalism found its expression in efforts to make the American political economy more friendly to farm interests and, by the late twentieth century, in various forms of resistance to the federal government. See *Rural Radicals: Righteous Rage in the American Grain* (Ithaca, N.Y.: Cornell University Press, 1996).

7. Historian Susan Sessions Rugh shows how, in the late nineteenth century, with increasing integration into the national marketplace, residents of rural Hancock County, Illinois, increasingly adopted new bourgeois middle-class values that undermined old ideas of masculinity and success, the commitment to farming as a lifestyle and a family enterprise, and the old communities based in mutual aid. Instead class distinctions became more pronounced and more central in the local culture. See *Our Common Country: Family Farming, Culture, and Community in the Nineteenth-Century Midwest* (Bloomington: Indiana University Press, 2001).

8. Black quoted in Sheila K. Dewan, "Old or New, the South Remains a Place Apart," *New York Times,* July 11, 2004, section 4, p. 4.

9. I am grateful to Charlie Thompson for starting me down the road of this line of analysis; see email communication with author, July 6, 2005, copy in author's possession.

10. [William and Kate Graham], interview by Melissa Walker, April 30, 2002, Asheville, N.C., tape and transcript in author's possession.

11. Pierre Bourdieu, *Distinction: A Social Critique of the Judgment of Taste*, trans. Richard Nice (London: Routledge and Kegan Paul, 1979, trans. 1984), 406.

12. Ronald Jager, *The Fate of Family Farming: Variations on an American Idea* (Hanover, N.H. and N.Y.: University Press of New England, 2004), 28.

13. Katherine Marie Dudley, "The Entrepreneurial Self: Identity and Morality in a Midwestern Farming Community," in *Fighting for the Farm: Rural America Transformed,* ed. Jane Adams (Philadelphia: University of Pennsylvania Press, 2003), 175–91, quote on 176.

14. For a discussion of some of these small-scale solutions, see Jager, *Fate of Family Farming*, chapter 10.

15. [William and Kate Graham] interview.

Bibliographic Essay

Historian Jacquelyn Dowd Hall has recently reminded us that stories matter, whether those stories are told by historians, by politicians, or by people. She says that stories "shape how we see our world. 'Facts' must be interpreted, and those interpretations—narrated by powerful storytellers, portrayed in public events, acted upon in laws and policies and court decisions, and grounded in institutions—become primary sources of human action" (see "The Long Civil Rights Movement and the Political Uses of the Past," *Journal of American History* 91 (2005): 1233–63, quote on 1239). In another work, Hall has challenged historians to find new ways of writing about the past, ways of writing that can both examine the gaps between history and memory and break down the barriers between the two (Hall, "'You Must Remember This': Autobiography as Social Critique," *Journal of American History* 85 (1998): 439–65, quote on 441).

This book has been one attempt to break down those barriers between history and memory. As a result, this study is rooted in the scholarly conversation on the relationships between history and memory, scholarship drawn from a variety of disciplines. To explore the shape of rural southerners' memories of agricultural transformation, I initially turned to scholarship that examines expressions of collective memory—the shared understanding and articulation of a particular group's past. Scholars have put forward a range of theories about how collective memory is produced. The earliest theories about the origins of collective memory were drawn from the work of Italian political theorist Antonio Gramsci. Gramsci argued that collective memory was a product of cultural hegemony—that people in power "write" history and that they write it in ways calculated to reinforce and maintain their own power. According to this view, collective memory is imposed from on high, and individuals express collective memory in terms acceptable to people in power, remaining silent about conflicting memories of past events. See Gramsci, *Selections from the Prison Notebooks* (New York: International Publishers, 1971). Another theory was developed by French sociologist Maurice Halbwachs who argued that collective memory is socially constructed. Individuals remember, but they do so in a specific group context, drawing on that context to recreate the past. In his view, social groups form their own distinct memories, memories shaped by class, gender, ethnic or racial position, education, and generational experiences. In other words, collective memory emerges from the shared experiences of ordinary people. See Maurice Halbwachs, edited, translated, and with an introduction by Lewis A. Coser, *On Collective Memory* (Chicago: University of Chicago Press, 1992), especially 22–25. In recent years, however, a number of scholars have argued that these structuralist explanations don't account for how historical actors actually behave. Instead, they argue, the development of collective memory is a contested process, and the shape and content of collective memory is constantly shifting. Authority figures in a group may promulgate a particular version of the past, but that version may be altered or rejected by people within the group. All the resources shared by people in a particular group—from popular culture to commemorations and rituals to history texts to the stories people tell each other—are not only expressions of collective memory but also help to shape collective memory. Moreover, according to these recent interpretations, the major function of collective memory is to serve contemporary purposes such as identity building, nation building, or coping with social, economic, or political change. See for example, John R. Gillis, *Commemorations: The Politics of National Identity* (Princeton: Princeton University Press, 1994); John Bodnar, *Remaking America: Public Memory, Commemoration, and Patriotism in the Twentieth Century* (Princeton: Princeton University Press, 1992); Iwona Irwin-Zarecka, *Frames of Remembrances: The Dynamics of Collective Memory* (New Brunswick: Transaction Publishers, 1994); John Walton, *Storied Land: Community and Memory in Monterey* (Berkeley: University of California Press, 2001); and Noa Gedi and Yigal Elam, "Collective Memory: What Is It?," *History and Memory* 8 (1996): 30–50.

Most historians who have studied collective memory have examined its articulation in public discourse—in political debates, the creation of monuments, commemorative practices, and popular culture. Many studies have focused either on the role of collective memory in the process of nation building or on the role of what French historian Pierre Nora has called *les lieux de mèmoire* or "sites of memory" in shaping collective memory. Nora has noted that collective memory "takes root in the concrete, in spaces, gestures, images, and objects." See Pierre Nora, "Between Memory and History: *Les Lieux de Mèmoire*," *Representations* 26 (Spring 1989): 9. Indeed, examining commemorative sites and the contested process of establishing and interpreting those sites can tell us much about the negotiated process of shaping collective memory. As a result, many scholars have fruitfully focused on commemorative expressions of collective memory such as memorials, monuments, and rituals. For example, Eric Hobsbawm, Terence Ranger, and others explore the invention of tradition—that is, the "set of practices, normally governed by overtly or tacitly accepted rules and of a ritual or symbolic nature, which seek to inculcate certain values and norms of behaviour by repetition, which automatically implies continuity with the past." See Eric Hobsbawm and Terence Ranger, eds., *The Invention of Tradition* (Cambridge: Cambridge University Press, 1983), quote on 1; Benedict Anderson, *Imagined Communities: Reflections on the Origin and Spread of Nationalism* (London: Verso, 1983); Michael Kammen, *Mystic Chords of Memory: The Transformation of Tradition in American Culture* (New York: Knopf, 1991); Paul Connerton, *How Societies Remember* (Cambridge: University of Cambridge, 1989).

The development of the collective memory of the "lost cause" in the post–Civil War American South has commanded sustained attention from numerous scholars. See for example, W. Fitzhugh Brundage, "White Women and the Politics of Historical Memory in the New South, 1880–1920," in *Jumpin' Jim Crow: Southern Politics from Segregation to Civil Rights*, ed. Jane Dailey, Glenda Elizabeth Gilmore, and Bryant Simon (Princeton: Princeton University Press, 2000), 115–39; Catherine W. Bishir, "Landmarks of Power: Building a Southern Past in Raleigh and Wilmington, North Carolina, 1885–1915," in *Where These Memories Grow: History, Memory and Southern Identity*, ed. W. Fitzhugh Brundage (Chapel Hill: University of North Carolina Press, 2000), 139–68; Gaines M. Foster, *Ghosts of the Confederacy: Defeat, the Lost Cause, and the Emergence of the New South, 1865 to 1913* (New York : Oxford University Press, 1987); Paul A. Shackel, *Memory in Black and White: Race, Commemoration, and the Postbellum Landscape* (Walnut Creek, Calif.: Altamira Press, 2003); Cynthia Mills and Pamela H. Simpson, eds., *Monuments to the Lost Cause: Women, Art, and the Landscapes of Southern Memory* (Knoxville: University of Tennessee Press, 2003). Recently scholars have also turned their attention more broadly to the contested terrain of Civil War memory and especially to African Americans' efforts to develop their own memories of the meaning of that conflict. A partial list of such scholarship includes Kathleen Clark, "Celebrating Freedom: Emancipation Day Celebrations and African American Memory in the Early Reconstruction South" (pp. 107–32) and Laurie F. Maffly-Kipp, "Redeeming Southern Memory: The Negro Race History, 1874–1915" (pp. 169–90), both in W. Fitzhugh Brundage, ed., *Where These Memories Grow*; David W. Blight, *Race and Reunion: The Civil War in American Memory* (Cambridge: Belknap Press of Harvard University Press, 2001) and *Beyond the Battlefield: Race, Memory and the American Civil War* (Amherst: University of Massachusetts Press, 2002); David Goldfield, *Still Fighting the Civil War: The American South and Southern History*, (Baton Rouge: Louisiana State University Press, 2002); Barry Schwartz, *Abraham Lincoln and the Forge of National Memory* (Chicago: University of Chicago Press, 2000); Timothy B. Smith, *This Great Battlefield of Shiloh: History, Memory, and the Establishment of a Civil War National Military Park* (Knoxville: University of Tennessee Press, 2004). For useful reflections on the functions of nostalgia among postbellum southerners, see David Anderson, "Down Memory Lane: Nostalgia for the Old South in Post–Civil War Plantation Reminiscences," *Journal of Southern History* 72 (February 2005): 104–36.

As I worked with my sample of oral history narratives, however, I came to see that studies focused on expressions of collective memory in public discourse did not really describe the ways my narrators were using memories to construct life stories. Rural southerners told highly individual stories, stories that contained recurring themes and persistent patterns of the type that sometimes appeared in public discourse, but nonetheless individual stories. I came to see that collective memory must be located in the individual and articulated by the individual in order to play any role in social or political life. Historian Alessandro Portelli has rejected the use of the term "collective memory" to describe the way individuals describe memories that they share in their oral history narratives. As he put it, "Texts (by which here I mean also the verbal component of oral narratives and interviews) are both highly individual expressions and manifestations of social discourse, made up of socially defined and shared discursive structures (motifs, formulas, genres)." Portelli fears that our understandings of both individual and collective memories can become mechanistic and oversimplified if we lose sight of the fact that individuals are doing the remembering. As he put it, "If all memory were collective, one witness could serve for an entire culture—but we know that it is not so. Each individual, especially in modern times and societies, derives memories from a variety of groups, and organizes them in idiosyncratic fashion. Like all human activities, memory is *social* and may be *shared*, . . . however, . . . it only materializes in individual recollections and speech acts. It becomes *collective* memory only when it is abstracted and detached from the individual: in myth and folklore (one story for many people . . .), in delegation (one person for many stories . . .), in institutions (abstract subjects—school, church, State, party—that organize memories and rituals into a whole other then the sum of its separate parts [his emphases]." See Alessandro Portelli, *The Battle of Valle Giulia: Oral History and the Art of Dialogue* (Madison: University of Wisconsin Press, 1997), quotes on 82 and 157.

I came to be convinced by Portelli's argument. To avoid the pitfalls of using the term "collective memory" to describe individual recollections of shared experiences, I instead chose to use the term "community of memory" to describe the figurative community that rural southerners built from their memories of a shared past. The term "community of memory" is drawn from Robert N. Bellah, et al., *Habits of the Heart: Commitment and Individualism in American Life* (New York: Harper and Row Publishers, 1985), 153. Historian Susan A. Crane proposes that historians reconceptualize collective memory by placing the individual who articulates collective memory back in our understanding of collective memory. As she put it, "A revised notion of collective memory may provide a theoretical basis for imagining a different kind of historical memory, which would focus on the way individuals experience themselves as historical entities." See Crane, "Writing the Individual Back into Collective Memory," *American Historical Review* 102 (1997): 1372–85, quote on 1375.

Other historians who have grappled with the nature of the relationship between individual and collective memory include Michael G. Kenny, "A Place for Memory: The Interface between Individual and Collective History," *Journal for the Comparative Study of Society and History* (1999): 420–37; Valerie Quinney, "Childhood in a Southern Mill Village," *International Journal of Oral History* 3:3 (November 1982): 167–74; and Daniel James, "Meatpackers, Peronists, and Collective Memory: A View From the South," *American Historical Review* 102 (1997): 1404–12.

Oral history provides a powerful tool for examining patterns in memory and the relationship between history and memory, especially among society's least powerful groups. Although oral narratives are shaped in myriad conscious and subconscious ways by the powerful, they nonetheless are individual forms of expression where the collective memory of subaltern groups may be more openly expressed. Alessandro Portelli pioneered the use of oral history for examining themes and patterns, silences and dissonances in oral history narrators' accounts of the past. In addition to *The Battle of Valle Giulia*, see *The Death of Luigi Trastulli and Other Stories: Form and Meaning in Oral History* (Albany: State University of New York Press, 1991). Sherry Lee Linkon and John Russo studied the relationship between work and memory in Youngstown, Ohio, examining both public commemorations of Youngstown's steelmaking past, but also individual expressions of that shared past in such forms as oral history. See Linkon and Russo, *Steeltown U.S.A.: Work and Memory in Youngstown* (Lawrence: University Press of Kansas, 2002). Historians and other scholars who examine the construction of memory in oral histories include essays in Jaclyn Jeffrey and Glenace Edwall, eds., *Memory and History: Essays on Recalling and Interpreting Experience* (New York: University Press of America, 1994); Barbara Allen, "Story in Oral History: Clues to Historical Consciousness," *Journal of American History* 79 (September 1992): 606–11; John Bodnar, "Power and Memory in Oral History: Workers and Managers at Studebaker," in *Memory and American History*, ed. David Thelen (Bloomington: Indiana University Press, 1989), 72–92; Devra Anne Weaver, "Mexican Women on Strike: Memory, History, and Oral Narratives," in *Between Borders: Essays on Mexicana/Chicana History*, ed. Adelaida R. Del Castillo (Encino, Calif.: Floricanto Press, 1990); Emily Honig, "Striking Lives: Oral History and the Politics of Meaning," *Journal of American History* 9 (Spring 1997), 139–57; Seena B. Kohl, "Memories of Homesteading and the Process of Retrospection," *Oral History Review* 17 (Fall 1989): 25–45; Nancy Grey

Osterud, "Land, Identity, and Agency in the Oral Autobiographies of Farm Women," in *Women and Farming: Changing Roles, Changing Structures*, ed. Wava G. Haney and Jane B. Knowles (Boulder: Westview Press, 1988), 73–87. In his landmark book, *Passing the Time in Ballymenone*, folklorist Henry Glassie provides a useful overview of the structural conventions and analytical framework of stories. He pays special attention to the use of story to convey memories of historical events. See Glassie, *Passing the Time in Ballymenone: Culture and History of an Ulster Community* (Philadelphia: University of Pennsylvania Press, 1982).

Memory is drawn in part from historical events. On the relationship between historical events and individual memory, see Raphael Samuel and Paul Thompson, eds., *The Myths We Live By* (Routledge: London, 1990); Raphael Samuel, *Theatres of Memory, Vol. 1: Past and Present in Contemporary Culture* (London: Verso, 1994); Michael Frisch, *A Shared Authority: Essays on the Craft and Meaning of Oral and Public History* (Albany: State University of New York Press, 1990); W. Fitzhugh Brundage, "No Deed But Memory," in *Where These Memories Grow: History, Memory, and Southern Identity*, ed. W. Fitzhugh Brundage (Chapel Hill: University of North Carolina Press, 2000), 1–28; Norman R. Brown, Steven K. Shevell, and Lance J. Rips, "Public Memories and Their Personal Context," in *Autobiographical Memory*, ed. David C. Rubin (Cambridge: Cambridge University Press, 1986), 137–57; Tracey E. K'Meyer, "What Koinonia Was All About: The Role of Memory in a Changing Community," *The Oral History Review* 24 (Summer 1997): 1–22.

Other research has focused on how people use knowledge about the past in their daily lives. Roy Rosenzweig, David Thelen, and scholars at Indiana University's Center for Survey Research conducted a massive survey of 808 randomly selected Americans to discover how ordinary people use the past in their daily lives. They found that people used shared experiences to build connections, to seek to understand how their personal past has shaped their present identities, and to search for alternatives for the future. See Rosenzweig and Thelen, *The Presence of the Past: Popular Uses of History in American Life* (New York: Columbia University Press, 1998). Sociologist Arthur G. Neal has explored the impact of national trauma on collective memory, using major American events from the twentieth century as a case study. He notes that national trauma has a similar effect on the collective consciousness of people as does a personal trauma on an individual. National traumas cause social disruption and "People both individually and collectively see themselves as moving into uncharted territory." Neal argues that citizens of a nation use the shared experience of national traumas to forge a collective identity built from memories of overcoming the impact of the trauma. Myths, legends, and storytelling become the raw material for the creation of the sense of collective identity. See Neal, *National Trauma and Collective Memory: Major Events in the American Century* (Armonk, N.Y. and London: M. E. Sharpe, 1998), quote on p. 5.

I found scholarship from psychology useful in understanding how memories are constructed. Daniel Schacter's and David Thelen's surveys of cognitive research on memory and on literature about history and memory were a useful introduction to this literature. See Schacter, *Searching for Memory* (New York: Basic Books, 1996) and Thelen, "Introduction," in *Memory and American History*, ed. David Thelen (Bloomington: Indiana University Press, 1989), vii–xix. More recently, Valerie Raleigh Yow provides an overview of the scholarship on memory from a variety of disciplines in *Recording Oral History: A Guide for the Humanities and Social Sciences*, 2nd ed. (New York: AltaMira Press, 2005), chapter 2. Psychologist John N. Kotre's book also describes cognitive research on memory in terms accessible to nonspecialists. See *White Gloves: How We Create Ourselves through Memory* (New York: The Free Press, 1995). I found two articles particularly helpful in understanding the nature and meaning of memory distortion. See Michael Kammen, "Some Patterns and Meanings of Memory Distortion in American History," and Michael Schudson, "Dynamics of Distortion in Collective Memory," both in *Memory Distortion: How Minds, Brains, and Societies Reconstruct the Past*, ed. Daniel L. Schacter (Cambridge: Harvard University Press, 1995), 329–45 and 346–64, respectively.

Useful works on the role of memory in the development of identities, most particularly through autobiographical narratives, can be found in the realms of literary criticism, history, anthropology, psychology, and sociology. See for example, Paul John Eakin, *Making Selves: How Our Lives Become Stories* (Ithaca: Cornell University Press, 1999) and *Touching the World: Reference in Autobiography* (Princeton: Princeton University Press, 1992); Jacquelyn Dowd Hall, "'You Must Remember This': Autobiography as Social Critique," *Journal of American History* 85 (1998): 439–65; Jean Peneff, "Myths in Life Stories," in *The Myths We Live By*, ed. Raphael Samuel and Paul Thompson (London: Routledge, 1990), 36–48; Rhys Isaac, "Stories and Constructions of Identity: Folk Tellings and Diary Inscriptions in Revolutionary Virginia," in *Through a Glass Darkly: Reflections on Personal Identity in Early America*, ed. Ronald Hoffman, Mechal Sobel, and Frederika J. Teute (Chapel Hill: University of North Carolina Press, 1997), 206–37; Naomi Norquay, "Identity and Forgetting," *The Oral History Review* 26 (Winter 1999): 1–11; Joseph E. Davis, ed., *Stories of Change: Narrative and Social Movements* (Albany: State University of New York Press, 2002); Elizabeth Tonkin, *Narrating Our Pasts: The Social Construction of Oral History* (Cambridge: Cambridge University Press, 1992); Margaret R. Somers, "The Narrative Construction of Identity: A Relational and Network Approach," *Theory and Society* 23 (1994): 605–49; and Robyn Fivush, Catherine Haden, and Elaine Reese, "Remembering, Recounting, and Reminiscing: The Development of Autobiographical Memory in Social Context," in *Remembering Our Past: Studies in Autobiographical Memory*, ed. David C. Rubin (Cambridge: Cambridge University Press, 1996), 341–59. For more on the impact of aging on autobiographical memory, see Barbara Myerhoff, "Life History among the Elderly: Performance, Visibility, and Re-membering," in *A Crack in the Mirror*, ed. Jay Ruby (Philadelphia: University of Pennsylvania Press, 1982): 99–117; Gillian Cohen, "The Effects of Aging on Autobiographical Memory," in *Autobiographical Memory: Theoretical and Applied Perspectives*, ed. Charles P. Thompson et al. (Makwah, N.J.: Lawrence Erlbaum Assoc. Pub., 1998), 105–23. On variations in memory by gender, see Alexander Freund and Laura Quilici, "Exploring Myths in Women's Narratives: Italian and German Immigrant Women in Vancouver, 1947–1961," *The Oral History Review* 23 (Winter 1996): 19–25; Susan Stanford Friedman, "Women's Autobiographical Selves: Theory and Practice," in *The Private Self: Theory and Practice of Women's Autobiographical Writings*, ed. Shari Benstock (Chapel Hill: University of North Carolina Press, 1988): 34–62.

Of course, this study examines a particular set of memories articulated by a particular group of people in a particular time and place. Understanding that time and place is essential for understanding their memories. The literature on the transformation of southern agriculture in the twentieth century is extensive, and this is not intended to be an exhaustive survey. The best starting points for understanding the changes that swept the southern countryside are Pete Daniel, *Breaking the Land: The Transformation of Cotton, Tobacco, and Rice Cultures since 1880* (Urbana: University of Illinois Press, 1980) and *Standing at the Crossroads: Southern Life in the Twentieth Century* (New York: Hill and Wang, 1986); Jack Temple Kirby, *Rural Worlds Lost: The American South, 1920–1960* (Baton Rouge: Louisiana State University Press, 1987); Gavin Wright, *Old South, New South: Revolutions in the Southern Economy since the Civil War* (Baton Rouge: Louisiana State University Press, 1986); and R. Douglas Hurt, ed., *The Rural South since World War II* (Baton Rouge: Louisiana State University Press, 1998). Three recent works, including my own, examine the impact of this southern rural transformation on the region's women. See Rebecca Sharpless, *Fertile Ground, Narrow Choices: Women on Texas Cotton Farms, 1900–1940* (Chapel Hill: University of North Carolina Press, 1999); Melissa Walker, *All We Knew Was to Farm: Rural Women in the Upcountry South, 1919–1941* (Baltimore: Johns Hopkins University Press, 2000); and Lu Ann Jones, *'Mama Learned Us to Work': Farm Women in the New South* (Chapel Hill: University of North Carolina Press, 2002). The classic work on the lives of African American women in the rural South is Jacqueline Jones, *Labor of Love, Labor of Sorrow: Black Women, Work and the Family, From Slavery to the Present* (New York: Vintage, 1985). Other important works on the transformation of particular southern subregions include Jeanette Keith, *Country People in the New South: Tennessee's Upper Cumberland* (Chapel Hill: University of North Carolina Press, 1995); Jeannie M. Whayne, *A New Plantation South: Land, Labor, and Federal Favor in Twentieth-Century Arkansas* (Charlottesville: University Press of Virginia, 1996); and Eldred Prince with Robert Simpson, *Long Green: The Rise and Fall of Tobacco in South Carolina* (Columbia: University of South Carolina Press, 2000). Historian Ted Ownby examines the evolving place of consumption in the lives of twentieth-century rural Mississippians, particularly focusing on the ways that consumption could reshape both power relations and assumptions about race, class, and gender. See Ownby, *American Dreams in Mississippi: Consumers, Poverty, and Culture, 1830–1998* (Chapel Hill: University of North Carolina Press, 1999).

The works of New Deal–era rural sociologists, journalists, and social scientists have enriched our understanding of twentieth-century transformations. See Paul W. Terry and Verner M. Sims, *They Live on the Land: Life in an Open-Country Southern Community* (Tuscaloosa: University of Alabama Press, 1993, reprint of 1940 edition); Margaret Jarman Hagood, *Mothers of the South: Portraiture of the White Tenant Farm Woman* (New York: W. W. Norton & Co., 1977, reprint of 1939 edition); Arthur F. Raper, *Preface to Peasantry: A Tale of Two Black Belt Counties* (Chapel Hill: University of North Carolina Press, 1936) and *Tenants of the Almighty* (New York: The MacMillan Company, 1943); Charles S. Johnson, Edwin R. Embree, and W. W. Alexander, *The Collapse of Cotton Tenancy: Summary of Field Studies and Statistical Surveys 1933–1935* (Chapel Hill: University of North Carolina Press, 1935); Charles S. Johnson, *Growing Up in the Black Belt: Negro Youth in the Rural South* (New York: Schocken Books, 1967, reprint of 1941 edition); Howard W. Odum, *Southern Regions of the United States* (Chapel Hill: University of North Carolina Press, 1936); Howard W. Odum, with an introduction by Bryant Simon, *Race and Rumors of Race: The American South in the Early Forties* (Baltimore: Johns Hopkins University Press, 1997). Photographers also left a rich record of rural southern economic problems. See Dorothea Lange and Paul Schuster Taylor, *An American Exodus: A Record of Human Erosion* (New York: Reynal & Hitchcock, 1939) and James Agee and Walker Evans, *Let Us Now Praise Famous Men* (Boston: Houghton Mifflin, 1988, reprint of 1939 edition).

Many scholars have examined the role of the federal government in reshaping southern agriculture beginning with the New Deal. Most blame federal policies for the destruction of small, diversified family farms, particularly those run by African Americans. For example, historian Pete Daniel has shown how federal policies undermined the legal foundation of the crop lien system and how federal agricultural policies replaced crop lien laws as the force shaping southern agriculture. USDA programs were structured to reward large farmers who used capital intensive methods and to disadvantage small diversified farmers. See Daniel, "The Legal Basis of Agrarian Capitalism: The South since 1933," in *Race and Class in the American South since 1890*, ed. Melvyn Stokes and Rick Halpern (Oxford, England and Providence, R.I.: Berg, 1994), 79–102; and "The New Deal, Southern Agriculture, and Economic Change," in *The New Deal and the South*, ed. James C. Cobb and Michael V. Namorato (Jackson: University Press of Mississippi, 1984), 37–61. A similar argument was advanced by Jack Temple Kirby in "The Transformation of Southern Plantations, c. 1920–1960," *Agricultural History* 57 (1983): 257–76. Historian Nan Elizabeth Woodruff has concurred, showing how Mississippi Delta landowners used federal and local agencies during World War II to develop and implement strategies to modernize the plantation economy while preserving their own political and economic power. See Woodruff, "Mississippi Delta Planters and Debates over Mechanization, Labor and Civil Rights in the 1940s," *Journal of Southern History* 60 (1994): 263–84. Political scientist William P. Browne also argues that the destruction of African American agriculture was a result of federal policy. See Browne, "Benign Public Policies, Malignant Consequences, and the Demise of African American Agriculture," in *African American Life in the Rural South, 1900–1950*, ed. R. Douglas Hurt (Columbia and London: University of Missouri Press, 2003), 129–51. Historian Donald Holley takes a more benign view of the federal government. He does not see mechanization as the product of federal agricultural policy nor does he believe that mechanization caused the exodus from the land in the South. Instead he argues that mechanization arose as a response to out-migration. He saw mechanization as freeing African American sharecroppers from an economically exploitive system. See Holley, *The Second Great Emancipation: The Mechanical Cotton Picker, Black Migration, and How They Shaped the Modern South* (Fayetteville: University of Arkansas Press, 2000). Sociologist Jess Gilbert and political scientist Mary Summers argue that a small group of USDA officials *did* attempt to address the problems of small farmers, but that these officials were silenced when Congress eliminated their programs during and after World War II. See Jess Gilbert, "New Modernism and the Agrarian New Deal: A Different Kind of State," (pp. 129–46) and Mary Summers, "The New Deal Farm Programs: Looking for Reconstruction in American Agriculture," (pp. 147–59), both in *Fighting for the Farm: Rural America Transformed*, ed. Jane Adams (Philadelphia: University of Pennsylvania Press, 2003). While Gilbert and Summers have succeeded in convincing me that a significant number of New Deal–era USDA officials—both in Washington and in the field—possessed noble motives and goals of creating agricultural programs rooted in grassroots democracy that would benefit the neediest farmers, I believe that they miss the point of the USDA's critics. Democratic agricultural reformers, clustered mostly in the Resettlement Administration and its successor, the Farm Security Administration, lost their battle to shape and control USDA programs. In the end, programs to serve the interests of landowning commercial farmers consumed the lion's share of the agency's attention and budget and thus shaped farm policy for generations to come.

Rural transformation was inextricably linked to southern industrialization. For accounts of this process, see Jacquelyn Hall et al., *Like a Family: The Making of a Southern Cotton Mill World* (New York: W. W. Norton and Co., 1987); James C. Cobb, *Industrialization and Southern Society, 1877–1984* (Lexington: University Press of Kentucky, 1984) and *The Selling of the South: The Southern Crusade for Industrial Development, 1936–1980* (Baton Rouge: Louisiana State University Press, 1982); Brian Kelly, *Race, Class, and Power in the Alabama Coalfields, 1908–1921* (Urbana: University of Illinois Press, 2001); Randall L. Patton with David B. Parker, *Carpet Capital: The Rise of a New South Industry* (Athens: University of Georgia Press, 1999); Ronald D. Eller, *Miners, Millhands, and Mountaineers: Industrialization of the Appalachian South, 1880–1930* (Knoxville: University of Tennessee Press, 1982); Paul Salstrom, *Appalachia's Path to Dependency: Rethinking a Region's Economic History, 1730–1940* (Lexington: University Press of Kentucky, 1994); Mary K. Anglin, *Women, Power, and Dissent in the Hills of Carolina* (Urbana and Chicago: University of Illinois Press, 2002).

Studies of the massive twentieth-century migration to southern cities also provide important insights on the process of rural transformation. Historian Louis M. Kyriakoudes recently reshaped our understanding of rural-urban linkages and the way they shaped the transformation of agriculture. In an examination of Nashville and the middle Tennessee hinterlands, he demonstrates that rural people charted their paths to city life based on their previous relationships to city markets. See Louis M. Kyriakoudes, *The Social Origins of the Urban South: Race, Gender, and Migration in Nashville and Middle Tennessee, 1890–1930* (Chapel Hill: University of North Carolina Press, 2003). Other important studies of urbanization in the South are David R. Goldfield, *Cotton Fields and Skyscrapers: Southern City and Region, 1607–1980* (Baton Rouge: Louisiana State University Press, 1982) and *Region, Race, and Cities: Interpreting the Urban South* (Baton Rouge: Louisiana State University Press, 1997).

The history of the rural South is incomplete without careful consideration of race relations. Two very fine recent works examine the ways rural African Americans resisted control of the white power structure, including white landowners. Both make important contributions to our understanding of the sharecropping system and the way that African Americans themselves ultimately transformed and then destroyed that system. See Nan Elizabeth Woodruff, *American Congo: The African American Freedom Struggle in the Delta* (Cambridge: Harvard University Press, 2003) and Steven Hahn,

A Nation under Our Feet: Black Political Struggles in the Rural South from Slavery to the Great Migration (Cambridge: Belknap Press of Harvard University Press, 2003). Mark Schultz has shown how rural Georgia whites and blacks developed fluid and complex relationships based on personal interactions rather than an institutionalized Jim Crow system. While white supremacy was still the rule, Schultz shows how the face-to-face interracial interactions that characterized rural life also provided many African Americans with freedoms unknown to urban blacks. See Mark Schultz, *The Rural Face of White Supremacy: Beyond Jim Crow* (Chicago and Urbana: University of Illinois Press, 2005).

A number of sources help to place southern rural transformation in a national and international context. Historian Deborah Fitzgerald has argued that the emergence of an industrial ideal is a fundamental feature of twentieth-century agriculture. In the early twentieth century, a new class of agricultural leaders from government, universities, agribusiness, and banking encouraged farmers to apply notions of specialization, mechanization, efficiency, and economies of scale to the practice of cultivating the land. The result was the development of interconnected systems of production and consumption that operated like industry and tied various economic sectors and geographic regions together. See Deborah Fitzgerald, *Every Farm a Factory: The Industrial Ideal in American Agriculture* (New Haven: Yale University Press, 2003). On the farm crisis of the 1980s, see Barry J. Barnett, "The U.S. Farm Financial Crisis of the 1980s," in *Fighting for the Farm: Rural America Transformed*, ed. Jane Adams (Philadelphia: University of Pennsylvania Press, 2003), 160–71; Bruce L. Gardner, *American Agriculture in the Twentieth Century: How It Flourished and What It Cost* (Cambridge and London: Harvard University Press, 2002); Russell L. Lamb, "The New Farm Economy," *Regulation* (2003–2004): 10–15; and Willard W. Cochrane, *The Curse of American Agricultural Abundance: A Sustainable Solution* (Lincoln and London: University of Nebraska Press, 2003).

Good general surveys of the history of rural America, including the South, include David B. Danbom, *Born in the Country: A History of Rural America* (Baltimore: Johns Hopkins University Press, 1995) and R. Douglas Hurt, *Problems of Plenty: The American Farmer in the Twentieth Century* (Chicago: Ivan R. Dee, 2002). Geographer Ingolf Vogeler's book is useful to understanding the relationships between large agribusiness corporations and small farmers. See *The Myth of the Family Farm: Agribusiness Dominance of U.S. Agriculture* (Boulder, Colorado: Westview Press, 1981).

Chapter 5 is informed by a variety of work on the nature of rural community. Historian Orville Vernon Burton argues that community studies still have much to tell us about the rural past in "Reaping What We Sow: Community and Rural History," *Agricultural History* 76 (2002): 631–58.

For more on the reality of life in rural communities, see for example, work by historians Mary Neth, *Preserving the Family Farm: Women, Community and the Foundations of Agribusiness in the Midwest, 1900–1940* (Baltimore: Johns Hopkins University Press, 1995); Jane Marie Pederson, *Between Memory and Reality: Family and Community in Rural Wisconsin, 1870–1970* (Madison: University of Wisconsin Press, 1992); Susan Sessions Rugh, *Our Common Country: Family Farming, Culture, and Community in the Nineteenth-Century Midwest* (Bloomington: Indiana University Press, 2001). For more on the role of mutual aid in rural communities, see John Mack Faragher, *Sugar Creek: Life on the Illinois Prairie* (New Haven: Yale University Press, 1986); Nancy Grey Osterud, *Bonds of Community: The Lives of Farm Women in Nineteenth-Century New York* (Ithaca: Cornell University Press, 1991); Allan Kulikoff, *From British Peasants to Colonial American Farmers* (Chapel Hill: University of North Carolina Press, 2000), 223–24. Studies of contemporary rural communities include Janel M. Curry, "Community Worldview and Rural Systems: A Study of Five Communities in Iowa," *Annals of the Association of American Geographers* 90 (2000): 693–712; Cornelia Butler Flora et al., *Rural Communities: Legacy and Change* (Boulder: Westview Press, 1992); Glen H. Elder Jr. and Rand D. Conger, *Children of the Land: Adversity and Success in Rural America* (Chicago: University of Chicago Press, 2000).

Recent work on the decline of civic engagement has also informed my understanding of the meanings that rural southerners gave to changes in their own communities and in the meaning of community in general. These include Robert N. Bellah et al., *Habits of the Heart: Commitment and Individualism in American Life* (New York: Harper and Row Publishers, 1985); Robert D. Putnam, *Bowling Alone: The Collapse and Revival of American Community* (New York: Simon and Schuster, 2000); and Paul K. Conkin, *A Requiem for the American Village* (New York: Rowman and Littlefield Publishers, Inc., 2000).

Scholarly work on the development of the Protestant work ethic and on the meaning of work to the working and middle classes has informed the section on the rural work ethic. The earliest theorizing about the origins and purposes of the Protestant work ethic was done by Max Weber. See Weber, translated by Stephen Kalberg, *The Protestant Ethic and the Spirit of Capitalism* (Chicago: Fitzroy Dearborn Publishers, 2001). For more recent scholarship on the meaning of work to working-class men, see Richard Sennett, *The Corrosion of Character: The Personal Consequences of Work in the New Capitalism* (New York and London: W. W. Norton & Company, 1998), especially 98–100; Michele Lamont, *The Dignity of the Working Man: Morality and the Boundaries of Race, Class, and Immigration* (New York and Cambridge: Russell Sage Foundation and Harvard University Press, 2000), especially 24–26.

On the American distrust of government, see Gary Wills, *A Necessary Evil: A History of American Distrust of Government* (New York: Simon and Schuster, 1999); Catherine McNicol Stock, *Rural Radicals: Righteous Rage in the American Grain* (Ithaca: Cornell University Press, 1996).

Index